D1218811

SOUTHERN BIOGRAPHY SERIES

MONTAGUE OF VIRGINIA

MONTAGUE OF VIRGINIA

The Making of a Southern Progressive

by

William Larsen

LOUISIANA STATE UNIVERSITY PRESS

PREFACE

—————•◆•—————

"Let us take the best of the old and give it to the conditions
of the present."
        A. J. MONTAGUE, Inaugural Address, January, 1902

FOR Virginia, the year 1862 was one of dramatic moment. That
year military move and countermove made the Commonwealth a focal battleground of the Civil War, then only a
year in progress. From Tidewater to the mountain fastnesses the
conflict of wits and brawn raged furiously. Though at the year's end
the Confederates' future seemed bright, the preceding months had
not always given reason for optimism. McClellan's huge Army of
the Potomac had landed on the Williamsburg peninsula and had
advanced to within a few miles of Richmond by the month of May.
The Confederate government made plans to abandon its young capital. Richmond held, McClellan was repulsed, yet danger remained.
To escape such danger, Gay Eubank Montague, then expecting her
fifth child, fled from her Middlesex County home to friends in Campbell, near Lynchburg, safely out of reach of Union armies. There,
on the third of October, she gave birth to a son, Andrew Jackson
Montague.

"Jack" Montague's birth came at a time of rapid change and un-
certainty. Born during the turmoil of war, the son of a man who presided at Virginia's secession convention and who served in the Confederate Congress, he inherited a legacy of the old Virginia—the
Virginia that slowly died, even as he was born. And yet the young
Montague also represented the new generation of Virginia, the gen-

eration that gradually replaced the embittered veterans in the seats of
power. Montague was a product, but not a contemporary, of the old
Virginia. As the nineteenth century eased into the twentieth, the old
generation gave way to the new. As the first postwar governor of
Virginia without a military rank to grace his name, Montague well
illustrates and epitomizes this shift. He injected new blood into the
old, thereby achieving a balance of calm conservatism and bold
progressivism. With this formula he approached the problems of the
"new Virginia."

The problems were manifold, and in attempting to cope with them,
Montague, as Virginia's first twentieth-century governor, earned a
reputation as a reformer—an eloquent critic of the established political and economic order. A man of lofty ideals and moving eloquence he voiced from rostrums throughout the Commonwealth his
scorn for the corrupt politician and his concern over the apparent decline of public and private ethics, the rise of materialism, the decline
of individual opportunity, the self-centered domination of government
and politics by the *nouveaux riches*. Reflecting these attitudes, he
joined with those Virginians demanding a new constitution that
would purify elections and provide effective regulation of railroads
and corporations. And he won the Democratic nomination for governor in 1901 on a platform bitterly critical of machine politics, a
platform dedicated to the adoption of direct primaries and to the improvement of schools and roads.

In all these respects, Montague's career displayed the basic themes
of the national reform impulse which historians have labeled the
"progressive movement." This national progressive movement has
long been recognized, defined, and investigated, but its Southern
counterpart has only recently received attention from historians, who
generally had tacitly assumed a Northern monopoly of anything savor-
ing of progress. That facile assumption has, by various studies of
Southern reform, been undermined sufficiently to admit the region below the Mason-Dixon Line within the pale of respectable progressivism. Indeed, it now appears that in some respects the South surpassed
the North in its zeal for certain reforms of the age.

Andrew Jackson Montague of Virginia and Robert M. La Follette
of Wisconsin, elected contemporaneously as governors of their respective states, closely resemble each other in their basically moralistic fight to protect "the people" against "the interests." Studies of
both the well-known Northerner and the little-known Southerner

should be helpful, then, in rounding out an appraisal of the essential spirit of the national progressive movement. Who was Montague? What were his attitudes, his motivations and objectives? How did he develop as a state, regional, and national public figure? The following pages, attempting to answer these questions, depict the making of a Southern progressive.

ACKNOWLEDGMENTS

THE author wishes to acknowledge his indebtedness to the many individuals who have facilitated the research or supervised and criticized the writing of this work: especially to Professor Edward Younger of the University of Virginia, who directed the research and writing of the manuscript in its dissertation stage; to Professors Allen W. Moger, Claude Hall, Dewey Grantham, T. Harry Williams, and to Mrs. James F. Fargason, Jr., all of whom have read and criticized portions of the manuscript in its various stages of composition and revision; to the personnel of the libraries of the University of Virginia, the University of North Carolina, Duke University, the Library of Congress, and the Virginia State Library; to Montague's daughter, Gay Montague Moore, for granting access to private family papers and for furnishing the illustrations for this book; and to many others—family, friends, acquaintances—who have afforded information and advice, and who have given their patience and encouragement.

WILLIAM LARSEN

CONTENTS

LIST OF ILLUSTRATIONS

MONTAGUE OF VIRGINIA

I

A TIDEWATER HERITAGE

ONE January day in 1885 a boarding house in Charlottesville, Virginia, served oysters to its patrons, students at the nearby University of Virginia. Jack Montague, one of the boarders, a young, athletic, red-headed law student from Middlesex County, commented disparagingly in a letter home that a true Tidewaterman "could hardly recognize them." [1]

The incident is trivial but revealing. Andrew Jackson Montague's cultural, social, political, and family inheritance was derived from roots deep in the Tidewater—a country of flat, gently undulating landscape, broad rivers, and sparsely settled rural population. There he matured to a young man, and there, after a lifetime career which carried him to state, national, and European capitals, he would return in his old age to ruminate, to fish in the Dragon River, and to die. There he found his being, his heritage.

And the heritage was a venerable one. The Montague family had inhabited the Virginia Tidewater from the genesis of the colony. Peter Montague, the first to come, emigrated to Virginia on the ship *Charles* early in 1621. Rapidly acquiring extensive landholdings in Nansemond and Middlesex counties, he twice sat in the Virginia

---

1 Andrew Jackson Montague to Elizabeth "Betsie" Hoskins, Jan. 6, 1885, in Gay Montague Moore Collection, Toddsbury, Gloucester County, Va. This collection is hereinafter designated as Moore Collection.

House of Burgesses before his death in 1658. In the two centuries following, his numerous progeny were to live as unobtrusive, substantial citizens of their localities, holding such positions as constable, road surveyor, justice of the peace, and sheriff.[2]

Jack Montague's paternal grandfather, Lewis Brooke Montague, a veteran of the War of 1812 and a resident of Middlesex, was one of the least successful members of the family. As a merchant and farmer he suffered bankruptcy soon after his marriage in 1818 to Catherine Jesse. Though lacking affluence, he nevertheless instilled in each of his six sons a sense of dignity, service, and patriotism; all six did credit to their family in military and professional positions. The most successful, Robert Latané Montague, became lieutenant governor of Virginia.[3]

Born in 1819 in Middlesex, the second son of the family, Robert Montague determined to enter the legal profession and obtained his law degree from William and Mary in 1843. Almost immediately thereafter he plunged into the politics of his state. His pleasing manners, ruddy complexion, lustrous red hair, and brilliant flair for oratory gave him, as his son later described it, "an irresistable capacity for popularity, which literally swept him into public life." Aligning with the Democratic party, he consistently proclaimed his belief in local government and individual freedom and his bitter antipathy to the materialistic, industrial Northeast, the moneyed interests, and the tariff.[4]

Robert Montague first displayed his oratorical eloquence while campaigning for James K. Polk in 1844. In 1850 he was elected to the Virginia House of Delegates, and in 1852 he became commonwealth's attorney for Middlesex County. When the state Democratic convention of 1859 nominated the "Westerner," John Letcher of Lexington, for the governorship, Montague, the "Eastern" orator, was a natural choice for lieutenant governor. Letcher was ill during a large portion of the campaign, and Montague substituted admirably in a series of debates with the Whig nominee, William L. Goggin of

2 George W. Montague, *History and Genealogy of Peter Montague of Nansemond and Lancaster Counties, Virginia, and His Descendants, 1621–1894* (Amherst, Mass., 1894), 494 pp.
3 A. J. Montague, "Some Recollections," a short MS written Nov. 17, 1920, Moore Collection; G. W. Montague, *History and Genealogy of Peter Montague,* 186.
4 Montague, "Some Recollections"; Richmond *Dispatch,* March 3, 1880; G. W. Montague, *History and Genealogy of Peter Montague,* 311–13.

Bedford. It was in one of these debates that he received the appellation "Red Fox of Middlesex." Goggin asserted that he was glad the Democrats had nominated a "young red fox from Middlesex," because he was "fond of fox hunting," and Montague replied that Goggin had complimented him without so intending: "A red fox always runs straight; it is the gray fox . . . that doubles and runs crooked." Having willingly accepted the designation (which he would later hand down to his son), the red fox ran straight and hard, helping to lead his ticket to victory in the general election.

As a delegate from Mathews and Middlesex, Robert Montague also took a leading part in the state convention which met early in 1861 to deliberate upon Virginia's relationship with the Union. Elected chairman of the convention upon the resignation of John Janney, he advocated secession even before Lincoln's initial call for troops. After secession, Governor Letcher appointed him a member of an executive council to organize Virginia's war effort. Later, in 1863, the lieutenant governor was elected to the Confederate Congress from the first Virginia district.[5]

Sharing Robert Montague's political career, his hopes, and his disappointments was Cordelia Gay Eubank of King and Queen County, whom he married in 1852. Though fifteen years younger than her husband, Gay Montague proved to be a compatible helpmate and a devoted mother to their eight children, only three of whom survived infancy. The family lived on a 612-acre farm in upper Middlesex County, where, shortly before his marriage, Robert Montague had constructed the family residence on a bluff overlooking the Rappahannock. This large but simple frame house he christened "Inglewood." From the house could be seen orchards, wheatfields, woods and swamp, as well as steamboats plying the river between Fredericksburg and Baltimore four times a week.[6]

When the war came, the same bluff afforded a different view: that

5 The information concerning Robert L. Montague's career was obtained from numerous newspaper clippings in scrapbooks of the Moore Collection.
6 This and following information concerning Inglewood and Jack Montague's early family life was obtained from many letters in his early correspondence in the Moore Collection; from interviews with his two daughters (Mrs. Janet Montague Nunnally, Deltaville, Middlesex County, Va., June, 1960; Mrs. Gay Montague Moore, Toddsbury, Gloucester County, Va., Dec., 1959, and June, 1960); and from a short paragraph describing Inglewood, written by Robert L. Montague, July 18, 1876, Moore Collection.

of Yankee gunboats cruising the river. It was to escape possible molestation by federal troops that Lieutenant Governor Montague, in the fall of 1862, accepted the kind offer to occupy temporarily a vacant home of his friend Judge Charles H. Lynch in Campbell County. On October 3, two days after arriving at their Campbell haven, Gay was delivered of a son. The name given him, Andrew Jackson Montague, was in remembrance of Robert Montague's youngest and favorite brother, a cadet at Virginia Military Institute who had volunteered for the defense of Richmond, only to be mortally wounded at the battle of Gaines's Mill in July, 1862.

Seven months after Jack's birth, when Federal pressure on eastern Virginia had been relieved, the family returned to Inglewood, to remain another twenty years. After Appomattox, Robert Montague turned again to his law practice for his principal means of livelihood. He also maintained his active interest in politics, campaigning against the Carpetbagger Underwood constitution and attending the Conservative party's state convention in 1872—striking "hammer blows for Kemper," the party's nominee in the gubernatorial campaign which followed. In 1872 he was elected to the Virginia House of Delegates from Middlesex, and in 1875 he obtained from the Virginia legislature an appointment as circuit court judge for the eighth Virginia circuit. This position he held until his death.[7]

Robert Montague felt uncomfortable in the political climate of the new Virginia. In various public speeches throughout the state he reaffirmed his Jeffersonian-Jacksonian desire to guarantee "equality of individual opportunity," but he also decried the "dangerous heresy" that all men were created equal. And he ridiculed the "French type of democracy" which gave each man a vote. His panacea for the problems of the disrupted South lay in education—not the education of the intellect which caused a "belief in self to replace belief in God" but an education in religious values and morality. During his brief postwar term in the Virginia legislature, he became known for his obdurate support of "old Virginia in everything—old-field schools, old-field magistrates, old county sheriffs, old general musters, warrant-trying Saturdays, and big barbecues." The lieutenant governor had outlived his time.[8]

7 Newspaper clippings (1875–80) from scrapbooks in Moore Collection.
8 *Address of Hon. Robert L. Montague, delivered before the Society of Alumni of William and Mary College, Williamsburg, Virginia, on the 4th of July, 1870* (Norfolk, 1871), *passim*, in Andrew Jackson Montague

Such was the father and such the environment which influenced young Jack Montague, and the influence was a profound one. From his father, Jack inherited many of the admirable qualities of Old South statesmanship; from him he also inherited a basic political conservatism. With these legacies, however, the son was to witness a far different era than that foreseen by the father, and in changing with the age Jack Montague gradually developed a more flexible attitude toward government and society. Yet, ever present in his later political career was an undercurrent of the conservatism developed by the vital formative years at Inglewood.

For the Montague family, Inglewood provided an atmosphere of quiet, rural living. As a boy, Jack performed the ordinary farm chores of tending sheep and hogs. During his many hours in the fields he developed a love for the wild animal life that abounded on the farm. His leisure hours he spent reading such Victorian novels as Scott's *Ivanhoe*. Life was quiet, but not entirely isolated. Each Sunday the family —Robert Montague, his wife, and their three sons, Dew, Jack, and Lynch—would visit Hermitage Church where Baptist sermons were delivered by the pastor, John W. Jyland. There were frequent visits from neighboring relatives, from King and Queen friends of Gay Montague, and from political friends of Robert Montague.

At the age of nine Jack Montague began his formal education. He first briefly attended a public school at Storemont in Middlesex; later his father financed his enrollment at a private grammar school in Williamsburg. Several years thereafter Jack and his younger brother Lynch were instructed by a tutor, Claggett B. Jones, a successful teacher and an "excellent disciplinarian."

Under this tutelage and in these surroundings young Jack matured into a serious, sometimes moody young man with a quick wit, a penchant for story-telling, and a volatile temper. Inwardly he tended to be pessimistic; outwardly, cheerful and gracious; inwardly, ambitious; outwardly, modest and unassuming. At full growth he stood five feet, ten inches, and though of large frame, in his youth he weighed a scant 150 pounds. His most prominent features were an oval face, a small, amiable mouth, a straight nose, clear blue eyes, and flaming red hair— altogether an appearance labeled handsome by his early acquaintances. His visage and deportment lacked rugged resoluteness; rather,

Papers, Virginia State Library, Richmond. This collection is hereinafter designated as Montague Papers.

his manner was one of inoffensive charm, congeniality, restraint, and dignity.[9]

From his mother, to whom he was particularly devoted, Jack Montague acquired a sensitivity, a sentimentality, an aesthetic awareness. From her he also received an understanding sympathy: "For a long time I felt as if nobody ever understood me save my darling mother. She always did. Even in my boyish days, before I learned to control my temper, when others would scold me, she would always smile and kiss me and tell me that 'little gentlemen never get mad.' I even felt then that if the world were made of such beings I would indeed never 'get mad.' " [10]

Though Montague's relationship with his father was evidently not as close as that with his mother, the affection and respect of the son for the father was no less deep and abiding. Robert Montague left with his son an impression of "mental honesty," of clear thinking, and of boldness. He also provided him with an appreciation for classical scholarship and beauty. Years after his father's death, Jack Montague vividly recalled a memorable moment: "In the last year of my father's life he would occasionally turn to his Virgil or Horace, read them with beauty and unction and then translate with rapidity, accuracy and grace. . . . Once in a severe illness, somewhat wandering in mind, he repeated with pathetic beauty . . . lines of Virgil. . . . which so overcame me that I went from his bed chamber to hide my boyish tears." [11] In all his later personal correspondence Jack Montague left no trace of disrespect for his father.

Robert Montague gave his son a considerable heritage: a native intelligence, a mental curiosity, a philosophical bent, a legal mind— qualities which were to make the son more a scholar than a practitioner, more statesman than politician; qualities which were to be eventually recognized by honorary doctorates from two prominent American universities.[12] From his father, Jack also acquired a disdain of materialism and expediency, a genuine sense of religious morality, integrity, and honor. Most of all Robert Montague endowed his son with a love for politics and statesmanship, a tradition of public service, and an abiding sense of history. Robert Montague had

9   This personality sketch is derived from numerous introspective letters written by the young Montague (Moore Collection) and from the Moore and Nunnally interviews.
10 Montague to Betsie Hoskins, April 18, 1885, Moore Collection.
11 Montague, "Some Recollections."
12 Brown University and the University of Pennsylvania.

dined occasionally with former President John Tyler and after the war had as his house guests such figures as Senator R. M. T. Hunter. From animated parlor conversations which accompanied these visits young Jack was to receive his initial orientation in public affairs and statecraft. From his father and his father's associates he acquired a familiarity with gentility and greatness, a nineteenth-century legacy of political idealism, patriotism, and ambition.

Robert Montague died on March 2, 1880, from an erysipelas infection. Jack wrote in his father's ledger that he died "without a struggle or gush. . . . a loss unspeakable to us, but an eternal gain to him." At the age of seventeen, Andrew Jackson Montague was thus thrown upon his personal resources for his collegiate aspirations. His father had adequately supported the family while living, but upon his death his diminished estate would of necessity go to the support of his widow, then an invalid. Without money, but rich with a heritage of intellectual, religious, and political endowments, Jack Montague faced an uncertain future, full of hope and of anxiety.

II

EDUCATION OF A STATESMAN

THE years from 1862 to 1880 had seen the basic pattern set, the qualities of character and intellect established. For Jack Montague, the five years following his father's death were years of rapid development upon the foundation already laid. As a student, he saw his knowledge expand, his nature become even more introspective. In religion, through study and prayer, he developed a fervent faith conquering temporary doubts. As a tutor for two years, he demonstrated an ability to communicate his ideals to others, to win their admiration and respect. As a young man, he selected his profession, laid plans for his future, and confessed an ambition dizzying in its ultimate objectives. Finally, as an emotional being, he experienced the warmth of a youthful love. In these years, critical years for a young man bent on career, Montague displayed a tenacity of purpose, a growing maturity, which augured well for the future.

Following Robert Montague's death, arrangements were made for a tenant, James L. Marchant, to farm most of Inglewood. Subsequently, in September, 1880, Jack Montague left Inglewood to enroll in Richmond College, a Baptist institution located in Virginia's capital city. In 1880 Richmond College was a small liberal arts school staffed by a faculty of only nine members. Montague took coursework in several departments of the college, developing an especial fondness for the abstract speculative world of philosophy and an admiration for modern scientific progress in chemistry and physics. Darwin's theory of evolution, however, he termed "bald, arid, skeptical." From his English professor, the distinguished educator J. L. M. Curry, he acquired an intense interest in the future of Southern education. Later, as governor, he attended Curry's funeral in 1902 and in a sense inherited his former teacher's mantle as a crusader for Southern education.[1]

Montague's coursework strengthened in him an analytical, studious tendency already well developed, for at the age of eighteen he was a well-read individual. A notebook which he kept, extending to 1887, records those books he read, evidently from his earliest literacy.[2] Fiction dominated his early reading—sea tales and pirate adventures. Interspersed with such romances, however, was a considerable number of histories, touching upon Roman, English, and American topics. His maturing interests gradually gravitated to more serious literature: Goldsmith, Dickens, Bacon, Shakespeare, Scott. While at Richmond he turned to works with such ponderous titles as *Elements of the Human Intellect, Constitutional Lectures,* and *Handbook of Moral Philosophy.* Following 1882 the same interest in serious literature, history, and exposition continued, with added emphasis on theology. The intensive reading habits developed by Montague during the quiet days at Inglewood and the busy days at Richmond gave him a depth of learning and knowledge which expanded his mental horizons and kept his convictions fresh and reaffirmed. In his later years, his favorite diversion was reading history and fiction to his children and grandchildren; his wife was to complain that his book purchases kept them perilously close to the poorhouse.

The two years spent at Richmond developed Montague's social and leadership capacities, as well as his intellect. Several long-lasting friendships were made with classmates, and in true gentlemanly fashion, Jack called on his "young lady friends," though he confessed an aversion for "city visiting." He became a contributing editor for the college's literary magazine, the *Messenger;* and he joined two organizations, Beta Theta Pi, a social fraternity, and the Philogians, a literary and debating society. His vigorous maiden speech before the Philogians attracted favorable attention; in the spring of 1881 the society

1 Charles W. Dabney, *Universal Education in the South* (Chapel Hill, 1936), I, 130; A. J. Montague, "Our Progressive Age," *Richmond College Messenger,* VIII, No. 2 (1882), 3–11, in Montague Papers.
2 Located in Moore Collection.

awarded him its annual medal for best debater; and in 1882 it elected him its commencement orator. His subsequent address, "Our Progressive Age," marked the opening of commencement week, which saw Montague graduated with degrees in several of the college's departments.[3]

Montague's valedictory at Richmond College provides valuable insight into the thinking of the maturing scholar and budding politician. In rejecting the "dress and external splendor" of the so-called progressive age, Montague clearly revealed his basic, idealistic conservatism and his indebtedness to his father for his political ideas. Arguing that contemporary progress was more shadow than substance, Montague discounted the notion that governments made men, that outward compulsion or legislation could bring inward reform. Speaking in a day when Republican government acted as the benefactor of big business through railroad subsidies and high tariffs, he called for a return of government to its only legitimate function, the protection of human liberty. The pseudoprogressive spirit of the times, he complained, cared little for "virtue, talents, or honesty." The whole age was shallow: "Literature is entirely too insipid for the drawing room; philosophy 'not too deep,'" and politics was expelled from all spheres of refinement or intelligence to the hustings and the wrangling demagogues. The shallowness of the age was most obviously demonstrated by the popularity of that "exceedingly fine theory" which held that all men were born free and equal. Such a theory he termed, in true Robert Montague fashion, the "flimsiest of dreams." [4]

Also indicative of Montague's developing political attitudes is an article he contributed to the *Messenger,* entitled "What Is a True Statesman?" Lamenting the poor quality of political leadership then evolving in the age of the robber baron, Montague depicted a statesman as one who rose above party, above section, above expediency —independent, if necessary, of his own constituency. Knowledge was only one ingredient of a statesman's makeup; more important were "conscientious principles having no . . . connection with any purpose or design . . . except the Universal Welfare." Castigating so-called statesmen who held office dearer than principle, Montague asserted that a true statesman should not only represent, but present.

---

3   R. L. Montague, III, "The Red Fox Runs Straight," *Essays in History,* III (Charlottesville, Va., 1956), 45–62; *Religious Herald,* Feb. 4, 1937, and Danville *Register,* April 14, 1888, in scrapbooks, Moore Collection. Montague to Betsie Hoskins, July 8, 1884, Jan. 6, 1885, Moore Collection.
4   Montague, "Our Progressive Age," 3–11.

He had an obligation to lead, not be led. The "selfish wishes of a corrupt people" should always be subordinated to the "sagacious principles of a statesman." [5] In his patrician disdain for the cultural crudity of the new industrial order then emerging in America, and in his appeal for more morality in government and less government in society, Montague displayed all the traits of the "mugwump" reform element then active in American politics—that element which would later give enthusiastic support to the statesman of their ideals, Grover Cleveland.

Both of these political essays clearly demonstrate the extent to which Robert Montague influenced his son's political views. For though his call for government retrenchment and for a resurgence of public morality were cardinal tenets of the old Jeffersonian democracy, Montague's underlying mistrust of a mobocracy was the mistrust of an innate conservative who cautioned against any tampering with the basic social and political order. From the redheaded youth expounding his nascent philosophies at a college commencement in 1882, to the cultured attorney general campaigning twenty years later for the governorship on a platform endorsing popular primaries and a return of government to the people, there would be a marked, even startling, transition. The same emphasis on qualities of statesmanship would remain, the same moral tone would persist, but the early mistrust of popular majorities would be replaced by a mistrust of political manipulators and moneyed interests. The early aristocratic contempt for the hypothetical equality of man would be replaced by a contempt for a political machine which undermined the governmental and moral fiber of the Commonwealth. The young Montague had cast his basic political likeness in a mold copied from his father, but the refinements, the etchings, were yet to be made. The materials were yet malleable.

After his graduation from Richmond College in 1882 Montague served as a private tutor for two years in order to repay debts he had necessarily contracted while attending college. His employer, John Churchill Willis, operated a thousand-acre farm called "Indiantown," located in the Orange County Piedmont within view of the somnolent Blue Ridge Mountains.[6]

5 A. J. Montague, "What Is a True Statesman," *Richmond College Messenger,* VII, No. 4 (1882), in Montague Papers.
6 Information on Montague's years at Indiantown has been obtained chiefly from the following letters to the author: from Mrs. Catesby Willis Stewart,

Willis and his wife, Mary Catesby Willis, were scholarly people, yet "practical and full of energy with a rather deep religious side." With them, and with his pupils, Montague developed a relationship which proved fond and enduring. He instructed his half-dozen pupils (sons of Willis and of neighbors) in Latin, French, math, and history, using as a teaching technique debate and recitation. In addition, he instilled in them a love of literature, especially poetry. To his pupils he presented an example of industry, morality, and "absolute integrity." One of them, Ben Willis, testified that he was "pure in thought and word and action," and was never known to "use an oath or an unworthy expression." Ben's daughter writes, "I was brought up to think no finer man ever lived." For his part, Montague affirmed that he knew no better people than his Indiantown associates.

In matters of religion Montague was particularly influenced by John Willis, his employer. "From him," he remarked a decade later, "I have learned great lessons in the great book of our great religion." [7] Montague's reading during this period reflected this heightened religious interest: *Christianity the Science of Manhood, Freedom of the Will, Doctrine of the Atonement,* and *The Tri-lemma.* Such reading fare reflected not only the moralistic, inquiring nature of the young Montague but also his religious disquietude. This was the period of his greatest religious doubts and the period in which he evidently resolved them. John Willis aided this settling of Montague's convictions: "He cleared up for me one doubt that sat upon me with almost crushing weight. I can never forget how sweet and uplifting was my prayer on that night after that conversation." [8] For the balance of his young manhood Montague was to remain a stalwart in the Baptist religion, active as a layman in both state and local assemblies. In 1890, before he had attained a statewide political reputation, he was awarded recognition for his active participation in church affairs when he was appointed trustee for his Alma Mater, Richmond College.

Fredericksburg, Va., March 11 and March 28, 1960; from Miss Nellie Norman, Culpeper, Va., March 6 and April 3, 1960; and from Mrs. Edgar O. Willis, Jr., Culpeper, Va., March 23, 1960. These individuals are relatives of Montague's pupils. Their letters represent not only their personal recollections, but considerable information gleaned from the reminiscences of others.

7 Montague to Ben P. Willis, Aug. 3, 1894, in possession of Mrs. Catesby Willis Stewart, Fredericksburg.

8 *Ibid.*

His days at Richmond and at Indiantown helped Jack Montague develop intellectually, politically, and religiously. His personal disposition, however, retained something of the pessimism, the melancholia of his youth. Like the austere Puritan, he conceived it his duty to aid mankind, to pursue his ideals, yet in his heart he distrusted his emotions and found difficulty in feeling a rapport with other individuals or a faith in their motives and character.[9] But beginning with his years at Richmond, he gradually acquired a new interest, a new love, one which fulfilled his quest for beauty and nobility, and one which assuaged his cynicism and introversion. On June 16, 1884, one month after he left Indiantown, Elizabeth Lyne Hoskins agreed to his proposal of marriage.

Elizabeth "Betsie" Hoskins, a girl with "rosy cheeks, red lips, meaningful eyes [and a] merry, happy, innocent laugh," [10] came from a family of ten children. Her father, William Hoskins, a graduate of Philadelphia's Jefferson Medical College, earned his living as a country doctor in King and Queen County. Her mother, Janette Roy Hoskins, had been a close girlhood friend of Gay Montague; both were natives of King and Queen County and had attended Hollins College together. The two families frequently visited each other, especially after the death of Robert Montague.

Betsie was a versatile girl, six years younger than her future husband. She played the piano, loved dancing, and occasionally wrote poetry. An energetic, gay, even volatile person, she became, as Montague's brother expressed it, "an expert in all the art to draw and let fly the cupid arrow." As early as 1881 Jack became interested in this young girl with the "meaningful eyes," but coldly tried to convince himself "under the cynical garb of reason . . . that there was no such thing as love." Visits between families continued. Affection grew. Finally, in June, 1884, his proposal was made and accepted.

---

9 Montague once stated to his fiancée: "You are right. I feel as if I am different from other men. I am not a least bit effeminate . . . flatter myself with a real manliness; yet notwithstanding all this, I feel very little in common with my sex. I like them—I enjoy a talk; but I have seen only four or five men in my entire life for whom I really felt any other feeling than that of a slight friendship and congeniality." Montague to Betsie Hoskins, April 18, 1885, Moore Collection.

10 Montague to Betsie Hoskins, April 23, 1887, Moore Collection. Most of the material in the following narrative is taken from numerous letters in the Moore Collection, which Montague wrote to Miss Hoskins between 1884 and 1888. The material for the period before 1884 is from recollections in the later letters.

The five-year romance which ensued was entirely Victorian. Separated as they were for most of their long engagement, the couple conducted a copious correspondence, expressing sentiments taken straight from the pen of Scott. "In you, Jack," wrote Betsie, "I find all my soul is entirely filled." And Jack replied that if "Betsie is untrue, I am done with people. If your purity and innocence, which is in your every utterance and expression and movements, is deceptive, then I am at a loss where to find these qualities."

The courtship consisted of more, however, than personal sentiment and effusive phrases. The two brought to each other a reciprocation not only of love, but of ideals and of ambition. Even in their divergences, they complemented each other—Betsie the vivacious socialite; Jack, the more serious, retiring intellectual. Betsie brought to Jack an infusion of youth, gaiety and spontaneity, Jack to Betsie a love of learning and of culture. Betsie also gave young Montague what he perhaps most needed—an anchor of faith in a world which the young idealist found increasingly disillusioning. As Montague himself expressed it in his grandiloquent fashion, "As a mere child you stole into my heart with a mild and healing sympathy (though it was never expressed) and from that day I felt the light of your innocent soul." By the September following their June engagement, he could observe, "Since my love for you, I have been more strengthened than I can say in my belief in a God, for I have awakened to the true conscientiousness of what man is above an animal, which my cold, moralizing, cynical speculations confirmed by some painful observations."

For Montague the idealist, the moralist, the firm believer in the powerful influence over young men "of an educated female society," a person who longed for the "quiet sanctity of the home," these sentiments savored only slightly of exaggeration. His was the Victorian age, an age of sentiment, of literary excesses, of "purer affections, and loftier purposes." In Betsie, Montague found these affections and these purposes epitomized. By softening his ascetic tendencies, she made him more ambitious and desirous of both personal accomplishment and public service in the years ahead.

The future was yet vague, but Montague made ambitious plans to prepare himself professionally for whatever role he would play. The occupation he selected was that of his father, the law; the institution in which to pursue a study of that subject, the University of Virginia. He enrolled in July, 1884, three weeks following his engagement; and there, encouraged by Betsie's letters and discomforted by John B. Minor's incisive questioning, he remained for the ensuing year.

The summer law school of 1884 was the sixteenth annual summer course to be held at the University. Directed by Professor Minor, the session of 1884 welcomed sixty-seven students to its classes, both novitiate and advanced. The coursework, consisting of common and statute law, began on July 9 and lasted for two months.[11] Montague took three classes that summer, embracing Minor's entire course for both beginners and advanced students. Minor as a lecturer impressed Montague favorably; his style was described as slightly "fascinating," his voice distinct and mellow but at times tinged with sarcasm. As for his personal progress, Montague could state by the first of August, "I have learned as rapidly as I ever learned in my life this summer."[12]

Montague's return to the University in the fall session was delayed by the sudden illness and death of his mother during one of her accustomed visits to the Hoskinses. Even though he had sensed the imminence of his mother's death, the urgent summoning, the long hours at her bedside while she alternately rallied and subsided, were both a shock and a strain. She died a "true and Christian" death on September 25. On that day Montague wrote to Betsie, "I now turn to you more than ever. . . . You must now be your boy's mother as well as his sweetheart."

Once the estate was settled, Montague returned to the University, though not without misgivings. His goal was a Bachelor of Laws degree, but financially, he could afford only one more year of study, and the courses (international and constitutional law) were already a month advanced. Most students at the University required two years to complete a degree; Minor himself recommended three. Montague's accelerated schedule therefore taxed his capacity and constitution. Even Christmas Day found him at his books. Worn by the grinding pace, he despaired of reaching his goal, and voiced regret that he had ever returned. "Old John B." he now described in terms not quite so complimentary ("Mr. Minor is so innately mean that I can barely

11 *Catalogue of Students of the University of Virginia Summer Law Class for 1884* (Charlottesville, 1884), 1–4.
12 Montague to Betsie Hoskins, July 13 and 26, Aug. 16, 1884, Moore Collection. Information for the rest of the chapter is taken almost entirely from Montague's many letters to Miss Hoskins, 1884–88, Moore Collection.

stand him."), and the death of his other law professor in late November was a distinct setback to his hopes of completing in one year.

Nor was Montague content with the University or with Charlottesville life about him. He was abashed at the rigid custom which dictated that one could not speak to a classmate unless first introduced. And the "swellhead" students who patronized the barrooms, he depicted contemptuously: "This place tonight is almost a young Sodom. The billiard saloons are full, the card tables are full, and the hacks will be rolling in from town all during the night with fellows that are full." Then too, Mrs. Chancellor's boarding house served bad oysters. Montague developed several warm friendships, but by his own admission, constant study prohibited any substantial diversion. His life was "almost a hermit's."

The intensive study paid dividends. Despite his accelerated schedule and personal apprehension, he passed the comprehensive examination in June and received his law degree with twenty-one other graduates in ceremonies on July 1. The profession had been chosen, the subject material mastered, now would come the career.

Despite an unobtrusive beginning, this career was destined to bring high accolades and honors. Such was the intention of the man who charted it, for if Jack Montague was often unduly pessimistic concerning particular qualities in himself, for his long-range plans he exuded supreme confidence and ambition. "Failure," he intoned, "is not written in the lexicon of youth." Acting upon a conviction that "no man is any account without conceit, also that no man is any account who shows this," he proceeded, with psychological acumen and with deliberative step, to climb the ladder of legal and political preferment.[13]

Montague possessed this requisite conceit without overtly expressing it. In a sense he considered himself predestined to greatness: "I was not born to be a drone," he declared to Betsie, "it was intended by the Omnipotent hand either that I should die early or make life a success." Later he exclaimed, "I don't want to crawl to the top, I want to leap there!"[14] Just where this top, this apex, was, he never made clear, but occasional references to national service and to "fame"

13 Montague once wrote to Betsie, "Mr. Marchant [Inglewood's tenant] thinks I am much ahead of what I am in reality. But then this is in accord with my principle to fool people in this line. Am I wrong?" Montague to Hoskins, June 26, 1884, Moore Collection.
14 July 20, 1884; March 4, 1886.

indicated that the echelon contemplated was high indeed. So compelling was Montague's ambition that he confessed it made him restless and gnawed at him unceasingly. Robert Montague's political legacy, a legacy of ambition as well as idealism, had proved durable.

But if Montague's personal ambition seemed almost overweening at times, with this selfish motivation for personal success was a selfless ambition, "a longing to do something for the people." [15] The political idealism inherited from his father, nurtured by religious conviction, and combined with personal ambition, gave promise of a creative career of public service. Whether the sterling idealism and the eager ambition could remain unified in the turbulent Virginia politics of the later nineteenth century remained to be seen.

15   To Miss Hoskins, March 2, 1885.

III

THE EMERGING POLITICIAN

THE immediate question facing Montague upon his graduation was where to settle. After considering Hampton and Fredericksburg and the prospect of a partnership in Texas, he turned his attention to the young Southside town of Danville near the North Carolina border. Described to him as "the most flourishing town in this State," Danville had a population of some seven thousand persons. He wrote for advice to at least one leading Danville citizen and personally visited the town in early August. He liked what he saw. The graduate had selected the city of his future, where "the atrocious crime of being a young man was rewarded rather than punished." [1]

Montague arrived at Danville on October 5, 1885. He quickly found living accommodations in a boarding house and arranged for a law office in the downtown business district. With a facility that belied his somewhat shy nature, he soon made numerous friends, both personally and professionally, in the cotton mill and tobacco town. Within a few months of his arrival he was asked to officiate at commencement exercises of the Danville College for Young Ladies; and in the Baptist church he soon rose to prominence, advocating increased donations to church orphanages and participating in regional meetings of the Roanoke Baptist Union.

As a civic-minded citizen and later as a family man, Montague as-

1 Danville *Register,* April 14, 1888, in scrapbook, Moore Collection.

sumed the ordinary role of participant in community activity. As a lawyer, his role was less prosaic. He quickly developed a reputation for legal acumen which eventually extended beyond the confines of Danville and within eight years resulted in an appointment as United States District Attorney for Western Virginia. These, then, were embryonic years for the emerging politician.

Initially, claims cases constituted the bulk of Montague's legal work, his fee being a customary 10 per cent of the amount collected. So adept did he prove himself in this field that two Richmond firms, Allison & Addison and Southern Fertilizer Company, contracted with him to collect their unpaid claims in the Danville region. Since some of the claims were substantial, these contracts greatly augmented the young lawyer's small annual income, which by 1887 amounted to $1,500.[2]

Montague's other legal activity consisted chiefly of minor criminal cases: assault, forgery, petit larceny. His first murder defense came in 1886. His record of acquittals was impressive; just as impressive, however, was the poverty of his clients. For the first few years of his career Montague lived "the routine life of a small city lawyer, with a throng of poor clients. But then every now and then a rich one patronizes me, and I suspect in a few years I will have my share of them." [3]

The greatest boon to Montague's developing legal reputation came in March, 1888, when he participated in the most celebrated murder trial in Danville's history. In that trial Montague, joined by Judge A. M. Aiken, defended Charles Saylor, a Danville man charged with slaying Richard L. Cohen. That Saylor had technically killed Cohen was not disputed; whether he was guilty of murder or had killed in self-defense was the issue. After a three-day trial Montague, in his closing arguments to the jury, made a stirring appeal for the legal right of self-defense, an appeal which "swayed the vast crowd in the courtroom." At its conclusion, the courtroom listeners began to ap-

2 Outgoing letters from Montague, 1887 and after, Montague Papers; fee book, Moore Collection. In these early years, Montague's most important claims case was that of *Noell and Starling v the Richmond and Danville Railway,* in which Montague won damages of $1,260 for his client, Noell and Starling. The railway appealed the case to the Virginia supreme court, and in 1888 Montague appeared before that court for the first time. The original decision was sustained. Montague to S. W. Guy, June, 14, 1888, Montague Papers.
3 Montague to Hoskins, Jan. 22, 1886, March 13, 1887, Moore Collection.

plaud before the judge could call for order. Montague's eloquence notwithstanding, the result was a hung jury and a new trial. The second trial, held before a jury of Amherst County residents, took place in December, 1888, and elicited the same forensic display by Montague. This time the defendant was acquitted.[4]

This trial and others amply demonstrated the attributes which made Montague's legal success almost inevitable—his impressive manner and style before the bar. His red hair, handsome countenance, clear, distinct voice, dignified gestures, and impeccably neat dress created a personal magnetism which carried his audience. Added to his physical attractiveness was a "cogent, lucid and persuasive" manner of speech, a manner which occasionally assumed the ornate, florid quality of his prose, but which rarely forsook clarity for embellishment. Montague used his natural talents effectively. Bragging to Betsie about his performance in the second Saylor trial, he recounted, "I not only carried many of the people in the audience from laughter, to serious thought and then to tears . . . the jury wept." So overwhelming had been Montague's final appeal that one of the jurors announced that his next son would bear Montague's name.[5]

Magnetism Montague had; affluence he had not. Economically, the "new Virginia" of the 1880's expanded rapidly, but money still spread itself thin, and fortunes were few. Wealth was concentrated chiefly in corporations, especially in railroads. Anxious to improve his economic standing, and anxious most of all to acquire sufficient practice to make possible his marriage to Betsie, Montague sought a position as local attorney for the Richmond and Danville Railroad. Possibly because of his own efficiency in prosecuting several important claims cases against the railroad, Montague obtained the position in August of 1889. (Evidently he also benefited from the favorable lobbying of C. G. Holland, one of Danville's wealthiest citizens, who took an avid interest in his career.[6])

Montague was to serve his new employer capably for the next eight years, defending the railroad against the same damage claims he had previously prosecuted, investigating official complaints by municipal

4 Clippings, Dec. 13, 1887, March 16, 17, and 18, Dec. 15, 1888, scrapbook, Moore Collection; Montague to Hoskins, Dec. 15, 1888, *ibid.*
5 Benjamin Simpson, *Men, Places, and Things* (Dance Bros., 1891), 382–85; Montague to Hoskins, Dec. 15, 1888, Moore Collection.
6 Montague to Hoskins, Dec. 15, 1888, Moore Collection; Montague to James P. Hamins, June 14, 1889, Montague Papers.

bodies concerning the railroad's property, and advising the management in its public relations.[7] Although his position evidently involved
no familiarity with company policy, it did provide a relationship with
individuals who were to become important figures in Virginia politics.
General William H. Payne, general counsel for the road and Montague's direct superior, took an active interest in state politics, later
joining Montague in the ranks of the Independents. Another significant acquaintance was Payne's son-in-law, Eppa Hunton, Jr., who
served as attorney for the Richmond area. The son of Senator
Hunton, he too later played a prominent role in the Virginia reform
movement. Political associations with these men were to prove valuable in Montague's next legal ambition—the position of United States
District Attorney for Western Virginia.

Montague's campaign for federal office—the climax of his early
legal career—reflects the success of his role as an emerging politician.
If his appointment as district attorney recognized his legal abilities, in
an even greater measure it represented a political reward. His early
success at the bar was equaled or surpassed by his rapid rise to political prominence. Remarkably, his meteoric rise developed against the
backdrop of a political scene in which he felt instinctively uncomfortable—the turbulent Virginia politics of the late nineteenth century. A
brief analysis of this political background is therefore requisite.

Virginia's post-Civil War political development witnessed a gradual deterioration of public ethics and service. Divested of many of her
abler statesmen by the war; faced with a suddenly increased electorate, composed, in many counties, of a majority of tractable Negro
illiterates; and plagued by economic devastation which forced her to
borrow heavily, Virginia encountered formidable problems, equipped
with a minimum of human and physical resources. The state had
early been "redeemed" from Carpetbagger Reconstruction, but the
new Conservative party which governed the Dominion in the 1870's
proved to be inflexible with reference to the state's most immediate
and pressing problem. Maintaining that Virginia was honor-bound not
to scale down the massive state debt contracted before the 1870's,
a debt whose interest sometimes equaled the total annual state expenditures, the Conservatives passed a funding act selling state-
owned stocks in railroads and sacrificing even the public school fund
—all to pay the debt.

7 Montague to W. H. Payne, Jan. 31, 1891, and Montague to A. B. An-
   drews, June 26, 1893, Montague Papers.

By the end of the decade the state's citizenry recognized the growing futility of the Conservatives' program. A demand arose that the debt be repudiated or readjusted. The "Readjusters," organized and led by William Mahone, a Civil War general, gained control of the state legislature in 1879 and elected a governor in 1881. Once in office the Readjusters arbitrarily scaled the debt down to a level maintainable by the state. They also levied higher taxes on railroads and corporations, gave greater aid to schools and colleges, and abolished the poll tax.

But if the Readjusters brought a fresh air of progress to Virginia, they also injected a new dose of political corruption and demagoguery. Mahone, elected in 1880 to the United States Senate, proved himself a master of political chicanery and manipulation. Combining a loose alliance of Republicans, Negroes, and disaffected Conservatives into a powerful political machine, he maintained power with ruthless thoroughness. Negro votes were often corralled by the bribing of Negro ministers, by outright purchase, or by actual intimidation. And, to placate Mahone's followers of that race, Negroes were occasionally appointed to local town offices.[8]

The Readjuster era in Virginia was short-lived. The Conservatives quickly capitalized on the Readjusters' callous attitude toward political corruption, particularly their deference to the Negro. The "Funders'" old cry for state honor was forgotten and the debt readjustment was tacitly accepted. Conservative John S. Barbour, in 1883 elected state chairman of the party (rechristened the Democratic party), laid detailed campaign plans for the legislative election of that year, intensively organizing each precinct, county, and district in the Commonwealth. Barbour's organization, the harbinger of the Virginia Democratic machine, successfully vanquished the discordant Readjusters in November, regaining control of the state legislature. A period of unbroken Democratic ascendancy had begun.

From 1883 to 1889 the Democratic party, led by Barbour and backed by railroad money, consolidated its control of the state. In

8 John H. Moore, "The Life of James Gaven Field, Virginia Populist" (M.A. thesis, University of Virginia, 1953), 108; Herman L. Horn, "The Growth and Development of the Democratic Party in Virginia Since 1890" (Ph.D. dissertation, Duke University, 1949), 22–25. Other discussions of electioneering methods can be found in Richard L. Morton, *The Negro in Virginia Politics, 1865–1902* (Charlottesville, 1919), and William C. Pendleton, *Political History of Appalachian Virginia, 1776–1927* (Dayton, Va., 1927).

1885 the Confederate hero, Fitzhugh Lee, won the governorship. In 1887 John W. Daniel replaced Mahone in the Senate, and in 1889 Barbour himself replaced Readjuster Senator Harrison H. Riddleberger. Mahone came back to wage a strong campaign for governor in 1889, but the Democratic candidate, Philip W. McKinney, emerged triumphant. After 1889, the Republican party in Virginia (the name was adopted by the Readjusters in 1884) "went to pieces." Already suffering from internal schism, it lost its most prominent leaders who gravitated back into the Democratic fold, and its reputation as a party of mountaineers and Negroes became firmly established.[9]

Both governors Lee and McKinney were personally honest and gave Virginia acceptable government. To the consternation of some, Lee turned out to be a "real liberal." Yet the Democratic party itself eventually adopted the same corrupt electioneering tactics it had so recently condemned in its opponent. Proceeding at first from a desire to rid Virginia of the threat of domination by uneducated Negroes and/or irresponsible government, especially on the county level, the Democratic legislature enacted the Anderson-McCormick election law in 1884. This act ended Mahone's effective control of Negro votes by giving the General Assembly control over all the state's electoral machinery. So quickly did the Assembly make effective use of this machinery, that in 1885 Lee was elected on the basis of majorities from counties in which the Negro population was larger than the white. These paradoxical Democratic majorities in Republican territories were obtained by stuffed ballot boxes and fraudulent returns.[10]

Such perversions of the electoral process continued long after 1885 and long after any threat, real or imagined, to white government had vanished. The Democratic politician, accustomed to purchasing Negro votes, began to purchase white votes. Moreover, whiskey and money began to "cut a figure" in intraparty competition, as well as in general election contests against the "black Republicans." As late as 1902 the national House Election Committee, in seating William F. Rhea as Representative of Virginia's Ninth District, criticized the methods used there as "repugnant to all lovers of fair play and honest

9   See Charles E. Wynes, *Race Relations in Virginia* (Charlottesville, 1961); H. J. Eckenrode, "Virginia Since 1865, a Political History" (MS in Alderman Library, University of Virginia, Charlottesville), 235 ff.

10 Moore, "Life of James Gaven Field," 120; Eckenrode, "Virginia Since 1865," 237; Horn, "Democratic Party in Virginia," 28–29; Lois G. Moore, "William Alexander Anderson; Attorney General of Virginia, 1902–1910" (M.A. thesis, University of Virginia, 1959), 22, 72.

elections." [11] The Commonwealth had reached a nadir of democratic processes.

On this troubled sea Montague would launch his campaign for political advancement. From his father he had had glimpses of a nobler era in Virginia politics, glimpses which made the modern spectacle even more painful and disturbing. His reaction was therefore one of disenchantment and disgust. But he did not withdraw from the political scene in total aversion. Rather, he bided his time, and hoped for better days.

Montague's reaction to his political environment as a young child is cloaked in obscurity. However, his father presumably instilled in the boy the accepted Conservative view on the debt question. Of Mahone and the political corruption which accompanied his regime, young Montague was bitterly critical. In a letter composed at Indiantown and sent to the *Witness*, an out-of-state religious organ, Montague termed Mahone a commercial Senator—a man whose industry was "whetted by malice," and whose shrewdness was "almost unique in its criminality." Later, recalling the state of affairs under Mahone, he charged that "the courts of justice were corrupt, ignorance and corruption [were] found in many high places, professors . . . [left] the universities, and public honor turned into disorder." [12]

Montague especially criticized Mahone's use of the race issue in state politics. Although he personally viewed the individual Negro kindly and with a genuine paternal concern, he resented the effect of the Negro's suffrage on the state's political ethics.[13] "The majority of the white people in Virginia," he asserted in his letter to the *Witness*, "do everything in their power for the improvement of the Negro," but by consolidating the Negro vote, Mahone had purposefully fomented racial prejudices. "Under the influence of this senator, colored people suspended and expelled the members of their churches;

---

11 Horn, "Democratic Party in Virginia," 28–29.
12 Letter of a "Young Virginian" at Indiantown, May 7 (1883 or 1884), published in the *Witness*, scrapbook, Moore Collection; unidentified clippings, scrapbook, Montague Papers.
13 An indication of his paternal attitude came when the "boy" at his Danville boarding house became ill with pneumonia. Montague visited him and his family several times, and sent them a "nicely dressed chicken." He described his visit as "a duty in the discharge of which I felt happy." Montague to Hoskins, April 23, 1887, Moore Collection.

made pastors resign; wives threatened to leave their husbands. . . .
A colored minister living within a few miles of this place told me that
he had been threatened by Mahone's canvassers that upon success of
the Democratic party, the Negro population would be relegated to
slavery." Such a travesty of the representative principle Montague
found antithetical to his concept of proper government. Reared according to a different standard of political ethics, he resented the corruption brought to Southern politics by the Negro's exploiters, and he
wistfully longed for the day when racial and regional factors would
cease to frustrate the formation of a new Southern and Virginian
statesmanship. "I am young," he wrote in concluding his Indiantown
letter, "I turn longingly and hopefully to the young men of the North
and South; in them alone can I reasonably expect to see our country
again made common."

Danville lay in the heart of Virginia's black belt. It had been the
scene of a bloody race riot in 1883, and there Montague found political manipulation at its worst. But though idealistic, Montague was
also ambitious and calculating. He was a young lawyer, desiring a
successful practice and an early marriage. Desiring also eventual political promotion, he realized that to plunge immediately into political
quarrels would invite a quick death to both careers. He therefore realistically accepted existing conditions, complaining of the political
situation privately and before selected groups, but publicly speaking
only the accepted Democratic gospel. "My object," he confided privately, "is to stay clear of every faction and feud, and to hold my
tongue," a policy he termed "discretion, not hypocrisy." [14]

His policy proved to be prudent. In January, 1886, only two
months after arriving in the city, Montague was asked by leading
Danville citizens to accept nomination to the Virginia House of Delegates. He declined, but contributed several speeches to the subsequent
campaign, speeches "full of sound advice and true Democracy." In
March of the same year he similarly declined an invitation to run for
commonwealth's attorney of Danville. In August, 1887, however,
encouraged by numerous friends, he seriously considered running for
the elective position of Danville corporation judge. But the possible
opposition of his close friend Judge Aiken eventually deterred him,
and when in the same year he was pressed to accept the chairmanship
of the town's Democratic party, he decided not to do so: "I don't

14 Montague to Matilda Hoskins, Nov. 30, 1885, *ibid.*

want it, and will only accept it when I think my duty prompts me."
The time was not yet ripe for political baptism.[15]

The opportunity came in 1888. Montague, then but a twenty-six-year-old youth, boldly announced his candidacy for the post of commonwealth's attorney in opposition to the veteran incumbent, Henry E. Barksdale. Optimistically, he predicted to Betsie in January, 1888, that "if left to the freewill of the people, with no money used to purchase votes," he would win by a large majority. The first Saylor murder trial preceded the primary election on April 24 and directly affected its outcome. Though Montague felt his speech at the trial had helped him professionally, he feared it had injured him politically since popular feeling had turned against Saylor. As election day approached he reported: "Everything I said or did during the murder trial has been tortured into everything else except what I did say and mean to injure my chances. . . . I never in my life dreamed that any man could be so lied about as I have been. My opponent is thoroughly unscrupulous and he pushes his henchmen to circulate these. . . . the integrity of my position is so plain to me that I feel painfully the maliciousness of these rumors."

In his despondency Montague exploded, "But for backing out, I would withdraw and quit the disgusting field of politics." The election saw Barksdale win renomination by a narrow margin, 567 to 494. The first youthful venture had failed, but more painful than the loss of the office was the wounded pride of the vanquished.[16]

Although he was becoming increasingly disenchanted with state politics, Montague could still campaign enthusiastically for the Democratic President Grover Cleveland in his race against Benjamin Harrison in 1888. In August of that year he was elected president of a pro-Cleveland Democratic club organized in Danville, and the Fifth District Democratic organization later drafted him to make a series of speeches throughout the Southside region. Apologizing to Betsie for his renewed interest in politics, Montague wrote, "When one contemplates the state of affairs that must exist as consequent upon the election of Harrison, I don't see how he can suppress his exertions or his patriotism." On September 19 he addressed a Chatham audience; on September 22 he spoke at North Danville, on the twenty-fifth at Stu-

15 Montague to Betsie Hoskins, Jan. 22, March 4, June 24, 1886, Aug. 20 and 27, 1887, *ibid.*
16 Montague to Hoskins, Dec. 11, 1887, Jan. 15, March 23 and 25, 1888, *ibid.*

art, on October 1 at Franklin, and on October 3 at Rocky Mount. An auditor of Montague's speech at Elba on November 3 described him as "not the rising but the risen orator of Danville." [17]

Montague's oratorical eloquence, first widely recognized in this campaign, was to prove an asset in his political career as it had in his legal practice. By 1891 a Danville contemporary would declare: "As an orator, Mr. Montague has no superior in this section of the State. He is a toast in every political campaign, and is hailed with delight whenever he ascends the rostrum." [18] His style of speaking has been described in many ways, some of them contradictory. References are found to the "grandeur and pathos of his speech, the unquenchable eloquence of his voice," to his "graceful, ornate, and animated" manner. One journalist described his oratory as "chaste, elegant, fluent . . . classical," his reasoning "terse, compact, vigorous." A different picture was painted by another observer who stated that "Mr. Montague's continued references to Mahone were the most stirring examples of invective to which I ever listened," and on at least one occasion his style was described as "homely . . . colloquial . . . humorous." [19]

In his criticism of Harrison, Montague showed more sarcasm than elegance. "The calf," he proclaimed, "might as well expect to get milk from an icicle as for the Southern people to expect to get justice from the hands of such a man." But his remarks contained more than censure. Though partaking of the customary campaign folderol, they revealed his attitude toward national issues and national problems, especially his continuing rejection and mistrust of the new industrial money power then in the process of consolidating America's economic wealth. In these and following addresses Montague referred frequently to human rights as having been "wrung from the power which wealth and influence have controlled" only by determined efforts of the people. He emphasized the precarious status of those rights at the hands of self-seeking officeholders and pressure groups. And he voiced fear of the money power's ability to arbitrarily fix tariffs, regulate currency, and control legislation in its own interest. He particularly resented the intrusion of plutocracy into statesman-

---

17   Clippings, August to November, 1888, scrapbook, Moore Collection; Montague to Hoskins, Oct. 3 and 28, 1888, Moore Collection; Montague to Fitzhugh Lee, Sept. 26, 1888, Montague Papers.
18   Simpson, *Men, Places, and Things*, 382–85.
19   These descriptions are taken from various journalistic accounts of Montague's speeches from 1888 to 1900.

ship; he recoiled "at seeing merit overlooked for filthy lucre's sake" in the nomination of candidates. As late as 1930 Montague would characterize the Republican party as the party of materialism and the Democratic party as the party of humanism.[20]

This disdain for materialism was perhaps the most progressive of Montague's inclinations. His concern was for the whole society, for the virtues of character rather than for wealth. Although he did not consider people socially or intellectually equal, at least he desired for them equal opportunity and individual liberty. Later, in 1892, Montague asserted that the greatest social and political danger to the country lay in the growing concentration of her wealth, the urbanization of her population, and the gradual disappearance of her middle class. To counteract these dangers, he advocated more education for the citizenry in "knowledge of our governments, State and Federal," the creation of a "real science of politics" in every college in the country, a federal policy of immigration restriction to retard accelerating urbanization, and the construction of good roads to ease the social and industrial blockade of rural areas. "So far as the government can lessen these disparities or equalize these ameliorations it is manifest that to this end its powers should be exerted." [21]

His lofty ideals of statesmanship and his concern for the individual were the most consistent threads of Montague's developing progressivism. As economic centralization increased, so did his progressivism, while his concept of laissez-faire weakened. But if he departed somewhat from the conservatism of his father, in a sense the transition was a natural one. Class notes taken by Robert Montague from Professor Thomas Roderick Dew's lecture on the United States Bank and the "dollar era," June 20, 1843, include these remarks: "Religion, virtue, morality, and even the . . . eye of beauty itself, have all become wards of barter." [22] The "external splendor and internal rottenness" which Robert Montague decried was little different from the "high living and low thinking" that his son found so distasteful.

Montague's aspirations were rapidly being fulfilled. As a church layman and an active citizen, he had become an accustomed feature

20 These quotations come from scrapbook clippings of campaign speeches in 1888, 1889, 1896, 1897, and 1930, Moore Collection.
21 *Address of A. J. Montague, Esq., delivered before the Literary Societies of William and Mary College on June 29, 1892* (Danville, 1893), *passim*, in Montague Papers.
22 Robert Montague notebook, Moore Collection.

of the Danville scene; as an orator and politician, he won a local re-
nown which would soon grow to state and regional proportions. Still
lacking, however, was the marriage and family life for which he
yearned. All information concerning his rising civic and professional
standing Montague reported in letters to Betsie. The correspondence
of the engaged couple continued, unabated in volume or intensity of
affection. Their marriage was delayed only by "cold money facts."
Finally, when Montague felt able to support a family in proper fashion, the long-awaited marriage took place on December 11, 1889, at
Betsie's home in King and Queen County. Returning to Danville after
a brief New York honeymoon, the couple established temporary residence in the home of W. H. Lipscomb, a Danville friend. There they
remained until approximately 1892, when they moved into a large,
eight-room house, newly built on the outskirts of Danville in Pittsylvania County. Montague could at last give to his wife the comfort
of three servants: Lavinia, a cook; Pency, a nurse; and Henry, a
gardener and general helper. Pency cared for the three children who
came to the family—Gay in 1891, Janet in 1895, and Robert Latané
in 1897—children to whom Montague gave devoted parental attention, and children who grew to regard their parents with an uncommon respect and reverence.[23]

Montague's role as a family man did not detract from his continuing interest in Virginia politics. In 1889, a few months before his
marriage, he had attended the state Democratic convention, supporting the eventual nominee, "the State's pride and hope," Philip W. Mc-
Kinney. In the campaign against Mahone which followed, Montague
spoke in avid support of McKinney at several points in the state. Especially excoriating was his speech before the Powhatan Club in
Richmond, in which he lauded the honesty of the Lee administration
and contrasted Lee's record with the office-holding favoritism of the
Mahone machine. At least once, following McKinney's election,
Montague recommended to the governor a man for judicial appointment, suggesting that his (Montague's) own "short career . . . of
faithfulness to you in your aspirations" should excuse the presump-
tion of such a request.[24]

Other indications of a growing political role are evident. In 1889

23 Moore interview.
24 "In that great Convention I felt that you were the people's choice," Mon-
    tague wrote to Philip W. McKinney, Nov. 7, 1889 (Montague Papers);
    Montague to McKinney, April 10, 1890, Montague Papers; clippings, 1889,
    scrapbook, Moore Collection.

Montague declined the offer of nomination to the House of Delegates. In 1889 and 1890 his advice and endorsements were solicited for the semipolitical appointments of school superintendent of his locality. Perhaps most indicative was his appointment late in 1891 as a board member of the state mental institution at Williamsburg. As a member of this board he worked to obtain an adequate "water-fire supply," and as a member of a committee of five to memorialize the legislature for appropriations, he urged the committee chairman to call an early meeting: "I notice that the chairman of the Finance Committee of the House has already reported an appropriation bill, minus the sum we need. . . . We must hurry." [25]

In the presidential campaign of 1892 Montague again took the stump, this time before statewide audiences. The Virginia Democracy (as the state Democratic organization was often called) in that year experienced an internal schism, prompted in part by the fear of a third-party Populist rebellion. A group led by the silver-tongued orator Senator John W. Daniel opposed the renomination of Grover Cleveland, a man they considered too conservative on currency matters. The state convention which met in May resulted, essentially, in a victory for the anti-Cleveland forces. The delegation to the Democratic National Convention was divided equally between the contesting factions, but the platform adopted showed Populist inclinations in its appeal for federal aid to agriculture and for an increased volume of currency.[26]

Montague's attitude toward the 1892 rift in Virginia's Democracy is unknown. Evidently, he continued to follow his policy of strategic aloofness from factions. After Cleveland's nomination, however, he gave wholehearted support to the national Democratic ticket. On the local scene he spurned the Populist movement then winning widespread approval in the Southside black belt, and campaigned actively for Claude A. Swanson, the youthful Democratic nominee for Congress from the Fifth District. On the state scene, Basil Gordon, Democratic state chairman, recognized Montague's oratorical abilities by appointing him representative from the Fifth District on the state's Democratic Executive Committee, a position usually reserved for the most prominent and professional politicians. In the Virginia cam-

25 Montague to John L. Hurt, Jan. 13, 1890, and Montague to Col. W. R. Taylor, Jan. 30, 1892, Montague Papers.
26 Richard B. Doss, "John Warwick Daniel, a Study in the Virginia Democracy" (Ph.D. dissertation, University of Virginia, 1955), 139–40; J. H. Moore, "Life of James Gaven Field," 156.

paign which followed, Montague spoke throughout the Commonwealth, sometimes twice a day, ingratiating himself not only with
Gordon but with the entire Virginia political hierarchy.[27]

With the Cleveland victory in November, Montague could confidently anticipate reward for political faithfulness. His fidelity paid
dividends in the hectic scramble for political office which followed
Cleveland's inauguration in March, 1893. Numerous Virginians
descended on Washington, seeking not only the six chief offices of
federal patronage (revenue collector, marshal, and district attorney
for both eastern and western Virginia), but also consulates and petty
departmental positions. When Cleveland requested the Virginia congressional delegation to nominate jointly a slate for the six major offices, recommendations, petitions, and personal visitations kept the
delegation in continual harassment and embarrassment.[28]

The host of aspirants gave Montague stiff competition in his candidacy for district attorney of the west. His most active supporter was
the newly elected Fifth District Congressman, Claude A. Swanson, a
handsome, personable, young politician, who had left the University
of Virginia one year after Montague, settling in his home county of
Pittsylvania. Swanson had quickly acquired a thriving law practice
and, like Montague, a political reputation. In 1892 both he and Montague had been prominently mentioned for Democratic nomination
to Congress. Montague declined to run, said some, because of his
strong friendship for Swanson. Others surmised, perhaps more plausi-
bly, that "Swanson took up and supported 'young Jack Montague,'
[for district attorney] for the sole and simple reason that 'young
Jack' had strong Congressional aspirations in the Fifth district, and
being a public speaker of magnetism and address far exceeding any
such qualities in Mr. Swanson, it was thought in this section that he
could capture the nomination." [29]

Aided by Swanson's substantial support, Montague also sought the
endorsement of Senator Daniel as early as December, 1892, but in
March, 1893, Daniel attempted to ally with Swanson's political en-

27 Richmond *Times,* Oct. 31, 1892; Richmond *Dispatch,* May 26, 1893.
28 James Hay to William Bibb, Nov. 16, 1892; Charles T. O'Ferrall to Bibb,
Nov. 28, 1893; John W. Daniel to Bibb, Nov. 14, 1892; all in William Bibb Papers, Alderman Library, University of Virginia, Charlottesville.
29 Richmond *Dispatch,* March 8, 9, 10, and 18, 1893; unidentified clipping,
Aug. 28, 1897, scrapbook, Montague Papers; Roanoke *Evening World,*
March 23, 1901, in scrapbook, Moore Collection.

emies in the Fifth District. Montague's relations with Senator Eppa Hunton, Sr. (appointed by McKinney on the death of Senator Barbour) are even more uncertain. He made at least one personal visit to Senator Hunton, seeking his support, and later, after Montague's final appointment in May, Eppa Hunton, Jr. recommended a candidate for his assistant district attorney. Whatever the exact positions of Daniel and Hunton before the caucus of the delegation, Montague's friends claimed that he would begin with at least four of the twelve votes. Seven votes would be decisive.[30]

On March 31, the day of decision, the Virginia delegation met at 8 P.M. in Daniel's capitol committee room, remaining in session until past 2 A.M. After a wearisome and unbelievable two to three hundred ballots, the final selections were made, and all regions but Virginia's Second District were in some way placated. Swanson had garnered his objective; he had convinced the professionals. Montague would become district attorney. A public career of over forty years' duration had begun.[31]

At the age of thirty Montague thus had been accorded a significant tribute to his ability. His appointment also demonstrated, however, that the young idealist had not yet assumed the mantle of the fearless statesman envisioned in his Richmond College essay a decade earlier. The "true statesman" of that essay was one who placed principle above all else—including office. But Montague, though chafing at the political corruption which he had experienced even in his own race for commonwealth's attorney, had expediently muted his protests and allied with the very type of politician which he had previously castigated. Swanson, the man on whom his appointment rested, was described by Judge Berryman Green in 1892 as "the creature and servant of the rings. . . . His election and the election of such men as he and [Peter J.] Otey will end in the overthrow of Virginia Democracy." [32] Montague's alliance with such a man must, in turn, savor something of expediency.

30   Jannette Hoskins to Betsie Montague, Nov. 30, 1892, Montague Papers; Berryman Green to John L. Hurt, March 2, 1893, and John W. Daniel to Hurt, March 27, 1893, in John L. Hurt Papers, Alderman Library, University of Virginia, Charlottesville; Eppa Hunton, Jr., to Montague, May 27, 1893, Moore Collection; Richmond *Dispatch*, March 22, 1893.
31   Richmond *Dispatch,* March 9, 21, 22, 23, and 25, April 1 and 2, 1893. Cleveland officially appointed Montague on May 27. Unidentified clipping, May, 1893, scrapbook, Moore Collection.
32   Berryman Green to John L. Hurt, Oct. 17, 1894, Hurt Papers.

Montague had played the game by the existing rules, but he disliked the rules. Although he had not yet become the statesman of his ideals, neither was he the inveterate politician. As a lawyer, he had sought and obtained a public position, legal in nature, which called for no political pledges or platform. Privately, he continued to support orphanages and general philanthropy, and as an obscure member of an asylum board he showed concern for public eleemosynary institutions. And in an eloquent address before the Literary Society of William and Mary College in June, 1892, he bemoaned the conditions of political corruption then existing on the national scene. As a public figure, however, he discreetly avoided controversial pronouncements on Virginia problems. As district attorney he would keep his counsel and perform his official duties. The political Independent had not yet developed.

To some extent, the political philosophy expressed in Montague's 1892 Williamsburg address displayed the same pattern as his "mugwump manifesto" delivered at Richmond a decade earlier, but there was a significant change of emphasis, and of content as well.[33] More now was said of political rights and the sacredness of the ballot—less said of the foibles of the average man. More now was said of the dangers of entrenched officeholders beholden to the new masters of money—less said of the perils of an uninformed electorate. Perhaps most significant, Montague now warned of a danger to the "plain and simple" heritage of the Republic, resulting from the growing concentration of wealth. The proposals he advanced as a possible solution for society's ills showed that his former laissez-faire attitude was giving way to an endorsement of government intervention to help channel and control economic growth and development.

Montague's Richmond College address of 1882 could well have been delivered with enthusiasm and gusto by Robert Montague. But the father would have balked at some of the sentiments expounded at William and Mary ten years later. Unlike the usual evolution—from youthful, idealistic, naive zeal to venerable, realistic, sound conservatism—Montague's political philosophy in those ten years had changed from an outlook that was idealistic but cynically withdrawn to one more dynamic, more imbued with human empathy. The incip-

---

33 "Those who say the purification of modern politics is an 'iridescent dream,'" he counseled, "should be relegated to the limbo of 'statesmen without a job.'" *Address of A. J. Montague, Esq., William and Mary College, June 29, 1892,* Montague Papers.

ient politician and statesman was in a process of transformation. The sculpture begun at Inglewood and Richmond assumed in Danville a more definite shape. The young idealist had shown himself fully able to hold his own in the calculating game of politics. This combination of idealism and pragmatism gave promise of a rewarding political future.

IV

MONTAGUE
AND VIRGINIA POLITICS,
1893–96

Wɪᴛʜ his appointment as district attorney, Andrew Jackson Montague had made his statewide political debut. His position in relation to the various dominant political factions in Virginia was yet obscure, however; the three years following his appointment would clarify his basic alignment. Similarly, the general Virginia political scene assumed a sharper focus, a clearer division between factions. These years saw the emergence of the Martin Democratic machine, destined to play a powerful role in the state's political affairs. They also witnessed the culmination of the Populistic silver agitation in the fratricidal Democratic rift of 1896. Finally, Montague's personal reputation and popularity increased to a degree which encouraged him to seek further political promotion. For Montague in his role in Virginia politics, these were settling years, maturing years.

The Western Judicial District of Virginia in 1893 constituted one of the largest in the country in volume of official business. District court sessions, held regularly in four different cities, Harrisonburg, Lynchburg, Abingdon, and Danville, provided the district attorney an immense amount of work for his modest annual salary of $4,500. Among other items, the court agenda included prosecutions for federal tax irregularities, evasions of liquor laws, and banking malfeasance.[1]

---

1   G. W. Montague, *History and Genealogy of Peter Montague*, 313; Richmond *Dispatch*, July 18, 1897.

Montague evidently performed his duties with vigor and ability. He undertook certain administrative reforms in the office, and his rigorous prosecution of government suits won respect even from those prosecuted.[2] His work also pleased his Washington superiors. He was criticized by the Attorney General's office in Washington on only one occasion, and that criticism was later expunged from the files as "wholly undeserved." [3] Montague's performance also impressed prominent Virginia figures; Senator Daniel avowed that he had never seen a young man handle himself with a greater degree of "dexterity, ability and foresight in court." In a self-evaluation, Montague claimed he had obtained "more convictions than ever before proportionate to the number of cases tried." [4]

The nature of Montague's work enhanced his rising political reputation. Present at numerous court days throughout western Virginia, he became well known to both lawyers and local politicians; and when Cleveland somewhat hesitantly granted him the right to appoint his own assistant district attorney, he shrewdly selected the brother of Henry C. Stuart, a wealthy farmer and businessman and a powerful figure in southwest Virginia politics, who later became a Virginia governor. Montague also continued his close association with that consummate politician, Claude A. Swanson. When bills affecting Montague's judicial district and salary came before Congress, he obtained Swanson's promise to safeguard his interests; and when Montague received complaints from dissatisfied constituents concerning Swanson's handling of patronage, he defended Swanson as a "good representative" who deserved a second nomination. Montague also spoke for Swanson in his 1894 campaign for reelection.[5]

But if Jack Montague fulfilled his duties creditably and formed valuable political contacts in his work, publicly he evidently remained

2 Montague to Waitman T. Stigleman, July 5, 1894, and George M. Edmonds to Montague, Aug. 27, 1897, Montague Papers.
3 Montague to J. S. Easley-Smith, Oct. 19, 1899, *ibid*. The nature of the criticism cannot be determined.
4 Richmond *Times Dispatch*, Dec. 16, 1905; Montague to his wife, Oct. 12, 189[?], Moore Collection. Senator Daniel's description of Montague's finesse came from firsthand experience. In 1895, when Daniel defended a bank embezzler prosecuted by Montague, following an eloquent argument before the court by Daniel, Montague "proceeded to sift and strip the arguments of the Lame Lion [Daniel] and establish the claims of the Government." Richmond *Times Dispatch*, May 9, 1936.
5 Montague to Henry C. Stuart, June 2, 1893; Montague to Swanson, Feb. 5, 1896; Montague to Waitman T. Stigleman, July 5, 1894; all in Montague Papers.

aloof from political quarrels of the day. The proprieties of his office and his political ambition both made an active partisan role imprudent. As a young district attorney he persevered in his policy of watchful waiting.

The scene which Montague observed in comparative silence could not have been satisfying. From 1893 to 1896 the political immorality and degradation which he had seen emerge in his adolescence showed no sign of abating. Ballot box stuffing, fraudulent returns and, particularly, bribery continued to disgrace Virginia's elections. Not corrupt politicians alone, but conscientious, otherwise honest citizens winked when doctored election returns were announced, or contributed when dollars were necessary to purchase a Democratic victory. The Negro vote could be obviated in no other way, it was frankly argued. And the fact that the indifferent, usually illiterate, Negro often offered his vote to whomever would buy, Republican or Democrat, made election bartering requisite for political survival.[6] Many people lamented such political duplicity, but accepted it as necessary for the maintenance of sane, stable government. Montague himself, on at least one occasion, made campaign contributions ultimately destined for use as "sinews of war" keeping apathetic Negroes from Danville polls.[7] In so doing, he indirectly sanctioned such methods as the necessary consequence of an illiterate, tractab'e suffrage.

The illiterate Negro, of course, was but one cancer in the body politic. Demagogic politicians frequently used the shibboleth of

6   Examples of bribery of Negroes are manifold. C. M. Boston wrote: "I have seen the Negro preacher I mentioned to you . . . he expects to hold meetings in the neighborhood from now until election, I think that with his influence we will almost carry this neighborhood solid Negro vote as he is *directly interested* in your election, and I think his chgs [charges] will be very light." Boston to William Bibb, May 6, 1895, Bibb Papers. Another example: "These fellows have paid the leading Negro 25 dollars, one 15 dollars one 5 dollars. It will take 50 dollars to secure these . . . for you, which amounts to from 75 to 120 votes for you." J. Clifton Harris to Henry D. Flood, Oct. 28, 1896, in Henry D. Flood Papers, Manuscripts Division, Library of Congress, Washington.

7   During the 1897 campaign Montague's law partner, N. H. Massie, wrote J. Taylor Ellyson, state Democratic chairman, that the Danville Negroes were apathetic, "and with a little pressure . . . we can keep nearly all of them away from the polls." Massie to Ellyson, Oct. 27, 1897, in J. Taylor Ellyson Papers, Alderman Library, University of Virginia, Charlottesville. Montague evidently later siphoned part of his $200 contribution to the party into Massie's hands. Massie to Ellyson, Nov. 4, 1897, and Montague to Ellyson, Nov. 11, 1897, Ellyson Papers.

"white supremacy" merely to maintain place and power by deflecting public attention from the legitimate need for state reforms. Moreover, corporations and railroads were only too eager to ally with those politicians who were willing to accept their contributions in return for immunity from restrictive legislation in the state legislature. Indeed, the presence of a large bloc of purchasable voters in the Virginia electorate placed a premium on corporate contributions. The Negro thus became a pawn for grasping politicians.

The strategic political power which railroads subsequently gained in the Virginia Democratic party was made graphically evident in 1893 by the election of Thomas Staples Martin to the United States Senate. A little-known railroad attorney for the Chesapeake and Ohio, whose only previous public notice had come during his service on the Virginia Debt Commission, Martin had never addressed a political audience. Yet in the Virginia legislative caucus which met to elect a successor to Senator Barbour, Martin vanquished a former Virginia governor and Confederate general, Fitzhugh Lee. Most Virginians were both amazed and shocked.[8]

Martin's election was part of a conservative reaction among Virginia Democrats following the 1892 schism between the pro-Cleveland and anti-Cleveland forces. In the 1893 gubernatorial contest, for example, Congressman Charles T. O'Ferrall of the Seventh District, a Cleveland man, easily defeated the silverite candidate James Hoge Tyler, going on to trounce the Republican-Populist candidate in the general election by a three-to-two margin.[9] The same November election that elevated O'Ferrall also swept in a portion of the Virginia General Assembly, the same Assembly which one month later confounded the prognosticators by electing Martin to the Senate. In so doing, the legislature seemingly thwarted the will of Virginia's populace, shelving the aspirations not only of Lee, but also of Senator Hunton and Governor McKinney himself, all of whom were better known than Martin. How then, did Martin manage his election?

The answer lies in adept organization. As early as June, 1892, shortly after Barbour's death, Martin had written to William Bibb, Eighth District member of the state Democratic committee and his loyal political ally, asserting: "I am in to fight to a finish and do not see how it is possible to beat me. I had the endorsement of a majority

8   James A. Bear, "Thomas S. Martin, a Study in the Virginia Democracy" (M.A. thesis, University of Virginia, 1955).
9   J. H. Moore, "Life of James Gaven Field," 224–36.

of the Legislature [for the interim appointment], and have added several since. . . . nothing should be taken for granted. . . . My policy is to strengthen, confirm, and reassure the support of those who endorsed me before the Governor. . . . How is your local paper?" [10]

Martin "strengthened, confirmed, and reassured" his support by various means. As a railroad attorney he somewhat naturally inherited the direction of the Barbour political machine, which had had as its mainstay railroad contributions. Cooperating with William A. Glasgow of the Norfolk and Western and with his close friend, Barbour Thompson, superintendent of the Richmond and Danville, Martin operated a slush fund which was dangled before beleaguered local legislative candidates in need of ample "sinews of war." According to one report the C & O and R & D contributed ten thousand dollars to various candidates in 1893.[11]

In return for financial assistance, the support of the legislators would be exacted to block certain items of legislation, and to promote others. In 1891, for example, Barbour Thompson wrote to C. G. Holland of Danville (the same man who earlier had taken an interest in Montague's career), suggesting that he spend five hundred dollars on a local legislative candidate, provided "you satisfy yourself thoroughly as to his position" concerning the proposed Kent bill.[12] The Kent bill, as originally drafted, was a strongly regulatory measure curbing excessive railroad rates. Martin, however, as head of the railroad lobby, was able to emasculate the bill with crippling amendments; the law that resulted was merely a sop to the clamoring public.[13]

In 1893 railroad money had been expended largely to obtain pledges of support for Martin's election. The results were not disappointing when in the legislative caucus held in December, 1893, Martin led from the first and finally defeated Lee on the sixth ballot by an eleven-vote margin. Nine or ten of the legislators surprised even their colleagues by voting for Martin. The loud outcry of protest together with the numerous rumors of fraud resulted in a half-hearted investi-

10   Martin to Bibb, June 20, 1892, Bibb Papers.
11   Bear, "Thomas S. Martin," 95, 100, 103, 135, 141; "Senator Martin's Railroad Connection as Shown by the Barbour Thompson Letters" (pamphlet prepared in the 1911 senatorial campaign), Montague Papers.
12   "The Deadly Parallel," typed copy of Barbour Thompson's letters, Montague Papers. These letters were revealed in the 1911 senatorial campaign.
13   Allen W. Moger, The Rebuilding of the Old Dominion (New York, 1940), 67.

gation by a legislative committee. The result—claimed his critics—a
whitewash for Martin.[14]

With a solid foundation in railroad and corporation support, Martin, following his election, built a party organization that played a
commanding role in Virginia politics (with occasional interruption)
from 1893 until his death in 1919. Least effective in controlling the
governor's chair, Martin's machine was most effective in retaining a
firm hand on the General Assembly. Indeed, so firm was his grasp
that on several occasions prior to his senatorial election he offered
committee positions to potential competitors.[15]

Financial backing had been the original and most important factor
in creating the core of Martin's organization. For example, in 1895
Martin told Henry D. Flood, then a candidate for the state senate, "I
expect to have a hand in directing a small fund," and promised that if
Flood was the nominee he would get a share. Otherwise, no funds
would go to the district.[16] Equally important, perhaps, was Martin's
own masterful ability as a tactician. With precise steps he constructed
a phalanx of solid party support based on personal loyalty. Also effective was the powerful lever of patronage. In the Virginia governmental pyramid, control of the legislature amounted to control of the state;
the legislature selected the judiciary, which in turn appointed school
trustees and other local county boards. William A. Jones, Congressman from the First District, once charged that no man could get on
the judicial bench unless he "grovelled at Martin's knees." [17] Martin
ultimately was able to win the allegiance of the majority of "courthouse rings" and local party committees. The party committees in
turn dictated the procedures for local elections and appointed electoral officials. By controlling or influencing much of Virginia's election machinery Martin gained the opportunity to indulge in all the
corrupt practices characteristic of the age, not only against the dis-
reputable Republicans but against fellow Democrats as well.

In 1896, after the railroads had temporarily failed to cooperate with
the machine, a disgruntled Martin wrote to Hal Flood:

> They will want special legislation and it is not well for them to be
> encouraged to think they can get it till it is clearly seen that they will

14   Eckenrode, "Virginia Since 1865," 251 ff.; Richmond *Times Dispatch*,
     Aug. 6, 1905; copy of the committee's report, Montague Papers.
15   Bear, "Thomas S. Martin," 100 ff.
16   Martin to Flood, Sept. 1, 1895, Flood Papers.
17   Quoted in Horn, "The Democratic Party in Virginia," 144.

align themselves properly. . . . If they want those who have taken the burden and worry and trouble of protecting them in the past to continue to do so they must learn not to strike at them one day and appeal to them the next, and they should be put on terms if we are to bother with them at all. I think I can manage it.[18]

Martin's 1893 election had reflected the general conservative reaction within the Virginia Democracy following the 1892 schism between the "silverites" and the "hard-money" factions. This schism had been produced nationally by a basic disagreement over financial policy. Silverites charged that a serious currency shortage was retarding American economic development, with particular damage to the producer of raw materials—especially the small farmer. To solve the problem, they suggested, the government needed only to adopt a policy of "free and unlimited coinage of silver," or, as the phrase became abbreviated, a policy of "free silver." Hard-money financial conservatives argued in rebuttal that such a policy would eventually lead to ruinous inflation. In 1892 the champions of silver had failed to capture control of either the Democratic or the Republican party. Consequently a new party, the Populists, campaigning on a general reform platform which included a demand for free silver, attracted strong support from agrarian interests in the South and the West during the presidential election that year. From 1892 to 1894 the Populist movement in Virginia attained considerable momentum. General James G. Field of Albemarle County had been the national vice-presidential nominee of the Populist party in 1892; and in 1893, the Populist-Republican candidate for governor, Edmund S. Cocke, won approximately 40 per cent of the vote. The business depression which ravaged the country after Cleveland's inauguration in 1893 threatened to turn still more dissident farmers and impatient liberals into the Populist ranks. Moreover, the 1893 election of O'Ferrall and Martin caused the Populists to despair of achieving such goals as railroad regulation on the state level, and to redouble their efforts to construct an effective party of protest.

In attempting to forge a new party, however, the Populists encountered insurmountable obstacles. One handicap was the radical tenor of their platforms and proposals. More important was the composition of the party itself. Leaders of the Populists came from some of Virginia's most respected families, but the rank and file supporters were drawn chiefly from lower-class farmers and Negroes. The ma-

18   Martin to Flood, Jan. 2, 1896, Flood Papers.

jority of whites, both rural and urban, liberal and conservative, maintained their historical allegiance to the Democratic party, disdaining to risk white unity by enlisting in a dubious reform movement sponsored by impoverished Negroes, "wild-eyed anarchists and stolid farmers." [19]

The failure of the Populists to capitalize on the growing divergence between the factions of the Virginia Democratic party thus explains not only the ultimate decline of the Populists but also the ultimate rise of a progressive movement within the Democratic party. The Virginia Populists performed the usual role of a third party— serving as a catalyst, prodding and hastening change in the major parties, providing new ideas and new vision, but failing to achieve personal fulfillment of their objectives. The task of carrying Virginia's reform movement through to at least partial fruition would rest with such later leaders as Montague.

But if Montague was later destined to assume a leading role in Virginia's reform movement, as a district attorney he surveyed these developing embroilments in Virginia politics with comparative detachment. Only once in the first three years of his office did he break his public silence. That exception was his participation in the closely-fought 1894 Congressional campaign for Swanson, who faced serious Populist opposition. Speaking for Swanson at Rocky Mount early in November, Montague ridiculed the Virginia Populist party as being chiefly controlled by "farmers who did not farm." The local leaders of the party, he alleged, were lawyers without clients and preachers without pulpits, and in reference to General Field, the state leader of the party, Montague expressed doubt that he had had a good law case in two years.[20] By scornfully caricaturing Field and the polyglot elements composing the Populist party, Montague typified the reactions of many in the Virginia Democracy. As a practicing Democrat, hoping to win political promotion through the channels of his own party, he felt no temptation to enlist in the ranks of a third party, even though two years later he would enthusiastically espouse one of the basic tenets of the Populist platform, free silver.

19 J. H. Moore, "Life of James Gaven Field," 177, 277. See also William D. Sheldon, *Populism in the Old Dominion, 1885–1900* (Princeton, N.J., 1935).
20 Field later wrote Montague, protesting this slur upon his professional reputation; Montague replied, "I simply said what I have so often and widely heard of you to support my argument as to the personnel of your party." Montague to Field, Nov. 7, 1894, Montague Papers.

But while rejecting Populism and maintaining his Democratic loyalty, Montague also gradually aligned himself with the wing of his own party from which would ultimately emerge Virginia's progressive movement. The roots of that movement took their original nourishment not wholly from a desire for social justice and extension of democratic processes. These desires, outgrowths of the economic depression and the Populist agitation which resulted, were genuinely felt and advocated by many Virginia Democrats, but the force which first coalesced Virginia's future progressive leaders into a common union was the presence of Thomas Martin in the United States Senate. Martin's election by a partially bribed legislature served to accentuate the grasp held on Virginia politics by corporate influence and to dramatize the degenerate condition of Virginia politics generally. By arousing widespread hostility to the tactics which his election symbolized, Martin almost incidentally served to foster the birth of political and election reform designed to end the conditions which had made his success possible. Within four years of his election the Virginia campaign for direct election of Senators had been launched.

Montague's initial reaction to Martin's election cannot be determined, but his attitude possibly may be reflected in the reactions of those individuals with whom he was closest politically. Governor McKinney, Senator Hunton, Eppa Hunton, Jr., and General William Payne all opposed Martin's selection, the latter three quietly supporting Lee.[21] Montague's close association with several of these individuals indicates that he probably did likewise, for within a few years of Martin's election, he joined the ranks of those seeking the Senator's downfall. In Montague's opinion, the blunt, plodding, colloquial Martin, aside from factors of political honesty or dishonesty, was simply not a cultured gentleman—not a man of senatorial qualities, not a man of vision. Montague's abhorrence of political chicanery, of materialism, of one-class control in society and government; his disdain for petty cliquishness and shallow statecraft—all these facets of his growing political disillusionment could now be epitomized by one man and that man's machine. In a sense, Martin's election to the Senate was thus the turning point in Montague's ca-

---

21 Eckenrode, "Virginia Since 1865," 249–51. According to *Dictionary of American Biography* (New York, 1928–37), IX, 422: "Against his retirement from the Senate he [Hunton] seems to have made no protest; but he never forgave, it is said, the manner in which Fitzhugh Lee was prevented from becoming his successor."

reer. The initial reaction had been prudently subdued by the ambitious district attorney. Later, as an elected attorney general, the delayed reaction would find freer vent.

The first clear indication of Montague's position in the Virginia Democratic factional rivalries came in 1896, when the "boy orator of the Platte," William Jennings Bryan, gained control of the national Democratic party to lead a crusade for silver, a crusade which hypnotized the South and West and threatened even to undermine the hard-money, industrial Northeast. Bryan, a reformer whose political ideology hardly coincided with that of the more conservative Montague, nevertheless sounded a common chord of hostility to the money power, to the tariff, to the trusts. Responding with apparent enthusiasm, Montague broke his political silence and joined the silver bandwagon, extolling silver with the proverbial silver-tongued oratory. And though Bryan went down to national defeat in November, the silverites in Virginia triumphed in what was perhaps the bitterest Democratic rift in Virginia's political history.[22]

Why were Virginia's silver crusaders able to arouse such a "rampant" sentiment for silver and Bryan, while at the same time Populistic movements for internal state reform developed so little response? Primary in importance was the Populists' participation with Republicans and Negroes in the threat to white supremacy. A second reason derived from the economic exigencies of the day. Virginia in 1896 faced her most compelling problem in the continuing national depression with its accompanying unemployment and hardship. Silver disciples argued that the depression had been either caused or aggravated by repeal of the Sherman Silver Purchase Act in 1893, by the continuing contraction of currency and of markets, and by the consolidation of wealth into the hands of the few. The minting of silver was proclaimed the panacea for the nation's ills. To many Virginians, this was the paramount reform, the overriding issue, state or national.

Led by such men as Senator Daniel (a Greenbacker himself in his youth), Congressmen Peter J. Otey, William A. Jones, and Swanson, the Virginia silverites of 1896 scored quick success. By the time of the June meeting of the state Democratic convention in Staunton, fully two-thirds of the counties had instructed their local delegations to work for a silver platform. Opposition to the silver stampede was eloquently expressed but poorly organized. State figures such as Gov-

22   Allen W. Moger, "The Rift in the Virginia Democracy in 1896," *Journal of Southern History*, IV (Aug., 1938), 295–317.

ernor O'Ferrall, former state party chairman Basil B. Gordon, and Beverly B. Munford lambasted the silver panacea as an illusory and dishonorable sham. Other figures, such as state chairman J. Taylor Ellyson, James Hay, and Henry D. Flood either remained dubiously noncommittal or made lukewarm overtures to the silver camp.[23]

Senator Martin, the man who had by now established a reputation as the most important, if not the most popular, politician in Virginia, maintained a sphinx-like silence concerning the raging controversy until the very eve of the Staunton convention. His voting record in the Senate had not favored the silver cause, but, as his own carefully compiled notations on the actions of the various counties indicated, the state convention was likely to become a silver carnival. At Staunton, therefore, to the hisses of some in his audience, he suddenly and belatedly announced his conversion to the silver cause, an action the prosilver Staunton *Spectator* later termed an "awkward and undignified tumble into the silver band wagon." Many machine politicians followed Martin's example.[24]

The final election contest in Virginia caused a major rift in the Democratic party. Led by Governor O'Ferrall, some of the more conservative elements of the Democracy refused to adopt so suddenly the Populist doctrines they had recently castigated. So decided was their opposition to Bryan and his platform that many openly deserted their party and campaigned for the Republican candidate, William McKinley. These "Goldbugs," as they became known, recruited followers in the cities and among the upper classes generally, but Bryan's strength in the hinterland could not be overcome. The final election results gave Bryan a narrow margin of victory, 159,000 to 135,000 votes. Confirmed Democratic silverites, former Populists, and the Democratic machine had carried the day. The Goldbugs were politically ostracized.[25]

Montague had contributed his share to the Bryan victory. In a way, his alliance with the silver wing of the party could be attributed to the same type of opportunism which motivated Martin. As a district attorney dependent for reappointment upon the next President, he would of necessity curry the favor of the heir apparent. To have sup-

---

23 *Ibid.*, 298; Doss, "John Warwick Daniel," 187–88.
24 Staunton *Spectator and Vindicator*, Jan. 29, 1904.
25 Eckenrode, "Virginia Since 1865," 264–70; Micajah Woods to J. Taylor Ellyson, Aug. 27, 1896, in Micajah Woods Papers, Alderman Library, University of Virginia, Charlottesville; Woods to Camm Patteson, Aug. 13, 1896, *ibid.*

ported any candidate before the National Democratic Convention would have been unseemly and foolhardy. Furthermore, he had already tentatively decided to run for Virginia's attorney general the following year. His postconvention canvass for Bryan was therefore but another indication of his expedient Democratic orthodoxy.

To state that Montague's support for Bryan was expedient, however, is not to say it was necessarily insincere. Montague's actual attitude toward the rift between Cleveland and Bryan cannot be positively determined. At various times in his career he expressed warm admiration for both statesmen. In 1896, however, he seems to have become convinced that drastic measures were necessary to combat the country's economic ills.[26] In this and other campaigns Montague's speech repertoire contained some of the usual embellishment common to all political sermons. But newspaper accounts of his 1896 addresses invariably describe their depth of research, their scholarly synthesis, and their lucidity. To his audiences, at least, Montague imparted an impression of fervent conviction.[27]

Even so, it was with some misgiving that Montague decided to speak in the Bryan campaign. The nature of his office had been one cause for his public silence on political topics; as semijudicial officials, district attorneys were not expected to be practicing politicians. Montague had participated in the 1894 campaign, for example, only after prior approval from Washington. A natural reason for his reticence in the 1896 campaign was Cleveland's dismissal of his colleague, the U.S. District Attorney for Eastern Virginia, Francis Rives Lassiter. The pretext for the removal was Lassiter's accepting the chairmanship of the Fourth District Democratic party; the real reason was probably Lassiter's silver sympathies. Showing some concern, Montague on October 2 wrote R. B. Glenn, a North Carolina district attorney, asking if he had heard any intimation from the Department of Justice whether a cause for removal would include not only the holding of political office, but the expression of "personal opinions before public audiences." Such opinions, Montague affirmed, it was his intention to express.[28]

Apparently, Montague began speaking soon after his letter to

26 In a letter to his old Indiantown pupil, Ben P. Willis, Montague spoke of his canvass for Bryan, and of Cleveland's reaction, with no intimation that his support for Bryan was feigned. Montague to Willis, July 17, 1897, in possession of Mrs. Catesby Willis Stewart.
27 Unidentified clippings, 1896 and 1897, scrapbooks, Montague Papers.
28 Montague to R. B. Glenn, Oct. 2, 1896, *ibid.*

Glenn, for on October 12 a group of Danville residents drew up a bitter letter of protest, charging that Montague had used "the influence of his official position to aid a cause which is in the opinion of a very large proportion of our people destructive to the best interests of the country." The Attorney General in Washington, responding to the letter, informed Montague that the government did not complain of public speaking unless it "threatens the efficiency of the officer involved." Even with this tentative Washington sanction, however, Montague later confided that the partisan nature of his addresses induced Cleveland to consider his dismissal "on the day before the election." [29]

All told, from early October until the election, Montague made twenty speeches for Bryan in many points of the state—speeches which further extended his growing political reputation. The basic theme of his addresses condemned the "money power" which wanted to limit currency for selfish economic advantage. The "Goldbug" argument that "a dollar that would buy the most was the best dollar" he labeled the lame rationalization of the hard-money interests to justify their monopoly of the country's finances. Montague attributed the depression not to overproduction but to the rejection of silver as a respectable medium of exchange. Proclaiming that the cause of silver was the cause of the people, Montague avowed that "if standing for the rights of the people be anarchy then I am an anarchist." The young conservative student at Richmond had come a long way.[30]

By aligning with the more progressive element of the Democratic party Montague revealed his basic aversion to centralization of the country's economy and his belief in the protection of individual opportunity. But to ascribe his enlistment in the silver crusade entirely to principle would be naive. To ascribe it entirely to self-seeking, opportunistic ambition would be unfair. Montague's participation in the 1896 campaign proved his political shrewdness without detracting from his political honesty and his emerging role as a spokesman upon national issues. In his first embroilment in Virginia factional politics, he had fared well.

29 Montague to Attorney General Judson Harmon, Oct. 19, 1896, *ibid;* Montague to Ben P. Willis, July 17, 1897, in possession of Mrs. Catesby Willis Stewart.

30 This information was obtained from various scrapbook clippings in the Moore Collection and Montague Papers. Some of the quotations are taken from accounts of 1897 speeches, when the familiar silver arguments were repeated almost verbatim.

The 1896 silver movement in Virginia represents the end of one reform movement and the beginning of another. Though the Populist
ideas and leadership seemed to have been vindicated by the wholesale
adoption of their silver gospel, in reality Populism and silver had
reached their fag end. The young Democrats who most fervently advocated the cause of silver in 1896 formed the nucleus of a group
more refined than the Populists, more educated and more practical, a
group which would lead the later Virginia progressive movement for
the improvement of education and the democratization of political
processes. Their endorsement of the borrowed Populist silver theme
represented an intermediate departure from the ranks of Democratic
solidarity and from the status quo. And though Martin's and other
usually conservative politicians' expedient shifting with the popular
tide somewhat obscured the natural rift developing between the party's two factions, that schism could not long be concealed. The 1896
rift in Virginia's Democracy was the prelude to an incipient reform
movement which would widen the rift even further. The Democracy,
with some exceptions, had accepted the apostles of free silver in
1896. The missionaries of internal reform, thus far unrecognized and
unwanted, would be acknowledged later.

V

RISE TO ATTORNEY GENERAL

IN 1897 Montague attained his first elective office. Capitalizing on his public recognition won in the silver campaign, he successfully challenged a field of six other candidates, one of them the incumbent, for the Democratic nomination of attorney general of Virginia. Though candidates for the position were as thick as "huckleberries in Henrico," the preconvention campaign itself was lackluster. In an age which considered it impolitic for a candidate to canvass openly for his nomination, the 1897 competition for state offices was seemingly devoid of issues. Extensive correspondence conducted by the candidates customarily dealt only in general platitudes, as did the occasional editorials endorsing regional favorites. To many electors, a candidate's eligibility depended entirely on his previous stand on free silver. Those who had been most vociferous in lauding the white metal in 1896 found their avenue to political success made easier in 1897. Those who had been less enthusiastic faced an unfriendly electorate demanding satisfactory explanations. In the final analysis, personal popularity was perhaps the decisive factor.[1]

The gubernatorial competition in 1897 pitted James Hoge Tyler of

1 Harry E. Poindexter has written a penetrating analysis of "The Virginia Democracy in 1897, Silver-Plated Conservatism," *Essays in History,* II (University of Virginia, 1955), 5–27. Poindexter is especially helpful on the move for a constitutional convention discussed in Chap. VI of this work.

Radford against J. Taylor Ellyson of Richmond. Tyler, a farmer and businessman of rural Montgomery County and a jovial, folksy speaker, appealed especially to the agrarian elements of the state. As a candidate for governor on two previous occasions, he stood to benefit from earlier political contacts. His prosilver stance in 1896 was also no handicap.

By contrast, the urbanite Ellyson, capable and efficient state chairman of the party, obtained his chief support among the professional politicos, and his "lukewarm" attitude toward silver constituted his main handicap.[2] Overt support from Henry D. Flood and William Glasgow, dispensers of railroad money, may have given Ellyson an undesirable machine image, whereas Tyler had acquired a reputation as a man hostile to "machine methods and political cliques." [3] The same type of spontaneity which had marked the 1896 campaign for silver also marked Tyler's 1897 campaign. As spring changed to summer, Ellyson's drive for the nomination lost momentum. Even in his home territory, Richmond, he lost 40 per cent of the delegation to Tyler. By July 6, a month before the convention, Tyler led in total delegate strength, 395 to 123. On the eve of the convention he led Ellyson by a ratio of almost four to one. His victory was assured; the silver wing's 1896 triumph had not tarnished.[4]

As the drift of the gubernatorial race early became evident, interest shifted to the more closely contested nomination for attorney general. In this contest the two-term incumbent, R. Taylor Scott of Warrenton, faced the fight of his political life against nine opponents, six of whom persevered as serious contestants. At first glance, there seemed no reason for such widespread opposition to Scott's renomination. "While not a brilliant man he was a very safe and a very sincere man and made the state a very efficient attorney general," wrote the Staunton *Daily News*.[5] Opposition to his renomination

2   J. N. Brenaman to Ellyson, Feb. 27, 1897; George W. Morris to Ellyson, Dec. 2, 1896; Marshall McCormick to Ellyson, Nov. 20, 1896; George B. Keezell to Ellyson, Dec. 16, 1896; all in Ellyson Papers.
3   F. E. Buford wrote to Montague, "The machine headed by Robert Turnbull as county chairman will be for Ellyson, as it was in the last gubernatorial campaign, but we think we can beat the machine next year as we did then." Buford to Montague, Sept. 3, 1900, Montague Papers. Francis Rives Lassiter to William A. Glasgow, Jr., May 10, 1897, in Francis Rives Lassiter Papers, Duke University library, Durham, N.C.; Ellyson to Flood, March 8, 1897, Flood Papers; Poindexter, "The Virginia Democracy," 15; Richmond *Dispatch*, April 18, 1897.
4   Richmond *Dispatch*, June 2 and 23, 1897; Richmond *State*, Aug. 7, 1897.
5   Staunton *Daily News*, Aug. 7, 1897; Richmond *Dispatch*, Aug. 10, 1897.

seemed to develop mainly because of his tardy endorsement of Bryan and free silver in 1896.[6] Still, as an incumbent, he possessed the advantage of a well-known name. Although he fell far short of obtaining a majority of the elected delegates, he nevertheless amassed a total larger than any other candidate. It was Scott against the field.

The "field" eagerly prepared for the fray. Besides Montague, Scott's competitors included H. R. Pollard, a Richmond lawyer; Lloyd T. Smith of Northumberland County, the choice of the First District and Congressman William A. Jones; W. R. Alexander, the favorite of the Valley Seventh District; Francis Rives Lassiter of Petersburg, former District Attorney for Eastern Virginia; and William Hodges Mann, a judge and attorney from Nottoway County. Pollard, Smith, and Alexander were purely regional favorites. Montague, Lassiter and Mann were more serious contestants. All six possessed acceptable silver records, however, and in a race where regionalism played a decisive role, all six enjoyed theoretical chances of victory.

The candidacies of Lassiter and Mann evidently produced confusion within the ranks of the dominant Martin organization. Mann, who later became governor of Virginia, was backed strongly by State Senator Flood of Appomattox, easily the most valuable person in Martin's organization.[7] For a time Martin seemed to give Mann his support, saying, "If Judge Mann can make the Fourth District solid, it will give him a powerful send off." [8]

Lassiter, however, was also a resident of the Fourth District, and when he later announced his candidacy with the active support of Congressman Sidney P. Epes, Mann's chances for the nomination collapsed. Consequently, Martin withdrew his active promotion of Mann's candidacy,[9] and Mann himself made an agreement with Lassiter to withdraw from the race as soon as he became convinced that Lassiter's strength was greater than his own. By July, Lassiter

6　Richmond *Dispatch*, July 15, 1897.
7　"You know Flood's relations with Tom," wrote Prentis Pettit to Bibb, intimating that Flood would support Martin's candidate for railroad commissioner. Sept. 10, 1897, Bibb Papers. In 1898 Martin could say that Flood had "done more for me" politically "than any other man in the State." Martin to W. H. Holman, March 8, 1898, Flood Papers.
8　Martin to Flood, April 11, 1897, Flood Papers.
9　In a letter to Flood (May 3, 1897, Flood Papers), Mann remarked in a complaining manner, "I should think it would be important to Mr. Martin for me to be elected as I would become well acquainted with all the members of the legislature and be able to do him a great deal of service when his election comes on."

could claim that Mann no longer had the support "of any well known political leader in the state except Hall Flood." [10] Indeed, behind the scenes, Martin evidently swung support to Lassiter in an effort either to oust Scott or to thwart Montague.[11] With a name recognized throughout much of eastern Virginia and with the support of many veteran politicians, Lassiter predicted his position as second only to Scott in delegate strength.

The remaining major candidate, A. J. Montague, would take advantage of the divisions within Martin's organization. Montague possessed intellectual qualifications for attorney general equal or superior to those of Lassiter,[12] and his statewide popularity, developed by the magnetism of his oratory and by his creditable performance as district attorney, exceeded that of the Petersburg lawyer. A Lassiter worker in southwest Virginia once complained to Epes: "I am working at a disadvantage as Lassiter is unknown, and Montague is well known out here and quite popular." [13]

Montague's political ambition had its roots in his boyhood days at Inglewood. Exactly when he first coveted the office of Virginia's attorney general cannot be determined, but the pattern of his unfolding career suggests that the step was not unpremeditated. In his letters to Betsie from Danville during the 1880's he occasionally expressed a desire to advance judicially rather than politically. He may have considered advancement to attorney general a natural step in the upward path to legal preferment. On the other hand, the office was also a possible stepping stone to the governorship.

Montague definitely considered entering the race against Scott as early as the spring of 1896. At that time "he sent letters to numerous friends throughout the State, stating his desire and asking opin-

10   Lassiter to William Shands, May 22, 1897, and Lassiter to Micajah Woods, July 21, 1897, both in Lassiter Papers.
11   Lassiter made appeals to railway agents, including William Glasgow, for financial support. Glasgow, a close friend of Martin, promised his aid, and later in the campaign Lassiter was able to promise free travel expenses from "my friends" to certain of his delegates. Furthermore, most of the congressional delegation seemed aligned behind his candidacy. Lassiter to Glasgow, May 10, 1897; Lassiter to H. S. J. Jakeman, June 10, 1897; Sydney Epes to Lassiter, July 17, 1897; all in Lassiter Papers.
12   Ironically, Montague and Lassiter were in the same class at the University of Virginia, and each regarded the other highly. Lassiter once described Montague as "one of the ablest" of his classmates. Lassiter to A. A. Campbell, May 17, 1897, Lassiter Papers.
13   A. A. Campbell to Epes, July 1, 1897, in Epes-Kilmartin Papers, Alderman Library, University of Virginia, Charlottesville.

ions . . . responses were more than gratifying and dispelled any doubt" that he would make at least a creditable showing. Besides his "diversified acquaintanceship" derived from political and legal contacts, Montague also enjoyed advantages from having lived in several parts of the state and from his father's reputation. His potential candidacy was recognized as "seriously interfering with the calculations and prospects of other aspirants." [14]

Montague's basic strategy in a field of multiple candidates was to obtain support as second choice from the backers of those candidates more regional in appeal than himself.[15] The core of his support, however, came from the Fifth District, a region frustrated by long years of nonrepresentation on the state ticket. There, Democrats of all factions rallied behind their redheaded representative in his fight to bring recognition to himself and to his region.[16] Help in solidifying Fifth District support evidently came from the young Congressman of the district, his political friend, Claude A. Swanson, although Swanson apparently did not participate actively in the canvass until the eve of the convention. It may have been, as the Newport News *Morning Herald* later observed, that "Montague and Swanson . . . never had much love for each other. For a dozen years past they have been in each other's way to a certain extent and their friends have always predicted that sooner or later they must have a fight to the finish." But if Montague personally disliked Swanson's tactics, he realistically recognized the latter's political control over the Fifth District.[17]

Swanson's support of Montague raises the question of Montague's exact position in the undulating factional currents of Virginia politics. That Montague failed to win Martin's endorsement has been estab-

---

14 Richmond *Dispatch,* Aug. 29, 1897; clipping, Aug. 28, 1897, scrapbook, Montague Papers.

15 He wrote his former Indiantown pupil, Ben Willis, asking him to "help me out in the Fredericksburg delegation to the measure of being their second choice . . . should Mr. Smith be dropped." Montague to Willis, June 3, 1897, in possession of Mrs. Catesby Willis Stewart; V. L. Fowlkes to Montague, April 5, 1897, Montague Papers.

16 The Henry *Bulletin,* the Stuart *Enterprise,* the Hillsville *Advocate,* and the Danville *Tobacco Journal* all joined the Franklin *Times Democrat* in advocating Montague's selection. Clippings, scrapbook, Moore Collection.

17 Newport News *Morning Herald,* Nov. 20, 1900, in scrapbook, Ellyson Papers. That Montague later repaid his debt to Swanson is shown by his support of Swanson's candidate for the position of superintendent of the Virginia penitentiary. Swanson to Montague, Sept. 15, 1897, Montague Papers.

lished. But Swanson, Montague's most important single supporter, was of a breed quite similar to Martin. And though in 1897 Swanson had not completely allied with Martin's machine personally, that alliance would soon be cemented. Moreover, in 1897 Montague received backing, if not from the Southern Railroad itself, at least from important personnel of that road.[18] As a possible recipient of some railroad support, could Montague too be termed a machine politician?

Later J. Hampton Hoge (Montague's Republican opponent for the governorship) charged that Montague "had been in the rotten Machine, and turned states evidence on Swanson and Martin by exposing it, that he [Hoge] commended [Montague's] conduct in that particular only, but that Aaron Burr once said, 'The man who turned states evidence upon his confederates in rascality was the damnest rascal in the bunch.'" [19] To deny that Montague tolerated political alliances in 1897 which he would disdain to countenance in 1901 would be to deny falsely. Montague's chances for the attorney general's position were at best risky. To have alienated any faction of the party would have spelled certain defeat. He therefore appealed to all segments, and he received support from all segments.

Montague's 1897 victory, however, was achieved largely through the support of men other than political ringsters. Swanson was his mainstay in the Fifth District. Outside that district Montague encountered the direct opposition of Martin, and those individuals who supported the former most avidly in the state convention and earlier were the same men who later comprised the core of Virginia's reform movement: Joseph Willard, R. Walton Moore, Greenlee Letcher, and William A. Jones.[20] Such men as Martin, Daniel, Flood, Rhea, Mann, and Lawless—individuals whose names would long remain synonymous with Virginia's political machine—found Montague's nomination unpalatable. In the August convention they proved the greatest obstacle to his selection.

Fate stepped into the attorney general's race in early August, arbi-

18   E. T. Lamb, writing on stationery of the General Agent, Southern Railway Company, Norfolk, declared: "I think you will have no trouble, or any cause to regret the action of the delegation from this section . . . . if you do not receive the support of our friends in this section, I shall be very much disappointed." Lamb to Montague, Aug. 9, 1897, Moore Collection.

19   Quoted in W. H. Hale to Montague, Sept. 5, 1901, Montague Papers.

20   Jones supported Montague after first backing his neighbor, Lloyd T. Smith. Clipping, Warsaw (Va.) *Northern Neck News,* scrapbook, Montague Papers.

trarily upsetting all calculations. On August 6 Attorney General Scott died at his Warrenton home from complications of a typhoid illness. The state's press carried eulogies; Scott's erstwhile opponents paid their tributes. And then came the scramble for delegates.[21] Scott's removal from the race naturally improved Montague's prospects. Robert N. Pendleton wrote from Wytheville, "The death of the late Atty Genl in my judgment makes the race for Atty Genl between yourself and Mr. Lassiter." B. Richards of King William County was more emphatic, "I see now Scott out of the way nothing to defeat you." As the delegates began assembling in Roanoke for the convention, newspaper accounts tended to confirm these predictions. "The general impression," reported the Richmond *Dispatch,* "is that Mr. Montague will lead on the first ballot." Many of the delegates themselves, however, remained inscrutable. The convention alone would decide.[22]

As it assembled, the 1897 state Democratic convention at first displayed little overt feeling, little factional bitterness. Ellyson closed ranks with Tyler, the attorney general candidates professed friendship for each other, and even a visiting Populist delegation obtained audience from the gentlemanly Democracy. But hidden beneath the superficial harmony were the same factional rivalries which had accompanied the prenomination campaigns. And, in choosing between factions, the convention delivered a narrowly administered but distinct setback to Martin and his organization.[23]

Martin's loose hold on the convention was made apparent early when he failed in his attempt to install William F. Rhea as temporary chairman. For the first time in years a lively fight developed for the honorary position, with Rhea's chief opponent being Greenlee Letcher, a member of the House of Delegates from Lexington and the son of Virginia's Civil War governor. In the state Democratic committee which would elect the chairman, Martin lined up strong support for Rhea from Bibb, James Hay, and R. Tate Irving. Support for Letcher came from Joseph Willard and William A. Anderson (indi-

---

21 Richmond *Dispatch,* Aug. 7, 1897.
22 Robert N. Pendleton to Montague, Aug. 7, 1897, and B. Richards to Montague, Aug. 9, 1897, Moore Collection; Richmond *State,* August 9 and 10, 1897; Richmond *Dispatch,* August 11, 1897.
23 Most of the following description of the convention is from accounts in the Richmond *Dispatch* and Richmond *State* between August 11 and 13, 1897. See also Poindexter, "The Virginia Democracy," 16 ff.

viduals who would later serve under Montague as lieutenant governor
and attorney general respectively). Since Letcher supported Montague for attorney general, his selection by a vote of 26 to 22 was an
ill omen for Martin.[24]

With Letcher as temporary chairman, the convention of fifteen
hundred delegates officially convened in Roanoke on the morning of
August 11. As the first order of business, the delegates turned to the
nomination of a gubernatorial candidate, but Tyler's victory was so
self-evident that Ellyson's name was not even presented.

The contest for lieutenant governor which followed provided more
serious competition. Several figures had offered their candidacy, but
dependent upon developments in the more closely contested race for
attorney general, the competition had remained in a fluid state. Chief
aspirants were James R. Caton of Alexandria, Merritt T. Cooke of
Norfolk, and Edmund R. Cocke, offered by the almost defunct Populist party as its price for fusion. None of the three aroused much enthusiasm, however, and a move developed to draft Edward Echols, a
conservative state senator from Staunton, who was closely identified
with the Ellyson faction. Echols defeated Cooke on the second ballot, 803 to 682, chiefly because Cooke's geographical bailiwick
hampered four of the six attorney general candidates.[25]

On the day following Tyler's and Echols' nominations came the
denouement in the race for attorney general. After two tedious hours
of nominating speeches, the first roll call began at 11:30 on August
12. After its completion, as predicted, Montague led Lassiter, 375 to
357; the other four candidates trailed with less than 300 votes each.
The voting had divided along the expected geographical lines, with
Montague receiving the support of at least seven counties in the
southwest, and perhaps most significant, thirty votes from Richmond,
a number exactly equivalent to the number of Tyler delegates in that
city.

On the second ballot intensive "politicking" began. "Those who
were conducting the canvass on behalf of the two favorite candidates
were hard at work," persuading followers of the other candidates to

24 Willard to Bibb, July 22, 1897, and Martin to Bibb, July 8, 1897, Bibb
    Papers.
25 Richmond *Dispatch*, July 25 and 30, 1897; Lassiter's support of Echols
    and opposition to Cooke may have been a crucial determining factor in
    defeating his candidacy; Cooke's Norfolk friends turned to Montague,
    but Echols was unable to bring Lassiter much support from the Valley.
    Robert R. Kane to Lassiter, Aug. 27, 1897, Lassiter Papers.

join ranks with a winner. Swanson busily bargained with local political bosses. These efforts paid dividends. Flood withdrew Mann in favor of Lassiter, and immediately afterward Alexander was withdrawn in favor of Montague. The circumstances of this move were recalled for Montague seven years later by a delegate from Rockingham: "[James] Hay came to our delegation and said that Swanson had told him if the 7th district . . . would come to you—the position of assistant Aty Gen should come to his district, and that as Rockingham was the largest delegation as far as he Hay was concerned it should go there. . . . We changed our 30 votes from Alexander. . . . This was was the beginning of the break which resulted in your nomination." At a crucial moment in the convention Swanson had proved himself adept at the age-old game of patronage. Montague, however, was personally unaware of Swanson's intention to promise Hay this position, and whether he delivered on the promise cannot be determined from available records.[26]

After numerous changes and an actual recount, the second ballot totals stood at 697 for Montague, 465 for Lassiter. On the third and final ballot Montague continued his steady progress to the magic number of 775 votes. Several substantial changes were made to the "Red Fox of the city of Danville," and his nomination became almost certain. With the roll call concluded, he was within a few votes of victory. The convention's secretary called the roll again for changes, and "when Joe Button had got down to Northumberland, all doubt was removed." Half the convention were on their feet, waving. Flood moved that the nomination be made unanimous, and the motion carried. In a brief speech of acceptance Montague assured the convention, "I shall not be in the rear of this fight, but with all the energy I possess I propose to go where the fight is thickest. If elected, I will discharge the duties of my office without fear or favor or hope of reward." A significant milestone in Montague's career had been reached.

Tyler's and Montague's nominations, both distasteful to Martin, clearly demonstrated that the more conservative machine forces within the Virginia Democracy did not dominate the 1897 convention. Still it cannot be asserted that the atmosphere of that convention

26 George B. Keezell to Montague, June 1, 1903, Montague Papers. The attorney general's office in Richmond reports that no official position of "assistant Attorney General" existed during Montague's term in office. Reno S. Harp, III, to the author, Aug. 16, 1960.

was strikingly progressive. Continuing the precedent established in 1896, state issues and the need for reform were largely obscured by pushing national issues into the political limelight: "Keynote speeches lauded free silver, extolled a federal income tax, and praised economy in government. . . . Every mention of free silver, Senator Daniel, and the Chicago convention of 1896 brought thunderous cheers." [27]

The platform adopted by the convention reflected this relative complacency. Composed largely by Daniel, and read by him personally to the convention, following Montague's nomination, it reaffirmed the radical Chicago platform of 1896 in its entirety, emphasizing free silver, a revenue tariff, and "the vigorous use of Congressional authority over taxation and foreign commerce to regulate trusts." Concerning state affairs the platform contained only effusive praise for the Democracy's accomplishments in fostering education, providing pensions, caring for the insane and deaf, and settling the state's debt.[28]

Still there were some delegates who sounded a discordant note of protest, who spoke for internal reform. And present in many of the speeches before the convention was an underlying demand for economy and for state constitutional amendments, a demand which reflected the growing statewide dissatisfaction with election methods and governmental inefficiency. Beverly B. Munford, for example, asserted the need for Virginia to reduce the number of her state offices, to prevent the use of bribe money in elections, and to provide generously for free schools, thus protecting those in the black sections "from rule by ignorant majorities." Gubernatorial nominee Tyler declared that politics, "a lofty, and noble science," had been left too long to the manipulations of a few; that the ballot was a sacred trust; and that the people eventually would awaken to the perversion of their will. Both Tyler and Montague in their acceptance speeches promised to work toward economy in state government.

But the development which most clearly demonstrated the progressive sentiment of a large portion of the convention was the spontaneous movement to endorse the nomination of United States Senators by direct popular primary. Undoubtedly a by-product of the Populistic agitation for the extension of democracy, the primary proposal also reflected the bitter resentment engendered by Martin's election in

27 Poindexter, "The Virginia Democracy," 16.   28 *Ibid.*, 18.

1893 by a partially bribed legislature. This resentment, dormant for four years, erupted in the Roanoke convention, and the fight waged there for a primary inaugurated Virginia's progressive movement.[29]

The campaign for a primary had been launched less than a month earlier by the Warsaw *Northern Neck News,* a paper controlled by Congressman Jones. The majority of the state's press appeared receptive to the suggestion, and Jones optimistically carried his fight to the resolutions committee of the Roanoke convention. There he encountered the determined opposition of such friends of Senator Martin as Hay, George Morris, R. E. Boykin, and Senator Daniel, who criticized the primary as an untried innovation requiring considered study and thought—more than could be given at a convention. Defending the primary were A. A. Lipscomb, Prentis Pettit, R. Walton Moore (the man who seconded Montague's nomination the following day), and Jones himself. Lipscomb asserted that "every corporation, every bank, every trust in the State is opposed to this movement," and Moore referred to "dark lantern" caucuses, buying of legislatures, and the use of money at the polls as the real motives for the reform. The upshot of the debate was a fifteen-to-fourteen committee vote to accept the primary as part of the platform, but to allow the delegates to vote upon the issue separately. The forum of discussion was thus transferred to the convention arena.

The primary fight on the convention floor came shortly after Montague's nomination. Jones spoke in its favor, arguing that the primary's practicality had already been demonstrated in other states, and challenging his opponents to suggest a better plan. "Why," he asked, "are the people of this State competent to vote for their Governor, for the President of the United States, for members of the Legislature, and not for the Senator of the United States by a direct vote?" In reply to Jones the Martin forces turned to Senator Daniel, an ambivalently independent figure, never at the nerve center of Martin's organization, but one who nevertheless gave it his tacit support and occasional active assistance. Daniel defended Martin from "besmirching abuse" (though Jones had made no reference to the Senator) and strongly insinuated that Jones's only real motive for

---

29 A good discussion of the Roanoke primary fight can be found in Harold G. Wheatley, "The Political Career of William Atkinson Jones" (M.A. thesis, University of Virginia, 1953), 47–48, and *passim.* See also Doss, "John Warwick Daniel," *passim,* and Poindexter, "The Virginia Democracy," 19–27.

proposing the primary was his personal opposition to Martin. With evasive repartee he avoided categorically replying to Jones's incisive questioning, at one point confessing that he had "never studied the primary system at all." Though most observers agreed that Daniel's performance was less than brilliant, nevertheless his unexcelled personal popularity probably saved the day for Martin. At the close of his arguments the convention, by the narrow margin of 850 to 609, deleted the primary proposal from the platform.

The vote rejecting the primary, however, cannot be accepted as clearly reflecting the sentiment of the state, or even of the delegates. Taken late in the afternoon, after all the nominations had been completed and when half of the delegates had departed for their distant homes, the total vote was comprised of many proxies cast by a few individuals, most of which were cast against the primary. With this handicap and "in the face of determined maneuvering by Daniel and Martin" the primary forces had performed well. A radically new departure from political tradition had won impressive support from a Virginia party renowned for its conservatism.

The 1897 fight over a senatorial primary proved to be a political crossroads in Montague's youthful career. Although he evidently attained his nomination with the benefit of Swanson's support, Montague also privately endorsed Jones's reform, a reform opposed by the vast majority of Virginia's machine politicians, including Swanson. As a candidate for nomination, Montague had taken no direct part in the deliberations of the convention, "but he and his friends gave it [the primary] loyal support." W. Seymour White, himself a delegate to that convention, graphically described the factional split over the primary proposal:

> Mr. Jones [in fighting for the primary] gathered about him such brilliant leaders as Lipscomb, Walton Moore, Jack Montague, Massey, Tazewell Ellett, and others while around Senator Daniel were gathered the grim forms of the machine politicians—Boykin, Otey, Hay, Epes, Taylor Ellyson and the Norfolk gang. Not the least conspicuous in earnest advocacy was Honest John Lamb, while Congressman Swanson, halting between two opinions, was conveniently absent when the fight came.[30]

In aligning with the more progressive elements of the party at the Roanoke convention Montague had made a crucial decision. His affiliation with the reform element proved a durable one. Long after

30 Clipping, Fredericksburg *Star*, scrapbook, Montague Papers.

Swanson and Montague ceased exchanging friendly letters, Jones and Montague would counsel together on the best strategy in their mutual struggle against machine domination. In making his alliance, Montague had selected his true element. The idealism of the youth could now find a creative outlet.

The general election which followed the Roanoke convention proved to be "one of the dullest . . . in Virginia history." [31] The majority of the Goldbugs reluctantly entered the silver temple of their party; the sadly decimated Populists declined to field a gubernatorial nominee, despite the cold shoulder given them by the Democrats; and the Republicans suffered from a civil war within their own party. The Democratic triumph in November proved anticlimactic.

On June 2, two months before the Democratic convention, "the question whether to have a ticket in this State" was being seriously considered by the Republican party. On July 11, a month later, a difference of opinion still persisted. Finally, on October 5, a Republican state convention assembled in Lynchburg. "Characterized by perfect harmony, considerable enthusiasm, and scarcity of eloquence," the convention proceeded to endorse William McKinley and the national Republican platform, and to nominate a three-man ticket: for governor, Pat H. McCaull of Culpeper, "a thorough gentleman, personally above reproach"; for lieutenant governor, O. B. Roller of Harrisonburg, "no demagogue"; for attorney general, James Lyons of Richmond, a "man of good standing, and considerable ability." Following his nomination, McCaull stumped the state, concentrating on national issues. But in Petersburg his address to a "small crowd, mostly negroes . . . fell flat upon his hearers." Similarly, Lyons, the attorney general nominee, "failed to awaken much enthusiasm among the Republicans" in an address delivered at Harrisonburg. So feeble were the Republican efforts that the Richmond *Dispatch* speculated on October 17 whether the enemy were "asleep" or " 'possuming." [32]

Even before the discordant Republicans had nominated their ticket, the Democrats had launched their campaign, opening on September 23 with addresses by all three state nominees in Richmond. Tyler, in an anecdotal dialogue, delivered the customary arguments

31 Eckenrode, "Virginia Since 1865," 273.
32 Richmond *Dispatch,* June 2, July 11, Aug. 19, Oct. 6, 17, 19, 20, and 31, 1897; Staunton *Daily News,* Oct. 6, 1897.

for silver and against tariffs, and once again praised economy in state government. Echols asserted in a bit of political philosophy that "the only high mission of government is to establish what is right between man and man." And Montague discussed national and state issues in "a brilliant effort." All three adhered closely to the platform as formulated in Roanoke; none discussed the issue of corrupt elections, which promised to be the chief talking point of the Republicans. Montague, however, in passing reference, "derided those who are so heartily in favor of honest elections and . . . spent $165,000 in the [Virginia] campaign last fall." For his efforts, Montague was cheered repeatedly.[33]

The same emphasis on national issues which characterized the opening salvo in Richmond continued throughout the campaign. Montague and others easily defended this approach, since the November ballot would also elect the legislature that would choose a successor to Senator Daniel. In a more candid mood, Montague confessed in an interview with the Richmond *State* that "the people wanted to hear about these national issues . . . don't want to hear anything else." [34] A wise politician gives the people that which they desire.

But Montague was not only a politician. One of the qualities of a statesman as defined in his Richmond College essay was the ability to lead the populace rather than be led by them. In the 1897 campaign, therefore, he began gradually to speak out on state issues, on state needs and deficiencies. In phrases reminiscent of his youthful essays he called for a revival of morality in politics, of character in education, and of conscience in public service. On October 25, speaking at Staunton, he "delineated with ability . . . the praiseworthy policy of the party in its provision for the Confederate soldiers, the deaf, dumb, and blind, and the insane." On another occasion "he held up to view the evil of illiterate suffrage," and advocated a liberal public school system as a remedy. Only through public schooling could voters be educated and truly universal suffrage established. He frequently expressed his desire to encourage "local patriotism," to obtain "pure judges," and "to see the Legislature stimulated." And at Pulaski on October 5 he gave an "eloquent address of an hour and a half to an enthusiastic audience," declaring himself anxious to improve the public roads and public education, to provide for economy in goverment,

33 Richmond *Dispatch*, Sept. 24, 1897.
34 Clipping of interview with Richmond *State*, scrapbook, Moore Collection.

and to create a "free ballot and a fair count" in elections. "Thousands of hearts are dead, patriotically speaking," he once exclaimed, "but you will yet see a free people casting a free ballot without fear or favor." Such phrases presaged his campaign for the governorship four years later.[35]

These phrases also captivated his Virginia audiences. W. B. McChesney wrote to Montague describing "the "magnificent impression that your speech . . . here made upon the people of Augusta and Staunton. It is spoken of as the gem of the campaign." Another observer, writing to Ellyson, was even more laudatory: "Many pronounced his [Staunton] address as the greatest political speech ever made in our Court House." A dispatch from Richmond to the Baltimore *Sun* prophetically commented: "Major Tyler is a pleasing speaker, but it is admitted that he will not begin to develop the oratorical powers of Mr. A. J. Montague." The great demand for the latter would "probably make him a candidate for a much higher position." [36]

On election day, November 2, the aggregate vote polled was smaller than usual, with Negro voting reported particularly slack. In Danville, only thirteen hundred of an electorate of four thousand bothered to visit the polls. Certainty of a Democratic victory had resulted in apathy.[37]

The Democrats overwhelmed their opponents. Tyler with 109,000 votes easily defeated McCaull with 56,000. Echols, faced with opposition from the Populist Cocke as well as the Republican Roller, ran behind Tyler with 105,000 to Roller's 46,000. Montague led the ticket with 110,000 to Lyons' 48,000. In defeating Lyons, Montague performed best in Tidewater, the Piedmont, the Southside, and especially in the cities. But his victory was virtually universal. Lyons carried only three counties, Alleghany, Floyd, and New Kent. The Democratic victory in the legislative contests was equally decisive.

The year 1897 thus witnessed significant developments in Virginia politics. The same rift which had divided the Democratic party in

35 References to Montague's speeches are from scrapbook clippings of the Richmond *Dispatch*, the Richmond *State*, and various unindentified newspapers, Moore Collection and Montague Papers.
36 W. B. McChesney to Montague, Nov. 16, 1897, Montague Papers; W. T. McCue to Ellyson, Oct. 26, 1897, Ellyson Papers; Baltimore *Sun*, Sept. 26, 1897.
37 Richmond *Dispatch*, Nov. 3, 1897; Poindexter, "The Virginia Democracy," 24.

1896 continued to influence party thinking in 1897. But a new voice
also made itself heard during the year, a voice demanding state election reforms and economy and retrenchment through elimination of
unneeded offices. The new spirit was especially evident when the
Roanoke convention nominated gubernatorial and attorney general
candidates hostile to machine politics and disturbed by election corruption. In addition the convention only narrowly defeated the motion for a party primary, a demand which later served as the cardinal
objective of Virginia's developing progressive movement. The missionaries of internal reform had attracted an audience.

One of the men who joined the forces serving as the nucleus of
Virginia's progressive movement was A. J. Montague. Having sailed
to the political left in Virginia's silver crusade of 1896, he continued
to orient himself among the reform elements of the Democratic party
and to drift farther away from the emerging Martin machine. Nominated for attorney general without Martin's support, he had endorsed
the senatorial primary proposal at the Roanoke convention. This action, and the candid content of his speeches in the subsequent final
election campaign, signaled his break from the dominant Democratic
faction. Having cast his lot with Virginia's political Independents, he
would soon rise to a position of leadership within that faction.

The attorney general of Virginia possessed only a modicum of
power in 1898. His chief duty was to defend the state in conflicts between state and federal jurisdiction, or in suits brought before the
state Supreme Court of Appeals. His only authorized contact with the
law-making process came through an annual report to the governor,
summarizing his year's activities. Thus, paradoxically, his position as
one of three members of the state board of education, a position
which required only one-tenth of his time, gave him more political
power than his role as the state's chief attorney.[38]

Within this framework Montague performed his duties capably,
with moderate success and with occasional flashes of brilliance.[39] He
personally supervised several important cases reaching both the Virginia and the United States supreme courts, and his legal advice was
frequently solicited by local commonwealth's attorneys and school

38 A good description of the attorney general's routine can be found in
    Lois G. Moore, "William Alexander Anderson," 31 ff.
39 Most of the following discussion of Montague's performance is taken
    from his annual reports: *Annual Report of the Attorney-General to the
    Governor of Virginia 1898, 1899, 1900, 1901* (Richmond, 1898–1901).

board officials, as well as various state officials, including the governor.

Politically, Montague's position on the state board of education proved to be the most important facet of his duties. A position which taxed his energies heavily, it also brought upon him considerable political pressure, including, for example, a lengthy letter from Senator Daniel suggesting the adoption of a multiple schoolbook list for the state. More important, as a member of the board he was partially responsible for the appointment of school superintendents at four-year intervals. In 1901 this power would prove a practical asset in his gubernatorial campaign. Still, in general Montague appears to have maintained a nonpartisan approach to the appointment of school personnel during his first years as attorney general. Similarly, he declined to undertake corporate practice which might have influenced or prejudiced his official duties.[40]

Although Montague's official opinions dealt of necessity with legal technicalities, much of their formulation naturally depended on the predilections of their author. Several are therefore indicative of his growing progressivism. For example, in upholding the right of the Virginia Board of Works to require the Norfolk and Atlantic Railway to construct an overhead crossing in Norfolk, he rejected the laissez-faire arguments of that railroad, terming the board's public duty "one of the highest importance for the welfare of the people and the protection of property." In another instance, he strictly interpreted Virginia's election laws, insisting that only the physically and educationally handicapped be given assistance by the judges in the marking of ballots, and that once the ballot was prepared, no voter had the right to expose it to anyone. Montague liberally interpreted Virginia's Confederate pension laws to include all Southern veterans maimed or disabled. Though some of his opinions proved distasteful to the parties concerned, as late as 1905 none of them had been reversed.[41]

In the field of litigation Montague participated in several cases of importance. Perhaps the most significant was *Harkrader v. H. G. Wadley*. Wadley, the president of a Wytheville insurance company, had been prosecuted by the state for embezzling $196,000 of company funds; but the federal courts, intervening on a technicality, had

---

40 Daniel to Montague, July 22, 1898; Montague to G. O. Green, Oct. 25, 1899; Montague to J. B. Baylor, Jan. 16, 1905; all in Montague Papers.
41 "Record of A. J. Montague," compiled during 1905 campaign, Montague Papers.

issued an injunction against the state's prosecution, an injunction "unprecedented in our system of jurisprudence," claimed Montague. Protesting this usurpation of Virginia's jurisdiction, Montague carried the case to the United States Supreme Court. On December 5, 1898, the Court unanimously sustained Virginia's contention "in the most comprehensive and definitive way."

In other important litigation, Montague successfully defended a state tax upon stockholders of state banks, saving thousands of dollars of revenue for the Commonwealth. He also convinced the Virginia supreme court to uphold the state's taxation on barges and tugs, "floating property [which] is likely to come more and more within our jurisdiction for the purposes of taxation." His most important reversal was the suit of *McCullough v. Virginia,* a case first instituted by his predecessor, R. Taylor Scott, which involved Virginia's long-standing debt litigation. In this suit the Supreme Court rejected Virginia's contention that her creditors should not pay their state taxes with coupons of state bonds.

Montague's performance as attorney general was well received by the Virginia legal profession and the public. Duval Porter wrote in November, 1898, "Your brilliant . . . especially able speech in the Carter case has placed you at a single bound in the forefront of the powerful Richmond bar." An editorial of the Lebanon *News* described his record as "exceedingly brilliant." [42]

But of all Montague's acts while he was attorney general, the one that generated the most publicity was his intervention in an incident connected with the Spanish-American War. A group of fifty to seventy-five men in the Third Virginia Regiment stationed at Camp Alger had become involved in a minor disciplinary fracas caused by racial friction. General M. C. Butler of the United States Army had subsequently charged the entire regiment with disgraceful, insubordinate conduct, restricted its members to quarters, and threatened wholesale court-martials. Montague came to the aid of the regiment; he, Senator Martin, and others discussed the affair with Secretary of War Russell A. Alger, and obtained his promise of a hearing. In the hearing Montague and R. Walton Moore won vindication for the regiment.[43]

The regiment was immensely grateful for Montague's defense. S.

---

42 Duval Porter to Montague, Nov. 21, 1898, Montague Papers; clipping, Lebanon *News,* scrapbook, Moore Collection.
43 Richmond *Dispatch,* Aug. 10–19, 1898.

R. Donohoe, one of its officers, thanked Montague for his "manly and vigorous" defense against "Butler's cowardly attack," then added: *"When you run for Governor* you will have no warmer supporters than the officers and men of the Third Virginia regiment." [44]

Montague's intervention in the affair had thus done no harm to his advancing political career. He had as yet made no definite decision to run for the governorship, as Donohoe suggested, but that he cherished high political ambitions was widely recognized. As a developing leader of Virginia's Independents, he had maintained an active interest in state politics. At the time of Donohoe's letter, moreover, the conflict between Virginia's two Democratic factions had sharpened in intensity, the progressives demanding various reforms, the conservatives stoutly defending the status quo. Montague's role in this conflict would assume major importance.

---

44 S. R. Donohoe to Montague, Sept. 12, 1898, Montague Papers.

VI

LEADER OF THE
VIRGINIA PROGRESSIVES

Fᴿᴏᴍ 1898 to 1900 Virginia's progressive movement rapidly gained momentum. The paramount drive for a senatorial primary, temporarily stalled by the 1897 Roanoke convention, continued to gain new adherents. That drive culminated in the enthusiastic May conference of 1899, which conclusively demonstrated the popularity of the reform among a considerable segment of Virginia's Democracy. Though Martin was once again able to check the immediate proposal for a primary in the 1899 senatorial election, that proposal seemed destined for ultimate acceptance.

A second important feature of Virginia's developing progressivism was the movement for a constitutional convention—a movement to purify elections and to reorganize an archaic, inefficient state government. The campaign for a convention had generated considerable support in 1897, and though the move was defeated in a state referendum of that year, the defeat proved only temporary. The same electoral and governmental conditions motivating a convention remained, and the defeat of the movement for a primary in 1899 and the roughshod tactics used by some of Martin's legislative candidates of that year served only to accentuate the growing oligarchical nature of Virginia's Democratic machine. These factors gave even greater zeal to those who demanded wholesale reform. As a result, the Virginia General Assembly of 1900 agreed to another state referendum on a convention, and the state Democratic convention of 1900 endorsed the proposition. The voters subsequently approved the call by a narrow margin.

As attorney general, Montague helped promote both of these reform movements. Cementing his alliance with the progressives, initially contracted in 1897, he became one of the original petitioners for the May conference of 1899 and took a leading role in the conference itself. In 1900, he again lent his influential voice in support of a constitutional convention. Finally, within a mere three years he increased his political stature among his fellow progressives to the extent of winning their united support in his race for governor in 1901. And in the gubernatorial campaign of that year he became their recognized leader.

These years as attorney general, then, witnessed Montague's continued evolution into a full-fledged, genuine crusader, castigating evil and exhorting reform. Such an evolution was a natural one for Montague, the moralist, the idealist—the attorney general now freed from absolute dependence on party politicians for office and position. But such an evolution was also symptomatic of the times. In advocating the party primary, improvements in education, and cleaner elections, Montague advocated reforms then gaining widespread acceptance in many states.

Nationally, the progressive reform impulse reached its apex in the years between 1900 and World War I. Generally speaking, the movement aimed to protect the public from abuses by railroads and corporations, to ameliorate social ills and deficiencies, and to purify and democratize electoral processes. Such state governors as Robert La Follette of Wisconsin, Charles Evans Hughes of New York, and Hiram Johnson of California fought for various reforms in their respective states—the direct primary, more equitable tax rates for railroads, and industrial and social welfare legislation.

The national progressive movement had its Southern counterpart. Indeed, some aspects of the movement were indigenous to the South. The direct primary, for example, originated in South Carolina twelve years earlier than in Wisconsin, the first Northern state to adopt it. The Southern drive to purify elections and destroy machine control equaled the crusading zeal found in the North, and the Southern crusade for education was the more remarkable, since the Southern educational systems were the more deficient. All strains of Northern progressivism could to some extent be duplicated in the South.[1]

The prevalence of the progressive trend throughout the South can partially be explained by the spadework done by the Populists and the silverites, especially in the 1896 campaign. But whereas the Populist movement sought federal remedies to national problems, the Southern progressive movement concerned itself chiefly with state reforms. The Populist movement had found its wellsprings in national economic unrest among lower-class agrarians; consequently, its leadership reflected both frustration and poverty. The progressive movement, in contrast, emerged in an era of relative prosperity. Economically pacified, the less affluent agrarian classes sank once again into their customary anonymity, while the leadership for progressive ideas passed from country to town, from farmer to editor, from tenant to teacher, from lower to middle class. Political reform had become respectable.[2]

Another factor explaining the universality of the Southern progressive movement lay in the widespread chronic problem of the Negro in Southern politics. That the Negro's enfranchisement (among other factors) had generally served not to democratize the South, but rather to help undermine democratic processes has already been demonstrated. Every Southern state witnessed the same perversions of electoral machinery which characterized Virginia, and reformers in every state eventually attempted to partially remedy the situation through the same method: Negro disfranchisement. Other motives existed for disfranchisement, of course. Numerous Democratic politicians advocated such a move solely to destroy Republican power, especially on the county level. Nevertheless, a prime motivation for the movement existed in the desire of many Southern progressives to purify elections and to remove the racial issue from politics.[3]

Mississippi initiated disfranchisement in 1890, and the other Southern states followed suit, either through constitutional conven-

1   C. Vann Woodward, *Origins of the New South, 1877–1913* (Baton Rouge, 1951), 373. A concise summary of the Southern progressive movement is Arthur S. Link's "The Progressive Movement in the South, 1870–1914," *North Carolina Historical Review*, XXIII (1946), 172–95.
2   Woodward, *Origins of the New South*, 371; Link, "The Progressive Movement," 178–80; see also: Francis Butler Simkins, *The South Old and New* (New York, 1947), 262 ff., and Benjamin B. Kendrick and Alexander M. Arnett, *The South Looks at Its Past* (Chapel Hill, 1935), 130 ff.
3   On the Virginia scene, at least, the author is convinced that this was the case as is explained later in this chapter and in Chap. X.

tions, or by means of constitutional amendments.[4] These conventions and amendments not only wrought revolutionary changes in the electorates of the various states, they also either initiated or gave further impetus to other reforms on the progressives' agenda. A constitutional convention afforded unparalleled opportunity to effect wholesale reforms at a single sitting. For this reason, fearful of change and partial to the status quo, the main Democratic opposition to disfranchisement and to the various convention movements came from machine politicians and conservatives. Conversely, leaders of the progressive elements generally favored the movement. Indeed several of these leaders rose to state power at the same time or soon after disfranchisement had been accomplished. Disfranchisement in the South must therefore be included as part of the Southern progressive movement. In this respect only did the Southern movement differ radically from its Northern counterpart.[5]

The progressive movement in Virginia had originated in the campaign for a senatorial primary. Aimed directly against the reelection of Martin in 1899, the primary was considered by the insurgents the easiest method of deposing the Senator, simultaneously destroying his career and his machine. With this aim accomplished, a freer political climate would be created, and other reforms would follow.

Opposition to Martin arose also because of his conservative and prosaic Senate record. He had voted in 1895 against the coinage of silver at the magic ratio of sixteen to one, and in 1897 he had enraged free-trade Democrats by voting for a high tariff on lumber.[6] Moreover, efficient executive that he was, Martin confined his senatorial activities to routine committee work and to services for his Vir-

---

4   Woodward, *Origins of the New South,* 32 ff.
5   Several Southern progressives other than Montague rose to power partially on this issue. One was Charles Brantley Aycock, governor of North Carolina. Another progressive governor, Hoke Smith of Georgia, advocated in his 1907 inaugural address a comprehensive seven-point platform of reform, which included Negro disfranchisement. See Link, "The Progressive Movement," 179–80; R. D. W. Connor and Clarence Poe, *The Life and Speeches of Charles Brantley Aycock* (Garden City, 1912), 61 and *passim;* Oliver H. Orr, Jr., *Charles Brantley Aycock* (Chapel Hill, 1961), 149, 249, and *passim;* Dewey W. Grantham, Jr., *Hoke Smith and the Politics of the New South* (Baton Rouge, 1958), 158 ff. There is, however, one example of an earlier reformer who opposed disfranchisement—James S. Hogg, governor of Texas from 1891 to 1895. Robert C. Cotner, *James Stephen Hogg, a Biography* (Austin, 1959), 225–26, 353 ff.
6   William A. Jones to Montague, undated, 1905 campaign, Montague Papers.

ginia constituents; rarely did he speak on the Senate floor or to Virginia audiences. To many Virginians, accustomed to past days of statesmanlike oratory, this silence was inexplicable and almost embarrassing. To Martin it was in keeping with the spirit of the age. Virginians, he often asserted, were too sentimental.

The campaign for the direct election of senators lost little momentum following the adverse vote of the 1897 Roanoke convention. Congressman William A. Jones, still the leader of the movement, renewed his efforts to obtain a primary as early as March of 1898. In that month he visited Richmond, where he talked with Montague, Governor Tyler, Congressman John Lamb, and others sharing his opinions. Plans were laid for a statewide conference the following year, the object being to dramatize the demand for a primary and to force the state committee to adopt one for the 1899 senatorial election. This proposed conference received further impetus when all measures to legalize a primary were defeated in the state legislature by Martin's friends, and with his encouragement.[7]

In his discussions with Jones, Montague had assured the Congressman of his "strong desire to defeat Mr. Martin," but Jones later became concerned lest Montague's own ambitions prevent him from participating in the proposed conference:

> Since our talk in Richmond I have been informed that you understand the object of our proposed conference . . . to be the selection of an anti-Martin candidate, and that . . . you preferred not to be bound by any action it might take. . . . The impression which I get from this is that you contemplate being a candidate for the Senate. . . . The impression made upon me during our conversation was that you did not contemplate becoming a candidate.

Jones's original impression had been correct. Although friends had early urged Montague to take on the race against Martin, he had concluded that public support was insufficient to warrant a contest. In advocating the primary, then, Montague was evidently actuated by no ulterior motive. In his own words: "Any misgivings upon this change . . . have been entirely removed by the recent deplorable conditions obtaining in those states which are now electing, and have recently elected, Senators. . . . it seems that we have reached an acute stage of public evil and demoralization which demands a

7   Wheatley, "William Atkinson Jones," 57; Martin to Flood, Jan. 28, Feb. 20, 1898, Flood Papers.

change of method of selection of Senators. . . . the primary plan is the only substitute now offered." [8]

In January of 1899 Montague, N. H. Massie, J. C. Parker, Eppa Hunton, Jr., and other opponents of Martin met in Washington to formulate their strategy. By March, plans for the conference had crystallized, and an appeal, signed by Montague and fifty-one others, appeared in the Richmond *Dispatch* urging a May conference of all Democrats who held to the principle "that the people are fully capable of choosing their senators, and who are willing to unite with us in an effort to secure to them that cherished right." In pungent language the appeal cited as the most obvious reason for reform the ostensible fact that "140 legislators . . . subjected to powerful . . . influence of corporations . . . have not the resisting force of half a million of voters." Others signing the petition included Henry C. Stuart, John Goode, William A. Anderson, Joseph E. Willard, and Congressmen John F. Rixey, John Lamb, and William A. Jones.[9]

Montague took an active role in promoting attendance to the conference once the appeal had been published, urging Judge N. H. Hairston of Martinsville to "throw yourself into this movement with your accustomed energy and fearlessness, for the Democracy of the State must assert itself here on that day." He also participated in making final preparations for the conference and in deciding the line of action best suited to its purposes. Differences of opinion existed among the Independents as to exactly what action the conference should take. Some favored having it directly ask the state Democratic committee to adopt a senatorial primary to select Martin's successor. Others felt that a request for a state Democratic convention would be more feasible. A third group, which included Montague, argued that the decision of the 1897 convention was legally binding on the party, and that the primary advocates should therefore appeal directly to city and county Democratic committees to institute local preferential primaries to instruct legislative candidates. Realization of a statewide primary would come later. Debate concerning the efficacy of the various approaches continued to the eve of the conference, with Montague leading those who urged a direct appeal to

8 Jones to Montague, Jan. 21, 1899; A. Brooks to Montague, Aug. 29, 1898;
   Montague to T. W. Richardson, Feb. 11, 1899; all in Montague Papers.
9 Wheatley, "William Atkinson Jones," 62; Richmond *Dispatch,* May 7,
   1899; Martin to Henry D. Flood, Feb. 2, 1899, Flood Papers.

local committees. As the *Dispatch* observed, "an interesting fight emerges." [10]

An interesting fight also emerged among Martin's followers in reaction to the proposed conference. Most machine politicians, including Swanson, opposed the movement as "simply a scheme against Martin." For his part, Martin argued cogently that the state convention of 1897 had already acted on the question. Citing only the "expense and worry" of a canvass as the reason for his opposition to a primary, he privately expressed confidence that the state committee would sustain his views on the matter.[11]

Not all Martin men opposed the movement, however. The Senator himself observed that though a Mr. Kean, a legislative candidate in Louisa County, had signed the call for a conference, "I never felt that he was unfriendly to me." And political realities persuaded another Martin supporter to endorse the May conference: "I favor the primary plan & think Martin can win in the primary as well as before the legislature. I suppose at the May Court this county will send delegates to the May 10th meeting in Richmond. I want to go. . . . This primary plan is too strong for Martin and his friends to oppose it. Therefore we must get in the swim." [12]

The "swim" threatened to engulf the Commonwealth. Unusual support developed for the May conference, support which both surprised and gratified the progressive leaders. On May 8 the advance guard began arriving in Richmond, including William A. Anderson and Jones, "the recognized leader in the movement." These two met with Montague and others in a three-hour meeting, evidently still attempting to resolve differences of opinion on the proper action of the conference. By May 9, most of the eight hundred delegates had arrived. Representing eighty-three of the one hundred counties, and all but two of the cities, the similarity of the assembly to a regular Democratic convention received frequent allusion. Among the delegates were R. Walton Moore and Eppa Hunton, Jr., both of whom, like Montague, were mentioned as potential senatorial aspirants.[13]

10   Montague to N. H. Hairston, April 11, 1899, Montague Papers; Richmond *Dispatch*, April 28, May 2, 3, and 9, 1899.
11   Richmond *Dispatch*, April 16 and 20, 1899; Martin to Henry D. Flood, Feb. 2, 1899, Flood Papers; Martin to Francis Rives Lassiter, Jan. 30, 1899, Lassiter Papers.
12   Martin to William Bibb, April 14, 1899, and Y. M. Blake to Bibb, April 19, 1899, Bibb Papers.
13   Richmond *Dispatch*, April 26, May 2, 6, 9, and 10, 1899.

Formally convening on the morning of May 10, the conference transacted its business quickly. A receptive audience of delegates listened attentively to several stirring speeches and to the presentation of a platform, which was adopted after a brief debate. The platform endorsed the popular election of senators by means of a legalized primary through legislative enactment. Pending such enactment, however, the conference resolved to ask the state committee to call a state convention or to order a primary election for the purpose of choosing a senatorial candidate. If the state committee refused to act, then the conference urged "that the preference of the Democratic voters in each legislative district for U.S. Senator be ascertained by a party primary. We hope the need for local action will be obviated by the State Central Committee." To carry its petition to the state committee and to work as a permanent force for reform, the conference also authorized the organization of a Senatorial Reform League, with an executive committee of thirty members.[14]

The various speeches of the conference reflected its progressive atmosphere, and no speech was more favorably received than that delivered by Montague. As reported by the Richmond *Times:* "A noticeable feature in connection with yesterday's convention was the attention attracted by Hon. A. J. Montague . . . applauded enthusiastically whenever the members . . . caught sight of him. . . . His address, delivered at the close of the meeting, when the delegates were tired out, excited . . . interest." [15]

Montague's oration consisted of a defense of the conference and its motives against those who would label it schismatic: "We think we have jurisdiction within the party to be here on this day. We think there has never been a period in the history of the Democratic party, that when a motion is made to let the people be heard, that that means the disruption of the organization. . . . We here represent Democracy." Declaring that the conference had met to promote the complete realization of the Declaration of Independence's dictum that government rests upon consent of the governed, Montague continued, "We think we have pure motives. It has been stated . . . that mine are not pure, because I am an aspirant for the Senate. I am not an aspirant for the Senate, and will not be." [16]

Developments preceding and following the May conference demonstrated that Congressman Jones was still leader of the Independ-

14 *Ibid.,* May 11, 1899.   15 Richmond *Times,* May 11, 1899.
16 *Ibid.*

ents, still the chief of staff. But Montague had proven himself a promising young staff officer. His role in the conference definitely stamped him as one of several leaders of the Independents, and at the same time all former friendly relations with machine politicians such as Swanson were permanently severed.

In spirit and enthusiasm the conference had exceeded expectations. The true temper of Virginia's popular opinion had been dramatically measured. But the leaders of the movement failed in their endeavors to carry the resolutions of the conference through to fruition. William A. Anderson, supervising the organization of the Senatorial Reform League, encountered difficulty in obtaining wholehearted cooperation, even from former leaders of the conference. Montague, for example, declined to serve on the executive committee, explaining that he would be unable to give the position the "attention it merits." Jones, on hearing of Montague's refusal, urged Anderson to insist that he accept, saying, "There certainly ought to be as many men of prominence and might on it as possible." Montague, however, remained adamant in his position, though he cooperated with Anderson in convincing others to serve.[17]

Predictably, the executive committee's petition to the state Democratic committee for a primary or convention proved unavailing. Martin in a letter to Flood commented nonchalantly: "Two-thirds of the . . . [Democratic] Committee are my friends and will take care of me in this or any other matter. . . . I must see after the Committee and see that they are posted." On Martin's advice, state chairman Ellyson called a meeting of the Democratic committee, and on June 12, the body met and with little debate defeated the motion to call a primary by a vote of 37 to 11. Martin waited at Murphy's Hotel while the committee was in session, and mingled in the lobby with his jubilant followers after his victory. The May conference, having as its foremost objective the political downfall of Martin, had met defeat at his hands. The senatorial contest was now thrown back to its old familiar grounds, the state legislature. There, Martin would prove impregnable.[18]

The Independents probably had erred in not selecting a candidate

17 Montague to Anderson, May 20 and 28, 1899, and Jones to Anderson, May 26, 1899, in William A. Anderson Papers, Alderman Library, University of Virginia, Charlottesville.
18 Wheatley, "William Atkinson Jones," 61; Richmond *Dispatch,* June 13, 1899; Martin to Henry D. Flood, June 5, 1899, Flood Papers; Martin to Francis Rives Lassiter, May 17, 1899, Lassiter Papers.

against Martin in the May conference. With a dilatoriness perhaps typical of undisciplined political amateurs, they postponed choosing a candidate until it was too late to produce effective opposition. Publicly, they maintained the fiction that theirs was simply a movement for the primary principle. In contrast, Martin had begun silent campaigning even before the May meeting. He was not to be displaced, in a primary, in a convention, or in the legislature, without coordinated effort. This effort the Independents were unable to produce.

Several potential candidates had been available, but Moore, Montague, and Hunton had all refused to be considered. Speculation thus centered on the man who had led the conference movement, William A. Jones. But after the state committee defeated the call for a primary, Jones also refused to enter the race. Although his decision was a bitter and final disappointment to many Independents, some persisted in their search for a candidate. In so doing, they eventually convinced Governor Tyler to offer his name. Tyler's antipathy to Martin and to Virginia's corrupt elections was well known, but because of his rather limited ability, he had not earned membership in the coterie of emerging progressive leaders. Nevertheless, he had expressed approbation for the objectives of the May conference, and was acceptable to most Independents. The candidates had been selected; the battle for legislative support would follow.[19]

Tyler waged his fight with the active assistance of Jones, Montague and other progressive leaders. Jones was particularly helpful, making a statewide speaking tour of crucial legislative districts. Montague did not support Tyler so openly, having decided that his position as attorney general made an active speaking campaign imprudent. High state officials, it is true, rarely campaigned publicly for individual candidates for Democratic nominations. Indeed, before 1901, intra-party contests were not preceded by speaking canvasses, even by the candidates themselves. Montague thus hesitated to follow Jones on the stump: "So far as I can learn I would be establishing a precedent in this particular," he explained to a friend.[20] Possibly, looking to his own political future, he also viewed Tyler's bandwagon as a liability.

In private correspondence, however, Montague felt no such reser-

---

19 Richmond *Dispatch,* May 11, 1899; William A. Jones to William A. Anderson, June 13 and 16, July 8, 1899; J. C. Parker to Anderson, July 10, 1899; Claggett Jones to Anderson, Aug. 8, 1899; all in Anderson Papers.
20 Montague to Samuel L. Adams, July 20, 1899, and Montague to Jones, Aug. 4, 1899, Montague Papers.

vations. He wrote to many of his friends in Danville, Pittsylvania, and elsewhere, urging their support for Tyler: "While the Governor may not be a great man," he commented in a letter to J. W. Gregory, "yet his heart is worth more to the people now than some wiser heads." Montague particularly cooperated with James L. Tredway, a Pittsylvania politico, in obtaining support from prominent county residents. But when Tredway asked Montague to send money for the Pittsylvania campaign, Montague replied: "I have seen Mr. Henry Tyler, the governor's brother. He says that the Governor thinks the use of money by Mr. Martin in supplying funds to aspirants for the [legislative] nomination most objectionable, and that the Governor will not follow his example in this respect. Therefore, I do not think that funds can be obtained as suggested in your letter." [21]

If Tyler refused to finance his followers, Martin felt no such inhibition. Montague's 1897 opponent Lassiter, for example, helped funnel money from the Senator to legislative candidates favorable to his reelection, and Martin personally picked up expense tabs when necessary. The telegraph and telephone corporate interests contributed to the Democratic coffers in return for expected favors from the legislature. Martin also retained contacts with railroad personnel during this period.[22] Relying on corporate assistance and on numerous personal loyalties built up through the years, Martin confidently predicted in mid-September, "Everything seems to be in perfect shape now for my re-election by a good majority." [23]

Several instances of corruption occurred in the election of Martin's legislative candidates. In the senatorial district comprised of Nottoway, Lunenburg, and Brunswick counties, for example, Martin backed William Hodges Mann of Nottoway, Montague's opponent in 1897. Mann was opposed by E. P. Buford of Brunswick, who ran as an independent in protest to irregularities at the district's Democratic convention. In the election Buford carried both Brunswick and Lunenburg by good majorities, yet a day or so after the election, Mann was suddenly credited with over sixteen hundred votes in Nottoway,

21 Montague to J. W. Gregory, Aug. 2, 1899, and Montague to James L. Tredway, Aug. 3, 1899, Montague Papers.
22 Francis Rives Lassiter to Martin, July 22, Oct. 17, 1899, Lassiter Papers; E. P. Meaney to Henry D. Flood, July, 1899, and Joseph Button to Flood, Oct. 27, 1899, Flood Papers. At one point in the earlier 1898 campaigns Martin had asked Flood, "Can the railroad people help you or is it best to have them show no interest at all?" Martin to Flood, May 11, 1898, Flood Papers.
23 Martin to William Bibb, Aug. 8 and 17, Sept. 11, 1899, Bibb Papers.

whereas Buford obtained only eight. And by strange coincidence, shortly after Mann's election was certified to the Secretary of the Commonwealth the poll books were stolen.[24]

Other examples of corruption could be cited. From Tyler supporters in Warren and Clarke counties complaints were heard that "their rights were ignored . . . the Tyler party being shut out having neither judge or clerk" in the primary election. And in a contested election in Southhampton, Isle of Wight, and Nansemond counties, even a Martin supporter agreed that the "party leaders [had been] defeated and rightly . . . 'things were crooked.' " When all the Democratic nominees had been selected, the outcome was scarcely in doubt. After charges of fraud had ceased or subsided, the Democratic legislators elected in November met and caucused; Martin won easily, 103 votes to Tyler's 27.[25]

At first glance, therefore, the May movement of 1899 had failed completely. But a cursory glance is deceptive. True, the drive for a primary had not been realized, and Martin's reelection had not been prevented. But the conference had excited enthusiasm among prominent figures in Virginia politics; it had given the Independents a concrete feeling of unity and purpose. In contrast, Martin's opposition to the reform carried the aura of self-interest, of stubborn opposition to popular will. And the tactics used by some of Martin's lieutenants in the 1899 legislative elections were repugnant to all segments of the party, thus contributing to the drive for reform. The 1899 Virginia legislature that elected Martin was the last to perform such a function independent of a party primary. Sensing imminent change, the Old Dominion did not applaud a dying ritual.

The proposal for a party primary had provided the first objective for Virginia's Independents. The second item on their agenda was the campaign for a constitutional convention. Agitation for this movement, basically derived from a desire to purify elections and to

24 E. P. Buford to Marshall R. Peterson, June 26, 1905, in E. P. Buford Papers, Alderman Library, University of Virginia, Charlottesville. Buford's account is substantiated by a letter written to J. M. Harris (undated, author unknown, Epes-Kilmartin Papers): "I did not favor his [Mann's] nomination and purposely avoided any connection . . . with his canvass. . . . I was absolutely astounded when I heard of the methods adopted by Judge Mann's principle [sic] friends."

25 E. A. Green to J. Taylor Ellyson, Sept. 6, 1899, and J. Walter Hosier to Ellyson, Nov. 11, 1899, Ellyson Papers; Lynchburg News, Dec. 8, 1899.

streamline state government, had begun as early as 1888. Quickened by the reform atmosphere generated in 1899, it would come to fruition in 1900.

Prior to 1900 various factors had defeated the drive for a convention. In the early 1890's a strong Republican-Populist coalition threatened to control a convention if one were called, and the economic depression plus the Bryan crusade diverted reforming energies to the national level. Following Bryan's defeat in 1896, agitation for state reform increased, but in an 1897 state referendum the proposal for a convention suffered defeat by an eight-to-three majority.[26] Even so, events in 1897 indicated that the drive for a convention had reached a turning point. The 1897 November election conclusively demonstrated that the Democratic party need no longer fear Republican competition on a state level. And with the rising prosperity which accompanied the new McKinley administration, radical fringes of rural dissatisfaction subsided, allaying conservative fears of a convention controlled by discontented lower classes. With these impediments removed and with the conditions motivating reform still in evidence, the move for a convention rapidly gained public favor.

The campaign for Negro disfranchisement, the foremost objective of the constitutional convention movement in Virginia, coincided with the crusade for a senatorial primary. Seemingly paradoxical and contradictory, the two reforms actually complemented each other as viewed by their proponents; for the object of the primary was to extend democracy and to undermine machine organizations, and the object of disfranchisement was to rescue the suffrage from its odium of illiteracy and barter by removing the bulk of purchasable votes. With the Negro disfranchised, it was reasoned, elections woud be purified, opportunities for political manipulation by machine politicians would be curtailed, and the need for Democratic solidarity would be destroyed. The electorate would be restored to a position of "virtue and intelligence," able to think independently and to divide naturally on political issues other than that of race.

Such arguments were frequently advanced by the advocates of a Virginia convention movement. Such a reputable historian as Philip A. Bruce, writing shortly after the Virginia constitutional convention had met, asserted that "this privilege of voting, which had been thrust upon the blacks without their seeking, was destructive of every interest necessary to the welfare of the South. . . . Peaceful relations

26 Poindexter, "The Virginia Democracy," 7–13.

with the white people remained impossible as long as the negroes continued to cast their ballots in a herd simply as black men, and not as citizens." [27] Montague resembled Bruce in his thinking on the problem. In retrospect, he stated that the bulk of the Negro population at that time had "neither intelligence nor character fitted for the discharge of the duty of voting. Again, with the same amount of mere mental education the negro still lacks the . . . tradition of free government." On another occasion he wrote, "The foundation of Republican government . . . consists in the virtue and intelligence of its electorate. Either dishonesty or ignorance is fatal to free institutions." Unlike some of his contemporaries, however, Montague did not look upon disfranchisement as permanent. By establishing educational qualifications for the suffrage and then providing the Negro with adequate education, "eventually we may expect the development of a negro electorate determined upon sound political principles," he once commented to a Northern audience.[28]

Montague (together with Governor Charles Brantley Aycock of North Carolina and E. A. Alderman, president of the University of Virginia) also contended that with the issue of white supremacy buried, the populace would look with greater objectivity and resourcefulness upon vital political issues of the day. "In Virginia," he wrote after disfranchisement had been accomplished, "we long lived under a sort of mental and moral servitude. All questions gravitated to the control of the local governments by the white race, and all other questions subordinated. . . . Our new constitution was intended to modify this unwholesome condition [and to bring a] revival of free discussion which must evolve a new order of leadership." [29] The fact that the Southern campaigns for railroad regulation, the senatorial primary, child-labor legislation, and better education all coincided with or closely followed Negro disfranchisement lends some credence to this viewpoint. Whether disfranchisement was merely a reactionary, racist accompaniment of the generally progressive reforms of the era, as most current historians are prone to assert, or whether it was a causative agent contributing to the success of

27 Philip A. Bruce, *The Rise of the New South* (Philadelphia, 1905), 447–49.
28 Richmond *News Leader*, Jan. 13, 1904; Montague to G. Cassel, April 10, 1905, Montague Papers; A. J. Montague, "The South and the Nation," *University of Chicago Magazine*, II (Jan., 1910), 93–101.
29 Montague, "The South and the Nation," 93–101; Orr, *Charles Brantley Aycock*, 149; Virginius Dabney, *Liberalism in the South* (Chapel Hill, 1932), 176.

the other Southern reforms, is a question which warrants further investigation.[30]

In Virginia, a second important incentive contributing to the constitutional convention movement, one scarcely less important than disfranchisement, was the desire to streamline state government, removing needless offices and making state administration more amenable to the will of the people. Montague, for example, voiced a hope that a convention would institute "certain changes . . . in the matter of simplifying the several departments of our State government (thus lessening the cost of government), and in regulating and purifying our elective franchises." Montague particularly desired to see Virginia's judicial maze streamlined, the State Board of Education strengthened, and the public hospitals for the insane improved. A convention was also supported by many people who simply wanted to destroy the Martin organization via any available means. Carter Glass, a vociferous champion of constitutional reform, hoped that a convention would "rid the State of a corrupt, costly, and intolerable domination of an office-holding clique." Unless such deplorable conditions were remedied, he predicted, the ruination of the Democratic party was inevitable.[31]

Opposition to a convention naturally arose from those officeholders whose positions were likely to be eliminated. Most of the courthouse rings and corporate representatives (Martin included) either expressed opposition or maintained a policy of silence. Opposition also developed among those who argued that Negro disfranchisement would remove the only cause for Democratic solidarity, though Montague himself looked upon this increased independence of the voter as "an end in the highest sense to be desired." The Republicans of the southwest area, faced with no Negro problem of their own

30 C. Vann Woodward, *The Strange Career of Jim Crow* (New York, 1962), 66, 74–76. Woodward and others agree that disfranchisement was endorsed by nearly all Southern progressive leaders, that it coincided with the Southern progressive movement as a whole, and that Southern progressives themselves considered it part and parcel of their program. Still, Woodward describes the relationship as paradoxical and regrettable, a "blind spot." Historians must make value judgments, yet a dismissal of all these idealistic progressives as misguided, prejudiced bigots in this one particular, appears to be a somewhat heavy indictment. And the relationship of disfranchisement to the Southern progressive movement, whether causal or coincidental, remains largely unexplored.

31 Montague to C. H. Burnley, Feb. 6, 1901, and Montague to T. D. Gibson, March 7, 1905, Montague Papers; Horn, "The Democratic Party in Virginia," 47–49.

and fearing that a convention would disfranchise all illiterates, black and white, naturally opposed the movement. In addition, some Independents, including Governor Tyler, opposed a convention on the grounds that it would be dominated by machine politicians.[32]

In 1900 the final phase of the drive for a convention originated in the General Assembly. A bill to call a state referendum on the subject passed both houses in March, and the referendum was slated for May 24. The convention's proponents next sought the vitally necessary endorsement of the Democratic state convention, which was to meet on May 2. In the selection of representatives to that convention, therefore, leaders of the movement, including Eugene Withers of Danville, J. C. Parker, Glass, and Montague, lobbied to elect delegates favorable to their cause. Montague composed a public letter in support of a constitutional convention, arguing that the necessity for the step lay in the "continued refusal of the legislature to submit [constitutional] amendments." He also urged that a new constitution be submitted to the people for ratification.[33]

Joining the progressives in their call for a convention were two stalwart friends of Martin, Senator Daniel and State Senator Flood. Indeed, Flood had sponsored the legislative bill which set the referendum. Martin, by way of contrast, was distinctly cool to the reform. Although sympathetic to the demand for disfranchisement in the black belt, "where the negro vote is large and troublesome," he opposed making a vote on the referendum a matter of party regularity. Such a course, he warned privately, would arouse and unify the Republican party, thereby endangering Democratic prospects in the November, 1900, state elections.[34]

In this instance, Martin's wishes did not prevail. The state Democratic convention convened in Norfolk as scheduled. Though it was dominated by Martin's forces, Martin evidently made no effort to defeat the popular demand for a constitutional convention, already endorsed by many organization men as well as by Independents. "Opposition to a . . . convention," the *Dispatch* observed, "has disappeared like dead leaves before the gales of autumn. . . . Those who are at heart opposed are silent." The platform, as finally adopted

32 Richmond *Times,* May 11, 1900; Richmond *Dispatch,* Feb. 3, 1901; Montague to Edward M. Shepard, Sept. 12, 1901, Montague Papers.
33 Richmond *Dispatch,* April 29, 1900; copy of public letter, written April 21, 1900, Montague Papers.
34 Martin to Francis Rives Lassiter, March 29, April 13, 1900, Lassiter Papers.

with little dissent, endorsed the calling of a convention but stipulated that no citizen entitled to vote in 1861, or any descendant of such citizen, should be deprived of his suffrage. The endorsement also recommended that the new constitution be submitted to the people for ratification as Montague had earlier suggested.[35]

The three short weeks intervening between the Norfolk convention and the referendum witnessed a brief flurry of campaign activity. Various speakers, Montague among them, stumped the state urging a favorable vote in the referendum. Although Glass maintained that "selfish politicians" were plotting to thwart the convention proposal, no prominent Democrat dared to speak in opposition to the meeting. The Republicans, who had officially disapproved of the proposal in their February convention, remained unorganized. Even so, unobtrusive opposition from machine Democrats combined with solid Republican opposition resulted in a close vote in the referendum—77,000 votes in favor, 60,000 opposed. The Southside and Piedmont gave a majority to the convention, but the cities, the seedbed of Southern progressivism, provided the most overwhelming margin, 24,000 to 6,000. The electorate had decided. The election of delegates to the convention itself would follow in 1901.[36]

This decision may be considered the first victory for the Virginia progressives. Though battle lines were often ambiguous, those who had participated in the May conference of the previous year supported the constitutional convention unanimously, while such machine figures as Martin and Swanson were conspicuous by their silence.[37] Whatever the motivations, the calling of a convention signified that epochal change was in the making for Virginia's fundamental law. Virginia's Independents, preparing for the 1901 election of convention delegates, hoped to achieve several constructive reforms.

Montague too looked forward with anticipation to the year 1901, for in that year statewide elections might determine his political fu-

35 Richmond *Dispatch,* May 2, 3, and 4, 1900. In the balloting for the four delegates-at-large, Senator Daniel led with 771 votes, Martin followed with 730; the two Independents, Tyler and Jones, trailed with 570 and 523.
36 Richmond *Dispatch,* May 24, 1900; Horn, "The Democratic Party in Virginia," 63.
37 Victor D. Weathers, "The Political Career of Allen Caperton Braxton" (M.A. thesis, University of Virginia, 1956), 16. Swanson's silence is paradoxical, since he was one of the few Democratic leaders to support a convention in 1897.

ture. Certain personal decisions had to be made. Should he seek re-election as attorney general? Should he aspire to the governorship? Or should he quit politics altogether?

The events of 1899 had temporarily filled Montague with doubt and discouraged him in his political aspirations. The failure of the May conference to obtain any concession from the machine forces and the failure of the Independents to prevent Martin's reelection made him despair for his own and his state's future. A letter to his wife, written late in August as the campaigns of the state legislators were progressing, poignantly reveals his indecision as to his personal career and his distress over the conditions of Virginia politics:

> Such an unhappy year this has been for me! And politics has done it all. I feel so keenly the plain decay of public official life, and the villainy of so many seeking office, and the betrayal of friends, that my heart has been restless and pained for some months. And I so poor, and so unprepared to lift a helping hand. All this has been to me a keener grief than I felt you should know. . . . I hope a brighter day is coming, a day that will either release me from public life or one wherein I may be serviceable, and successfully serviceable, to my poor and beloved State. . . .
>
> . . . . . .
>
> . . . the fame of the public official is fleeting, no matter how proud, glorious and brilliant it be. But a warm home, with books, bright fire-sides and sanctified by the care of wife and childen alone bring peace in old age. Friends of the plain citizen will last. Friends of the public official leave him gladly in the hour of his defeat. Think over all these things, and not the immediate gratification of our ambitions, and we will talk when we are together again.[38]

Talks with his wife must have revived Montague's optimism and his ambition, for in November he confided to a friend, "I have not fully determined what I shall do. There is an effort to drive me out of politics in this State, and . . . [as presently] advised the best way I can meet it is to take the bull by the horns and announce myself for the Governorship." By early January of 1900 Montague was still uncertain, but the rumor of the gubernatorial candidacy of his erstwhile supporter Swanson pushed him toward a final decision: "If he [Swanson] be strong enough to nominate himself I cannot be taken as Attorney General from the same county. In addition to this, I do not care to be Attorney General on a ticket headed by him. . . . Self-

38 Montague to his wife, Aug. 20, 1899, Moore Collection.

preservation seems to require that I myself shall be a candidate for the . . . nomination." [39]

Conferences with various friends who were members of the legislature—Anderson, Moore, Hunton, and Carter Glass—encouraged Montague to announce his candidacy. Revealing his inclinations to Jones, still the titular leader of the Independents, he inquired, "What do you think of this, and does it interfere . . . with your aspirations? If you will be a candidate for the Governorship, I will not be." Jones evidently gave his blessing, for on January 27, 1900, a full two years before his final inauguration, Montague formally announced his candidacy.[40]

For Montague and for Virginia's progressive movement, the years from 1897 to 1901 were years of rapid development. The individuals who had temporarily allied in favor of a senatorial primary in 1897 had combined into a distinct faction of Independents, dedicated to electoral reform and determined to undermine the dominant Democratic organization. Montague, functioning capably as the state's attorney general, developing administrative experience, and attracting a political following, had risen to a position of leadership in that faction. In 1901, campaigning for governor on a progressive platform dedicated to the preferential primary and better schools, he would displace Congressman Jones as the leader of the Independents. His campaign would bring the progressives a solid victory over the Martin organization.

39 Montague to K. B. Stoner, Nov. 18, 1899; Montague to Thomas W. Shelton, Jan. 3, 1900; Montague to William A. Anderson, Jan. 18, 1900; all in Montague Papers.
40 Montague to William A. Jones, Jan. 18, 1900, *ibid.*

VII

CAMPAIGN FOR GOVERNOR, 1901

ANDREW JACKSON MONTAGUE had formally announced his gubernatorial candidacy in January of 1900. Through the remainder of that year he quietly endeavored to obtain support from the Virginia Democracy's rank and file. Aided by his widespread reputation for oratory and by a prevalent hostility toward the Martin organization, he gained the backing of a large segment of the state's electorate. Alarmed by Montague's evident popularity, Martin and most of his machine forces subsequently aligned behind the candidacy of Claude A. Swanson, Montague's former neighbor and ally. In the spring of 1901 as the campaign shifted into high gear, Montague and Swanson clashed in one of the most bitterly fought contests in party history. The upshot would prove to be a personal victory for Montague and a severe blow to Martin's organization.

In conducting his campaign, Montague proposed a progressive platform favoring the popular primary, better schools, better roads, and the enactment of an employer's liability law. The outstanding feature of his campaign, however, was a sustained criticism of the Martin machine. He censured a political domination which resulted in "government of the friends, by the friends, and for the friends"; which sometimes ignored the welfare of the whole for private preferment; and which appropriated all public offices to its exclusive clientele. With Jacksonian zeal he promised to restore idealism to politics, to make government once more responsive to community, not private, interests. The young Montague, an aspiring lawyer eager for legal and political advancement, had prudently bided his time, had silently acquiesced in the course of his state's political degradation. Now, at last, would come the reaction. The 1901 campaign stamped Montague as a genuine Southern progressive.

Throughout 1900 Montague's campaign activity consisted largely of organizing his forces, conducting an extensive correspondence, and maintaining general public relations. In February, one month after his announcement, state chairman J. Taylor Ellyson received a report that the attorney general was "daily gaining ground," and in March, a month later, Montague assured James L. Tredway of Pittsylvania that "my candidacy is favorably progressing. I am in the lead of all the other candidates combined." C. A. Cutchin was probably correct when he surmised in September, 1900, that it was "the field against Montague, with Montague in the lead at this time." [1]

Montague drew his popular support primarily from those Independents who were concerned with corruption in Virginia politics. Eppa Hunton, Jr., a close adviser, expressed succinctly the viewpoints of the progressive leaders when he wrote Montague shortly after the latter's announcement: "I am glad you have announced your candidacy. I believe you are the strongest man in the state of the anti-Martin party; that the people of the state will rally to you sooner and more readily than to any one else, to lead them against this political machine which is leading us constantly to political degradation." From Mecklenburg, E. Betts, speaking for "those of us in the black belt, sick and sore of ring and place politics," applauded Montague's candidacy. And C. L. Corbitt, a minister who was an old friend and schoolmate of Montague, was even more emphatic: "I want to see the Martin-Swanson ring buried out of sight & I believe you are the man to do it." [2]

But Montague derived support not only because of his antimachine stance. Educators endorsed his advocacy of better schools. (W. S. Gooch reported from Charlottesville that the University vote was for him.) Labor unions, especially railroad unions, praised Montague for his support of an employer's liability law. Montague was also en-

---

1 J. C. Carpenter to J. Taylor Ellyson, Feb. 25, 1900, Ellyson Papers; Montague to Tredway, March 10, 1900, and C. A. Cutchin to Montague, Sept. 29, 1900, Montague Papers.
2 E. Betts to Montague, Feb. 17, 1900, and C. L. Corbitt to Montague, Feb. 2, 1900, Montague Papers.

dorsed by persons unconcerned with factional rivalries. One observer, for example, declared that Governor Tyler was "not worthy to unfasten the latch strings of Tom Martin's shoes," but that "your man Montague struck me as a very brilliant and practical man as District Attorney." Even Swanson supporters occasionally expressed admiration for their opponent. W. S. Hale, party chairman in Pittsylvania, Swanson's home county, gave his titular endorsement to Swanson, but added: "I am a great admirer of Mr. Montague. He is an able man, a clean man and a fine speaker." [3]

With this strength in depth Montague faced his developing campaign with optimism. He helped to maintain his initial advantage by continuing his role as spokesman for the Virginia Democratic party, both on state and national issues. During the first part of 1900, he was one of the leaders in the agitation for a constitutional convention.[4] And in the fall he contributed to the Bryan campaign in Virginia by conducting another speaking tour of the state. The tenor of Montague's addresses shifted drastically from that of four years earlier. Like Bryan himself, he no longer emphasized silver. Instead, he bore heavily on the issue of trusts and monopoly and the influence which money had carved for itself in the national Republican party. In castigating the economic trusts and their corollary the political trusts, Montague evidently made biting references to political trusts everywhere, thereby indirectly criticizing Martin.[5]

Montague's speaking tour thus served well to advance his gubernatorial candidacy, already announced but not yet actively prosecuted. One observer characterized his oratorical image as "so sincere, so deeply in earnest he pleads more like a Preacher than a Politician." Describing his oration at a cornerstone-laying at Charlotte Courthouse, Thomas D. Jeffress exclaimed, "They [the veterans] were delighted and gave you the *acme* of praise saying, 'Montague surpassed Daniel.'" After the November election, however, the Newport News *Morning Herald* observed ominously: "To all outside appearances

---

3 J. G. Agae to unknown recipient, Sept. 15, 1900; W. S. Hale to Judge W. S. Gooch, Aug. 17, 1900; Gooch to Montague, Dec. 5, 1900; all *ibid.*

4 R. Walton Moore wrote to Montague (Feb. 12, 1900, Montague Papers) before the state Democratic convention, "After the General Assembly adjourns would it not be well for you to bring together a few of your friends to talk over the situation and aid you possibly in arranging a plan of action? . . . we should perfectly understand what if any thing your friends are to attempt in [the convention]."

5 Clippings, 1900, scrapbooks, Moore Collection; C. Taylor Gwathmey to Montague, Oct. 18, 1900, Montague Papers.

the Democratic hosts of Virginia have been pulling most harmoniously in the traces," but now that the need for party unity had passed, "we are going to see the fur fly." [6]

The fur was to fly between Montague and a total of four opponents, including Colonel James "Cyclone Jim" Marshall from the populous Norfolk district, Lieutenant Governor Edward Echols, state chairman Ellyson, and Swanson. All four, like Montague, had made their ambitions known early in 1900. Of the four, Swanson was to prove the most formidable contestant.

It was peculiarly fitting that Swanson should become Montague's chief opponent. Although they were former political allies, and though their positions on many issues were similar, the characters of the two men provided antithetical contrast. Montague, though not devoid of political acumen, represented essentially a personification of Old South statesmanship. Nostalgia explains much in his basic motivation. On frequent occasions throughout his life he accepted invitations to deliver historical addresses describing the giants of Virginia's past. Fulfilling such assignments, he invariably acquitted himself with erudition, polish, and sentiment. (Later in his career, his reputation as a historian-statesman resulted in his being asked by S. F. Bemis to contribute a historical sketch of John Marshall in Bemis' monumental compilation of *American Secretaries of State.*[7]) Steeped in Virginia's biographical past, Montague both deliberately and unconsciously emulated his predecessors. A selfless desire to serve was to him the chief characteristic of a good public official; and though he was ambitious, desiring most of all to lead personally a renaissance of Virginia statecraft, still his motivation cannot be called wholly self-centered. Ambition and altruism were combined in a happy symmetry in his career.

Swanson, on the other hand, epitomized the machine politician. A "kind, friendly man," cavalier and vigorous, sometimes called the "young gamecock," he was probably as thoroughly expedient as any politician in Virginia. He actually bragged on occasion how quickly

---

6 Thomas D. Jeffress to Montague, Nov. 24, 1900, Montague Papers; Newport News *Morning Herald,* Nov. 20, 1900, scrapbook, Ellyson Papers; clipping, Sept. 11, 1900, scrapbook, Moore Collection.

7 Samuel F. Bemis (ed.), *The American Secretaries of State and Their Diplomacy* (10 vols.; New York, 1927–29). Montague's portion is found in Vol. II, 247–84. Dr. Carl R. Fish commented: "Mr. Montague's John Marshall leaves nothing to be desired either from the viewpoint of comprehensiveness or workmanship. It makes of this short and troubled term a memorable chapter in the development of American international thought." *American Historical Review,* XXXIII (Oct., 1927), 152.

he could change his tack to suit prevailing winds. As a five-term Congressman from the closely contested Fifth District, he had developed all the arts of the practicing politician to a fine degree. So questionable had his tactics proved that three of his five elections had resulted in congressional investigations—mute testimony of his control over the electoral machinery and final election returns. During his fifth congressional campaign in October, 1900, Tredway could observe, "many democrats who will vote for Swanson for Congress as the nominee are utterly opposed to him and his methods." [8]

At the time of Montague's announcement Swanson's own candidacy was uncertain. Reports that Martin would support the Congressman were discounted by the *Clarke Courier* and Richmond *Dispatch*. These journals asserted that Swanson had not yet definitely decided to run and that Martin and others had actually counseled against his making the race. When Swanson finally announced his candidacy in the fall of 1900, however, Martin, Daniel, and at least four of Virginia's ten Congressmen (Lassiter, Hay, Rhea, and Peter J. Otey) all endorsed his candidacy. [9]

Once the decision had been made, Martin worked avidly for Swanson. He wrote numerous personal letters to friends throughout the state, declaring that Montague's election would be a personal affront to himself. Martin's letter to William Bibb is perhaps typical:

> The organization which is promoting Montague's candidacy is inspired by the sole purpose of breaking down, what they see fit to call, "the Martin organization." In other words, Mr. Montague himself and his managing friends are hostile to me and to my friends, and we do not propose to see him become Governor of the State to use the power of his office to injure us. Senator Daniel knows that these parties are as hostile to him as to me and he feels the same interest in it that I do. In fact all of your close friends with whom you have always stood in the politics of the State are involved in this purpose to defeat Montague. . . . Swanson is the strongest man to make the fight with, and I see no reason whatever to doubt his success.

To Lassiter, Montague's opponent in 1897, Martin declared, "This fight is practically my fight and I propose to look after it." [10]

8 James L. Tredway to Montague, Oct. 4, 1900, Montague Papers.
9 *Clarke Courier* (Berryville, Va.), Jan. 24, 1900. Supporting Montague at this time were Congressmen Jones, Rixey, and Quarles. Congressman John Lamb later shifted from Ellyson to Montague, and Congressman Flood from Echols to Swanson (Richmond *Times*, Feb. 8, 1901).
10 Martin to Bibb, Dec. 24, 1900, Bibb Papers; Martin to Lassiter, March 25, 1901, Lassiter Papers.

Swanson endeavored to make capital from Martin's endorsement. In his thousands of letters to the state's citizenry he made frequent reference to his support by a majority of Virginia's congressional delegation. And in true Tom Martin fashion, he promised that the individual's support would be "highly appreciated and remembered. . . . Any who knows me will tell you that I am grateful and stand loyally to my friends." [11] The public, however, reacted adversely to Martin's attempt to select Virginia's next governor and to Swanson's own blatant appeal for support on the grounds of patronage. When publicly revealed, Martin's letters proved to be a "millstone" rather than a boon to the Congressman.[12] To Montague the development reemphasized the basic issue on which he pursued his campaign—that one man or one group of men was attempting to dictate the state's political affairs, that all aspirants for public office had to turn to Washington for support, and that this situation was inimical to the political welfare of the Commonwealth.

Besides Swanson, three other individuals figured in the campaign jockeying of 1900 and 1901. Ellyson was a potent factor in any race. A defeated candidate for governor in 1897, a longtime chairman of the party, he was considered by many as due for political reward. As state chairman he maintained invaluable contacts with Democrats of all factions. As a resident of Richmond, and, like Montague, an active layman in the state's Baptist councils, he found support in areas where Swanson was little known. In some respects, he seemed an ideal compromise candidate.

Ellyson had hoped to win Martin's support for his candidacy, and Martin may actually have preferred Ellyson over Swanson. But Swanson had persevered, forcing Martin to choose between the two. Assaying Swanson's strong hold on the Fifth District, and perhaps concluding that he would prove more reliable politically, Martin had chosen the Congressman. Lacking organization support, Ellyson withdrew from the race on January 4, 1901, causing consternation among Swanson's friends, who assumed correctly that Ellyson's strength would now go chiefly to Montague.[13]

11 "The Swanson Letter," Danville *Free Press,* Jan. 14, 1901, in scrapbook, Moore Collection.
12 John Ritchie, "The Gubernatorial Campaign in Virginia in 1901," *Essays in History,* II (Charlottesville, 1955), 58; *Clarke Courier,* June 19, 1901.
13 Henry D. Flood to R. E. Byrd, Jan. 5, 1901, Flood Papers. In May, 1900, Alfred P. Thom, a conservative railway attorney from Norfolk, wrote Ellyson asking, "Did I tell you in 1897 I'd support you now? I felt it then,

Two more regional figures offered their candidacies: Edward Echols of Staunton and James Marshall of Portsmouth. Echols' received his most influential backing from Congressman Flood of his home district. A conservative of quiet dignity, he aroused no bitter antipathy; neither did he create enthusiasm, though his campaign was afforded ample publicity by the newspapers. He was important chiefly as a potential dark horse, should Montague and Swanson deadlock. The candidacy of Colonel Marshall, the fourth and most regional aspirant, was never taken seriously, even in his own Second District.[14]

The charge was frequently made that Echols and Marshall were in league with Swanson and had entered the race only to stave off strong Montague sentiment in their respective sections. Montague himself viewed the candidacies of Echols, Marshall, and Swanson as being jointly directed by Martin. He personally felt "very kindly" toward Echols and preferred him "as between Ellyson and Swanson, yet I do not think he can be nominated, and am afraid if nominated he will be under the control of Mr. Martin. . . . But all represent the machine type, and it seems to me that unless something is done to relieve us from its bondage we cannot hope to free the State from its present deplorable condition." [15]

Montague's suspicions were well-founded. Although Echols himself took his candidacy seriously, he agreed to cooperate with the Swanson forces to their mutual advantage against Montague. In those regions where Swanson was strongest, Echols stood aside; in return, a tacit agreement was reached that certain counties would be exclusive Echols territory. Congressman Flood, for example, urged Martin to agree in Buckingham County to the selection of a delegation "of known Swanson men . . . instructed to vote for Echols as long as his name is before the Convention." [16] In May, when a Montague landslide seemed to be developing, the Swanson and Echols forces pooled their finances in a desperate effort to buy delegations, especially in the Southwest. A naive Echols was prevailed upon to raise personally

---

I know. Since then I have come under very great obligations of a personal nature to another." Thom's position possibly represents the shift of Martin's machine from Ellyson to Swanson (Thom to Ellyson, May 12, 1900, Ellyson Papers).

14 Richmond *Dispatch,* Jan. 10, 1901; E. T. Lamb to Montague, Aug. 29, 1900, Montague Papers.

15 Harrisonburg (Va.) *Rockingham Register,* Feb. 8, 1901; Montague to Anderson, Jan. 18, 1900, Montague Papers.

16 Echols to Flood, May 22, 1901, and Flood to Martin, March 15, 1901, Flood Papers.

ten thousand dollars; Flood, Swanson, and Martin together were to raise another ten. Echols fulfilled his part of the bargain, even contributing an additional three thousand when Swanson fell short of his quota—all to no avail.[17]

These were the candidates and personalities in the gubernatorial campaign of 1901. That campaign, as it developed, differed little from previous contests in some respects—the usual letter canvasses, mass meetings, factional quarrels. But it promised to be different in at least one important feature. On January 19, 1901, Montague announced that he personally would canvass the state, appealing to the voters on specific issues. Prior to that time (as will be recalled from the 1897 contest) Democratic candidates had refrained from preconvention campaigning, presumably camouflaging divisive party issues in a show of unity against the Republican party. Montague's announcement thus broke precedent, and his calls for a rejuvenated morality in state politics, for better schools and roads, and for a party primary, were heard in every corner of the Commonwealth.

Montague's speaking role, however, was not to develop until early spring. The opening months of 1901 were relatively calm politically. The first significant development came late in January when Montague sent a letter to the Roanoke *Times,* denying rumors that he had dishonored a pledge made to Swanson in 1897 not to run for the governorship in 1901: "I have never heard that he contemplated being a candidate until some three years [actually two years] after my nomination [for attorney general]. My political life is a protest against such promises of combinations. I only ask and desire the full and fair expression of the people of the Commonwealth, as the one tribunal to pass upon my candidacy." [18] The charge persisted, however, and as late as April Montague received letters asking if the story were true.

The first legitimate issue of the race developed near the end of February when the national Machinists' Union publicly supported Swanson as "one of the greatest labor advocates in the U.S. House of Representatives, one who used every effort to secure the passage of our fifteen-day leave bill" (yearly leaves of absence with pay for men employed in United States Navy yards).[19] Some unions on the state

17 Flood to Swanson, June 2, 1901; Echols to Flood, June 21, 1901; H. L. Kane to Flood, June 4, 1901; all in Flood Papers. Montague's forces also purchased votes in some regions. R. S. Campbell to Flood, June 29, 1901, *ibid.*
18 Reprinted in Richmond *Dispatch,* Jan. 16, 1901.
19 *Ibid.,* Feb. 28, 1901.

level, however, opposed Swanson. Measuring the three major candidates by their attitudes toward the enactment of an employer's liability bill, a measure which had been defeated in the Virginia Assembly in 1899, railway unions asserted that "Martin, Swanson [and] Echols . . . all fought us very hard," while Jones and Montague had both favored the measure.[20] And the Richmond Labor Council endorsed Montague as one who "not only did all in his power for the passage of the liability bill, but who, on every occasion, has shown a uniform fairness." [21]

Swanson and Echols both publicly denied having ever "lifted a hand" against the bill in the Assembly; indeed, Echols congratulated Flood for supporting the bill, and expressed surprise at the news that Montague had been an original supporter of the measure. If Swanson and Echols had not opposed the bill, however, in no sense had they supported it. Montague was to make his advocacy of the reform a chief issue in the ensuing campaign.[22]

Political news in March and early April consisted largely of speculation upon the prospects of the various candidates. Delegate R. Walton Moore reported that Montague had many supporters in Fairfax County and powerful backing in the Eighth District as a whole. After returning from a short trip to Princess Anne County, Attorney General Montague himself was "greatly pleased." Late in April Montague watchers heard private admissions by machine men that a landslide to Montague was developing.[23]

The state Democratic executive committee met on April 25 to select a date and location for the nominating convention. The date selected was August 14, the place, Norfolk. This decision, made by a Martin-controlled committee, was a victory for Swanson, since the later the date of the convention, the easier it would be to overcome Montague's early lead. The 1,468 delegates were elected at the discretion of local party committees, and the Swanson forces hoped to utilize the

20 The bill would have made railway companies liable for damages should their employees be injured while on the job.
21 *First Annual Report of the Virginia State Legislative Board, August 8, 1899* (Richmond, 1900), 13, Montague Papers; Richmond *Dispatch*, Feb. 28, 1901; Montague to D. R. Snapp, March 13, 1901, Montague Papers.
22 Bristol *Courier*, March 14, 1901, in scrapbook, Moore Collection; Richmond *Dispatch*, March 3, 1901; Echols to Flood, Feb. 27, 1901, Flood Papers.
23 W. A. Taylor to Montague, April 1, 1901; J. R. Jordan to Montague, April 6, 1901; J. P. Harrison to Montague, April 26, 1901; all in Montague Papers; Richmond *Dispatch*, March 3, 1901.

bandwagon technique by holding mass meetings and conventions in counties that were considered Swanson strongholds.[24]

The bandwagon technique was soon implemented, but by Montague's forces, not Swanson's. On April 27 the pro-Montague Manchester committee called what the Swanson people labeled a "snap primary," to be held on May 9. In Alexandria, a Swanson city, retaliation quickly followed when on April 30 a primary was set for May 6, three days before the one in Manchester. On May 7, the result of the Alexandria vote reached the papers: Swanson had triumphed, 1,035 to 925, thus receiving under the unit rule the entire twenty-vote delegation.[25]

The first blood had been drawn, and Swanson had drawn it. But his was an expected victory, and his margin was less than anticipated. Only a day later Montague himself broke into the scoring column by capturing Fredericksburg's six votes. Then on the tenth came news of a lopsided Montague victory in Manchester, 628 to 384. Scattered results continued filtering in until, by May 15, the totals stood at sixty-seven delegates for Swanson, forty-five for Montague, and eleven for Echols. Since Swanson's total came almost entirely from the Fifth District, Montague was actually ahead of his estimated strength.

As the campaign progressed, the individual candidates began making numerous speeches, all carefully covered by the state's journals. On May 7, the date of the Alexandria vote, Montague made "one of the ablest speeches heard here for years" at Emporia. In his address, he dwelt upon the dangerous and growing tendency in the country toward one-man power, "comparing the boss and his candidate to a child tied to its mother's apron strings." Speaking to a Roanoke audience on May 11, he again scored the machine, declaring emphatically, "I would rather be defeated a thousand times by the 'bosses' than elected by them." The only way for the people to control certain "plum-tree shaking" senators, he asserted, was to provide for their popular election. In a Richmond address a week later he repeated this theme: "Indifference to dirty politics prolongs dirty politics. . . . I wish every man and boy could come to look with horror upon the man who holds office against the wish of the people." The maxim of modern political bosses—to stand by one's friends—he labeled repre-

24 Richmond *Dispatch*, April 26, 1901.
25 *Ibid.*, May 1, 2, 3, and 7, 1901. All delegate statistics hereafter mentioned are taken from the *Dispatch*. With some exceptions, accounts of campaign speeches also are taken from the *Dispatch*, which will be cited only if the date is not clear in context.

hensible. And when someone in the audience shouted out the name "Martin," Montague replied, "I call no names. You know these things." Great tribute was paid to the past giants of Virginia's history, men who had given selfless and principled service, not men "who could do nothing but get post-offices for friends. . . ."

On the day Montague made this speech, Swanson issued a public statement denying any connection or dependence upon the machine and Martin. "Senator Martin did not inspire, nor did he suggest my candidacy. The assertion that he did so is not true . . . a slander which I resent." Inviting the public to view the record, Swanson claimed he was fully as independent as Montague; his 1897 support of Montague while Martin supported another proved that.

Although Montague may have exaggerated Swanson's complete subordination to Martin personally and to his machine, he realized that if Swanson were elected with machine help, he would be under obligation. "Government by men, however honest, owing their places to the endeavors of a powerful few, could result only in bad government," he declared in a May 18 speech at Leesburg. There he renewed his plea for a revival of fundamental Democratic principles of self-government: "An active participation in politics by the mass is essential to good government." Bosses like Martin and Mark Hanna maintained power only by promises and more promises. Personally he pledged that he had not promised, and would not promise, any place to any one in advance of his election. In private correspondence he reiterated this pledge when individuals asked for various positions.[26]

In lambasting the machine as an unhealthy element in Virginia politics, Montague created no synthetic issue. Rigid party organization, a product of the new industrialism and of the race-baiting, demagogic political contests of the 1880's, had taken powerful hold upon the state. Courthouse cliques, created through patronage of the General Assembly, constituted a nucleus of tractable party workers who afforded almost automatic support for the policies of machine leaders. And the machine leadership itself, supported by some on the grounds of conservative political conviction, by others for reasons of simple expediency, had developed into an exclusive board of directors —still backed by corporate finances—whose endorsement became increasingly necessary for the success of any candidate for public office.

One might legitimately ask if perhaps this machine provided Vir-

26   Montague to M. I. Murphy, Jan. 12, 1901, Montague Papers.

ginia with good government. Many Virginians in 1901 would have replied affirmatively; moreover, the historian should candidly admit that concrete accomplishments of the various reform agitations associated with the progressive movement (both state and national) have been less than is sometimes claimed. Still, even if it be reasonably argued that Montague and other progressives shared a naive faith that government action could significantly remedy social and political ills, this does not dismiss as superficial those factors which produced their protest. To some, Martin's organization provided Virginia a safe and sane political leadership. On the other hand, Montague and the Independents saw in it lethargy, electoral corruption, "special interest government," and most frustrating of all, a lack of vision.[27] As the progressives viewed it, Martin's organization possessed no idealistic credo, no platform of goals other than its own preservation; this organization endeavored chiefly to maintain the status quo, especially to retain control of Virginia's political machinery. Insofar as it dominated Virginia's General Assembly and selected Virginia's senators, it succeeded. In controlling the governorship, however, it encountered greater difficulty.

The power of the machine over the courthouse cliques was vividly depicted by William D. Hix of Appomattox. Writing to Ellyson concerning the gubernatorial campaign early in 1900 he observed: "The machine has taken charge, and it grinds out for itself; every office-holder in this or Buckingham counties (save our old clerk here whom we elected in spite of the machine) are afraid to acknowledge that their lives are their own, and when any order is issued, they fall in like blood hounds on the track." [28]

A letter from Martin to a protégé in 1898 indicates the extent of his influence over the Virginia Assembly at that time. Martin urged

27 This indictment may be considered exaggerated, and yet an extensive investigation of the private papers of numerous Virginia machine politicians reveals few expressions of sentiment, of idealism, of high public purpose. Rather, their correspondence reveals a realistic appraisal of practical politics, an acceptance of life for what it is. Almost entirely lacking is the sense of zealous dedication so often found in the writings of such men as Montague, Jones, Henry St. George Tucker, and A. C. Braxton. Camm Patteson, oversimplifying the case, put it this way in a letter to Tucker: "Flood possesses great industry but he is not a man of sufficient breadth of intellect ever to become a statesman nor is Thomas S. Martin. . . . They do not know how to appeal to anything but the selfish side of human nature." Patteson to Tucker, May 3, 1902, in Henry St. George Tucker Papers, University of North Carolina library, Chapel Hill.

28 William D. Hix to Ellyson, Jan. 31, 1900, Ellyson Papers.

his friend to convince State Senator D. Q. Eggleston to vote for his reelection: "It is, I think, easily demonstrable that such a course on his part would be wise, looking to his career in the Senate and to his personal and political future." [29] Montague frequently complained of this debilitating monopoly of state politics and patronage. Merit and talent were often overlooked; political loyalty became the paramount consideration. He feared that with the direction of Virginia politics centralized in the hands of a small clique, individual talents and natural leadership would be subjugated to the egocentric considerations of a self-perpetuating machine acting always in its own interest. So long as the machine continued to dominate Virginia's politics and tolerate political corruption, a revival of Virginia statesmanship would be delayed. Montague's feelings were all the more fervent since he undoubtedly considered himself such a potential statesman, endowed with native ability, oratorical persuasion, and humanitarian outlook—thwarted only by the disfavor of a narrow set of politicians. His fight against the machine was thus motivated both by personal ambition and by public patriotism.

Not only did the machine provide Montague with the central theme of his campaign, it also provided the chief point of discussion for the only joint debate of the contest. The campaign trails of Montague and Swanson met in Boydton on May 20. Swanson had previously challenged Montague to joint debate without success; at Boydton, however, Montague was forced to accept or lose face. The resulting encounter was termed "red-hot." Speaking to a rather small crowd of about two hundred persons, Montague declared that government was never more corrupt than now. Martin, who, ironically, lived in Jefferson's home county of Albemarle, had done all within his power to obstruct the popular will—by defeating the direct election of senators and by controlling the legislature with corporate assistance: "How much of your State legislation of to-day is shaped by the men you send to Richmond? . . . How much is dictated by lobbyists?" [30]

Once again, Montague raised no false allegations. Several machine members, including Flood, Swanson, James Hay and William F. Rhea, were not above accepting payments from corporations in return for various "services rendered" in the state legislature. The very embryo of the Virginia machine had been nurtured by railroad contributions given to enlist political influence in obtaining legislative fa-

29 T. S. Martin to M. M. Martin, Jan. 20, 1898, Flood Papers.
30 Richmond *Dispatch,* May 21, 1901.

vors.[31] That railroad money continued to "cut a figure" among machine men in later years was shown by a 1900 communication from Flood to Martin, describing Flood's successful campaign that year for nomination to Congress in the Tenth District: "The railroad employees stood by me almost to a man. Of course you, Wickham [attorney for the C&O] and others will understand this." Later, in 1903, Flood wrote Alfred P. Thom, a Norfolk attorney for the Southern Railway, asking for a $200 subscription for a local legislative campaign. The machine's candidate, Flood lamented, was not popular, and his opponent was a "great crank" who "cannot be controlled" on some questions—"your interest is one of them." Two hundred dollars, he concluded, would be money well spent. Thom later sent the money.[32]

Other corporations also contributed to the coffers of the machine in return for specific favors. The American Telephone and Telegraph Company, beginning at least as early as 1898, began a systematic distribution of money to Flood, Swanson, Hay, Rhea, and Martin in return for their aid in forestalling regulatory legislation in the General Assembly.[33] In 1899 Swanson himself was asked by the Association of Street Railways in Virginia to accept a "retainer" of five hundred dollars to oppose bills before the legislature limiting the hours of employees to ten hours daily.[34] Thus Montague's bitter charge in his Boydton debate, that the machine and corporate monies exercised an unhealthy influence on state legislation, possibly contained more truth than even he realized.

At Boydton, after Montague concluded his lambasting of Martin and the machine, the colorful Swanson almost leaped to the platform. Prefacing his remarks with "You have heard the sweet platitudes of my friend," and directing most of his speech directly toward Montague—often shaking his finger at him—he asked if Montague had not supported Tyler over Martin for the Senate two years ago: "If you don't want Martin to hit you, don't you hit Martin. And if he does hit you back, don't play the crybaby." Trying to cast off the millstone of Martin, he showed how they had often differed—on support of Cleveland as president, on the nomination of Montague four years earlier, and on the recent selection of a judge for the state su-

31 Martin to Flood, Jan. 2, 1896, Flood Papers.
32 Flood to Martin, June 22, 1900, and Flood to Thom, June 29, July 16 and 20, 1903, Flood Papers.
33 E. P. Meaney to Flood, May 7, 1898, Dec. 15, 1899, April 3, 1903; Flood to Meaney, May 5, 1900, July 12, 1902; all *ibid.*
34 J. T. Lawless to Swanson, Dec. 19, 1899, Lassiter Papers.

preme court. There was no machine in Virginia, he asserted, and if one existed, it belonged to Montague, not to Martin. As attorney general, Montague served as one of three members of the state board of education, empowered by the constitution to select all school superintendents. This power of appointment, Swanson charged, Montague had used for his political advantage.

Another highlight of Swanson's address was his advocacy of a statewide Democratic primary for the nomination of governor. In his rebuttal, Montague termed this ironic, since efforts in 1899 to enact the senatorial primary principle had been defeated by the machine with Swanson's cooperation. Indignantly rejecting Swanson's allegations of a personal machine, Montague declared, "If Mr. Swanson does not know there is a political ring in Virginia, he is so misinformed he is not fitted for the governorship." Such was the acrimony at the first joint debate in a pre-nomination race in Virginia's history. It was also to be the last of the campaign, though Swanson vainly challenged Montague for more.[35]

Swanson's criticism of Montague's use of his position on the board of education was reiterated later in the campaign. From Swanson's standpoint there existed a valid concern. Superintendents of schools, appointed for four-year terms, were then in the process of being selected. Although the deadline for applications had passed on April 14, final decisions on the applications had been delayed until the latter part of May and the first part of June. The delay in final action may have been usual; and again, it may have been political strategy. Disappointed applicants turned down by the board (another member of which was Governor Tyler, a Montague sympathizer) could easily be swayed by the efficient Swanson organizers. And from Swanson's viewpoint the board, by delaying its decisions, was keeping all applicants in the Montague camp during the vital first month of local primaries and conventions.

In the past, school superintendents' appointments had been made chiefly as political rewards, and many of Montague's own supporters urged him to use his power to gain votes. That Montague sometimes followed this advice cannot be denied. Machine men in Franklin and Rockbridge counties charged that Montague's appointments in their localities had been politically inspired. Even Henry St. George Tucker, Montague's friend and supporter, once observed privately

35 Richmond *Dispatch*, May 24, 1901.

that though Montague was a "good" man interested in better education, he was also in politics, and this naturally prejudiced his actions
relative to the appointments.[36]

However, though Montague tended to support those individuals
most inclined toward his own political attitudes, he did not ruthlessly
purge all non-Independents from the school administration. In general, he sought to remove that administration from all political considerations. Martin men, he once complained to Tucker, never held
school positions without prostituting their offices for partisan ends. In
contrast, on one occasion, when a candidate for appointment contributed campaign money to John J. Stuart, a Montague lieutenant in Abingdon, Montague insisted that Stuart return the money. In concise
terms he outlined to another supporter his general appointive policy:
"Where a school superintendent is faithful and efficient, and has not
used his schools in politics," he would favor reappointment. Thus
Montague attempted not so much to build a personal machine in the
school administration as to destroy Martin's hold there.[37] Even so,
his strategic delay in announcing appointments in May and June of
1901 worked to his political advantage. The Richmond *Times*, perhaps overstating the case, described his membership on the state
board of education as his "greatest political asset" in the campaign.[38]

After the Boydton debate, Swanson and Montague intensified their
campaign efforts; both candidates toured all sections of the Dominion. On May 25 Swanson spoke in Lynchburg while Montague appeared in Danville. The same charges and countercharges characterized the speeches of each, a major feature being Daniel's introduction
and praise of Swanson at Lynchburg. On the twenty-eighth Swanson
spoke in Richmond and again denied that he had opposed an employer's liability bill. Furthermore, he pledged that if elected governor
"and such a bill is presented to me, I will sign it." Swanson also
promised to make the public schools more efficient, to reform the system of taxation so that burdens would fall equitably, and to provide

---

36 John W. Burger to Montague, July 19, 1900, Montague Papers; J. O. Hoff-
    man to Daniel, June 4, 1901, in John W. Daniel Papers, Alderman Library,
    University of Virginia, Charlottesville; Henry St. George Tucker to Wil-
    liam A. Bowles, Feb. 20, 1905, Tucker Papers.
37 Montague to John J. Stuart, Jan. 31, 1901; Montague to E. E. Holland,
    June 5, 1901; Montague to Henry St. George Tucker, March 10, 1905; all
    in Montague Papers.
38 Horn, "The Democratic Party in Virginia," 166.

good roads for the Commonwealth—pledges similar to those made by Montague.

On June 1 Montague took Swanson's place on the Richmond hustings. In a speech described as superior to any he had previously delivered, he laid greatest emphasis on the need for better schools and educational opportunities, an emphasis also found in his 1897 campaign for attorney general. The consolidation of schools, facilities for technical and vocational education, a longer school term—these were his specific objectives. Like Swanson, he emphasized the need for good roads to provide easier commercial transportation, pointing to the Shenandoah Valley pike to indicate how adequate transportation facilities enhanced property values.

In general, Montague's 1901 speaking campaign captivated his audiences. Not only the content of his messages but the magnetic manner in which they were delivered served to reinforce his already favorable reputation throughout the state. Swanson's canvass did not lose votes, yet he never successfully refuted the impression that he was a machine candidate. His close connection with Martin, despite his attempts to minimize it, gave his candidacy an aura of ring politics that proved fatal. In addition, Swanson lacked something of Montague's dignity; to some his youthful and impulsive personality seemed inappropriate for the august executive of a sovereign state. In the final analysis, however, Montague's positive attributes, his wider reputation, not Swanson's deficiencies, influenced most voters. The fact that four years later this same Swanson succeeded Montague in the governor's chair indicates that many of the electorate approved of Swanson, but they preferred Montague.

The voters' verdict soon became manifest. As matters stood in mid-May, some predicted the tide could go either way, with the possibility of a dark horse victory not unlikely. On May 16, however, an unexpected result presaged the turn of events to come. Henrico County, previously claimed as exclusive Swanson territory, returned a verdict that was hardly unanimous—ten delegates for Montague and twelve for Swanson; five of the latter were contested for flagrant irregularities, and Swanson himself later repudiated several of them.

On the same day of the rowdy Henrico elections Dickenson and York counties elected solid Montague delegations. And on May 28 the first large breakaway by either candidate occurred. Elections in both Lynchburg and Danville gave Montague a clean sweep. In Danville, the metropolis of the Fifth District, Montague won by a margin of 77 votes in 1,841 cast; the margin in Lynchburg was more comfortable: 1,269 to 472. By the end of the month Montague had almost as many delegates as his three opponents combined. Richmond joined the groundswell on June 6, awarding thirty-eight delegates to Montague and only thirteen to Swanson. The following week Roanoke was easily taken, and Marshall had a hard time capturing a good minority of the delegates from the city of Norfolk. Little doubt remained. On June 25 Echols formally retired from the race with most of his eighty-eight delegates expected to go to Montague. By July 11 Montague was officially only one vote from nomination. July 14 found Swanson "rusticating" at his home in Chatham, while Montague went fishing in the waters of the Delaware.

August, 1901, was the month of conventions in Virginia—the constitutional convention, the Republican and Democratic conventions. The Democrats met on the thirteenth. "From the truck patches of Tidewater will they come . . . from the bluegrass fields of the Southwest; from the smiling Valley; from the Piedmont; from the Southside." [39] Comments were frequent about the "younger element of the Democracy" predominating in the convention as it assembled in Norfolk. "In many of the counties men, old and young, who never before took an active part in politics were workers for Mr. Montague." One correspondent asked, "Where are the old faces? Where was the tall . . . figure of Joe Lawless . . . the clearcut intellectual profile of William F. Rhea? Where was Hal Flood, Frank Lassiter . . . 'Ned' Echols . . . and where was . . . Thomas Staples Martin?" Replacing these men as leaders in the Norfolk convention were John Goode, William A. Jones, Glass, Braxton, and Moore. Senator Daniel was still there, popular "but unsought." Swanson was also there, in his gregariousness displaying a jollity that belied his recent defeat. Montague cordially greeted all visitors with an old-fashioned dignity for which he was admired.

The inevitable orations greeted the delegates on the first day of the convention, orations which differed from those of previous conventions in their concentration on state rather than national issues.

39 Richmond *Dispatch,* Aug. 11, 1901. The following account of the Norfolk convention, except where otherwise noted, comes from the Richmond *Dispatch,* Aug. 11–16, 1901. Especially helpful was a scrapbook of clippings found in the William A. Anderson Papers. See also scrapbook in Thomas S. Martin Papers, Alderman Library, University of Virginia, Charlottesville.

Chairman Goode gave a stirring address, advocating a liberal range of reforms for the consideration of the constitutional convention then in session. Governor Tyler spoke briefly, and Glass, installed by the Independents as permanent chairman, praised the composition of the convention as indicating a revival of party patriotism.

The nomination itself came anticlimactically; Swanson's name was not even presented. George C. Cabell of Danville, a former Congressman, nominated Montague as "distinctly a man of the people," a defender of the rights of property who "at the same time . . . dares to place flesh and blood above avarice and ambition. . . . He walks a highway of his own, and keeps the company of his self-respect." In a polished speech of acceptance Montague outlined his personal platform for progress in the new Virginia. He would improve the mental institutions, better the public roads as highways of commerce, invigorate the public school system, utilize the state's wealth "of water, of forest, of field, of mine," further scientific agriculture, and establish the uniform primary plan. The new constitution being formulated by the constitutional convention gave welcome promise, he asserted, of meeting the hopes of a progressive people. Following Montague, Swanson made a gracious speech of acquiescence to the majority will, promising to help the ticket against the Republicans in the fall. The ovation was deafening when the two shook hands in conclusion.

The platform adopted the next day reflected the progressive thinking of the convention. Reputedly drawn by a man "very close to Mr. Montague . . . revised by several of his friends," its provisions included the customary endorsement of the Tyler administration, the customary praise of accomplishments by the party, the customary platitudes favoring economy, efficiency, and education. Not so customary, however, were the resolutions favoring an employer's liability law and the party primary for all officials elected on a statewide basis. To implement the latter resolution the state Democratic committee was instructed to formulate a primary plan for the next regular election. The platform was adopted as drawn without overt opposition on the floor of the convention, a distinct contrast to the furor that greeted the primary proposal in the 1897 Roanoke convention. Another startling contrast could be found in the basic content of the two platforms. Whereas that of 1897 dealt almost exclusively with national issues, that of 1901 was primarily concerned with state problems and state reforms. The Virginia Democracy had become self-critical.

The races for lieutenant governor and attorney general in 1901 did not vitally affect Montague's own campaign. Though he was intimately acquainted with antimachine candidates for both positions, Montague found sentiment among his own following divided geographically with regard to the secondary positions. Therefore, rather than antagonize any element of his following, he maintained a strictly neutral position, although some of his adherents were not so noncommittal.

The fight for lieutenant governor was not closely contested. The most prominent candidate, Joseph Willard, was Montague's distant relative and his financial benefactor in the final campaign against the Republicans. Some of Montague's advisers, however, disliked Willard and feared that his candidacy would damage Montague's prospects. Accordingly, Montague avoided any direct endorsement of Willard, though the two occasionally exchanged encouraging comments. Willard easily won the nomination even without united Independent backing.[40]

The race for attorney general developed considerable competition. Swanson sponsored John L. Jeffries of Culpeper County; other candidates included Judge Samuel Williams of Wythe, a favorite of some Martin men in the southwest; Judge William G. Robertson of Roanoke, a personal friend of Montague; and William A. Anderson of Rockbridge County. As a leader of the 1899 May conference movement, Anderson attracted the support of most Montague men, and on the second ballot forged ahead of Jeffries for the nomination. A friend, congratulating him upon his election, exulted: "Mr. Martin had better pack his grip and go to England and stay there. The people through you and Montague are on top." [41] And Governor Tyler expressed the belief that "the ticket and the declaration of principles are the direct results of the fight which I made two years ago."

Tyler claimed too much personal credit for the victory, but that the actions of the convention represented the culmination of a growing reaction against corruption in politics cannot be denied. All three nominees can be classified as Independents; none trained with the Martin machine. The platform in particular represented a triumph of the reform movement which originated in the previous decade. The

40 R. Walton Moore to Montague, Feb. 1, 1900; William A. Jones to Montague, July 28, 1900; Montague to Willard, May 3, 1901; all in Montague Papers.
41 C. C. Doyle to Anderson, Aug. 16, 1901, Anderson Papers.

results of the August convention, coupled with the meeting of the constitutional convention, mark the summer of 1901 as a turning point in Virginia's political history. The party primary, an employer's liability law, a higher corporation tax rate, Negro disfranchisement and cleaner elections—all these aims of the reformers seemed on the verge of accomplishment.

Montague's personal victory had yet to be completely realized. Between him and the governor's chair stood the Republican party. Although greatly weakened compared to its strength in the 1880's and early 1890's, the Republican party was still sufficiently potent to provoke numerous warnings against Democratic apathy. As early as April 3 the Richmond *Dispatch* surmised that a former Democrat, Colonel J. Hampton Hoge of Montgomery County, would probably receive the Republican nomination if that party chose to field a ticket. "A lawyer of ability . . . an exceptionally effective stump speaker," Hoge was described as "a formidable competitor for the honor." The *Dispatch's* prediction was borne out by the Republican convention which met at Roanoke a few days after the Democratic Norfolk convention. Nominated with the support of federal officeholders, Hoge encountered opposition only from a small group of former Confederates. The stage was now set for the final election.

Hoge waged an aggressive speaking campaign against Montague. Mincing no words in his bitter attacks on both the Democratic nominees and their platform, he termed the Tyler Democratic administration reprehensible, specifying corruption in the auditor's office, cruelty in the penitentiary, and mismanagement in the mental hospitals. Seizing upon the key word, economy, he roundly denounced the clique of unneeded, vested-interest Virginia officeholders. He claimed Republican credit for inaugurating the public school system in 1870, whereas Democratic inefficiency, he charged, had developed them only to the extent of a five-month term. And he gave wholehearted approval to the McKinley administration, contrasting the national Republican unity with the Democrats' schism over Bryan.[42]

But the biggest issue raised by Hoge, and the most important of the campaign, was that of the constitutional convention. The convention delegates had been elected on May 23, and first met on June 12. Disfranchising the Negro, a chief aim of the convention, was the aim

42 Richmond *Dispatch,* Aug. 22 and 23, 1901.

most feared by the Republicans. To accomplish this objective various means were proposed. Many delegates desired merely to eliminate the Negro illiterate, thus achieving white supremacy and cleaner elections; some favored eliminating all illiterates by educational qualifications; a few even suggested a property qualification. If all illiterates, white and Negro, were excluded, the vast majority of Republican voters would disappear. Republicans naturally saw in the convention, then, a desire to eliminate their party from statewide competition. True, the Democratic party had officially pledged that no white man would lose his vote, but those convention members who advocated a property qualification apparently did not remember the pledge. Aware of their danger, the Republicans tried to arouse the illiterate white voters of both parties. And though Democratic organs attempted to belittle the Republican cries as mere propaganda, history affords a different picture. The Virginia electorate was reduced approximately 50 per cent by the new constitution.[43]

As might be expected, some of the substance of Montague's addresses remained the same through both his canvass for the nomination and the final campaign. He continued the same exhortation for suffrage reform, the primary, better roads, and better schooling. In other respects, however, he altered his course considerably. His speeches now adopted more of the "traditionally Southern" flavor—Confederate veterans were praised, the Carpetbagger Underwood constitution and the Fifteenth Amendment deplored. No longer was the legislature condemned nor mention made of the corrupt machine. Montague and the machine were now ostensibly united under the Democratic banner; Martin himself came out of obscurity and made a speech praising Montague as "eminently fitted for his high office." [44]

Countering the chief issue raised by the Republicans, Montague defended the objectives of the constitutional convention, expressed confidence in its mature deliberations, and counseled patience with its progress.[45] To allay the fear on the part of many whites that the Republicans were correct in warning of white disfranchisement, a broadside was printed and circulated by the Democratic state committee, reassuring all Virginians of the convention's aims. Included on the broadside was this comment by Montague:

43 Horn, "The Democratic Party in Virginia," 71, 104, 111; Anderson to Daniel, Dec. 24, 1900, Daniel Papers.
44 Richmond *Dispatch*, Oct. 18, 1901; Charlottesville *Progress*, Nov. 2, 1901.
45 Richmond *Dispatch*, Sept. 17, 1901.

The Democratic party, thru its representatives in the convention, is slowly, but surely, framing a law that will so effectually exclude the idle, shiftless and illiterate of the negro race from the suffrage that the gates of republican wrath cannot prevail against it. The trouble with our opponents is that they realize now that we will accomplish this and keep the pledge that no white man will be disfranchised. I stand here and declare it, for I do know it is the truth.[46]

During the closing days of the campaign, an incident occurred which destroyed any hopes the Republicans might have had of victory. On October 17 the new President, Theodore Roosevelt, had dinner at the White House with the eminent Negro, Booker T. Washington. A national scandal resulted; white Virginians were outraged. State Democrats seized upon the event as excellent propaganda against the Republicans, and Roosevelt, who previously had won some favor among Southerners, was immediately castigated as a "black Republican." Solemn editorials proclaimed the permanence of social inequality among the races. Roosevelt could "lie in the gutter" if he so desired, but Virginia should be kept pure in its white supremacy.[47]

Montague joined in the demagoguery. "Do we want Negroes dining in our executive mansion?" he asked. The Republican party he portrayed as "the party that loves a negro better than a white man." The white race, he alleged, was "by divine right . . . entitled to supremacy. . . . One race must guide . . . and one must be guided." State furor over the incident reached such a level that the *Dispatch* reported on November 3 that the Washington dinner seemed to have surpassed the constitutional convention as an issue in the campaign.[48]

A *Dispatch* cartoon on the evening of November 6 depicted J. Hampton Hoge being "snowed under" by ballots of the Virginia Democracy. A predicted victory margin of fifteen to twenty thousand votes had been exceeded. The final vote stood at 116,683 for Montague, 81,366 for Hoge, or a percentage of fifty-nine to forty-one. Montague had captured all of Virginia's eighteen cities, sixty-six of her counties, and nine out of ten congressional districts. In whatever fashion the figures were computed, the outcome was decisive. That

46 "No White Man to Lose His Vote in Virginia," 1901 election broadside, Ellyson Papers.
47 Richmond *Dispatch*, Oct. 18 and 31, 1901; *Clarke Courier*, Oct. 25, 1901; Staunton *Spectator and Vindicator*, Nov. 1, 1901.
48 Richmond *Dispatch*, Oct. 19, 30, and 31, Nov. 3, 1901.

Montague's triumph in 1901 was less pronounced than Tyler's four years earlier can be attributed to several factors: the Republican candidate Hoge, a one-time Democrat, provided effective opposition; the Democratic call for disfranchisement was controversial and was vigorously opposed by most Republicans and some Democrats; finally, Montague lacked solid Democratic support, for many in the Martin organization gave him only tacit endorsement.

At no time did the fortunes of the Democratic Independents seem brighter. Their most eloquent leader had mounted the state's top pedestal. A constitutional convention dominated by their forces was in the process of drafting a new charter for the state. Martin had evidently lost the support not only of the people, but of many politicians as well. For Montague personally, the 1901 election represented a crucial victory for his ambitions. The campaign also distinctly marked him as a Southern progressive.

Capitalizing on the spirit of innovation introduced with the successful calling of a constitutional convention, he had channeled this reform spirit into a crusade against all semblances of selfish political alliance and machine control. He had called upon Virginia to repudiate the ring politician and to adopt a program of progress for the Commonwealth. In response to his challenge, the state's citizenry had given him a four-year mandate of office. Already Montague optimistically envisioned an even greater victory against Martin in four years. The Red Fox of Middlesex would begin his term in office with high hopes for a successful administration.

VIII

A NEW GOVERNOR,
A NEW CONSTITUTION

ONTAGUE began his administration during a period of rapid
political transformation. The constitutional convention
which had first met prior to his nomination in 1901 continued to hold sessions into the spring and summer of 1902. The
convention, dominated by Montague's political friends, produced significant changes in Virginia's fundamental law. State educational and
eleemosynary institutions were reorganized, the state's judiciary system
was streamlined, and the Negro was disfranchised. Perhaps most significant was the convention's creation of an independent corporation
commission with power to charter, regulate, and supervise all domestic corporations (especially railroads) and to assess corporate taxes.
Montague, authorized to appoint the members, responded by selecting a capable three-man body which acted quickly to raise corporate
taxes and to reduce railroad rates. As a novel experiment in business
regulation, the commission stands as a notable monument to Virginia
progressivism.

Although the corporation commission thus supplanted the legislature in some of its traditional functions, the state Assembly under the
new constitution retained its dominant position in Virginia's government. True, the constitution empowered the governor to make several
important appointments, to make recommendations to the legislature,
and to veto legislative bills. But as an incumbent ineligible for reelec-

tion, he was largely denied political authority. Even within his own executive department he lacked the power of coercion over administrative departments. In essence, Virginia's chief executive was merely a "director of the board."

Within this framework Montague served capably but unobtrusively. During his four years in office he helped to create public demand for reforms in education and general state services; he sought also to destroy Martin's machine. But, hampered by constitutional qualms and factional quarrels, he failed to establish a working relationship with the General Assembly, feeling that the executive should not interfere in the law-making process. Hampered also by an essentially nonpartisan policy toward appointments, he failed to establish a loyal political organization to counterbalance Martin's. As a progressive governor, Montague continued his valuable role as a spokesman for various reforms; as an administrator, he functioned adequately; but as a political leader, he failed to accomplish several of his important objectives.

Montague's brief inaugural address on January 1, 1902, was delivered not before the General Assembly but before the deliberating constitutional convention. In a sense, the circumstance was symbolically appropriate, for Montague's elevation to office had resulted from the same reform movement which had motivated the calling of a convention. The most enthusiastic support for the convention movement had come from antimachine Democrats, whereas the most vehement opposition came from the threatened Republican party, from corporate interests, machine officeholders, and conservatives generally. After the call for a convention had been approved in the 1900 state referendum, these hostile elements naturally combined in an attempt to influence the election of delegates. Montague reflected the Independents' fear that such an influence would be predominant when he wrote to a friend, urging every precaution: "We should strive to have in the convention able, disinterested, and patriotic men . . . . else it [the constitution] might be made even worse than now." [1]

Final elections for the delegates to the convention had been held

1 Montague to C. H. Burnley, Feb. 6, 1901, Montague Papers. The best analysis of the Virginia convention can be found in Ralph C. McDanel, *The Virginia Constitutional Convention of 1901–1902* (Baltimore, 1928). For a description of contemporary Virginia government and how it was affected by the convention, see F. A. Magruder, *Recent Administration in Virginia* (Baltimore, 1912).

Andrew Jackson Montague, 1925

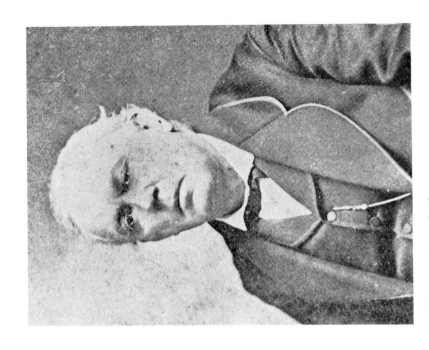

Montague's parents, Gay Eubank and Robert Latané Montague

Young Jack as a student at Richmond College

Betsie Hoskins, the future Mrs. A. J. Montague

Mrs. A. J. Montague in her inaugural ball gown, 1902

Montague with two of his three children,
Janet Roy and Robert Latané

Reunion of the sons of Virginia's Civil War officials: John S. Letcher, son of Governor Letcher; Henry St. George Tucker, son of Attorney General Tucker; and Andrew Jackson Montague, son of Lieutenant Governor Montague.

Governor Montague with his family. To his left: daughters Gay (Mrs. Charles Beatty Moore) and Janet (Mrs. William J. Nunnally); Mrs. Montague; and son Robert Latané. Next to Mrs. Montague is granddaughter Janet Roy Nunnally.

Governor Montague and his staff with the Richmond Blues
on the steps of the Virginia House, St. Louis Exposition, 1904.

Former Governor and Mrs. Montague in New York, 1934

on May 23, 1901, during the month when the Democratic gubernatorial campaign was at its height of interest and activity. A correlation naturally existed between the two elections, especially since
Swanson, like Martin, was not originally an advocate of a convention.
In Albemarle County, for example, two legislative candidates who believed that "all officials should be elected by the people," won a three-
to-one victory over candidates favored by Martin. And reports from
Rocky Mount indicated that Montague's friends had dealt the Swanson forces "a stinging blow" in the local convention held to nominate
candidates for the constitutional convention. When the one hundred
delegates finally assembled in June, the *Dispatch* observed that the
majority of the delegates were Montague men.[2] That machine Democrats did not dominate the convention seems confirmed by Richard
McIlwaine, himself a delegate, who asserted that the "little squad of
petty politicians . . . scattered throughout the State, who had been
accustomed to manage county and State affairs according to their
own sweet will for personal or party ends" were a minority element in
the convention, while the majority were "self-poised, independent,
conscientious, with no object before them other than the welfare of
the Commonwealth." [3]

Though references were sometimes made to a "Montague faction"
in the convention, Montague evidently had little direct connection
with that body's deliberations. True, during the 1901 final election
campaign he felt sufficiently acquainted with the intent of the convention to assure all white voters that none need fear disfranchisement.
And Allen W. Moger has stated that Montague's victorious campaign
for the governorship "probably helped induce the . . . Convention to
create a State Corporation Commission." Others have asserted that
the slightly increased executive powers granted under the new constitution can be labeled "a victory for Montague." [4] If Montague deserved such credit, he earned it only indirectly. By vigorously exposing the machine's tactics and influence, he undoubtedly helped elect a

2 J. H. Moore, "Life of James Gaven Field," 267; Madison (Va.) *Free Press,*
April 25, 1901, in scrapbook, Moore Collection; Richmond *Dispatch,*
June 13, 1901. W. A. Belcher to Montague, April 15, 1901; G. R. Scott to
Montague, April 23, 1901; J. M. Quarles to Montague, April 24, 1901;
all in Montague Papers.
3 Richard McIlwaine, *Memories of Three Score Years and Ten* (New York,
1908), 361.
4 Moger, *Rebuilding of the Old Dominion,* 120; Doss, "John Warwick Daniel," 293.

convention composed of men determined to correct such abuses. The *Northern Neck News,* for example, considered the approval of the constitutional convention and the election of Montague as twin victories: "It was a revolt against this machine, and its detestable methods, which has practically given Mr. Montague the Democratic nomination for Governor two months in advance of the state convention, and it was a strong protest against bossism which has made Mr. Goode president of the Constitutional Convention and surrounded him with able coadjutors." [5]

Some of Montague's correspondents assumed that he had influence in the convention. Indeed, several of his close friends had been elected to that body, including Moore, Hunton, Anderson, Stuart, and Glass. Even so, no evidence can be found to indicate that Montague had close dealings with the convention, or attempted leadership of any faction there. The press of his 1901 campaign and of his duties upon entering office precluded such a role. His closest collaboration with the convention occurred just before its adjournment, when that body voted to proclaim the constitution without a referendum. Although this action violated the Democratic party pledge and although Montague favored submission, he acquiesced in the decision and had a conference "with some of the leading men relative to my duties and that of the Legislature in setting the new Constitution into operation." Montague was a colleague, not a leader, of the forces dominating the convention. As a friend, he possessed the influence of friends. [6]

How did this quasi-liberal constitutional convention alter the governmental structure in Virginia? With what powers did it endow the executive chair which Montague was to fill for four years? Were the powers of the legislature curbed? Was Montague legally empowered to enact all the reforms which he advocated?

Dissatisfaction with the legislature had grown prior to the constitutional convention, partly because of its procorporation leanings, partly because of its tendency to give undue attention to party patronage and local trivia. The dissatisfaction resulted in some significant changes in the new constitution. For example, the people, not the legislature, were now to elect the secretary of state, the state

5 *Northern Neck News,* quoted in Doss, "John Warwick Daniel," 273–74.
6 T. A. Lynch to Montague, July 23, 1901; Montague to Scott Shipp, June 23, 1902; Montague to W. A. Taylor, Nov. 11, 1901; all in Montague Papers.

treasurer, the commissioner of agriculture, and the superintendent of public instruction. The new constitution also restricted legislative sessions to ninety days, allowed the governor the power of vetoing individual appropriation items, abolished the county court system (with its numerous judges appointed by the legislature), and established as a substitute the more efficient circuit court.[7]

However, another crucial reform advocated by some of Montague's friends, the popular election of the judiciary, failed by a vote of 38 to 29. Contributing to the defeat of this reform was fear in the Black Belt and southwest Virginia that local elections would result in Republican judges and subsequent Republican control of the electoral machinery. The only alternative, appointment by the governor, was also rejected as possibly leading to a personal political machine. Thus the legislature retained its centralized hold over the state's choicest patronage, though the number of officeholders involved was reduced.

The executive was strengthened slightly when the governor received power to suspend from office all executive officers (except the lieutenant governor) for misbehavior, incapacity, or neglect of official duty. In granting this power, however, the convention refused to extend it to include suspension of county sheriffs and other local officials. Thus, in a sense, county government remained independent of state government. Often Montague complained that as governor he had the responsibility to enforce law and order, yet his only control over the law-enforcement agencies was one of persuasion. Even the state militia, of which he was titular commander, could be used only on the appeal of local officials.[8]

In the matter of appointments, one of the few substantial powers possessed by the governor, the action of the convention also affected executive patronage. Under the old constitution the governor had been one of three members of the state board of education which appointed all local school superintendents. Under the new, he was merely one of eight members. In an attempt to remove the board from politics the convention made its composition more professional, less political, a move in keeping with Montague's desire to dissassociate the state's educational system from politics. In fact, Montague had campaigned to completely remove the school administration

---

7 McDanel, *The Constitutional Convention,* 90 ff.; Eckenrode, "Virginia Since 1865," 300–301.
8 Montague to M. G. Thompson, July 7, 1902, and Montague to W. A. Baugh, Feb. 17, 1903, Montague Papers.

from the aegis of the state legislature or central direction, by selecting all school superintendents in local elections. This reform, however, was not adopted.[9]

In at least one instance, Montague's power of appointment was enlarged. The office of railroad commissioner had been established by the Virginia Assembly as early as 1877. Theoretically, the commissioner, appointed by the legislature, could demand improvements in station facilities and require reduction in rates; in reality he had no way of enforcing these orders. Repeated legislative attempts to regulate railroad rates effectively had failed; consequently railroads in Virginia resorted to practices similar to those found on the national scene. In 1902 the Staunton *Spectator* observed, "One railroad in the State charges 4 cents per mile for passengers. . . . Where there is no competition, they charge what they please." [10]

The convention moved to remedy this situation by establishing an entirely new three-man corporation commission with full regulatory powers—legislative, executive, and judicial. And the power of appointing this commission was lodged with the governor. This action was but another indication that the Old Dominion shared in the Southwide reform impulse, for at this time the Southern states were "virtual pioneers" in the difficult problem of railroad regulation. From 1897 to 1907 all Southern states remodeled their commissions, increasing their authority, frequently making their members elective instead of appointive.[11] Of all the commissions, Virginia's was the strongest.

In the convention the fight for a corporation commission had been spearheaded by a delegate from Staunton, A. C. Braxton. As chairman of the committee on corporations, Braxton drafted the article which endowed a commission with effective powers to create, regulate, and supervise all domestic corporations, to investigate railroad property and business records, to create new regulations with respect to freight classifications and rates, and to compel enforcement of these regulations—"a commission, namely, endowed not alone with administrative and legislative powers, but also with judicial." This

9   Richard A. Meade, "A History of the Constitutional Provisions for Education in Virginia" (Ph.D. dissertation, University of Virginia, 1941), 276; Charles W. Dabney, *Universal Education in the South* (Chapel Hill, 1936), II, 322; Richmond *Times*, May 4, 1901.

10 Magruder, *Recent Administration in Virginia*, 31, 195; McDanel, *The Constitutional Convention*, 61; Staunton *Spectator and Vindicator*, Jan. 17, 1902.

11 Link, "The Progressive Movement," 183–88; Woodward, *Origins of the New South*, 380.

commission was authorized to assess property for tax purposes, to collect all corporation taxes, to order improvements in railroad facilities, and to prohibit issuance of railroad passes to public officials. Furthermore, railroads were now to be held liable for on-the-job injuries sustained by their employees.[12]

A significant feature of Braxton's article was its granting to the governor, not the legislature, the power of appointing the three-man commission. Many in the convention felt that such a power should not rest with one man. Richard E. Byrd, editor of the Winchester *Star,* charged that "concentration of the power in the hands of the Governor . . . will be fun for the Governor, but . . . death to some of the rest of us." Eugene Withers in particular pressed hard for the popular election of the commission, but Braxton and others argued that this would make the commission a less judicious tribunal: "The result will be that the Commission will be composed of politicians and office seekers, rather than efficient business men." The choice, therefore, lay between giving the power to the governor or to the legislature. The majority of delegates preferred the former alternative.[13]

Even with this important addition to his appointive power, however, the duties of a governor as delineated by the new constitution remained largely administrative. True, he selected the members of various boards (besides the corporation commission, all hospital boards, university boards, board of fisheries, board of pharmacists, and others), but once these appointments were made, there his power terminated. Rather than defer to a "lame-duck" governor ineligible for reelection, his appointees would naturally pay obeisance to the legislature (whence came the money) and to his probable successor. "The governor of Virginia is not at the head of a system. He works with department heads who may be subordinate or insubordinate as they like," wrote a contemporary observer.[14] As late as 1924 the report of a committee established to simplify state government complained, "Each state department is a little kingdom unto itself and their respective employees are as separate and distinct as if all were not servants of the same master." [15]

12 Magruder, *Recent Administration in Virginia,* 150 ff.; McDanel, *The Constitutional Convention,* 151–64; Maxwell Ferguson, *State Regulation of Railroads in the South* (New York, 1916), 65–67.
13 Doss, "John Warwick Daniel," 291; Braxton to Glass, Feb. 26, 1902, in Allen C. Braxton Papers, Alderman Library, University of Virginia, Charlottesville.
14 Magruder, *Recent Administration in Virginia,* 197.
15 Horn, "Democratic Party in Virginia," 130.

In general, then, the constitutional convention made significant advances in regulating railroads, in providing for an adequate tax structure, in weakening the hold of the machine on the school administration, in overhauling the judiciary system, and in purging the electorate. But the governor remained relatively powerless, and legislative prerogatives continued to dominate state government. Ironically, even the anticipated purification of the electorate served to strengthen the hands of the machine, not the Independents. By eliminating illiterates, both white and Negro (the 1900 Democratic pledge not to disfranchise whites was honored through a temporary "grandfather clause" allowing all whites to register until 1904, after which time literacy would be required of new voters), an honest ballot was gradually, though not immediately, obtained. But the resulting electorate composed "of beautifully small and aristocratic proportions" proved ideally suited for control by a small but loyal core of party workers and officeholders. And the hoped-for development of a genuine two-party system, divided on issues other than race, failed to materialize.

Legislative control over both the judiciary and the power of the purse greatly overshadowed the gubernatorial duties of pardoning criminals and appointing notary publics. Only a machine governor who "spoke the language of the tribe" could have exerted powerful influence in the Virginia governmental councils of 1902. Without legislative support, Montague was denied the opportunity to make a significant contribution to Virginia's codified law.

The constitutional convention finally concluded its tedious labors in June, 1902, six months after Montague's inauguration. Its most controversial decision was its last one—a vote to proclaim the constitution rather than submit it to the people in referendum. The state Democratic party in 1900, in an action Montague had approved, had called for a constitutional convention and for submission of any new constitution to the public, but the majority of the convention itself frankly feared that solid opposition on the part of those disfranchised by the new document might bring about its defeat. Had Montague or the legislature refused to accept the proclamation of the constitution, the work of a year might have been wasted; but Montague never seriously entertained such thoughts, possibly because he highly approved of the major modifications made in the new document.[16] Moreover,

16 In a letter to T. D. Gibson, Montague commented: "One of the chief advantages of the Constitution is that it greatly increases the revenues of the State. . . . simplified the judiciary and imposes new checks upon the

as a constitutional lawyer, he probably sympathized with the legal argument that the convention had the implicit right to bypass the referendum route. On June 27, he publicly acknowledged the constitution as a legal instrument: "I hereby call upon all the people of Virginia to render true and loyal support." At the same time he called the General Assembly into special session to take an oath to support the new fundamental law.[17]

The new constitution added many problems to Montague's administration. New systems of public boards, new taxes, problems of budgetary finance—all required his attention. The legislature, adjusting the state's code to comply with the new constitution, remained in almost continuous session from 1902 through 1904, and Montague was kept occupied constantly studying the immense volume of legislation presented for his signature. Also time-consuming was the ordeal he experienced in selecting the new corporation commission. Hundreds of applicants sought his endorsement and not until November, 1902, five months after the constitution's proclamation, did he finally send his nominations to the legislature.

As a routine administrator, Montague performed adequately. His performance aroused little or no complaint of inefficiency, ineptness, or malpractice. In his most important administrative service while governor, he helped facilitate a settlement of debts claimed by Virginia against the federal government and by the federal government against Virginia—a controversy which was finally ended by mutual cancellation of the debts. As chief executive of the state his primary responsibility was the proper administration of justice and the maintenance of law and order. Long years of experience at the bar had instilled within him an appreciation for the majesty of law; he thus approached all situations, especially the frequent petitions by prisoners for pardons, with a cautious judicial eye.[18]

Legislature. . . . The Constitution has improved the Board of Education, the judiciary . . . and the public hospitals for the insane. . . . The chief advantage . . . [is] the elimination of the negro from politics." March 7, 1905, Montague Papers.

17 *By the Governor of the Commonwealth of Virginia, a Proclamation* (Richmond, 1902), Montague Papers.

18 On each pardon application Montague followed the unvarying ritual of writing to the commonwealth's attorney where the criminal had been convicted, asking for his opinion as to the character of the individual. If both the attorney and the presiding judge recommended no pardon, Montague absolutely declined to overrule them: "I must be slow to assume any

Montague's stringent devotion to maintenance of law and order was well illustrated by two inflammatory incidents. One, a 1903 strike by the streetcar workers of Richmond, became a scene of physical violence when rumors spread of the approach of strikebreakers. Property was destroyed and persons were injured by brick-throwing rioters. Montague, in answering a call for military help, sent a large portion of the militia to restore order.[19] His sympathies were undoubtedly mixed; as a friend of labor unions, he frequently expressed his disgust at the materialism of the managerial class, yet his abhorrence of mob rule and his respect for orderly processes of government made him not at all hesitant in performing his obligation as commander of the militia. His action in sending them to the riots proved unpopular, especially when one militiaman shot and killed a rioter who had attempted to escape arrest.

The same considerations influenced Montague's actions toward several threatened lynchings. The spectre of lynching, Montague particularly condemned: "Nothing has so kept back the South as this nefarious practice. A people who do not use the law to vindicate their wrongs will go back, and deserve to go back. . . . If I left Virginia tomorrow . . . I would go where lynching was not." In 1904, when a vicious rape occurred in Roanoke and when lynch threats were loud and vehement, Montague promptly sent a full 80 per cent of the Virginia militia to protect the accused Negro as he was transported to trial: "I regret I had to take such action; perhaps the actual number of troops may have been a few too many . . . [but I] could not take chances." He reasoned that troops in small numbers would only incite, not quell, mob violence; an imposing array of military might would fully protect the accused, and also avert the unnecessary bloodshed of a mob fight.[20]

These actions provoked widespread criticism and may have been responsible for a certain decrease in his popularity. Some of the labor organs "and more extreme . . . friends of the working people . . . have attacked the governor vindictively because of his . . . activity in the Richmond strike affair," reported the *News Leader*. His Roanoke

---

of the prerogatives of the judiciary." Montague to Judge John W. Woods, Jan. 24, 1902, and Montague to L. C. Cooley, Feb. 3, 1902, Montague Papers.

19   See W. W. Minor Diary (MS in Alderman Library, University of Virginia, Charlottesville), June 23, 1903.

20   Montague to W. A. Laud, Feb. 18, 1902, and Montague to W. F. Battel, Jr., March 8, 1905, Montague Papers.

action also evoked considerable criticism; the *News Leader* defended him by asserting: "The question is between the power, dignity and laws of the State . . . and mob rule. . . . Virginia is as much bound to protect him [the Negro] as she would be if he was the purest and highest citizen." One voter who remained unconvinced grumbled that Montague had "only offered a reward of $250 for the arrest of the Brute, and then spent thousands to protect him." [21]

Montague's unflinching maintenance of law and order resulted in a decrease in Virginia lynching incidents. Four occurred during his administration, compared with an average of nearly four a year in the state from 1882 to 1901.[22] Out-of-state journals commented favorably on his efforts to maintain public safety and sanity. In 1904 the New York *Evening Post* concluded that Montague, already known in the North as Virginia's "Educational Governor," should also be known as her "Law and Order Governor," a "prouder title." [23]

In other phases of his career as governor, however, Montague's legal conscience, his penchant for strict constitutional interpretations of power and prerogative, limited his effectiveness. A man who believed in written law and constitutions as the only safeguard of a free people, he was slow to assume power not specifically and legitimately designated as his own. In short, he did not have the qualities of a strong leader—or of a political boss.

He had inherited his father's red hair and the political nickname, "Red Fox of Middlesex." But though it remained with him all his life, the sobriquet seems strangely incongruous, however the phrase is dissected. The common connotation of "fox" implies cunning, sly, perhaps deceitful qualities. Montague was no political fool, but neither was he a master political craftsman—and deceit was foreign to his nature. Robert Montague had proudly accepted the term "red fox" in quite another sense: the red fox runs straight unlike its gray-furred cousin, a master of the crooked trail. But this definition is also unsatisfactory as descriptive of Jack Montague. For if the younger Montague did not run a crooked path, neither did he, in the last analysis, qualify as a bold leader aggressively pursuing a firm, fast, hard line. His heart and voice he gave to causes noble and meritorious; yet

---

21 Richmond *News Leader,* July 20, 1903, Feb. 16 and 19, 1904; J. R. Bondurant to Montague, Jan. 6, 1905, Montague Papers.
22 James E. Cutler, *Lynch Law* (New York, 1905), 183. Montague himself itemized four lynchings during his entire administration; Cutler lists four during the first two years.
23 New York *Evening Post,* Feb. 16, 1904, in scrapbook, Moore Collection.

a gap sometimes appears between oratorical expression and actual performance.

Why the gap? Hypocrisy is not the explanation—that too was an element foreign to Montague's nature. Some vestige, perhaps, of his earlier "mugwump" adherence to governmental laissez faire remained to dampen and inhibit his later propensity for reform. Possibly, he never conquered the tendency toward introversion which had troubled him as a youth, and which made it difficult for him to essay the role of "gladhander," a role so effectively assumed by his 1901 rival, Swanson. Perhaps, indeed, the gap between Montague's oratorical abilities and his leadership potential can be explained by the personality-cultural differences in the man and in the mass of Virginians. A refined, erudite patrician, Montague as a youth had confessed difficulty in feeling rapport with humanity at large. His rapid ascent up the political ladder testifies to his overcoming his social inhibitions to a remarkable degree. Even so, he lacked somewhat the temperament of the politician, the brashness of the extrovert, the gay abandon seen in that national progressive, Theodore Roosevelt. He was not genuinely a man "of" the people.

Montague's reticent side was particularly noticeable in his relations with the General Assembly. He had several close friends in that body, and he was not averse to "friendly persuasion" and fireside chats with these friends.[24] But one cannot say that he had a legislative team. Although he expressed specific objectives in his addresses to the Assembly, following the delivery of those addresses he abdicated lawmaking responsibility to the lawmakers. Journals of the day fail to reflect any active attempts on his part to organize a legislative phalanx to promote a comprehensive program. And since Montague and the Assembly performed their duties in the same building, private letter collections do not reveal the extent of cooperation between them. Except for a few major issues, Montague consistently declined to comment publicly on bills then before the legislature. More than once, when pressed for opinions by correspondents, he replied, "As Governor I do not think I should undertake to favor in advance bills which are likely to come before me for approval or disapproval. I am sure you appreciate the propriety of my position." This attitude may have been prompted partially by a disinclination to invite public dis-

---

24 In 1904 Montague wrote W. H. Gunn stating that he would like to see Gunn "on the committee you mention," and promised to "do what I can," although he had no special influence with the Speaker of the House. Montague to Gunn, Jan. 1, 1904, Montague Papers.

approval; more likely, Montague sincerely felt that lawmaking was not his prerogative and that his only action should come after the enactments had been legally forwarded to him for signature or veto.[25]

Montague used the veto power only occasionally. For a progressive-minded governor, obstructed by a conservative Assembly, the veto might have been utilized best as a bargaining tool to obtain desired legislation, a lever of threatened disapproval for some bills in order to pry open committee bottlenecks for others. Otherwise, it would become purely a negative block. Montague's constitutional interpretations limited its use even further: "In my opinion an Executive cannot veto bills solely upon the ground that if he were a member of the Legislature he would have opposed their passage." Moreover, "the invariable rule of nearly every Executive is not to interpose the power of veto unless the public exigencies require it." With Montague the veto became essentially a process of judicial review—nearly all of his infrequent rejections of Assembly bills were made on constitutional grounds. Upon only a few did he express his personal disfavor, and these he usually allowed to become law without his signature.[26] There were at least two occasions, however, when he evidently used the veto to please political allies. In 1902 he vetoed a bill to redistrict the state's Congressional districts, and in 1903 he vetoed a bill amending local primary laws in Norfolk, at the request, reputedly, of the pro-Montague W. W. Dey faction of that city.[27]

Montague's appointive policy also was generally nonpartisan. "A public officer," he frequently declared, should not use his official place "to the advantage of the private interests of any individual or concern." The private interests not only included himself, but his closest friends. Several times his former chief of staff, George C. Cabell, appealed to him in the role of attorney to pardon several clients; Montague replied negatively. His basically nonpartisan attitude toward applicants for school superintendencies had long been firm: "I voted for Mr. Britt [a Swanson man] in your county because he had been a good administrator . . . no reason to change. . . . That I did not support Cutchin, my warm friend [and valuable political ally in 1901], may have hurt me in your County, but I could not consider this." [28]

25 Montague to C. H. Perry, Feb. 3, 1902, *ibid.*
26 Montague to W. M. Fishburne, March 25, 1904, and Montague to J. F. Allemong, January 26, 1903, in Montague Papers.
27 Appomattox *Southside Virginian,* May 27, 1903, in scrapbook, Moore Collection.
28 Montague to L. E. Homes, June 6, 1901, Montague Papers.

His board nominations followed the same pattern. He usually appointed friends to the various state agencies, but after the boards had been installed, he politely turned down numerous requests that he ask them for favors: "I have made it a rule, which I think the interests of the public demands not to be broken, not to make requests of the Boards appointed by me." Although he often called this an "inflexible" rule, his sportsman's love of fishing bent it a little when he requested J. W. Bowdoin, his appointee as chairman of the board of fisheries, to lend him and his friends one of the oyster boats—to be "done with as little notoriety as possible." And to William Stegar, applicant for a position as clerk on the corporation commission, Montague advised, "I took the liberty . . . of having a talk with one of the . . . State Corporation Commissioners. . . . very much encouraged. I am doing all I can for you. . . . Make out an application." This tendency to "put in a good word" increased as Montague's term progressed, but generally speaking, his impeccably rigid rules of official conduct defied reproach.[29]

Even Montague's political allies were disturbed by his conscientious appointive policy. In the 1905 senatorial primary campaign, for example, C. V. Meredith observed some dissatisfaction in Petersburg with Montague's failure "to put your friends on the Board of the Asylum in that city." Meredith urged the governor to capitalize on this fact in countering Martin's argument that Montague had built a machine of his own. Montague naturally favored those sharing his political opinions for appointments, but he strongly denied allegations that "I had organized a ring of my own, and had turned every Martin man out of office in Richmond. . . . As many as one-third of my appointees are friends of Mr. Martin. . . . This is true of Hon. H. H. Downing; Hon. Daniel Harman; Hon. Robert Gilliam; Hon. George B. Keezell." Earlier, in 1903, Braxton also conveyed the impression that the governor was risking his political future by his patronage policy: "Montague is certainly losing strength rapidly, as far as I can learn. His friends charge him with ingratitude and selfishness." [30]

However, Montague sometimes did make appointments which

29 Montague to C. R. Vance, July 24, 1902; Montague to William A. Rogers, June 5, 1902; Montague to B. F. Buchanan, Feb. 18, 1904; Montague to J. W. Bowdoin, May 18, 1903; Montague to William Stegar, June 6, 1905; all in Montague Papers.

30 C. V. Meredith to Montague, Aug. 1, 1905, and Montague to J. K. Taliaferro, Aug. 10, 1905, Montague Papers; Braxton to J. C. Wysor, Feb. 3, 1903, Braxton Papers.

benefited him politically. Douglas Southall Freeman, an admirer of Montague who wrote a brief tribute to him upon his death in 1937, recalled that as governor, Montague "quickly built up an organization of his own . . . [dealing] hammer blows with a gloved hand." Freeman may have overstated the case, but Montague's appointment of such men as James L. Tredway, R. S. Turk, and J. W. Bowdoin to various state boards was unquestionably political reward. And though Montague rarely asked personal favors of the boards themselves, he frequently communicated with these individuals on political matters. He was not without his eyes and ears throughout the Commonwealth.[31]

Predictably, to some neutral observers the inordinate determination of the Independents to destroy Martin's machine, and the means they proposed to achieve that end, made a choice between the two factions a case of tweedledum and tweedledee: "The present administration has constructed its own machine, and the contest [with Martin] has become a mere struggle of machine against machine for place and power," asserted the Norfolk *Virginian-Pilot*.[32] Such a picture was exaggerated. First of all, Montague never succeeded in cementing a truly strong alliance to counterbalance Martin's organization.[33] After his election as governor, he became the natural leader of such an alliance, but various Independent leaders challenged his right to such a position. This internal strife ultimately proved disastrous. Furthermore, Montague's relatively powerless position as governor afforded him no opportunity in the short span of four years to acquire a following of officeholders in his debt, even had that been his intention.

Montague recognized the need for an effective factional organization if the Independents were to destroy Martin's machine, and in the 1903 legislative elections he made efforts to defeat incumbent "Martin men" who he felt obstructed his legislative objectives, and who would once again elect Virginia's Senator should Martin succeed in junking the primary reform. But he did not attempt to destroy

31 Richmond *News Leader,* Jan. 25, 1937; Montague to Bowdoin, Nov. 13, 1903, May 5, 1904, and Montague to Tredway, June 16, 1904, Montague Papers.
32 Issue of June 11, 1904.
33 This was shown by Martin's easy domination of the state Democratic convention of 1904 despite Montague's efforts to alert antimachine people to the possible dangers of Martin's controlling that body. Montague to Moore, June 4, 1904, Montague Papers.

one machine merely to erect another of his own. His basic motive continued to be a desire to free Virginia's politics from domination by one man, a domination he felt was injurious not only to the natural rise of statecraft, but to the progress of the state. Had Montague gone on to the Senate, it would have been interesting to observe whether a "Montague machine" would have emerged—whether, in other words, Montague's fulminations about the evils of machine government would have withstood the realities of modern American politics.

Montague's procedure in selecting his appointees to the corporation commission best exemplifies his determination to execute the duties of his office in a nonpartisan fashion. The men he finally selected made the corporation commission an effective regulatory agency. Yet in making the appointments, Montague disgusted even his political friends by his refusal to accede to their various wishes. Probably no other of his public acts resulted in such a loss of political allegiance.

The constitution had called for the appointment of three commissioners with regular terms of six years each; a new commissioner was to be selected every two years. Of the three members, one was to be a lawyer, one a man of business affairs, and one a man with working knowledge of railroad rates and traffic. The commission was required to begin its duties on March 1, 1903; thus the governor had ample time to make his selections. Before he completed his search for available men, Montague reviewed the applications of several hundred persons and made four offers which were rejected. Friends, political supporters, and legislators bombarded him with petitions for their particular candidates. With almost monotonous regularity Montague answered all letters with a cordial "my utmost consideration," repeatedly expressing the determination "to give the State the best, fairest, and brainiest Commission possible." A. C. Braxton, father of the commission, earnestly recommended the appointment of E. S. Goodman, traffic manager of the Richmond Chamber of Commerce. Montague replied even to Braxton's exhortations with the usual noncommittal cordiality. Braxton wrote to a friend that he did his "durndest" with the governor, but it was like "singing psalms to a dead horse, so far as producing any effect." [34]

W. A. Taylor, a Montague supporter and a Danville resident,

---

34 Montague to Herbert Henkle, July 11, 1902, Montague Papers; Weathers, "Allen Caperton Braxton," 85.

campaigned actively for the position. Although he claimed support of fifty legislators, twelve circuit judges, nine Democratic county chairmen, sixty lawyers, thirty doctors, twenty banks, ten newspapers, and one thousand merchants and manufacturers, he failed to sway Montague. Another man of prominence frequently mentioned for the post—John R. Edmunds of Halifax—had the favor of Carter Glass, and, like Taylor, widespread popular support. Montague confessed that he regarded Edmunds "very highly," but that he was not suited for the commission's work: "I lost more friends by my failure to name Mr. Edmunds as a member . . . than by any other . . . act." [35]

Montague resisted the pressure of the many applicants, preferring to seek out his own candidates. None of those to whom he made offers solicited the positions. His first choice for the lawyer's position was former Judge A. A. Phlegar of Bristol, a corporate and railroad attorney, and a man of ambiguous political connections. Phlegar hesitated to accept the post, however, because as an admirer of former Governor Tyler he had already proposed Tyler's name for the commission. Montague assured Phlegar of his "warm personal feeling for Governor Tyler. Few people could be thrown with him without being drawn to him." But in the 1899 race Montague had privately expressed his opinion that Tyler was "not . . . a great man." He did not fulfill the "brainiest" qualification.

On August 18 Montague officially made an offer to Phlegar, at the same time asking mutual friends to help persuade Phlegar to accept. Phlegar wavered. Montague wrote again on September 6: "I must have a great lawyer upon the Commission . . . you are the central figure. . . . With you out the keystone in the arch I've constructed will fall." A week later Phlegar finally declined the offer, and Montague confided to a friend, "I am almost hopeless now about the Commission. I know of no suitable lawyer whom I can get. . . . I think I could have secured Judge Phlegar but for . . . Governor Tyler." [36]

On the day of Phlegar's refusal, Montague sent a letter to Judge James Keith, a resident of Staunton, asking him to "sound out" two other lawyers—Judge B. F. Buchanan, and Martin P. Burks, profes-

35 W. A. Taylor to Montague, Aug. 18, 1902, and Montague to James I. Pritchett, Dec. 12, 1903, Montague Papers; Richmond *Evening Leader*, Aug. 4 and 26, 1902.
36 Montague to Phlegar, June 21, Aug. 18, and Sept. 6, 1902; Phlegar to Montague, Sept. 12, 1902; Montague to Joseph Kelly, Sept. 15, 1902; all in Montague Papers.

sor of law at Washington and Lee. He first offered the position to Buchanan, a member of the state Democratic committee, who evidently turned it down with little hesitation. Burks was not so quick to refuse: "I find myself torn by conflicts of duty, and by doubts." Montague had written offering him any of the three positions and urging a personal conference. The conference was futile; by October 11 Burks had given his final answer, a negative one.[37]

With increasing desperation Montague now turned to the author of the commission article, A. C. Braxton. Montague had earlier informally offered the position to Braxton upon the adjournment of the convention. But Braxton had then "promptly declined, inasmuch as he stated in the Convention when securing the passage of the measure that in no event would he accept a place upon the Commission if tendered him." Montague now made another attempt to persuade Braxton that the public would forgive him his pledge in the interests of the commission he had helped establish. Braxton replied, "Nothing has ever occurred to render my decision not to accept an appointment . . . [less] fixed and irrevocable." [38]

Montague had acted previously to fill the other positions. On October 24 he revealed to a friend that he would offer the "traffic" member position to Henry Fairfax, a former state senator, a personal friend, and a member of the recent convention—a retired country gentleman "always found . . . on . . . the side of the people." As a civil engineer and contractor experienced in railroad construction, Fairfax was amply qualified for the position. Evidently, he accepted with little hesitation.[39]

For the business member of the commission Montague sought Henry C. Stuart, one of the men he had enlisted to persuade Phlegar. Stuart had also been a member of the convention and had taken a leading part in obtaining the commission article. Montague made the offer in late October; Stuart pleaded for a few more days "to determine some matters . . . of vital importance." Montague assured him that as long as there remained any possible hope of his accepting, he might take all the time he desired.[40]

37 Montague to James Keith, Sept. 12, 1902; M. P. Burks to Montague, Sept. 26, 1902; Montague to S. V. Kemp, Oct. 11, 1902; all *ibid.*
38 Braxton to Montague, Nov. 10, 1902, *ibid.*
39 Montague to W. H. W. Moran, Oct. 24, 1902, *ibid;* Lyon G. Tyler (ed.), *Men of Mark in Virginia* (Washington, 1906–1909), I, 46–50.
40 Henry C. Stuart to Montague, Oct. 27, 1902, and Montague to Stuart, Oct. 30, 1902, Montague Papers.

When Stuart finally accepted, there yet remained one vacant position. After Braxton's final refusal, mailed on November 10, Montague resorted to local talent. When he formally sent his nominations to the legislature on November 18, the third name was Judge Beverley R. Crump of Richmond, one of the state's leading young lawyers, recently elected a judge, and endorsed without dissent by the Richmond Bar Association. As the lawyer member, Crump became chairman of the commission. Montague's appointments received praise from the state's newspapers and unanimous approval from the Assembly.[41]

Although there was little outward criticism of Montague's selections, distrust of Montague's motives was expressed in some quarters. A Norfolk newspaper commented dubiously: "We regard the appointments as purely political and as made in furtherance of Mr. Montague's ambition to build up a machine that will be a staunch and dependable rival of . . . Martin." [42] A more significant evidence of disapproval came from Braxton himself. Braxton had lobbied actively for Goodman, and bitterly attributed Montague's refusal to heed his advice to political motives:

> As you doubtless know, I resented the appointment of Judge Crump when it was made, because I believe then, and still believe, that the Governor in making it, was actuated chiefly, if not solely, by a desire to avoid appointing Goodman, who, it seems, was very distasteful to many avowed opponents of the Commission whose advice and wishes seemed to have much more influence with the Governor than my own and those of nearly every man who had labored hard with me for the establishment of that tribunal.[43]

In charging that Montague's political advisers opposed the corporation commission article, Braxton probably was referring to Eppa Hunton, one of the antimachine group who had urged Montague in 1900 to make the race against Swanson. Later, as a member of the convention, Hunton had joined Alfred Thom in opposing Braxton's committee report. Moreover, both Hunton and Walton Moore, another Montague adviser, had opposed that portion of the report which established the employer's liability doctrine.[44] Conceivably,

41 Richmond *Evening Leader,* Nov. 15 and 18, 1902.
42 Clipping, unidentified Norfolk paper, Nov. 20, 1902, scrapbook, Moore Collection.
43 Braxton to J. C. Wysor, June 15, 1905, Braxton Papers.
44 Weathers, "Allen Caperton Braxton," 80; pamphlet entitled, "Co-operative Legislative Board of Railroad Employees of Virginia" (Jan., 1905), Montague Papers.

these men felt that Goodman was a particularly undesirable appointee and convinced Montague not to select him, as Braxton inferred.

However, if such were the case, it must not be presumed that these advisers influenced Montague's later selections for the commission, or that he was himself hostile to the commission. His attitude toward Braxton's report during the convention is not known, but he had always favored the more equitable taxation of corporations, an objective realized by Braxton's article. A more direct indication that Montague earnestly desired to see the commission function effectively can be found in the caliber of his appointments. Stuart and Fairfax both had been members of the constitutional convention, and both had favored the employer's liability doctrine. Far from pleasing the corporate interests in Virginia as charged by some of his critics, Montague's appointments actually aroused business antagonism: "When Governor Montague named three men on the Corporation Commission, that the railroads could not control, a club was put in soak for him," asserted the *Virginian-Pilot*. Moreover, since Montague offered the attorney's position to Braxton himself, not once but several times, Braxton's own charge that the governor acted in political self-interest and from a hostility to the commission is difficult to believe.

Also, whatever his motive, Montague's appointments did not result in feathering his political nest. Disappointment at his refusal to appoint Goodman, Taylor, or Edmunds was widespread. Paradoxically, Braxton himself, in contradiction to his own statement agreed that "Montague has lost many friends by his appointments . . . and in other respects, my impression is that he has decidedly lost popularity in the last few months." If Montague's appointments were meant to be shrewd politically, the move was a dismal failure.[45]

Final testimony that Montague's appointments were made with a desire to protect the public interest was the subsequent actions of the commission itself. On May 22, 1903, in its first official action, the commission directed that all corporations must make reports indicating the value and location of their taxable property within the state. The commission's subsequent assessments raised state railroad and corporate taxes 100 per cent in one year, from $277,000 in 1902 to $583,000 in 1903.[46]

45 Norfolk *Virginian-Pilot*, June 11, 1904; Braxton to J. C. Wysor, Dec. 27, 1902, Braxton Papers.
46 Richmond *News Leader*, May 22 and 23, 1903; McDanel, *The Constitutional Convention*, 84.

In ensuing years the commission took decisive steps to regulate railroad rates. After lengthy hearings extending from 1905 through 1907 it established a uniform classification for freight rates, forbidding long-haul, short-haul discriminations. Also in 1907 Virginia set an example to the country in the establishment of a maximum passenger rate "at the unprecedented low rate of two cents a mile." Other states, particularly Southern states, followed Virginia's example. The railroads appealed the decision through circuit courts to the Supreme Court of the United States. In November, 1908, that court turned down the appeal on a legal technicality, asserting that the railroads should first have appealed to a state, not a federal, court. Meanwhile, the commission, in an effort to stave off further assaults upon its jurisdiction, held new hearings and raised the maximum rate from two, to two and one-half cents per mile. After this action, the railroad suits were dropped.[47]

By its vigorous action, the commission dispelled fears that it would move cautiously in asserting its authority. Crump, chairman of the commission, had asked Braxton personally for advice and counsel soon after his nomination, and Braxton later termed Crump's services to the commission as efficiently rendered. When Crump came under attack from elements of Martin's machine in the 1905 senatorial campaign, Braxton defended his integrity. For his part, C. V. Meredith, a prominent Independent, agreed that his original distaste for Montague's appointments had proven groundless: "He builded better than I thought." [48]

On January 1, 1904, Montague appointed Crump for a full six-year term. Late in 1905 Fairfax resigned for personal reasons. In selecting his successor, Montague acted with dispatch, appointing Lieutenant Governor Joseph Willard to the vacancy.[49] One of his last acts as governor was naming Willard for the full term beginning in January, 1906. Thus, until the year 1908 (Crump also resigned before his term expired) the commission was controlled by Montague's appointees. The success of the commission can therefore be partially credited to his care in making nominations.

The corporation commission stands as a monument to Virginia

47 Ferguson, *State Regulation of Railroads,* 37; Magruder, *Recent Administration in Virginia,* 154.
48 Braxton to Crump, Jan. 2, 1903; Braxton to Wysor, June 15, 1905; Braxton to Richard E. Byrd, July 21, 1905; all in Braxton Papers; Meredith to W. I. Steele, May 12, 1905, Montague Papers.
49 Richmond *Times Dispatch,* Sept. 15 and 19, 1905.

progressivism. The forces of national reform that finally achieved the Hepburn Act of 1906 (increasing the powers of the Interstate Commerce Commission) found an earlier example for their aims in the new Virginia constitution. Montague had taken no active part in creating the commission; he had taken little part in the constitutional convention. But his 1901 gubernatorial campaign had helped create the political climate that made the convention possible. He had served as the vocal leader of the Independents; his own triumph and the simultaneous election of a constitutional convention dominated by Independents was no coincidence. He spearheaded the drive of the Independents during the year that saw their most complete victory, their high tide of success.

Montague's later performance as a functioning governor was more prosaic. He upheld law and order, and he strengthened the boards of state agencies by his appointments. But in his relations with the Assembly he assumed little initiative. Constitutional scruples forbade him to participate in the lawmaking process, and his nonpartisan appointive policy antagonized many Independent followers. Montague was never able to achieve a cohesive alliance among the Independent factions. As a consequence, Martin's organization retained its dominance in the state's Assembly, and there Montague encountered a persistent opposition to his objectives.

IX

MONTAGUE
AND THE
VIRGINIA ASSEMBLY

T HE tide of reform that swept Montague into the governor's chair did not so successfully penetrate the state's General Assembly; that body remained largely a haven of conservatism. As a natural consequence, the governor never entertained a high opinion of the legislature. During his 1901 campaign he had charged that lobbyists exercised a perverse influence over legislative actions, and during his term in office he felt that the Assembly deliberately obstructed his key proposals out of partisan spite. At one point in his administration he privately confided to a friend, "I do not think we can well defend the course of the present General Assembly in the things which they have not done as well as in the things which they have done." [1] Montague's messages to the Assembly displayed an eagerness for change usually far in advance of the thinking of his listeners; the goals he outlined for the new Virginia demonstrated a desire to adjust speedily to the temper of the age. The Assembly felt no such urge to rush headlong into the twentieth century, but eventually it would follow the governor's lead. Demands for state regulation of banking and business, for protection of labor unions, for child labor restriction, for electoral purification—all began to be heard. From 1901 through 1904 the Virginia Assembly shifted its ideological base

1 Montague to W. H. Turner, Oct. 8, 1903, Montague Papers.

slightly. To some extent, Montague's role as a spokesman for the new Virginia hastened this transformation.

Still, if Montague advocated a program of progressive legislative objectives in his infrequent addresses to the Assembly, it cannot be said that he vigorously pushed such a program. Besides generally tending to shun an aggressive leadership, he realized the futility of dealing with an Assembly whose members were, on the whole, hostile toward him politically. This, plus his constitutional reservations about meddling with the legislative process, prevented his commenting publicly on most issues before the legislature. Caution must be used in delineating Montague's exact relationship with the legislature, however. He had close friends there; his office and the Assembly chambers were both in the Capitol building; and occasional references in his correspondence describe discussions with solons relative to legislative matters. Moreover, in the 1903 legislative campaigns Montague actively sought to bring about the defeat of certain incumbents hostile to his administration. To presume that he had no influence with his political friends in the Assembly would be naïve. And on the major issues of better schools and roads he did indulge in public criticism of the Assembly's positions. Even so, his influence was certainly not predominant; his major legislative objectives were all thwarted. Ironically, they would find fruition in the term of his successor, Claude A. Swanson, when both the executive chair and the Assembly would be controlled by members of one Democratic faction.

The Virginia legislature of 1901–1904 may not have achieved a record in statesmanship, but it approached one in endurance. Possibly no period in Virginia's history required such protracted sittings of its legislative body—from December 4, 1901, to April 2, 1902; from July 15 to July 28, 1902; from November 12, 1902, to May 19, 1903; and from November 10, 1903, to March 15, 1904. The cause for such extended sessions lay partly in the Assembly's own lack of dispatch, but the chief factor was the new constitution. With a new constitution the entire code of the state required readjustment; hence, the "Long Parliament of Virginia history." [2]

The conservative tenor of the Assembly can easily be detected in the scant consideration it gave to a wide variety of progressive pieces of legislation, including some specifically proposed by Montague. For

2 A term used by Douglas Southall Freeman, Richmond *News Leader*, Jan. 25, 1937.

example, a bill to strengthen the hand of the corporation commission by requiring all telegraph and telephone companies to connect with each other and thus furnish an interchangeable service, was defeated in the state senate in 1903. The Bell Company had vigorously lobbied against the bill, and Montague indirectly criticized the Assembly's inaction in his 1904 address to the legislature, observing that the constitution "saliently declares for . . . the regulation of semi-public agencies." The senate, however, did not reconsider the measure.[3]

In another action relative to the corporation commission the Assembly inserted a "merger clause" in the statute governing the commission's activities, a clause allowing two or more corporations to combine, once their original charters had been granted. The clause was eventually watered down to apply only to corporations chartered prior to 1903. Even so, Montague feared that the effectiveness of the corporation commission would be undermined by the measure, and he expressed his disapproval by allowing it to become law without his signature. (The veto, he felt, was warranted only if a bill was patently unconstitutional.) [4] The Assembly also defeated attempts to establish—subordinate to the corporation commission—bureaus of banking and insurance, designed to protect the public from financially irresponsible state banks and insurance companies.

In other areas the Assembly rejected various bills which would have benefited labor unions. One measure, introduced by Senator J. M. Harmer of Tazewell, proposed to establish an arbitration board with power to mediate strikes, thereby recognizing labor's right to bargain collectively. Another, introduced by the same senator, would have prohibited any employer from threatening to discharge employees because of their unionizing activities. Delegate John Whitehead of Norfolk introduced yet another measure which would have protected unions from management's lockout tactics.[5]

These and other measures befriending labor unions were all either defeated or ignored. A similar fate greeted a rash of regulatory measures aimed at corporations. The most comprehensive antitrust bill was offered by Delegate W. B. Fulton of Wise. Its title: "A bill to

---

3 *Ibid.,* Dec. 5 and 21, 1903, Jan. 13, 1904.
4 *Ibid.,* April 30, May 4, 8, and 12, 1903; Montague to W. G. Loving, April 1, 1903, Montague Papers; "Concerning the Conference Report on House Bill 102" (Memo), Montague Papers.
5 Magruder, *Recent Administration in Virginia,* 159; McDanel, *The Constitutional Convention,* 80; Richmond *Evening Leader,* March 6, Nov. 14 and 19, Dec. 10 and 18, 1902; Richmond *News Leader,* April 14, 1903.

prevent and declare illegal all pools, trusts, agreements, combinations, . . . in restraint of trade." Fulton generated considerable public support for his bill, but the house committee refused to act on it, and a motion to discharge the committee failed by a close margin, 29 votes to 24.[6]

The General Assembly also acted sluggishly in improving the services of the state's charitable institutions. In a move to increase central authority and to coordinate the state's various welfare, mental, and criminal institutions, Montague recommended to the 1904 legislature the creation of a board of charities and corrections to act in an advisory capacity to all hospitals, reformatories, and prisons. A Richmond conference had proposed such a board as early as February, 1903, and Montague declared in his welcoming address at the conference that his "heart was earnestly in the work." Most officials of the institutions concerned sanctioned the recommendation, but it did not gain a favorable reception at the hands of the legislature.[7]

The legislature also treated lightly Montague's proposal that the state construct a school for the Negro deaf and blind. Although Montague believed firmly in the superior status of the white race socially, culturally, and intellectually (as did nearly all his white Virginia contemporaries), he had a genuine concern for the welfare and progress of the Negro. In correspondence with William C. Ritter, a Negro leader, he had early agreed that a school for the Negro handicapped was desirable, but he hesitated recommending it to the Assembly: "I have conferred with influential members of the Legislature. . . . They think in view of uncertain revenues [it is] impractical to try at this session." When he did make the suggestion in January of 1904, an overwhelming majority of the state press endorsed it. The fact that the suggestion needed repetition in his 1906 address to the legislature indicated that the Assembly did not agree.[8]

In one particular, the Assembly followed Montague's recommendation. Conditions at the state penitentiary were defended by no one and were termed "inconceivable to the human mind." The death rate approached thirty-two in one thousand annually, even though the fatally ill were pardoned to die at home. To help remedy the intolera-

6 Richmond *News Leader,* April 17, Dec. 19, 1903.
7 Montague to Wyndham B. Robertson, Oct. 17, 1902, Montague Papers; Richmond *News Leader,* Feb. 13, 1903, Jan. 13, 1904.
8 Montague to William C. Ritter, April 10, 1903, Montague Papers; Richmond *News Leader,* Jan. 17, 1904.

ble conditions Montague, in his first address to the legislature, recommended the erection of an additional cell building, that "the good name of our state" might be salvaged. Within a month after his suggestion the senate passed a bill appropriating $180,000 for the purpose, and the house shortly concurred.[9] One of Montague's rare legislative victories had been quickly achieved. The remainder of the sessions would not prove so fruitful.

The Assembly's truculent attitudes toward Montague's "top priority" projects for better schools, better roads, and the party primary created antipathy and distrust in the heart of the governor. A future Wilsonian Democrat, a man with goals both national and international, he recoiled from the limited outlook of many of his contemporaries, he continually lamented the demise of Virginia statecraft, and he longed for the return of a "tolerant public sentiment and a catholic patriotism." [10] Measured by his standards, the legislature's actions seemed picayune and narrow.

But Montague's view was distorted by the Assembly's opposition to him personally and by its obstinate refusal to pass any legislation that would enhance his administration politically. Actually, the legislature was not entirely isolated from the changing trends of the twentieth century. Numerous progressive bills, some already mentioned, received its consideration. A few hurdled all obstacles and achieved the status of law. Others died aborning. But they all represented a gradual shift toward a more positive concept of government, especially of governmental responsibility for the public welfare.

One of the more important evidences of this changing spirit in the Assembly could be found in its move to curtail election corruption. Purifying elections had been one of the chief motives leading to disfranchisement of the Negro in the South and in Virginia. With disfranchisement accomplished, the electoral corruption once tolerated as a necessary evil became indefensible, and a wave of "corrupt practices" legislation swept the Southland.[11] Montague endorsed moves to curb bribery by suggesting in one of his messages to the legislature that all corporation contributions to political campaigns be totally prohibited. The Assembly also reflected the public hostility to elec-

---

9   Richmond *Evening Leader,* Feb. 20 and 27, March 14 and 15, 1902; Richmond *Times,* Jan. 31, 1901.
10 Richmond *Evening Leader,* Jan. 1, 1902.
11 Link, "The Progressive Movement," 190.

tion bribery and corruption when it passed the Barksdale "Pure Elections" Bill in 1903.

Introduced in July, 1902, Barksdale's bill was designed to limit the expenses of all candidates in elections. As the bill read, no candidate for any public office "shall expend, pay, promise, loan, or become pecuniarily liable in any way for any money . . . to influence voters in his behalf . . . in any election, primary, or nominating convention." [12] The bill found widespread support in the state's press and among her citizenry. Some Democratic Independents, however, remained dubious. Charging that Martin men (including Barksdale himself) supported the bill for ulterior motives, they complained that the stringent provisions of the measure placed conscientious candidates at a distinct disadvantage to opponents who were not so scrupulous. Moreover, provisions for enforcement were weak.

To meet these objections amendments were adopted allowing expenditures for campaign correspondence, for advertising, and for the renting of halls for public meetings. As amended the bill passed both houses by overwhelming margins. [13] That such large majorities approved a bill only two years after a similar measure had failed to pass reflects the shifting trend of public opinion. Probably the biggest factor in this shift lay in the disfranchisement of the Negro by the new constitution. By the end of 1904 only fifteen thousand Negroes remained on Virginia's registration books. [14] So long as the purchasable illiterate remained as part of the electorate, laws against bribery had proved meaningless gestures. With these people purged, enforcement of such laws could be taken more seriously.

Acid testing for the Barksdale law came quickly. In the 1903 legislative elections, complaints were heard from several counties that the provisions of the law had been "completely ignored." And as late as 1905 Montague supporters would maintain that their opponents had taken advantage of their adherence to its terms. Evidence also indicates, however, that the 1903 legislative election was "the fairest" in twenty years; and such Independents as Braxton considered the law a step in the right direction. [15]

12 *Acts and Joint Resolutions passed by the General Assembly of the State of Virginia, during the Extra Session of 1902–3–4* (Richmond, 1902), 88–89.
13 Richmond *Dispatch,* Jan. 15 and 16, 1903; A. C. Braxton to John F. Ryan, Jan. 24, 1903, Braxton Papers.
14 Richmond *News Leader,* Nov. 28, 1904.
15 *Ibid.,* Sept. 4 and 8, Nov. 12 and 20, 1903.

Like many Independents, Montague viewed the Barksdale bill as a hypocritical attempt by the machine to gain credit for "purifying" elections. In his message to the newly elected legislature in January, 1904, he cautioned against a naïve faith that the statute would automatically bring reform: "Laws of themselves, however strongly declaratory of pure elections, are of little avail if unsupported by public sentiment." [16] He considered the attempt to legalize the senatorial primary a more practical step toward clean politics, yet this attempt was defeated in the Assembly through machine opposition. Nevertheless, Montague conscientiously endeavored to uphold the Barksdale law. In his 1905 campaign he refused to spend funds in contravention of the act, though he sometimes was urged to do so by his supporters.

Virginia's elections were not, of course, immediately purified by Barksdale's law. Especially in the Ninth District where the Republican party maintained a strong competitive position, election corruption continued for years afterward, with mass payments of poll taxes replacing direct bribery as a favorite technique. But in general, cleaner elections followed disfranchisement in 1902. Barksdale's law of 1903 was but the first codified reflection of this changing public attitude.

Another reform which swept Virginia and the South at the turn of the century was the move to regulate child labor. Long hours, poor working conditions, and meager wages—all accompaniments of America's new industrialism—constituted privation enough for adults. But the same conditions imposed upon young children eventually provoked public censure. Nowhere in the nation was child labor a greater problem than in the South, where 29 per cent of all cotton mill operatives were children under sixteen years of age. Although Virginia's tobacco factories, woolen mills, and cotton mills employed far fewer children than did similar mills farther South, the Old Dominion witnessed an insistent drive toward child labor regulation during Montague's administration.[17]

In late 1901 Delegate George C. Cabell of Danville, a man who had vainly sponsored regulatory measures in previous years, and who nominated Montague for governor at the Democratic convention of that year, introduced yet another bill into the General Assembly.

16 *Ibid.,* Jan. 13, 1904.
17 Elizabeth H. Davidson, *Child Labor Legislation in the Southern Textile States* (Chapel Hill, 1939), 1–2, 11–12, 53, 244 ff.

(Later appointed Montague's "Chief of Staff," Cabell was naturally in close contact with the governor. His continued advocacy of child labor legislation over a two-year period probably had Montague's personal blessing.)

Simply stated, Cabell's bill proposed to establish the minimum age of employment in any "factory or other business place of the State" at fourteen years. Favorably reported by a house committee in March, 1902, the bill provoked a spirited three-day debate. Advocates of the measure charged that a system of child labor fostered illiteracy and tended "to raise up a race of runts and degenerates"; opponents countered with the argument that hardship would be inflicted on families who heavily depended on their children's earning power for economic survival. After the third day's discussion, the vote was taken. The progressives lost, 42 to 29.[18]

Child labor regulation had been temporarily but not permanently defeated. In a private letter to South Carolina's governor in October, 1902, Montague revealed that he was considering the advisability of making a recommendation to the legislature upon the subject. He also revealed that a new bill would be introduced by Cabell in the fall session. As presented to the House of Delegates, Cabell's modified proposal reduced the absolute minimum age from fourteen to twelve but retained for the twelve-to-fourteen age group a prohibition against all night work or employment during school sessions. The house, in a remarkable reversal of its stand only nine months earlier, approved the bill in December, 1902, by a vote margin of 58 to 10. It was the first breakthrough in a previously hostile legislature.[19]

In the senate, however, Cabell's bill met formidable opposition. Long hearings in committee afforded the manufacturing and corporate interests ample time to voice their opposition, with the Lynchburg Board of Trade complaining that a minimum of fourteen years would work great hardship on the enterprises of their city. Consequently, the committee's innocuous version of the bill, later accepted by the entire senate, provided only that no child under twelve years of age be employed. The compromise arranged by the conference committee of the two houses retained this minimum age, though it also included Cabell's prohibition against night work for the twelve-to-

18 Richmond *Evening Leader*, Feb. 26 and 28, March 11, 12, and 13, 1902.
19 *Ibid.*, May 22, July 26, Aug. 27, Dec. 9, 12, 15, and 16, 1902; Montague to Gov. M. B. McSweeny, Oct. 3, 1902, Montague Papers.

fourteen age group. Cabell agreed to the compromise only because he realized it was the best bill that could be obtained at the time.[20]

Montague accepted the "half-loaf" and signed the bill on April 16, 1903. His 1905 campaign propaganda would provocatively inquire, "Hasn't he [Montague] taken an active part in furthering the abolition of child labor, and did he not approve a bill upon this subject although not drawn wholly in accordance with his views?" [21] Although he did not give the movement for child labor regulation the priority he awarded campaigns for better schools and roads, Montague kept abreast of developments in the Virginia crusade and evidently lent his encouragement to the reform. Later, as a Congressman, he would support proposals to prohibit interstate transportation in goods manufactured by child labor. And he would point with pride to the strides taken by Virginia and the South in combatting the problem.

The stand taken by the Assembly upon child labor clearly reveals its basic political complexion. As finally passed, the law was only semiprogressive at best. The *News Leader* estimated that only a few hundred children under twelve were employed by the manufacturing industries in the entire state. And the Staunton *Spectator* sarcastically praised the legislature for its promptness and wisdom in passing such a bill: "This will be a great boon to the children as soon as we get any factories for them to work in." [22] Yet a beginning had been made. In Virginia and the South, succeeding years would witness an increasingly effective series of statutes on the subject.

A more positive accomplishment by the legislature in the field of labor regulation was its enactment of an employer's liability bill. Previous attempts to enact such a measure had been unavailing; but after Montague's 1901 election campaign, and at his personal insistence, the state Democratic platform of that year endorsed the reform.[23] The governor reminded the legislature of the party's promise in his first message to that body.

20 Richmond *Dispatch*, Jan. 8 and 11, 1903; Staunton *Daily News*, Feb. 6, 1903; Richmond *News Leader*, Feb. 16, 1903.
21 *Record of A. J. Montague* (Richmond, 1905), Montague Papers.
22 Richmond *News Leader*, Feb. 16, 1903; Staunton *Spectator and Vindicator*, Dec. 19, 1902.
23 Montague claimed chief credit for the institution of a liability act: "I humbly think I did more than any man in Virginia to bring it about." Montague to C. A. Shafter, Jan. 24, 1904, Montague Papers.

On March 5, 1902, Senator R. B. McIlwaine, who had "for years been the leader of unsuccessful efforts to have the principle . . . enacted into law," introduced another measure in accordance with Montague's wishes. His bill provided that whenever a railroad employee was injured "by the wrongful act, neglect, or default of a superior, employee, or co-employee," the employer would be held liable for the injury. Knowledge by the injured of defect in machinery or appliances was not to be held as a bar to recovery of damages.[24]

On March 13 the senate passed the bill unamended. The house soon followed suit, and the governor signed it on March 28, 1902. Only one factor tarnished the motives of the Assembly in so quickly disposing of a bill that had four times been defeated prior to 1901. The constitutional convention, then still in session, had tentatively incorporated a similarly worded provision into the new constitution. "Only after it became a foregone conclusion that such legislation would be embodied in the constitution did the General Assembly . . . accede to the demands of the people." The Assembly had decided to steal the convention's thunder.[25]

The American progressive movement was one of varying currents and crosscurrents. What seemed progressive to one reformer seemed either reactionary or radical to others. And of all reforms, the one that aroused the greatest controversy, even among progressives, was the campaign for prohibition. In Virginia and the rest of the South most progressives tended to support the temperance crusade, while machine politicians tended to ally with liquor interests. However, a considerable portion of the conservative religious element advocating temperance had no sympathy with the other progressive reforms, and many progressives, including Montague, were antagonistic to prohibition. Furthermore, as the tempo of the crusade increased, the temperance movement, especially in the South, tended to focus all reforming energies on one glorious panacea. In the last analysis, then, the temperance movement was more of a hindrance than a help to the general Southern progressive movement.

In Virginia the temperance crusade had ample cause for germination. Prior to 1900 "practically every cross-roads store dispensed its full quota of ardent spirits. It was not unusual for a small town or village to possess several saloons which were often located on principal corner lots. . . . They did a flourishing business, especially on

24 Richmond *Evening Leader*, March 5, 1902.
25 McDanel, *The Constitutional Convention*, 63.

Saturday afternoons. Whiskey circulated throughout the State by the thousands of tons." In 1901, an estimated three thousand saloons dotted the Commonwealth.[26] That year these conditions prompted the formation of a Virginia Anti-Saloon League. In January of 1902 the league held its first state convention, and soon thereafter began an active campaign which resulted in the closing of numerous saloons by a local option process.[27]

An unusual circumstance brought the league into early prominence. Its superintendent, the Reverend C. H. Crawford, sent from the national headquarters to organize the Virginia area, encountered the wrath of Judge Clarence J. Campbell of Amherst County. Judge Campbell had rendered a questionable decision which allowed druggists to sell intoxicants without obtaining a license, and when Crawford criticized this decision, Campbell cited him for contempt of court. At the court hearing, however, the faultless logic of Crawford's lawyer forced Campbell to admit his error and acquit Crawford. Enraged, the judge met Crawford on the courthouse lawn, and bull-whipped him.[28]

A furor enveloped the state. Petitions urged Montague to recall the recessed legislature to investigate the matter and reassert the integrity of the judiciary. Montague admitted the action was a "stain upon the Commonwealth," but he declined to take action: "I am authorized to make recommendations to the Legislature respecting legislative, not judicial action. The action of impeachment is judicial." As to what the legislature might do, Montague feared the worst: "I am almost hopeless about the Legislature. They seem to neglect the 'weighty matters of the law' and give their main time to the election of judges." [29]

Montague had again underrated the Assembly. Although for a time the "friends and supporters" of Martin seriously considered supporting Campbell, a personal friend of Congressman Flood, they soon abandoned their plans. The sentiment of the state demanded Campbell's impeachment. When the Assembly reconvened, a house committee voted to indict Campbell, and the senate, sitting as the jury, removed him by a 25 to 10 vote. The surprised Montague privately

26 Richard L. Morton, *History of Virginia* (Chicago, 1924), III, 332–34.
27 Virginius Dabney, *Dry Messiah, The Life of Bishop Cannon* (New York, 1949), 49; Richmond *Evening Leader,* June 27, 1902; Morton, *History of Virginia,* III, 334.
28 James Cannon, Jr., *Bishop Cannon's Own Story—Life as I Have Seen It* (Durham, N.C., 1955), 119.
29 Montague to J. Thompson Brown, July 28, 1902, Montague Papers.

praised this as the one good act of a legislative session otherwise barren of accomplishment.[30]

This controversial incident naturally gave considerable publicity to the temperance forces. They struck while the iron was hot. Even before Campbell's formal impeachment, Senator William Hodges Mann of Nottoway, Montague's opponent for the attorney general in 1897, introduced into the Assembly a measure that captured newspaper headlines for months to come. The "Mann bill," as it was called, found few people taking a neutral position, and it became easily the chief political issue of the day.

Mann's bill aimed primarily to maintain law and order in rural areas, especially to protect women from the carousing drunkards of public saloons. This would be accomplished by stiffening the qualifications for a liquor license in towns with less than five hundred inhabitants, while raising the cost of licenses everywhere to a prohibitive level. Furthermore, before a county court judge could grant a liquor license in any locality, a favorable petition from a majority of that locality's voters had to be submitted. In addition, a judge had the privilege of arbitrarily determining to his satisfaction whether the sale of liquor would "not be contrary to a sound public policy or injurious to the morals or the material interest of the community." [31]

Mann's bill was introduced in November, 1902. During the ensuing months forty thousand petitions, organized by the antisaloon lobby, bombarded the legislature with a monotonous regularity. By March, 1903, both houses of the Assembly had become thoroughly "converted" to the cause. The senate passed the bill, 22 to 6. The house followed suit two weeks later, approving the bill by the comfortable margin of 59 to 28. After conference adjustments, the governor signed the entire revenue measure, of which the Mann bill was but a part, on April 16, 1903.[32] The temperance forces had won a significant victory. Six years later, half the state was "dry," and the number of saloons had been reduced from the 1901 high of 3,000 to only 750. By 1914 Virginia would adopt total prohibition.

30 W. G. Loving to Montague, March 23, 1903, and Montague to W. B. Richards, Oct. 12, 1903, *ibid.;* Richmond *News Leader,* Feb. 27, March 6 and 9, 1903.
31 H. Wesley Ward, *The Administration of Liquor Control in Virginia* (Charlottesville, 1946), 25–27; Cannon, *Cannon's Own Story,* 120; Richmond *News Leader,* Feb. 2, 1903.
32 Richmond *News Leader,* Feb. 2, 16, and 17, March 12, 20, and 26, April 3 and 8, 1903.

Governor Montague's signature did not necessarily indicate his approval. Although he was known as "an apostle of temperance," he never allowed the issue to interfere with his politics. The temperance issue in Virginia broke across factional lines; in a sense, it brought a realignment of factions, and Montague wished to avert this unnatural division over what he considered to be a minor issue. In reply to inquiries, he occasionally asserted that his past life was "satisfactory to the real temperance advocates," but he once insisted he was "not a Prohibitionist, but a Democrat." Publicly, his position on the Mann bill was never known, although he once privately criticized the legislature for "its enactment of laws that appear undemocratic and which have worked up a great deal of trouble in the State." More than likely, this was a pointed reference to the Mann law.[33]

The only other indication of Montague's attitude to the temperance problem during his administration can be found in his signing an amendment to the Mann bill, passed by the 1904 legislature, closing all saloons on Sunday. In defense of his approval, Montague asserted: "The bill actually closes all saloons on Sunday while the old measure merely prohibited sale of liquor. . . . My experience as a prosecuting attorney for nearly five years led me to believe that the opening of the saloon . . . could be proved . . . [whereas it was] difficult to prove the sale of liquor." [34] Like many of his fellow progressives, Montague favored a reasonable regulation but not a total prohibition of the liquor traffic.

Vehement opposition to the purposes of the Mann bill continued long after its enactment, but the temperance forces weathered the storm of protest. Basically, the Mann law remained undiluted, and its author and patron was elected governor of the state in 1909. Eventually Virginia, in contrast to other Southern states, would see machine forces form a close alliance with the prohibition advocates, while the schism between progressive leaders persisted. Of all Virginia reforms in this period, prohibition alone increased in fervor with the passage of years, while the political influence of the state's Independents declined. With religious rather than intellectual idealism as its mainstay, it lost none of its drive. Only when it demonstrated its

---

33 Richmond *Evening Leader,* Jan. 25, 1902; Cannon, *Cannon's Own Story,* 128. Montague to J. R. Ellis, March 31, 1905; Montague to R. R. Ratcliffe, May 2, 1901; Montague to W. B. Richards, Oct. 12, 1903; all in Montague Papers.
34 Montague to W. M. Fishburne, March 25, 1904, *ibid.*

impracticability during the 1920's did public opinion reverse direction.

Time gives perspective to all things. With the notable exception of the Mann liquor bill, none of the foregoing items of legislation attracted more than cursory attention from the general public. Gaining far greater public notice were the Assembly's actions on three items of appropriation: $300,000 for more liberal Confederate veteran pensions, $50,000 for a Virginia exhibit at the St. Louis World's Fair, and $200,000 for the 1907 Jamestown Exposition. The first passed the Assembly with little opposition in March, 1902; the second in December, 1902; and the third in April, 1903. All three appropriations were hailed by state journals as positive indications that Virginia had at last conquered the poverty and degradation left by the Civil War.

Montague had enthusiastically urged all three expenditures in his first address to the legislature. Referring to the St. Louis fair, he urged that "no such opportunity outside of our borders will occur in the next half a century for us to show our resources and products." Later, both he and Governor Aycock of North Carolina spoke at Norfolk in October, 1903, on behalf of the exposition celebrating the three-hundredth anniversary of the founding of Jamestown.[35]

These appropriations were not without opposition. Conservative economists and representatives of western districts labeled them a wasteful drain on the treasury. The Staunton *Spectator* termed the Jamestown Exposition appropriation "the most gigantic scheme to loot the treasury that has fallen within our day." The St. Louis appropriation, however, passed the house, 61 to 16, and the senate, 23 to 3. The Jamestown bill, a much larger appropriation, aroused the larger opposition. But after all delaying tactics failed, the house, by a vote of 58 to 30, and then the senate, 22 to 11, granted Montague his request.[36]

Soon after this action the *News Leader* commented editorially: "The present legislature has made a brilliant and a memorable record. It has broken away from the theory that a State government is a

35 Richmond *Evening Leader*, Jan. 1, 1902; Robert T. Taylor, "The Jamestown Tercentennial Exposition of 1907," *Virginia Magazine of History and Biography*, LXV (April, 1957), 169–208.
36 Staunton *Spectator and Vindicator*, April 24, 1903; Richmond *Evening Leader*, Dec. 10 and 15, 1902; Richmond *News Leader*, April 2, 1903.

thing to be kept barely alive as a mere convenience. . . . It has committed itself to the policy of making the State government a living, active, aggressive organization." [37]

Though overstated, this observation contained some validity. The General Assembly of 1901–1904 was neither hot nor cold. In varying degrees it acted favorably on three prominent pieces of progressive legislation—pure elections, child labor regulation, and restriction of saloons. Yet the absence of action and outright disapproval of other reforms indicated that the Assembly was still basically a nineteenth-not a twentieth-century institution. When it adjourned in May, 1903, for summer recess, a Richmond editorial entitled "Her Face to the Morning" summarized some of its accomplishments.[38] The caption is appropriate.

Montague saw this gradual coming of the morning, yet he chafed at its delay. He had favored child labor restriction, but was disappointed by the Assembly's amendments to Cabell's measure. More than any other Virginia politician he had advocated pure elections, yet he feared that the Barksdale law would prove unenforceable. Although his conception of a governor's duties forbade his taking an active part in legislative maneuvers, on several important issues of the day he played a major role as spokesman. But his personal crusades for good roads, good schools, and the party primary obtained little reciprocal enthusiasm from the legislature. Since Montague laid greatest emphasis on these issues, his caustic appraisals of the legislature can be appreciated. He felt his administration was continually hampered by the Assembly's hesitancy, its reactionary attitudes, its proclivity for partisan politics.

But Montague underrated the Assembly; that body had indeed set its face to the morning. Progressivism was still adolescent and faltering, but a gradual shift was apparent.

---

37 Richmond *News Leader,* May 6, 1903.   38 *Ibid.,* May 18, 1903.

X

GOOD SCHOOLS

I F the Virginia legislature of this period showed evidences of a new spirit of change, the Virginia populace demonstrated a more impressive reawakening—politically, socially, economically. Nowhere was this more evident than in the ardent crusade for better schools that swept the state after the turn of the century. In this crusade Montague played a significant role. He had viewed devitalized postwar Virginia and found her lacking; dreaming of a new Virginia, he looked to education as the foremost solution to her problems. As a candidate for attorney general in 1897 and for governor in 1901 he had repeatedly championed the need for better public education to free the ballot box from its odium of illiteracy, to help instill character in the mass of men, and to provide a means of economic uplift for the state's citizenry. Later, as Virginia's chief executive, he helped lead the educational campaign which quickly enveloped the state; for his efforts he became widely recognized as Virginia's first "educational governor."

In appealing to the populace for support of the public school system, Montague could point to obvious deficiencies. Virginia's public schools had their inception in the 1869 Underwood Constitution. Able leaders had succeeded in the monumental task of creating the rudiments of an educational system, yet after the administration of Willian Henry Ruffner (the "Horace Mann of Virginia") Virginia's

schools stagnated. Continuing poverty produced inertia and complacency. The turn of the century found conditions little better than they
had been thirty years earlier. Expenditures had increased, but so had
enrollments. Teacher salaries had remained almost static. The average school term had increased from four and a half to six months, but
the students enrolled in 1900 comprised only half the state's school-
age population. Fears were rightfully expressed that the state was
rearing a generation of illiterates.[1] The entire South faced similar
problems, and the entire South shared in the education revival which
came to Virginia at the turn of the century. Before describing in detail Montague's role in Virginia's school campaign, then, the general
Southern scene should first be examined.

Low teacher salaries, short school terms, poor attendance, inadequate facilities, increasing illiteracy among the white population, and a
continuing high (50%) illiteracy among the Negro population—these
were some of the problems that plagued Southern school systems. In reaction to these conditions a group of Southern educators and Northern
philanthropists organized in 1901 a Southern Education Board to promote a comprehensive program for educational improvement. Labeled
the Ogden movement in honor of Robert Curtis Ogden, a Northern
businessman who headed the board, the program devised aimed to create in every Southern state a public demand for improved school facilities—to encourage consolidation of rural schools, compulsory education, and industrial and agricultural education. Funds distributed by the
board (and by the General Education Board established by John D.
Rockefeller as a complement to Ogden's organization) were not to go
directly to individual schools, but were to be spent solely for propaganda, encouraging local development of local resources.[2]

State and local officials and citizens responded to the Ogden movement with alacrity. A group of progressive "educational governors"
came to power shortly after the formation of Ogden's board and the
inception of his movement—James B. Frazier of Tennessee, N. C.
Blanchard of Louisiana, Braxton B. Comer of Alabama, Charles
Brantley Aycock of North Carolina, and Montague. Ogden himself
especially praised "Governors Montague of Virginia, Aycock of
North Carolina, Heyward of South Carolina and Terrell of Georgia,"

1   Cornelius J. Heatwole, *A History of Education in Virginia* (New York,
    1916), 240–45.
2   Bruce, *The Rise of the New South*, 319 ff.; C. W. Dabney, *Universal Ed-
    ucation in the South*, II, 12 ff.

all of whom had been "very pronounced in their public utterances" in behalf of education.[3]

These educational governors served as the spokesmen for a large group of middle-class reformers—professional people, schoolmen, churchmen, editors—"inspired with humanitarian zeal and passion for uplift." [4] Their purpose was to elevate the Southern people intellectually, to create a fertile environment for more rapid economic development and, finally, to place a theoretical democratic government upon a firmer and broader democratic foundation. To Lyman Abbott, an Ogden colleague, the revival of education in the South meant "a revival of industry, a humanizing . . . ennobling of all vocations . . . a revival of political liberty." [5]

The crusade which enveloped the South after 1900 thus affords perhaps the best insight into the Southern progressive movement as a whole. With the possible exception of the drive for popular primaries, no other reform was so universally accepted by Southern progressives. Moreover, the center of the revival lay not in the rural areas which had nourished Populism but in urban localities where money and leadership were concentrated. The educational drive also serves as the second basic feature differentiating the Southern progressive movement from its Northern counterpart (the first being disfranchisement of the illiterate). By 1900, the North had already experienced great advances in its public schooling. High schools were commonplace, and every Northern state required compulsory attendance. In 1900 the Northeastern states spent for each pupil in their schools an amount ten times that spent in Alabama.[6] Thus, when the progressive-minded Southerner sought to bring "uplift" to his homeland, the school system presented the most obvious deficiencies. While the Northern reformer investigated problems of municipal government, his Southern counterpart turned to the need for public literacy as a safeguard of free institutions. While Northerners emphasized problems of railroad and monopoly excesses, Southerners lamented the plight of one-room schools and inefficient, underpaid teachers.

Several factors had retarded the arrival of this Southern educational advance. General poverty, a hostile public attitude toward the

3 *Ibid.,* 362–69, 396–97; Connor and Poe, *C. B. Aycock,* 114 ff.; Philip W. Wilson, *An Unofficial Statesman, Robert C. Ogden* (Garden City, 1924), 227.
4 Woodward, *Origins of the New South,* 396.
5 C. W. Dabney, *Universal Education in the South,* II, 103.
6 Woodward, *Origins of the New South,* 398.

principle of public education, the problem of the Negro—all handicapped efforts of educational crusaders. To many Southerners an education for the Negro seemed theoretically desirable, but a wasted
effort, not practicable; to others, even if practicable, it was not desirable. Demands were loud from the Southern black belts to segregate
the sources of public-school funds by race, leaving Negro schools
supported only by Negro taxes. Consequently the education reformers,
in true progressive tradition, were not only fighting to improve schools
but also defending the very principle of their existence "against the
old fortress of laissez-faire" and against racial prejudice. The magni-
tude of their victory is thus the more remarkable.[7]

The success which eventually rewarded the educational reformers'
efforts can be attributed to several circumstances. Credit must first
given to an able coterie of middle-class leaders who spearheaded the
campaigns in the several states. Allowance must also be made for the
rising prosperity of the South. Then too, educational reformers capitalized on the general spirit of innovation which characterized the entire Southern progressive movement. Another possible factor, not to
be overlooked, was the Southern disfranchisement of the Negro.

Many Southern progressives entertained the hope that disfranchisement would remove racism from politics, thereby permitting public
attention to be directed into more fruitful channels. There is some evidence that disfranchisement did act as a spur to the educational
movement. "Popular opinion held that it was the duty of public authorities to prepare for the time when 'Grandfather clauses' in state
constitutions would no longer confer on [white] illiterates the right
to vote." [8] This preparation would be made through better education.
Governor Hoke Smith of Georgia came to power on a reform wave
which saw the simultaneous enactment of an array of progressive
measures, including greater assistance to public education and the
disfranchisement of the Negro. One of the most active of the educational governors, Aycock of North Carolina, was also one of the most
vocal in calling for the Negro's disfranchisement. Aycock attributed
the success of his educational endeavors directly to the removal of the
Negro from politics:

> With the solution of our suffrage question there has come larger
> liberty of thought and action. . . . We have gone out of politics and

7 Connor and Poe, *C. B. Aycock*, 114; Bruce, *The Rise of the New South*,
   343; Woodward, *Origins of the New South*, 416.
8 Simkins, *The South Old and New*, 274.

taken up business. . . . We are going to educate the entire populace. . . . We spent on education this year more than half of the
entire revenue of the State.[9]

Sharing Aycock's sentiments was Edwin A. Alderman, a leader of the
educational movement in North Carolina and later president of the
University of Virginia. As quoted by Virginius Dabney, Alderman asserted that with the Negro no longer " 'a menacing political factor,
disturbing the judgment of men and arousing their passions,' the
South could at last 'think on him righteously and justly as a human
being, as a racial problem.' " [10]

Many Southern politicians, of course, cynically advocated disfranchisement simply because of its appeal to the prejudices of white
voters. Smith of Georgia, for example, played the part of a demagogue in his campaign for governor. So did Montague in his contest
with J. Hampton Hoge in 1901. Both men were politicians as well as
progressives, yet Montague, certainly, displayed no insincerity in his
conviction that purging the Negro as a political factor in elections
would produce beneficial results. Speaking to a University of Chicago
audience in 1909 (hardly an arena for demagoguery), the former
governor explained the basic reason for Virginia's disfranchisement
as a desire to free the state from a "mental and moral servitude" in
which "all questions gravitated to the control of the local government
by the white race, and all other questions [were] subordinated." Noting that the Negro's disfranchisement seemed to herald "a new order
of leadership," Montague further asserted that it would be only a
temporary development. With education, "eventually we may expect
the development of a negro electorate determined upon sound political principles." [11]

Several Northerners prominent in the Ogden educational movement confirmed the observations of Aycock, Montague, Smith,
Alderman, Bruce, and others that disfranchisement had partially removed the explosive racial issue from politics, thus creating an atmosphere beneficial to Southern reforms and particularly to the educational movement. Following the annual conference of the Southern
Education Board held in Richmond in 1903, Dr. Albert Shaw, editor
of the *Review of Reviews,* noted:

9 Grantham, *Hoke Smith,* 178–79; Connor and Poe, *C. B. Aycock,* 124–25.
10 Virginius Dabney, *Liberalism in the South,* 176.
11 Montague, "The South and the Nation," 93–101.

This year's conference has confirmed my belief that the Constitutional amendments recently enacted in the various Southern States respecting Negro disfranchisement were timely and necessary. It really gives him a vote, for heretofore he has never had a vote. Before this time the South has taken the stand that Negro suffrage was forced upon her. Now she has given the Negro a chance to place himself upon a footing with any citizen of Massachusetts.[12]

Ogden himself had as his primary object "to keep the field clear . . . of political controversy on either side." Thus, when a move developed in Republican circles to reduce Southern representation in Congress following the Negro's disfranchisement (a reduction made possible by the Fourteenth Amendment), Ogden wrote to President Roosevelt late in 1904 strongly advising him against such a move: "The race issue in the late campaign [of 1904] would have turned back the wheels of progress many years. Life, liberty, and the pursuit of happiness would have been increasingly difficult with an important part of our people. . . . The Fourteenth Amendment is a dangerous bit of political machinery. It may prove a boomerang. Its enforcement may be the Negro's undoing." [13] Such arguments reflected the tendency among many Northerners at this time to take the position that Negro suffrage had, initially at least, proven a failure. As titular leader of the educational movement then gathering momentum throughout the South, as a man determined to allow nothing to obstruct the success of that movement, Ogden expressed views which cannot lightly be dismissed.

Louis R. Harlan, author of *Separate and Unequal*, a history of the Ogden movement in the Southeastern states, shows that Ogden and his associates expediently acquiesced to the demand for disfranchisement, hoping that a subsidence of racial tension would create a favorable climate for general educational improvement from which the Negro might also benefit indirectly.[14] Although Harlan also shows that the Negro did not fully share in the educational renaissance which followed, he does not deny that such a renaissance did come.[15] The

12 New York *Times*, May 1, 1903, quoted in C. W. Dabney, *Universal Education in the South*, II, 104.
13 Wilson, *Robert C. Ogden*, 224.
14 Louis R. Harlan, *Separate and Unequal, Public School Campaigns and Racism in the Southern Seaboard States, 1901–1915* (Chapel Hill, 1958), 75–101.
15 *Ibid.*, 162–63. Harlan's contention that Southern educational facilities were "separate and unequal" for white and Negro need hardly be disputed. His statistics, however, usually exaggerate the disparity by overlooking or

point remains, then: would it have come as quickly had not disfranchisement somewhat pacified demands of white supremacists, turning
public attention to other issues of moment? The fact that white educational facilities improved more rapidly than Negro facilities does
not indicate that Negro schools languished in complete stagnation,
nor does it necessarily reveal a deterioration in race relations. Harlan's statistics indicate that after 1900 as great a gap developed between city and country schools as between white and Negro; yet this
would hardly justify a conclusion that rural schools were not helped
by the Ogden movement, or that the movement purposefully discrimi-
nated against rural regions. More plausible as an explanation for both
disparities is the cultural gap between town and country, between
white and Negro.

Able leadership, Northern financial assistance, rising Southern
prosperity, the removal of the Negro as a political force—all these
factors combined to promote the success of the Ogden movement in
the South and in Virginia. To the year 1901 has been credited the
real beginning of Virginia's campaign for better schools. Probably no
man contributed more to this initial reawakening than did Montague.

The governor's interest in education was not suddenly acquired.
His father, Robert Montague, had vigorously opposed the very principle of public education, but the son developed a different attitude.
As early as 1889 Montague, the young lawyer, proclaimed to a
Danville audience that all citizens must prepare their minds to meet
the responsibility of government: "This must be done by popular
education, the force of the nation; the Archimedian lever which is to
elevate us as a nation." [16] This faith in the efficacy of education was
possibly acquired at Richmond College, where Montague had studied
under J. L. M. Curry, a longtime and lonely crusader for Southern
education in the latter decades of the nineteenth century. The relationship between the two men, teacher and pupil, was evidently close,
for in 1885 Montague penned a letter to the Danville *Register,* hotly
attacking the arguments of those who opposed President Cleveland's

---

ignoring the lack of compulsory attendance laws in the South. Since the
percentage of school-age Negroes in attendance ordinarily fell below the
percentage of whites, statistics of total expenditures or total teacher salary
per Negro or white child of *school age* (Harlan's customary measurement)
fail to paint an accurate comparison of the two systems. See pages 144,
166, and *passim.*

16 Clipping, 1889, scrapbook, Moore Collection.

appointment of Curry as minister to Spain. After 1890 Montague and Curry both served as trustees of Richmond College, and the two apparently conferred together on educational matters.[17]

Montague's interest in education continued to grow through the 1890's. In 1895 he obtained a copy of a paper read in Atlanta before a National Congress of Education, entitled "What the South is Doing for Education and What Education is Doing for the South." The author, Dr. W. T. Harris, United States Commissioner of Education, made a strong plea for consolidation of schools in sparsely settled rural districts, a proposal Montague later espoused as a primary means of improving Virginia's school system. In his 1897 campaign for attorney general Montague frequently spoke out for public education, emphasizing that universal education must accompany universal suffrage if the latter were to support stable government. In a Richmond speech he "held up to view the evil of illiterate suffrage and advocated a liberal public school system. . . . Through our public schools alone could our voters be educated." Education was also presented as the only effective means to improve Virginia's political ethics: "a free government cannot be an ignorant and corrupt government." The remedy was not to be found in meaningless statutes, but in a purification of the wellsprings of character. This, he believed, came most surely through education.[18]

By adopting education as his panacea for the South's many problems, Montague became a thoroughgoing Jeffersonian, a believer in the people's ability to govern their destinies, once given the opportunity to rise above ignorance. The youthful pessimist was transformed into the optimist, imbued with a belief in human progress, in the perfectibility of man. This attitude was later revealed, to cite another illustration, in Montague's completely Wilsonian devotion to the goal of erecting a system of international law that would reduce government frictions to a minimum and eventually outlaw war.

In a sense, however, this Utopian quality could be found in both the young pessimist and the adult optimist. For even while indulging in adolescent disparagements of mankind's deficiencies, the young Montague had been by nature an idealist—an individual hoping for

17 Clipping, Danville *Register*, 1885, scrapbook, Moore Collection; Montague to Curry, July 3, 1893, Montague Papers.
18 W. T. Harris, "What the South is Doing for Education and What Education is Doing for the South," Montague Papers; unidentified clippings, 1897, scrapbook, Moore Collection.

ultimate improvement even though that hope at times seemed not founded in reality. By the very definition of the term, an idealist cannot view his ideals as unattainable, else he becomes a fatalist. Though to some extent Montague revealed throughout his life a mental undercurrent of complaint, doubt, even despair, this strain of thought was rarely dominant during his productive years as a public servant. As if continually attempting to persuade himself as well as his listeners, he spent his lifetime in a sustained, sonorous exhortation of both public and private betterment—with all the many ramifications that phrase implies. His message was positive; his promise of future reward for present effort often breathtaking. Though at times weighted down with feelings of personal inadequacy, the man had vision—and faith. As a fervent apostle of a strengthened system of universal education, he was to utilize his evangelical talents most productively.

In both his 1897 race for attorney general and his 1901 race for governor, Montague, the oratorical evangelist, had summoned popular support to the banner of public education. Speaking to the Norfolk Democratic convention which gave him the gubernatorial nomination, he had emphatically declared, "It is our duty to foster and improve our system of public instruction, for the cause of true popular education and free government is one and the same." [19] Addressing the constitutional convention upon his inauguration, Montague voiced one of his basic educational tenets, a belief in education suited to the individual:

> The material advancement of a State is measured by the school privileges of its people. But one education differs from another as one star differeth from another in glory. There is an education of the learned professions . . . science, and philosophy; and there is an education of agriculture and the mechanic arts; the latter is the foundation of wealth and comfort; and it is laid in the common schools. The age of the hand is past, and the age of the machine is come.[20]

Montague feared that the new industrial age "flowing across the threshold of the new century" had outmoded Virginia's school system. Like one of his correspondents, who fumed at the "folly of Latin," he urged an education program responsive to the vocational

19 Marjorie F. Underhill, "The Virginia Phase of the Ogden Movement" (M.A. thesis, University of Virginia, 1952), 40.
20 *Addresses, Messages, and Proclamations of Andrew Jackson Montague, Governor of Virginia, 1902–1906* (Richmond, 1906), 10–11.

needs of the people. Especially urging a more practical vocational curriculum for Negroes, in his first message to the legislature he recommended that Hampton Institute, a Negro school, be designated an "Industrial," not a "Collegiate," institution.[21] In these respects, of course, he shared the attitude of Booker T. Washington, the prominent Negro educator.

Montague had early contacts with the Ogden movement. Wallace Buttrick, the strategist of the Southern Education Board, appointed Robert Frazer, president of the Virginia State Normal College, and former Congressman Henry St. George Tucker, professor of law at Washington and Lee, as Virginia field agents for the board soon after its organization in 1901. On January 3, 1902, just three days after Montague's inauguration, these men and others, comprising a "Southern Educational Conference Committee," met in Richmond to discuss the Virginia situation and plan a campaign to stir up public interest in the plight of the schools. Montague attended this meeting, as did several prominent educators from North Carolina. In March he spoke before the Richmond Educational Association, an organization formed in 1900. His talk on "The Necessity for Normal and Industrial Training" received loud and frequent applause, and he praised the association as "a noble move," saying he hoped to see such organizations implanted in every city and county in the state.[22]

A month later the Ogden train passed through Virginia on its way to the fifth annual conference of the board, which was held in Athens, Georgia. On the evening of April 23, Montague gave a reception for the entire excursion, publicly expressing hope that the next conference would be held in Richmond. He accompanied the train to its Georgia destination along with several other Southern governors. There his invitation, seconded by the Virginia legislature, was formally accepted.[23]

Meanwhile, the Virginia phase of the movement gathered speed. On July 7, 1902, a conference of county and city superintendents met at Charlottesville for a summer school on methods. In the main speech of the morning session, Montague praised the objectives of the Southern Education Board, and expressed the hope "that this Commonwealth is now catching the first taste of an educational revival.

---

21 Richmond *Evening Leader,* Feb. 20, March 6, 1902; Richmond *News Leader,* March 28, 1904.
22 Richmond *Evening Leader,* Jan. 4, March 19, 1902.
23 *Ibid.,* April 21, 1902; Underhill, "The Ogden Movement," 60.

The public free school system of Virginia needs a little remedy-
ing. . . . The number of schools is too large for the average attendance. . . . We can never have a real efficient system without better
schools and longer terms. Quantity does not count; quality alone
counts. It is better to have one good school than ten poor ones." Consolidation of schools, in Montague's opinion, plus industrial and agricultural programs, comprised the two most pressing reforms needed
in Virginia's educational system. These two objectives found recur-
ring emphasis in his addresses.[24]

In January, 1903, Montague and Tucker attended together the
meeting of the Southern Education Board in New York. The New
York *Evening World* commented upon Montague's brief address
there: "It was a surprising thing to a Northern audience to hear the
Governor of Virginia say that educational topics now transcend politics in interest and importance in the Old Dominion. A new South indeed!" Montague had not portrayed Virginia incorrectly. Shortly
after his New York trip an important conference of Virginia's school
superintendents, sponsored by the General Education Board, met in
Richmond. Wallace Buttrick, secretary of the board, spoke at the initial session, highly praising Montague's contributions to the education
movement: "We in the North have already named Mr. Montague the
'educational Governor.'" Joseph W. Southall, Virginia's state superintendent of public instruction, introduced Montague in glowing
terms: "No man in the Commonwealth," he declared, "is more earnestly and enthusiastically interested in the subject of education."[25]

Montague, in his address, praised the assembly of superintendents
as solid indication of an educational revival in Virginia. The most
startling feature of his address was his reference to the controversial
subject of compulsory education. Though not openly advocating it, he
predicted that his children would see the day when it became a reality, and he gave several convincing arguments in its favor. Earlier,
Montague had privately expressed his belief that public education
without compulsory attendance was a contradiction. His conviction
on the matter became stronger as the months passed. "No longer," he
wrote in 1904, "is it a question of right that the State should afford
public education, but it is now the duty of the State to do so. . . .
Every child has a right to an education."[26]

24 Richmond *Evening Leader,* July 8, 1902.
25 Richmond *Dispatch,* Jan. 13 and 15, 1903.
26 Montague to John W. Jenkins, Jan. 7, 1903, and "Memorandum," May 4,
    1904, both in Montague Papers.

Adoption of compulsory attendance, however, was obstructed by the black belt Virginia counties, where the white minority gave only grudging support to Negro education. To advocate universal compulsory education in Virginia was thus tantamount to political suicide. Later, however, in January 1906, Montague, recently defeated in his bid for senatorial election, no longer feared for his political fortune. In his third message to the legislature he unequivocally advocated the principle: "Compulsory attendance," he complained, "prevails in every State . . . with the exception of the Southern States, and even here Maryland and Kentucky have broken the reactionary fetters." To mollify the black belt he suggested that if statewide compulsory attendance were not feasible, each individual county and city should be given the option to institute its own system.[27]

Following the address, Montague wrote to Ogden: "The message seems to evoke a good deal of opposition in this particular, which, however, I anticipated. The secret of the opposition is a mistaken view of the negro question, which seems to be invoked to obscure the just solution of every great issue which would make for the welfare and progress of the South. . . . But my views . . . must ultimately triumph." [28]

Though compulsory education for both white and Negro was an ultimate aim of Montague and Virginia's educational reformers, it was not the aim nearest at hand. The 1903 Richmond conference of superintendents which Montague addressed, for example, resolved that the time was "not ripe" for the advocacy of compulsory education in Virginia. The objectives of the Ogden movement were more practical: "Everywhere the appeal was for increased taxes for education, longer terms, a better attendance by children, and a more effective teaching." As Montague observed, the only way to jolt Southern education out of its lethargy would be to conduct a mass public relations campaign appealing directly to the people.[29]

In Virginia, this public appeal was conducted largely by Dr. Frazer and Professor Tucker. As agents of the Southern Education Board they spoke at courthouses, at religious gatherings, at teachers' meetings, in various ways reaching nearly every section of the state. Their efforts received tremendous impetus when the Conference for Education in the South, accepting Montague's invitation, met in Richmond

27   Richmond *News Leader,* Jan. 10, 1906.
28   Montague to Robert C. Ogden, Jan. 24, 1906, Montague Papers.
29   Richmond *Dispatch,* Jan. 17, 1903; Wilson, *Robert C. Ogden,* 236; Montague to B. J. Garner, Jan. 11, 1904, Montague Papers.

from April 22 to April 24, 1903. All told, two thousand Southern educators attended the gathering, including college and academy presidents, professors, and state superintendents of education, as well as local Virginia superintendents. Montague had been urged by Edgar G. Murphy, secretary for the Southern Education Board (and also a leader of the Southern child labor reform movement), to address the conference for a minimum of forty-five minutes. Such an address, declared Murphy, would give Northern visitors at the conference an "important impression of new Southern leadership." In addition, it would give the many Southerners present "just such inspiration as was brought to the Educators, Legislators, and people of Alabama" when Montague had spoken before the Alabama legislature on January 1, 1903. That speech was the highlight of a three-day education conference in Montgomery sponsored by the Southern Education Board.[30]

Although Montague made only a brief speech of welcome, not the extended address requested of him, his name did not go unmentioned during the proceedings.[31] In reporting to the assembly on the Virginia situation, Dr. Hollis B. Frissell, principal of Hampton Institute, optimistically observed that progress was being made. Consolidation of schools was being effected in some areas, and the Virginia populace showed signs of accepting the need for higher local taxation. Complimenting Frazer and Tucker for their energetic efforts, Frissell also credited the state press, especially the Richmond *Times Dispatch,* with helping the cause. Of Governor Montague he concluded: "He is rightly called the educational governor, for, in every possible way, by word and deed, he has made himself felt in the struggle for better schools." [32]

After the conference adjourned, Montague wrote to Dr. Edward Abbott, one of the Northern leaders of the Ogden movement, "The Conference was upon the whole inspirational, I think . . . [displaying] a breadth of view, a liberality of spirit and purpose. . . .

30 Wilson, *Robert C. Ogden,* 236; Underhill, "The Ogden Movement," 61; C. W. Dabney, *Universal Education in the South,* II, 96–98; Edgar G. Murphy to Montague, March 18, 1903, Montague Papers.

31 "The governor of Virginia, A. J. Montague, welcomed the Conference, before a large audience, in an address in which he stressed the necessity of the education of all the people in a democracy. Recalling how the ruling class of Old Virginia opposed for years free public schools . . . Governor Montague's address marked a new epoch in education." C. W. Dabney, *Universal Education in the South,* II, 98.

32 Richmond *News Leader,* April 23, 1903.

Thanks, many thanks, . . . for the breath of fresh air you brought us." By January, 1904, when Montague addressed the legislature, he was able to confirm this optimistic outlook. The increased public interest evidenced during the past two years, he described as "a decided step" forward. Especially did he applaud the progress made in consolidating schools, "which adds to the length of the school term and increases the pay of the teachers." [33]

In this same address Montague also recommended that the maximum tax rate authorized by the constitution (five mills) be enacted. The legislature had earlier levied only the minimum, one mill. Similarly, the new constitution allowed local school districts to levy a maximum of five mills, but the legislature had subsequently authorized them to set the rate only as high as two mills. It was partly for this reason that Montague and others urged the necessity of carrying their cause directly to the people, not the legislature. A few statistics demonstrate that this appeal to the various localities was not without reward. Of the total funds supporting public schools in 1900, $1,015,538, or over half, was contributed by the state; $926,993 came from the districts. By 1905, the ratio had been reversed. State funds had risen only $100,000 to $1,128,262, while local sources had contributed an additional $300,000, for a total of $1,214,973. [34]

The conservative legislature of the period failed to reflect immediately the educational revival that was sweeping the state. It not only rejected the increased tax rate that Montague recommended but also defeated measures that would have provided a longer school term, a minimum teachers' pay of forty dollars a month, a retired teachers' pension plan, and additional appropriations for the state's universities. J. L. Jarman, president of the State Female Normal School located at Farmville, wrote to Montague in 1903, criticizing the senate finance committee for turning down his requests for increased appropriations. As a result, stated Jarman, "We're at the mercy of the Peabody fund" (a philanthropic fund for Southern education). Montague had anticipated the legislature's action, and had written to Buttrick, "The condition of the Normal School is far from satisfactory. . . . if possible, aid these schools; and if so, advise me to what extent, in order

33 Montague to Edward Abbott, May 6, 1903, Montague Papers; Richmond
    News Leader, Jan. 13, 1904.
34 Richard McIlwaine, *Addresses and Papers Bearing Chiefly on Education*
    (Richmond, 1908), 101; Magruder, *Recent Administration in Virginia*, 57;
    J. L. Blair Buck, *The Development of Public Schools in Virginia* (Richmond, 1952), 138; Harlan, *Separate and Unequal*, 165.

that I may use your statement as a leverage to ensure . . . appropriations." [35]

The legislature did pass one beneficial act—authorizing the establishment of a state board of examiners to provide uniform standards for certification of teachers. Montague also approved of the legislature's action advising the state board of education to establish a single, not a multiple, textbook list for all school districts. As a member of the state board Montague, early in 1904, fought unsuccessfully for the single list on the grounds that the multiple list had resulted in widespread bribery with book companies giving sales commissions to school officials.[36]

If the progress of the campaign for better schools gave Montague some encouragement by January of 1904, the next two years would give him reason for jubilation. The year 1901 had seen the seed planted; 1902 and 1903 had seen germination and sprouting; 1904 and 1905 would witness a full and vigorous growth. Partially responsible for this upsurge was the organization of a statewide Co-operative Education Commission early in 1904. In January, 1903, a group of state educators including Frazer; Frissell; J. D. Eggleston, school superintendent of Prince Edward County; and Dr. S. C. Mitchell, professor of history at the University of Richmond, had gathered in Richmond at Montague's invitation to discuss Virginia's schools. Meeting in the governor's office, they decided to perfect an organization to coordinate more effectively the campaign which Montague, Tucker, and Frazer had already launched.[37]

Fulfillment of these plans came a year later. In March, 1904, "at the suggestion of Governor Montague and Dr. Southall . . . a number of college presidents and professors and other Virginians interested in the advancement of popular education" met in Richmond for a conference "to consider the educational, economic, and civic interests of the Commonwealth." The first session on March 28 assembled in the senate chamber of the Capitol, where informal addresses were delivered by Montague, Southall, Frazer, Mitchell, and others. A

35 Richmond *News Leader,* March 14, 27, and 30, April 20, 1903. J. L. Jarman to Montague, April 17, 1903; Montague to Buttrick, Feb. 7, March 27, Nov. 12, 1903; all in Montague Papers.
36 Buck, *Public Schools in Virginia,* 131–36; Richmond *News Leader,* March 10, 1904; Montague to William A. Bowles, Feb. 20, 1904, Montague Papers.
37 Edward F. Overton, "A Study of the Life and Work of Joseph Dupuy Eggleston, Jr." (Ph.D. dissertation, University of Virginia, 1943), 201. C. W. Dabney states that this meeting was held in 1902. *Universal Education in the South,* II, 323.

total of thirty-five representatives were in attendance, including Attorney General William A. Anderson. In his address Montague once
again urged the necessity and practicality of vocational education,
lamenting the fact that education in Virginia had been regarded
chiefly "as a device of leisure." After the session, the governor,
Southall, and Mrs. B. B. Valentine were designated to meet and suggest a permanent committee organization.[38]

The following day the Co-operative Education Commission was
formally organized. The title "co-operative" had been suggested by
Montague as best expressing the spirit and purpose of the conference.
Dr. Mitchell was selected president of the commission, and Governor
Montague officiated as chairman of the executive board. As chairman, Montague presided at the morning session of the commission,
which adopted a program of principles. The first plank accepted, one
for a nine-month school term, aroused some dissension, notably from
Attorney General Anderson, who felt that eight months was a sufficiently long period. The second plank, "a high school within reasonable distance of every child," also provoked spirited debate. The remaining planks of the platform were adopted with little discussion.
They included such objectives as well-trained teachers, efficient supervision, the introduction of industrial training (Montague's favorite
objective), the promotion of libraries, and the organization of an
educational association in every county and city. This statement of
principles was to serve as the central theme for literally hundreds of
speeches to follow.[39]

Throughout the remainder of 1904 the Co-operative Education
Commission successfully endeavored to establish local branch
"leagues" throughout the state. And on December 6 and 7 it held the
first of its annual conferences at the First Baptist Church in Norfolk.
There it was resolved to ask Governor Montague and President
Alderman, newly elected head of the University of Virginia, to conduct "a thorough tour of the State next May in the interest of better
education." Montague and Alderman accepted the invitation, thereby
encouraging the commission to make ambitious plans for an intensified crusade; the result was the extravagant May campaign of 1905.[40]

Aiming at an "all-day meeting in every county" during the month

---

38 C. W. Dabney, *Universal Education in the South*, II, 323–34; Richmond
News Leader, March 28, 1904.
39 Underhill, "The Ogden Movement," 67; Richmond *News Leader*, March 29,
1904.
40 C. W. Dabney, *Universal Education in the South*, II, 324; Richmond *Times
Dispatch*, Dec. 7 and 8, 1904.

of May, the commission enlisted as speakers hundreds of school officials, ministers, and politicians. The May campaign coincided oppor-
tunely with the torrid political campaigns of 1905; and the "militant,
aggressive, and proselyting" spirit of the educators aroused public enthusiasm to such a pitch that legislative candidates were forced either
to endorse the movement publicly or risk possible defeat.[41] Even
Senator Martin reluctantly consented to make a few educational addresses, though in a letter to Alderman he voiced his suspicion that
the decision to ask Montague to lead the May campaign had been the
work of a "political schemer. . . . I do not even now feel entirely
satisfied as to the wisdom of the proposed canvass." Further, Martin
charged that "a great deal of 'hot air' has been passing round for
some years in relation to the betterment of the schools. I have failed
to see from any of those leading in this agitation any practical and
tangible suggestion whereby the schools may be better with the funds
now available or whereby additional funds may be provided." Should
local taxation be increased to improve public schools, Martin warned,
this would "not likely . . . prove beneficial to the University of Virginia," which Alderman headed.[42]

J. D. Eggleston, then a candidate for election as state superintendent of schools, observed that most of the politicians, like Martin, at
first resented the efforts of educators to inject the issue of schools into
the campaign; the people, they believed, were apathetic to education:

> But the politicians did not know the real heart-hunger of the people
> for better schools. . . . In a week after our campaign started the
> people were flocking to our meetings, and neglecting the political
> meetings. . . . The politicians now came on the run, begging that
> they might be permitted to take part in our meetings and make
> speeches in behalf of public education. They now became fervid in
> behalf of schools. I think that most of them believed that the interest
> would soon die down. . . . They did not realize what forces had been
> turned loose.[43]

The tremendous enthusiasm generated by the May campaign truly
represented a fulfillment, an apex, of the agitation begun four years
earlier. Over 300 addresses were delivered at 108 meetings in 94

---

41 S. C. Mitchell to Montague, Jan. 12, 1905, and a circular of the Co-
    operative Education Commission, Jan. 9, 1905, Montague Papers; Rich-
    mond *Times Dispatch,* Dec. 18, 1904.
42 Harlan, *Separate and Unequal,* 152–53; Underhill, "The Ogden Move-
    ment," 77.
43 Quoted in C. W. Dabney, *Universal Education in the South,* II, 327.

counties of the state. Two hundred thousand pages of educational literature were distributed, and fifty citizen school associations were organized. The public was aroused as never before to the necessity for higher state appropriations, for higher local tax rates, for higher salaries, for higher standards. In glowing terms Montague could observe in his 1906 address to the legislature, "There has been a greater popular interest taken in public education in the past four years than perhaps in the entire history of the State." [44]

The May campaign soon produced practical results. Eggleston, using the promises he and others had elicited from legislative candidates during the election campaign, almost forced the 1906 Assembly to enact several progressive pieces of legislation. The most far-reaching was the Mann high school bill, which provided $50,000 in state funds on a matching basis to any county that wished to establish a high school. As a result, the number of high schools in the state increased at the rate of 100 a year, from 75 in 1906 to 360 in 1910.[45]

The 1908 legislature continued the trend of its predecessor, passing a teacher pension law and creating two new state normal colleges, at Harrisonburg and at Fredericksburg. In addition, counties were now allowed to consolidate their school systems to obtain full-time superintendents, a move that was vehemently opposed by most politicians. Finally, the Assembly enacted the type of law Montague had suggested two years earlier, allowing compulsory attendance regulations on a local option basis. From 1905 to 1911 total school funds, both state and local, more than doubled. The average school term was increased to seven months. Consolidation of schools continued unabated.

The Ogden movement produced similar results throughout the South. From 1900 to 1913 Southern school expenditures rose from twenty-one to seventy-one millions of dollars. Between 1900 and 1910 total illiteracy fell from 27 to 18 per cent of the population, and the average school term was extended an additional twenty-five days. Normal schools were established, and teacher standards were raised. Consolidation of rural schools proceeded rapidly. Tennessee, North Carolina, Arkansas, and Louisiana, like Virginia, wrote optional

---

44 Heatwole, *History of Education in Virginia,* 315; Underhill, "The Ogden Movement," 95; Richmond *News Leader,* Jan. 10, 1906.

45 Overton, "Life of Eggleston," 229; Underhill, "The Ogden Movement," 98–99; Byron M. Flory, "The Development of Secondary Education in Virginia" (M.A. thesis, University of Virginia, 1925), 51; C. W. Dabney, *Universal Education in the South,* II, 329.

compulsory education provisions into their statutes. The practical accomplishments achieved in nearly every Southern state stamp the education crusade as the most successful phase of the Southern progressive movement. Yet much remained to be accomplished. In the words of Ogden, the founder of the movement: "The results achieved would read like a romance; the undone margin to be covered is terrible to contemplate." [46]

Virginia had responded to the Ogden movement even more quickly than did most Southern states. This can be attributed to several factors. First, Virginia enjoyed the greatest per capita wealth of the Southern states and was better able to meet the need for increased educational expenditure. Second, the Ogden movement coincided with the reform atmosphere of the state's constitutional convention of 1901–1902. Finally, the Ogden movement also coincided with Montague's gubernatorial election. Having emphasized the need for better schools in his 1897 and 1901 campaigns, Montague had helped provide the necessary spadework for the crusade which followed. Cooperating with Virginia's educational leaders, he helped supervise the formation of an effective state organization which successfully directed the Virginia phase of the Ogden movement to its climax in the May campaign. By contributing his eloquent oratory, he lent the crusade the prestige of his position. So frequently, in fact, did he function as a spokesman for education that he was criticized in the 1905 senatorial campaign for neglecting the regular duties of his office. The *Times Dispatch* ridiculed such criticism: "He has met every obligation of his office conscientiously and courageously . . . he has done a public service going from place to place making speeches in the interest of public schools, good roads, good government . . . good morals." [47]

Montague's close cooperation with the Southern Education Board ironically served to embarrass that board's relations with his successor and political enemy, Claude A. Swanson. Swanson, though he himself vigorously pushed a program of educational improvement, took pains not to credit Montague and the Ogden forces with laying the groundwork. The Swanson regime, claimed Alderman, was "perfectly aware that much of the intense educational enthusiasm was due to the work of this [Co-operative Education] Association, backed by

---

46 Woodward, *Origins of the New South*, 405–406; Simkins, *The South Old and New*, 274; Wilson, *Robert C. Ogden*, 227.
47 Richmond *Times Dispatch*, April 14, 1905.

this [Southern Education] Board and fostered and encouraged by Montague." They intended to excel Montague and his group, but by appealing to local pride, not by soliciting the aid of outside forces. Ogden also diagnosed the reason for Swanson's (and Martin's) coolness as partisan pique:

> It has been made public that many of us in the Board were personal sympathizers with Governor Montague in his contest for the Senate, and it is now thrown back upon the Board that it has been in politics as the friend of Governor Montague. This is, of course, unreasonable. It, however, has the foundation in fact that we were personally friendly to Montague. We could not have been otherwise; he was so much more than a politician in his cooperation with the work of the Board.[48]

Montague filled an important position in the Virginia phase of the Ogden movement. As governor of the state, he served as the most prominent proponent of that movement in its embryonic stages. He became a mouthpiece, a spokesman, articulating the objectives of the professional educators and arousing the latent interest and concern of the populace. True, the campaign would undoubtedly have achieved ultimate fruition without his endorsement, and irony would have it that concrete results of the crusade came during his successor's term of office. But he had made significant contributions in laying the foundation upon which such phenomenal advances were later made. His pioneering role is perhaps best described in his own words: "When I first spoke for a better public school system . . . I was as one crying in the wilderness, and now I hear voices of sympathy and support all about me." [49]

48 Quoted in Harlan, *Separate and Unequal,* 156–57.
49 Richmond *Times Dispatch,* July 19, 1905.

XI

GOOD ROADS

IF Montague's advocacy of better schools constituted his most important contribution as governor, his concurrent espousal of better roads was scarely less important. During his four-year term of office he conducted a personal campaign to improve Virginia's highways, thereby bringing economic, social, and educational betterment to the Commonwealth. Unlike the crusade for better schools, the movement for good roads at first did not enjoy the support of a corps of organized supporters; nor did it arouse, initially, a groundswell of popular response. By comparison this campaign was a lonely one for Montague, and the success which attended his efforts was even more a personal triumph. With roads as with schools, in the period from 1901 through 1906 there developed a widespread public recognition of the state's deficiencies; this period also witnessed the first effective steps taken to remedy those deficiencies. In both the school and road crusades, Montague's role was one of a promoter, an agitator, a harbinger. In both crusades, he served as a leading spokesman for a new Virginia.

Montague himself placed the two movements for good schools and good roads on an equal plane: "Two things of supreme moment are needed by this State—the improvement of her highways and the improvement of her public schools. If these two agencies of our civilization could be brought to an efficient standard we would in a few years witness marvellous changes for the better." He looked upon transportation facilities as one measure of a civilization's vitality; all great civilizations, he declared more than once, left durable highways as monuments to their creativeness. "The statesmanship of our country seems to have neglected our common public highways," he complained. "Virginia is behind many of her sister States, and the American States are far behind England and Europe." [1]

Montague's preoccupation with Virginia's need for improved roads had its origin in his youthful days at Inglewood. Unserviced by railroads, his Tidewater homeland was particularly hampered by inadequate highways. When the budding lawyer later moved to Danville, he found the situation not much better. Railroad connections there afforded access to the state's largest cities, but the necessary country travels of the small-town lawyer were frequently made over dirt lanes, or made not at all during rainy periods.[2]

In reaction to these conditions Montague proposed as early as 1892 a government program of road construction as the best means to render country life more comfortable and attractive, thus lessening the alarming exodus of population from rural areas to the growing congestion of urban centers. He estimated that Virginia's rural roads were impassable half the year, constituting a "social and industrial blockade against the rural home and rural pursuits." To remedy the situation he urged that "so far as the government can lessen these disparities or equalize these ameliorations it is manifest that to this end its powers should be exerted." [3] Later, during his 1897 campaign for attorney general and in the legislative campaigns of 1899 Montague repeatedly advocated better roads for the Commonwealth, arguing that the state's prosperity was "concomitant with good highways." [4] His incorporation of road improvement as a primary objective in his 1901 gubernatorial campaign was thus no new emphasis on his part.

Despite the early attempts by Montague and others to arouse public concern for the state's wretched road conditions, the scene in 1901 showed little improvement from that a half-century earlier. The Staunton *Daily News* wryly observed, "And we still go on, as did our

1 Montague to H. B. Smith, April 11, 1903, and Montague to J. M. Smith, Feb. 10, 1904, Montague Papers.
2 Montague to Betsie Hoskins, Oct. 28, 1888, Moore Collection.
3 *Address of A. J. Montague, Esq. William and Mary College, June 29, 1892, passim,* Montague Papers.
4 Richmond *Times,* Oct. 5, 1897; unidentified clippings, scrapbook, Montague Papers.

ancestors before us, scraping the dirt from the sides and piling it in the center, ready to be washed back by two or three heavy rains." The hard-surfaced Shenandoah Valley turnpike had proved an unqualified success, yet the rest of the state had not benefited by the example. "Mud, mud, mud, and double mud is all the go now," commented one editor after a particularly hard winter. The phrase was applicable to practically every road in the state.[5]

Since 1865 Virginia had followed the policy of absolute local control in the construction and maintenance of her public roads. A law passed in 1869 provided for a property tax dedicated to roads of only ten cents on the hundred dollars, to be paid either in money or labor. In 1894 this tax was limited to between five and twenty-five cents, the rate to be levied at the discretion of the county board of supervisors. There was no central direction of road construction, and no uniform plan for state aid.[6]

About 1890 a nationwide movement for better roads developed. Leagues and associations of all kinds made their appearance, and a national *Good Roads* magazine was initiated. The first good roads convention in Virginia, held in Richmond in 1894, agreed to form a state association. But despite persistent agitation in such journals as the Richmond *Dispatch,* enthusiasm soon waned. Isolated examples of road improvement could be found, and occasional road conventions were held, but by 1897 the *Dispatch* could see few practical results. Not until 1902 did the state experience a revived interest.[7]

Montague had helped condition the state to renewed activity. During his 1901 campaign for governor he had repeatedly advocated better roads. Later, in his inaugural address, he noted the declining conditions of Virginia agriculture, and laid the blame to the

> condition of our public roads. . . . In many of our counties from two to three months in the winter season our roads are a social and industrial blockade. This blockade should be raised. . . . We have spent in the past five years about $2,000,000 upon the public roads, but this great sum has been of no appreciable good. . . . We should at least start a good road in every county which now has none. . . . Words are inadequate to express my sense of the importance of this subject.[8]

5 Staunton *Daily News,* Jan. 24 and 30, March 14, 1903.
6 Susie C. Palmer, "The Development of Virginia Highways" (M.A. thesis, University of Virginia, 1930), Chap. 1, p. 10.
7 Palmer, "Virginia Highways," Chap. 1, pp. 12–13; Richmond *Dispatch,* May 18, 1897, April 26, 1899; broadside, May 11, 1895, Epes-Kilmartin Papers.
8 Quoted in Richmond *Evening Leader,* Jan. 1, 1902.

In the interim between his January inauguration and the convening of the legislature in February, Montague journeyed to Charleston, South Carolina, to attend the national convention of the Good Roads Association, hoping to obtain ideas and suggestions for his forthcoming address to the legislature. When he made the address on February 20, his most important recommendation was for a state highway commission: "No house can be built without a mechanic . . . and no highway without efficient and scientific control." Montague suggested that a commissioner of public highways be established with powers of investigation, supervision, and control over all major state highways in order to assure coordinated planning and methodical construction.[9]

Concerning the financing of road construction and maintenance, which would be supervised by a state commission, Montague suggested three possible plans:

> The first is a county tax to be levied solely for road-building; the second, the issuance by counties, upon the guarantee of the State, of long-term bonds, the proceeds from which to be applied to road constructions . . . and the third, the State aid plan, by which the State undertakes to appropriate a given sum of money . . . upon the condition that the county supplement the sum. . . . It is not my province to frame a bill. This duty devolves upon you.[10]

In his message to the legislature Montague also endorsed a proposal (then widely advocated throughout the South) to work convicts on the public highways.[11] Many Southerners viewed this as both an expedient and humane solution to the prison problem—an alternative to the brutal convict lease system. Montague felt that the establishment of convict labor forces would not only afford a cheap means of road construction but would also relieve the congestion of the state penitentiary, thus improving the health of the prisoners. Besides penitentiary convicts, he suggested that tramps, vagrants, and certain other jail prisoners be employed "either in the preparation of road material or in construction."

Montague's road recommendations elicited wide applause from the state press. Many citizens shared with the governor a conviction that a

9 *Ibid.*, Feb. 7 and 20, 1902.
10 *Ibid.*, Feb. 20, 1902. Privately, Montague favored the state-aid plan; he most desired, however, the establishment of a highway commission. Montague to J. M. Barker, Sept. 2, 1902, Montague Papers.
11 See Jane Zimmerman, "The Penal Reform Movement in the South During the Progressive Era, 1890–1917," *Journal of Southern History*, XVII (1951), 462–92.

road campaign should complement the school crusade then developing. Construction of hard-surfaced roads would encourage a higher school attendance, especially in the winter months, and good transportation would also make school consolidations more feasible.[12]

Although the legislature as a whole was not particularly enthusiastic, several attempts were made to enact Montague's recommendations. In early 1902 a bill was introduced providing a comprehensive system for the improvement of roads, the chief feature of which was the establishment of a highway commission to consist of the governor, the commissioner of agriculture, and a state engineer. The bill also provided that all improvement or construction of "what are denominated as State roads" would have to be approved in advance by the commission. One per cent of the public revenues was to be set aside for highway construction; "through" highways were to receive state aid for maintenance at the annual rate of six dollars a mile. Finally, all vagrants and prisoners in county jails could be sentenced to work on the roads or be hired to other counties for that purpose.[13]

After a spirited two-day debate on the measure, in mid-March the House of Delegates by the narrow margin of thirty-seven to thirty-three registered its disapproval.[14] Ironically, a good roads convention, one of four held in Virginia during the early spring of 1902, assembled in Richmond just one day following this adverse vote by the house. Sponsored by the Southern Railway in cooperation with the national Good Roads Association and the United States Office of Public Road Inquiries, these conventions had as their object practical demonstrations of roadbuilding. A "good roads train," consisting of "fifteen car loads of modern machinery, expert operators, engineers, and road builders," traveled throughout the South between October, 1901, and April, 1902, stopping at eighteen different points to construct small sections of roads according to the most modern methods. Any community that desired an object-lesson road paid only the actual expenses for materials involved. Good roads conventions were arranged at each of the cities on the itinerary by W. H. Moore, presi-

12   Richmond *Evening Leader*, Feb. 7, March 20, 1902; Overton, "Life of Eggleston," 172.
13   Richmond *Evening Leader*, Feb. 28, 1902.
14   *Ibid.*, March 17 and 19, 1902. One of the proponents, Charles T. Lassiter, represented a different political faction, yet Montague recognized his prominence in the good roads movement by appointing him a delegate to various national road conventions. Lassiter to Montague, April 20, 1903, in Charles T. Lassiter Papers, Duke University library, Durham, N.C.

dent of the Good Roads Association, to capitalize on the public interest aroused by this construction. The Southern Railway, of course, hoped to encourage economic development and commercial interchange.[15]

In Virginia the good roads train visited Lynchburg, Danville, Richmond, and Charlottesville. First organizing a good roads group in Lynchburg, the entourage next moved on to Danville, where, from March 8 through March 13, it macadamized a section of the city streets. The customary convention, held there on March 13 and 14, heard Montague, one of several speakers, strongly champion the good roads movement in the state, and a resolution adopted near the end of the session applauded "the attitude taken by Governor Montague on the question of road improvement," and urged the legislature to carry out his recommendations.[16]

From Danville the train traveled to Richmond, where a week was spent paving sections of Floyd Avenue. Featuring addresses by Moore, Congressman John Lamb, and Senator Daniel, the convention on March 21 and 22 organized a statewide Virginia Good Roads Association and adopted resolutions calling for state aid to local highway construction.[17]

Montague, in a "highly interesting" address, had opened the Richmond convention by appealing strongly for a centralized system of road administration, asking "that he be given a chance to sign his name to a good roads law for the people of the Commonwealth." In answer to those who charged that the governor would obtain excessive patronage through the establishment of a state highway commission, Montague said he was willing to let the professors of the state appoint the state engineer if that were necessary to obtain passage of the bill defeated by the House of Delegates. He urged those in attendance first to arouse public sentiment and "then go after the Legislature." If the public demanded it, the legislature would be compelled to enact favorable laws.[18]

15 Martin Dodge, *Road Conventions in the Southern States and Object-Lesson Roads* (Washington, 1902), 3–4, Daniel Papers; Palmer, "Virginia Highways," Chap. 1, pp. 13–14; Bruce, *The New South*, 303.
16 Dodge, *Road Conventions in the Southern States*, 81–86.
17 *Ibid.*, 87.
18 Richmond *Evening Leader*, March 20, 1902. Montague also addressed the convention held in Charlottesville; at that convention's conclusion a resolution was adopted extending "thanks to the Hon. A. J. Montague . . . for his patriotic efforts to secure a good roads law for the State." Dodge, *Road Conventions in the Southern States*, 88.

The good roads train, which continued to Charlottesville before leaving Virginia, thus added considerable momentum to the slowly generating campaign for better roads. Much the same effect was felt throughout the South. The Virginia legislature, however, reacted slowly. The day after Montague made his appeal to the Richmond convention, the house voted down by narrow margins attempts to substitute a new road bill in place of the recently defeated measure.[19] The following year, efforts to obtain road legislation were renewed when Delegate H. C. Rice introduced a bill "to establish a highway commission of Virginia, to prescribe its duties and to make an appropriation for the same." This bill gave a highway commission only advisory powers, placing the services of the state engineer at the disposal of local authorities if requested. A News Leader editorial criticized the bill as not strong enough, but "the best that can be done at this session." The paper was overly optimistic, for in April, 1903, the house rejected even this relatively mild measure, 33 to 24; "the town and city members supported, the country opposed." [20]

True to his generally consistent standard of behavior, Montague had evidently taken little part in these legislative maneuvers other than to make his initial recommendations and furnish Assemblymen with information when requested. Delegate Rice, the bill's patron, later wrote the governor complaining that he, Montague, had made no attempt to influence the legislature to accept the bill: "I expected your sympathy, as I knew you were a Good Road man." Montague replied, "My position as Governor prevents my interceding with members of the Legislature in behalf of any measure. . . . The Martin supporters would never enact such a law during my administration." [21] Montague had close friends in the Assembly; Rice evidently was not one of them. Other unapparent factors may explain his failure to deal with Rice. Still, the episode is indicative of Montague's seeming reluctance to become embroiled in the rough and tumble of everyday politics—especially to tangle with an Assembly in which he placed no great confidence.

Within one year the house had thus defeated two attempts to establish a highway commission, the keystone of Montague's proposal.

19   C. T. Lassiter to J. E. West, May 22, 1902, C. T. Lassiter Papers.
20   Richmond *Dispatch*, Jan. 15, 1903; Richmond *News Leader*, April 20, 1903; C. T. Lassiter to W. F. Baugh, Nov. 19, 1903, C. T. Lassiter Papers.
21   Richmond *News Leader*, April 22, 1903; Rice to Montague, March 9, 1905, and Montague to Rice, March 13, 1905, Montague Papers.

One of the opponents of both attempts had been Delegate H. A. Edmondson, a Martin man from Halifax. This same man, however, authored another bill which would have complied with several of Montague's secondary recommendations, namely, to establish convict road gangs and to grant counties the right to issue bonds for road construction. The house approved Edmondson's bill in April, 1903. The Senate Committee on Counties, Cities, and Towns thereupon took the bill under advisement.[22]

On April 23, the committee listened patiently to four long hours of testimony. The chief objection to the bill was voiced by the Davis Boot and Shoe Company, which held a contract with the penitentiary for the services of its prisoners. Made in 1898 and good for fifteen years, the contract stipulated that the penitentiary would annually furnish the Davis Company the labor of one thousand prisoners at the rate of forty-two cents a day for men, and thirty-five cents for women. By making the agreement, the state had hoped to relieve itself of a major expense, a hope that was realized when the prison subsequently showed a profit, not a deficit. But now that other uses were envisaged for the convicts, the contract became an obstacle. Montague had early inquired of Attorney General Anderson if it legally could be broken, and the reply had been negative.[23]

The senate committee voted to stand by the contract. Rejecting the provision of the Edmondson bill for employment of convicts on the roads, it retained only the article authorizing the issuance of county road bonds. As amended, the bill finally passed the senate in December, 1903, and after much delay the house acquiesced to the senate's version in February, 1904.[24]

The bill as enacted can hardly be termed a clear-out victory for the good roads crusaders. When Montague addressed the newly elected 1904 Assembly, he again appealed for the objective he most desired, an effective highway commission: "Our indifferent public highways are a hindrance to the growth of our rural population and a bar to immigration. . . . A systematic construction and maintenance . . . should be begun . . . as early as practicable." Though initially en-

22 Richmond *News Leader,* April 24, 1903; C. T. Lassiter to H. A. Edmondson, March 12, 1903, C. T. Lassiter Papers.
23 Magruder, *Recent Administration in Virginia,* 110–11; Montague to Anderson, Feb. 12, 1902, Montague Papers; Richmond *News Leader,* April 24, 1903.
24 Staunton *Daily News,* May 1, 1903; Richmond *News Leader,* Dec. 21, 1903, Feb. 4, 1904.

couraged by the attitude of the new Assembly (elections had been
held in November, 1903), after a month of inaction Montague reluctantly confided to a friend:

> I fear the present Legislature is not inclined to enact any legislation
> upon this [highway commission] subject. Public sentiment will have to
> be thoroughly aroused before any action is taken; but I look for this
> at no distant date. I have recommended . . . many plans, and espe-
> cially that now operative in New Jersey, and have talked with members
> of the legislature personally and advised them where information upon
> the subject could be obtained.

Montague's efforts were unavailing. The legislature adjourned in
March, 1904, without taking action on his requests. Victory was
again postponed.[25]

Defeated in its ultimate objective—legislation by the Assembly—
the Virginia good roads movement failed to take solid root. The
March, 1902, Richmond convention which Montague addressed had
formed a permanent organization in the state Good Roads Association. Early in 1903 this group sent a circular letter to every prominent
person in every city and county of the state, urging the formation of
local associations and the construction of sections of "object-lesson"
surfaced highways. Probably as a result of these efforts, several local
organizations sprang into existence. In March, 1903, a group of Harrisonburg citizens met, established an organization, and appointed a
committee to draft a road bill for presentation to the legislature. A
similar group formed in Albemarle County. The militant Staunton
Daily News asked, "Why does Augusta dally?" [26]

Though several local groups were formed, the Richmond-backed
association failed to generate a groundswell of statewide support. The
hostility of the Assembly to effective legislation was undoubtedly a
discouraging factor. Yet tangible progress was lacking, even on a
local level. In January of 1904 a Richmond paper observed, "In Virginia the masses of the people are ready and willing to spend their
money for good roads. They lack leadership and definite plans . . .
each county fighting on its own hook." [27]

Montague received many invitations, some of which he accepted,

25 Richmond *News Leader,* Jan. 13, 1904; Montague to C. T. Harris, Feb. 19,
    1904, Montague Papers.
26 Staunton *Daily News,* March 18, 21, and 31, 1903.
27 Richmond *News Leader,* Jan. 27, 1904.

to speak at local good roads rallies, but there existed no central direction, no coordination, no practical result. In January, 1904, the governor spoke in Louisa; August found him in King and Queen; November in Loudoun. The *News Leader* praised Montague for his role as good roads ambassador: "We are convinced that Governor Montague was thoroughly honest and earnest in pledging his efforts for this cause, but he has been unable to accomplish results, although he never has failed to direct the attention of the legislature and people to the subject. He ran against a snag in the unwillingness of the people of the counties to move for local special road taxes." The same paper lamented that "when it comes to the road question our record is one of humiliating failure and backwardness. We have held meetings and 'resoluted' . . . hot air galore . . . yet virtually done nothing, except in one or two counties." [28]

The picture was not quite so dark as described. The spring of 1905 saw a new spurt of activity, a new enthusiasm. The four years of spadework had not been in vain. In January, 1905, a particularly enthusiastic good roads convention met in Danville, "the first of a series to be held throughout Virginia." This convention led in the formation of a new statewide organization, having as its aim the formation of good roads clubs in every county. Subsequently, rallies were held throughout the state.[29]

The 1905 legislative elections gave impetus to this increased activity. The good roads campaign of 1905 may not have been as intensive as the May campaign for education, but in a sense it was similar. By first creating a popular dissatisfaction with Virginia's poor road system, then injecting the issue into the elections, the campaign forced individual candidates to take definite positions in the controversy. Road conventions were not held in every county, but such conventions were evidently numerous enough to demonstrate a popular mandate. Even Senator Martin, who had never advocated national road legislation in his ten-year Senate tenure, announced, in his campaign for reelection, his support for federal aid to public highways—a stand his opponent, Montague, had taken as early as 1901. In that same contest, Montague himself contributed greatly to the good roads crusade by criticizing the Martin-dominated legislature for obstructing his road program. Such criticism, often re-

28 *Ibid.,* Jan. 28, Aug. 25, Nov. 11, 1904, Jan. 12 and 16, 1905.
29 *Ibid.,* Feb. 1 and 14, March 28, 1905.

peated, forced the legislators even closer to the mirror of public opinion.[30]

After the elections were over, the new legislature met in Richmond in January, 1906. In his address Montague made his customary recommendation favoring a highway commission; however, this time he was more specific. The commission, he said, should consist of not one but three engineers—one from the University of Virginia and one from either Virginia Military Institute or Virginia Polytechnic Institute. These two, who would serve without compensation, would then select the salaried third member. To facilitate the actual process of road construction, Montague again suggested that a convict labor force be established. He also reiterated his support of a state-aid plan whereby the county or city would match the state money dollar for dollar. He suggested that $100,000 be appropriated for this purpose.[31]

Following his address Montague privately predicted that the 1906 Assembly would follow the examples of its predecessors in taking no action on his recommendations. He never made a more erroneously pessimistic forecast. Within two months the Assembly had established a Virginia State Highway Commission quite similar to the one he had recommended. The terms of the act provided for a commission composed of three professors of civil engineering from the state's universities, who would in turn select a state highway commissioner "to gather and tabulate information and statistics on road building, maintenance and improvement, and to disseminate the same." The commission would supervise construction and repair of main roads and could recommend needed improvements to local road authorities. The act also created convict road gangs, which were made available to counties upon application to the commission. Regular penitentiary employees were to guard the convicts, and the state would pay the expense of shelter and food. (By 1908 the superintendent of the penitentiary reported that not enough convicts were available to supply the demand.)[32]

Montague had witnessed a remarkable shift from public apathy to

30 Richmond *Times Dispatch,* July 7, 1905; Richmond *Evening Leader,* March 20, 1902; Montague to W. H. Carrington, March 28, 1903, and Montague to Eugene Pendleton, March 9, 1905, Montague Papers.
31 Richmond *News Leader,* Jan. 8, 1906.
32 Montague to D. A. Withcar, Jan. 23, 1906, Montague Papers; Rudyard B. Goode, "The Distribution and Disposition of Highway Funds in Virginia" (Ph.D. dissertation, University of Virginia, 1953), 18–19.

public enthusiasm, a transformation partly attributable to his own efforts. The educational crusade had enjoyed the active sponsorship of several prominent Virginians. The good roads movement had no such wealth of talent. With the possible exception of the state's press, Montague was the movement's most prominent and persistent advocate.

His reputation was nationwide. Moore, president of the national Good Roads Association, had been favorably impressed with Montague's zeal at the 1902 Virginia conventions. He later corresponded frequently with the governor, entrusting him with the responsibility of guiding the Virginia phase of the national campaign. Moore invited Montague several times to make addresses at national conventions of the Good Roads Association. On one occasion Montague journeyed to Florida to accept such an invitation; the others he was forced to decline. He also accepted Moore's offer of a position on the National Advisory Committee for the association, although he regretted that he could not serve actively.[33] As in his educational campaign, then, Montague's recognition and reputation had extended beyond the state's boundaries. Though the term was never applied, he could well have been dubbed Virginia's first "good roads" governor, as well as her first "educational governor."

Montague, not usually a boastful man, abandoned all reserve in estimating his contribution to the Virginia phase of the good roads movement. "The records will show that I have done more to bring the people to realize the wretched condition of our roads than all the influence combined in Virginia for the past twenty-five years," he asserted in 1905.[34] When the 1908 Assembly enacted a state money-aid law appropriating $250,000 annually on a matching basis for the counties Montague's 1906 recommendations reached full fruition. As in the parallel campaign for better schools, the rich harvest began after he left office. Yet Montague had helped clear the paths which became highways.

---

33 Montague to W. H. Moore, March 7, Oct. 13, 1903, Montague Papers; Richmond *News Leader,* Feb. 2, 1904.
34 Montague to E. W. Smith, March 9, 1905, Montague Papers.

XII

---•---

THE PRIMARY
BECOMES A REALITY

MONTAGUE's actions as governor were motivated by both personal and public considerations. Essentially, his concern was an unselfish one, an interest in the well-being of his state and her people. Indeed, during his term of office he occasionally assumed an almost priestly role in addressing religious gatherings on the duties of "Christian citizenship." In advocating good schools he sought to give to each child an equal opportunity to prove his capacity. In advocating good roads he sought to benefit the material and social welfare of every citizen. In fighting the Martin machine he sought to free government from rule by partisian cliques.

And yet as governor he was also concerned with his own political future. In fighting to destroy the Martin machine, he fought especially to advance his own career. In championing moves to deprive the Virginia legislature of its time-honored right to elect United States senators, he did so with particular urgency, knowing that his own chances of election by that legislature were meager. Thus, both to bring about popular participation in government and to promote his personal career, Montague endeavored to establish the direct senatorial primary in Virginia. Due partially to his efforts, by 1904 the primary system had been accepted by almost all segments of the Virginia Democracy.

The origins of the primary crusade in Virginia reach back to the decade of the 1890's. State after state, especially in the South, adopted the reform around the turn of the century. Opposed bitterly by politicians, machine men, and conservatives generally, in Virginia the primary had been rejected by the state Democratic convention of 1897, by the state Democratic committee in 1899, and by the General Assembly on several occasions. It had received tentative adoption by the same 1901 Norfolk convention that had nominated Montague for governor, but for several years after this adoption the primary was still considered experimental. Politicians and legislators did not take easily to the new-fangled device. From 1902 to 1904 the office-holding clique made their last serious effort to retain the old system, to stave off the increasing demand for popular participation in popular government.

The 1901 Norfolk convention had left to the state committee the details of a primary system. A subcommittee, dominated by Montague's friends, subsequently met at State Chairman Ellyson's home to implement the instructions. As finally adopted, the committee's regulations made primary elections mandatory not only for the selection of Democratic senatorial nominees (results to be binding on Democratic legislators), but also for all Democratic candidates for national or statewide office. Voting would be viva voce, and individual candidates were assessed the cost of the primary. This system, first utilized in the 1902 congressional elections, generally gave "the utmost satisfaction," though most voters found the viva voce feature somewhat embarrassing.[1]

Still, the primary faced an uncertain future. In November, 1902, the Richmond *Evening Leader* frankly speculated that should the primary be discontinued, Democratic legislators would still select the U.S. Senator in 1905: "Senator Martin's warmest supporters make no endeavor to conceal their opposition to the new primary system, and some of them say openly that they will seek to break it down before the contest is fought out." Congressman Flood, Martin's close ally, complained that a primary encouraged personal animosities, caused party cleavage, and destroyed county and city organizations: "Without having anything to do the committees of the county or city, the men who do the fighting when there is real fighting to be done, will lose interest." Another complaint against the primary was the expense levied on the candidates; one legislator charged that it excluded men of "moderate means" from office.[2]

1 Richmond *Evening Leader*, Jan. 15, Sept. 12, 1902.
2 *Ibid.*, Nov. 27, 1902; Richmond *News*, Aug. 9, 1902, in scrapbook, Martin

Montague viewed the opposition to the primary with concern; he had tentatively endorsed the primary as early as 1897 and had warmly advocated it in the "May movement" of 1899. His gubernatorial campaign of 1901 had helped make the primary possible; yet he realized that the next Democratic state convention, if dominated by Martin's forces, could abolish the primary as easily as it had been adopted. As early as November, 1901, Montague voiced his fear to William A. Jones that Martin was "exceedingly active . . . to so load down the primary plan as to make it . . . offensive." And when Martin later publicly stated that a primary "ought to have a just and fair trial," an unconvinced Montague remarked privately: "You will observe by the headlines of this morning's Times-Dispatch that Martin comes out for the primary; but when you read the article you will notice he says he is not personally antagonistic to it. This means that he will not personally oppose it, but will stay in the background and let his friends fight it." The hostility expressed publicly by many in the Martin-dominated legislature seemed to confirm Montague's suspicions.[3]

To avert the possibility of the 1904 state Democratic convention's abandoning the primary, Montague privately urged several legislators to enact a statute on the subject. Writing to Delegate R. Walton Moore, he asked: "Do you not think the Legislature should pass a primary law? Unless this is done I am afraid it may be repealed . . . with the exception of some little crudities, the system has given satisfaction." In addition to guaranteeing the primary's perpetuity, a statute, Montague felt, would bring the primary more closely under the state's general election laws—at least theoretically prohibiting corruption and graft.[4]

Montague was not alone in favoring a primary law. The 1901 Norfolk convention's resolution directing the erection of a primary system had also called for the enactment by the General Assembly of a statute legalizing the primaries. Several bills were introduced soon thereafter, but the first serious Assembly action on primary legislation was delayed until May, 1903, when Senator Barksdale of Halifax introduced a bill which would have preserved the local electoral unit in

Papers; Richmond *Dispatch,* Jan. 22, 1903; Richmond *News Leader,* Feb. 2, April 9 and 13, 1903.

3 Montague to William A. Jones, Nov. 20, 1901, and Montague to A. H Clement, Sept. 11, 1903, Montague Papers; Richmond *Times Dispatch,* Sept. 11, 1903.

4 Montague to Moore, Oct. 26, 1902, Montague Papers.

a combination primary-convention system. Local primaries would elect delegates to a state or district convention, and each locality would be bound by the unit rule. Congressmen Hay and Flood had secretly drafted Barksdale's bill, and in April of 1903 Flood had blandly informed Martin, "I'm going down to Richmond to pass the primary bill. If you're going to be there, let me see you." [5]

Montague had no use for Barksdale's bill, terming it a "primary abortion." Congressman Jones entertained the same opinion: by resurrecting the state convention, he believed, the bill would "work the repeal of our primary system." Both Jones and Montague feared that the bill represented the main move by Martin's forces to emasculate the primary without actually repealing it. Congressman John Rixey agreed, yet he cautioned that many in the Independent ranks considered the proposal a workable and satisfactory compromise.[6] However, opposition to the Barksdale bill on the part of most Independents and many Martin partisans as well, resulted in its rejection by the Assembly in December, 1903.

Montague had been concerned for some time that the legislature might undo the work of the 1901 convention. That fear spurred him to fervent activity during the campaign which preceded the November, 1903, elections to the General Assembly. (The new legislature would hold its first session in January, 1904.) Writing to Eppa Hunton as early as December, 1902, he enclosed a list of the state senators up for reelection, noting those who were opposed, neutral, or friendly to him personally and to his administration. Writing to Jones in March, 1903, he warned that we "must have a majority of the 19 Senators elected this fall in favor of a primary . . . otherwise it may be repealed." In the ensuing months he communicated with numerous friends throughout the state, endeavoring to "bring out" candidates against hostile incumbents.[7]

Montague's correspondents included familiar names: Glass, Jones, Moore, Tredway, Bowdoin, Rixey, and his old Indiantown friend, A. G. Willis. But the correspondence was extensive and not confined to politicos alone. Writing to Reverend Charles L. Corbett of North-

5 Richmond *News Leader,* May 15, 1903; Staunton *Daily News,* May 16, 1903; Henry D. Flood to William F. Rhea, April 15, 1903, and Flood to Martin, April 14, 1903, Flood Papers.
6 Montague to John F. Rixey, May 6, 1904; Montague to Camm Patteson, Nov. 28, 1903; Jones to Montague, Aug. 30, 1903; Rixey to Montague, May 5, 1904; all in Montague Papers.
7 Montague to Eppa Hunton, Dec. 1, 1902, and Montague to Jones, March 30, 1903, *ibid.*

ampton the governor urged persuasive tactics to win a local delegate
back from Martin's camp. To J. K. Fulton of Patrick (himself a candidate for a seat in the house) he suggested the entry of Sheriff Wool-
wine in the race for senator. From Bowdoin he asked assistance in a
fight against an incumbent, "if you can find it consistent with your
sense of duty." He enlisted Rixey's aid in the Eighth District by asserting that "the deplorable condition of our politics in this State results
almost wholly from Mr. Martin's control of the Legislature." If
Slaughter (a Culpeper resident) were a candidate, warned Montague,
his "position [on senatorial preference] should be made known, for
you will recall that Mr. Martin has a method of turning legislators
away from instructions and solemn pledges." For advice on the best
antimachine candidate in the Fluvanna region, Montague turned to
Henry St. George Tucker, who was then helping to organize Virginia's educational campaign. When Tucker suggested support for a
Colonel Scott, one of four candidates, Montague conveyed this recommendation to a Fluvanna supporter, John A. Twyman: "Do not
mention this as coming from me, for reasons which you will readily
appreciate. I am anxious that we may have in the General Assembly
a body of disinterested men who will not make war upon my administration at every step." [8]

Mixed success attended Montague's efforts. In Pittsylvania he
complained, "I seem to be unable to get my friends . . . to do anything and I have grown quite hopeless about the matter." Several of
the candidates he supported suffered defeat, among them A. H.
Clement, to whom he wrote: "I hoped for your election and believe
if the primary law [Barksdale's pure elections law] had been properly enforced you would have won out." And yet congratulations sent
to various individuals—S. S. Hurt, Camm Patteson, and J. Hunton
Wood—indicate that his efforts were not in vain. In writing to Carter
Glass on November 9, Montague commented: "Did the election returns in Virginia suit you? Upon the whole I think we have no right to
complain. Fulton, however . . . would have been elected but for the
knifing by the Martin people." [9]

8 Montague to Rev. Charles L. Corbett, April 21, 1903; Montague to J. K.
Fulton, April 16, 1903; Montague to J. W. Bowdoin, June 30, 1903; Montague to Rixey, May 20, 1903; Montague to Tucker, June 12, 1903; Tucker
to Montague, June 29, 1903; Montague to John A. Twyman, June 30,
1903; all *ibid.*
9 Montague to Tredway, July 6, 1903; Montague to A. H. Clement, Sept. 8,
1903; Montague to S. S. Hurt, Sept. 2, 1903; Montague to Camm Patteson,

The newly elected Assembly convened in Richmond in January of 1904. A freshman senator from Alexandria, Lewis H. Machen whom Montague had specifically urged to run during the 1903 elections, renewed the fight for a primary. His bill, introduced in January, not only proposed that the primary be made the mode of selection for all statewide offices, it also established effective means to supervise these elections—to provide for the honest administration Montague felt was lacking in Barksdale's Pure Elections Act. Perhaps the most important of these safeguards was the procedure proposed for selecting judges and clerks of election: to insure impartiality Machen suggested that the candidates themselves should nominate a board, which would in turn select the judges.[10]

The senate passed Machen's bill on March 10 by the close vote of 19 to 15. Two days later the house also passed the measure, but with an important amendment which deleted Machen's procedure for selecting judges. Instead of the candidates' making the selection, the county and city Democratic committees were entrusted with the responsibility. Though greatly disappointed, Machen urged the senate to concur in the amendments.[11]

The senate did not concur. The session was about to terminate and several Martin men seized the opportunity to talk the bill to death. Chief agents in the filibuster were Senators Barksdale and F. S. Tavenner. For two days they dominated the floor, forcing the senate to adjourn without taking final action. Barksdale blatantly proclaimed that he opposed the bill out of friendship for Martin, and antipathy to Montague.[12] Actually, though both Flood and Martin opposed the original Machen bill (probably because it removed their power over the selection of judges), they did not approve of the blustering tirade made by Barksdale. One correspondent commented sarcastically in a letter to Flood, "Don't you think Montague would cheerfully have given $1,000,000 to Barksdale for the fool speech he made in the Senate on Saturday?" [13]

Sept. 2, 1903; Montague to J. Hunton Wood, Sept. 8, 1903; Montague to Glass, Nov. 9, 1903; all *ibid.*
10 Montague to R. Walton Moore, May 4, 1903, *ibid.;* Richmond *News Leader,* Jan. 26, 1904.
11 Richmond *News Leader,* March 10 and 12, 1904.
12 *Ibid.,* March 14, 1904.
13 L. S. Marye to Flood, March 14, 1904, Flood Papers. To John O. Reynolds Flood commented (March 23, 1904, *ibid.*), "I was not in favor of the Mason [*sic*] bill and do not believe you or any of my friends . . . would

After Barksdale's coup, the *News Leader,* previously neutral in the Martin–Montague rivalry, tersely announced that "if Senator Martin represents opposition to nomination of all Democratic candidates by Democratic primaries, we shall fight Senator Martin." Though acquitting him of personally defeating the bill, the paper insisted that since Martin's election would mean the triumph of the Martin element, "and the triumph of the Martin element would mean the destruction or long postponement of the general primary system," Martin should either disavow or sustain the action of his declared friends in the Virginia legislature.[14]

In response to this needling Martin publicly declared that he had not so much as read the Machen bill, that he never discussed the subject with his legislative friends, and that ever since the 1901 Norfolk convention he had expressed a desire to see the primary plan have a just trial "and to see it improved and perfected." Upon this pronouncement the *News Leader* resumed its former position of "absolute neutrality" in the senatorial contest.[15]

That Martin was cognizant of Flood's earlier efforts to emasculate the primary by passing Barksdale's bill is evident. That he had opposed efforts to establish a primary in 1897 and 1899 is also manifest. Yet, in every pronouncement since 1897 he had carefully refrained from opposing a primary publicly; he consistently asserted that he would be willing to accept any mode of election adopted by the Democratic party. Although Martin personally opposed a primary (not only because it would relax the hold of his machine on state politics but because it might also mean his own defeat in 1905), as a practical politician he leaned with the wind. Reports circulating back to Washington from various local politicos revealed widespread popular support for the primary innovation.[16] Martin realized that to oppose the primary openly would be folly.

By early 1904 Montague sensed that Martin would not dare oppose a primary to the extent of completely abolishing it. His chief remaining fear was that the "Martin people, while pretending to favor the primary, will load it down with many objectionable features . . .

---

have been if they had understood the bill." For his part, Montague believed Martin was behind Barksdale's maneuver: "A coterie of Martin men planned that Barksdale should speak the Machen bill to death." Montague to John Wood, March 22, 1904, Montague Papers.

14 Richmond *News Leader,* March 14 and 16, 1904.
15 *Ibid.,* March 21, 1904.
16 Martin to William Bibb, June 22, 1903, and R. G. B. Broome to Bibb, Aug. 13, 1903, Bibb Papers.

[and] make the system obnoxious to the people." Specifically, he felt that the Martin forces in the 1904 state convention would attempt what they had failed to accomplish in the legislature—the establishment of a combination convention-primary system where each county or city would "stand or fall by itself." He also feared that a convention might officially adopt a primary but then withhold its utilization until the 1906 legislature made an appropriation to defray its expenses. Although Jones minimized this last possibility as "not very dangerous," both he and Congressman Rixey corroborated Montague's fear that the convention-primary scheme would be revived; Jones admitted that "many . . . in our own ranks" favored the proposal.[17]

In August, 1903, during the convention of the Virginia Bar Association in Hot Springs, Montague, Jones, and other progressive leaders had held a conference to map strategy in opposition to these possible Martin moves. They decided to conduct a vigorous campaign in advance of the elections for the 1904 convention to insure that the delegates selected would be friendly to the primary. Though this campaign was not at first envisioned as a speaking canvass, Montague later suggested to Jones that "perhaps 4 or 6 of us should take the stump . . . the people are too complacent." [18]

Montague never carried out his intention to conduct a speaking tour for the primary; yet he devoted considerable time to promoting the cause, personally assisting the Richmond forces in their fight against the Martin-dominated city Democratic committee. Advocates of the primary had proposed that, in electing the Richmond delegates to the convention, the voters should express themselves as pro- or antiprimary; the resulting verdict would be binding upon the delegates. The city committee at first defeated this proposal, then adopted it after it was amended to be merely advisory, not binding. Later, in a referendum, the citizens of Richmond overwhelmingly endorsed the primary by a vote of 1,909 to 194. Montague commented, "I have made a most earnest fight for the primary in Richmond and am gratified at the results." [19]

Montague also conducted an extensive letter campaign to politi-

17 Montague to J. H. Spencer, April 14, 1904; Montague to W. B. Richards, April 18, 1904; Montague to Jones, May 30, 1904; Jones to Montague, May 28, 1904; all in Montague Papers.
18 Richmond *News Leader*, Sept. 4 and 7, 1903; Montague to Jones, Feb. 17, 1904, Montague Papers.
19 Richmond *News Leader*, May 5 and 7, 1904; Montague to Jones, May 25, 1904, Montague Papers.

cal friends and acquaintances throughout the state, urging them to see that delegations favorable to the primary were sent to the convention. Perhaps most important was his attempt to exert influence upon the state central committee. That committee was to meet on April 30, 1904, and was scheduled to select a subcommittee which would recommend to the state convention changes in the primary system. Montague wrote letters to several members of the committee, urging them to see him when next they were in Richmond. He warned that attempts would be made to weaken the primary plan and that friends of the primary should unite to avert such a catastrophe.[20]

Montague's efforts with the committee were evidently successful. On May 17 Jones wrote to the governor: "You were, of course, pleased with the result of the deliberations of the committee. . . . I was charged with manipulation of some of the members. . . . A majority of the sub-committee to suggest changes are good primary men who will make only good changes. . . . I have been given assurances that there would be no opposition to my suggestions." Still, Montague was not completely satisfied. Though both Chairman Ellyson and Martin had professed no knowledge of any move to alter drastically the primary system at the convention, Montague apprehensively awaited proof.

As Montague had forewarned, the convention which met in Richmond on June 8 was dominated by Martin delegates. Montague's earlier attempts to arose the mass of Independents to activity brought little success. In the general selection of convention delegates, he complained, "No interest was taken in the primary. In Lunenburg County the delegates were elected by the County Committee. In Suffolk there were only seven present when the meeting selected delegates." To Jones he asserted that nothing had been done for the primary except in the Richmond fight "in which I participated," and "in a few counties where I've had parties offer resolutions." On the eve of the convention he wearily confided to Moore, "Our people have had no organization. I have had no assistance or cooperation and have felt that perhaps our friends could not be better aroused . . . than to have such an object lesson as this Convention will afford." The governor assumed that this apparent apathy would provide an opportunity for a Martin coup against the primary.[21]

20 Montague to Bowdoin, May 5, 1904; Montague to B. F. Buchanan, H. O. Humphreys, and W. B. Richards, April 11, 1904; all in Montague Papers.
21 Montague to Jones, May 30, June 2, 1904; Montague to Walter E. Addison, May 30, 1904; Montague to Moore, June 4, 1904; all *ibid.*

When the convention finally met, Montague's apprehensions proved to be greatly exaggerated. The only significant attempt to alter the primary procedure was made in the method of voting. The viva voce method had originally been favored by the Independents as a means of preventing cheating at the polls; if voting were publicly recorded, honest election returns would be assured and ballot box stuffing eliminated. However, it soon became apparent that the vocal ballot could also be used to promote other means of intimidation: "A boss at a shop of 500 men could easily spot every man who failed to vote for Martin's man and then find some excuse for cutting off his bread and meat. If there is an inclination to use money, as they have done heretofore, they can know by the living voice whether the contract is carried out." [22] Moreover, the average citizen expressed a disinclination to approve or disapprove publicly local candidates, many of whom might be neighbors or business patrons.

Montague had originally favored viva voce, and continued to do so although he recognized its defects. Congressman Jones was of the same opinion. However, many Independents dissented, and in the subcommittee which recommended changes to the Richmond convention, Jones had a difficult time obtaining even a compromise. As presented to the convention, this compromise made the viva voce system mandatory for statewide offices but optional for local elections. An attempt in the committee to adopt the principles of the Barksdale bill was voted down with little debate.[23]

A combination of Martin and Independent forces brought about complete repeal of viva voce on the floor of the convention, and Jones accepted the secret ballot "for harmony's sake." After this alteration, Martin himself proposed that the committee's report be accepted, and the resolution carried with only three or four audible dissents. Montague was gratified. Though the convention had reconstituted the state committee so that Martin dominated, and though it had even pointedly failed to endorse his administration as governor, Montague regarded the readoption of the primary as victory enough: "The State Convention did the one thing . . . of supreme moment. . . . it has given us a primary." [24]

The Democratic conventions from 1897 to 1904 thus reflected a

22 B. W. Arnold to Montague, Sept. 3, 1903, *ibid.*
23 Montague to B. W. Arnold, Sept. 1, 1903, and Montague to Jones, May 30, 1904, *ibid.;* Richmond *News Leader,* June 9, 1904.
24 Richmond *News Leader,* June 9, 1904; Montague to Thomas F. Ryan, June 13, 1904, Montague Papers.

complete transition. The forces that so bitterly and successfully opposed a primary in 1897 had now quietly acquiesced to the obvious popular will. The reaction that had begun with Martin's questionable election in 1893 by a partially bribed legislature had finally brought results. The national reform forces that eventually would obtain the Seventeenth Amendment to the Constitution had won an initial victory in the Virginia Democracy.

Two men deserve chief credit for this success. Congressman Jones had initiated the primary movement in 1897; he had given it his leadership during the years when victory proved elusive. Montague contributed to the reform shortly after the movement's inception and, by his stirring 1901 campaign, helped elect a convention which brought the reformers their first victory. Later, Jones and Montague kept the issue alive, insuring it against a loss of ground already gained. By obtaining the primary's initial adoption, by publicizing it, they had demonstrated its effectiveness and assured its popularity. Martin, looking ahead to the critical 1905 election, dared not flout the public's will and incur popular rebuke. He surrendered to the inevitable.

Though some of his enemies circulated the rumor that Montague himself had reservations about the primary principle and advocated it only expediently, a recounting of his activities from 1899 on belie the rumor. Still, the paradox remains (in a way, the paradox of Montague's entire career) that here was a man, espousing a democratic reform, who in his heart lacked a simple, absolute faith in the collective wisdom of the people. "To the manor born," as a congressional colleague later described him, Montague was no leveler. He felt most in his element before the learned society, among polite parlor company. Analyzing his record and contrasting his public and private utterances, one gains the impression of a man, almost schizophrenic, instinctively recoiling from the crassness and oversimplification required of the politician appealing to the masses on the hustings, and yet at the same time a man able to an uncommon degree to attune his oratory to the level of his audience. In short, Montague the scholar did on occasion resort to demagoguery.

The question remains: what prompted Montague's advocacy of the primary reform, an advocacy which in the late 1890's signaled his alignment with progressive forces in the Virginia Democracy? The transformation from the young college student casting aspersions on the "so-called" progressive age of the early 1880's, to the governor embracing numerous progressive reforms of a later age, remains somewhat perplexing, however explained. In the same vein, something must explain the shift from the young mugwump, deriding the fiction that governmental legislation could remedy social ills, to the progressive governor, advocating several items of remedial legislation. Most to the point is the problem of how to reconcile the youth's fulminations about the potential dangers inherent in absolute majority rule with the adult's advocacy of majority rule in the primary.

In attempted explanation, perhaps the most satisfactory rejoinder would be simply to say that Montague was a man of flexibility, that as his environment changed, so did his attitudes. To repeat earlier analyses, the young Montague's distrust of illiterate electors was later overlaid by a keener distrust of callous, corrupt, entrenched office-holders. In another sense, though, the change of attitude was not complete. True, the young college student would have maintained a solid buffer of restrictions—of constitutional law—protecting individual liberty and property against the "fiendish clamors of an excited and infuriated" popular majority; yet he was a democrat and no Hamiltonian in that he subscribed fully to the expression *vox populi, vox Dei.* In the last analysis, the people were the sole source of political authority. When that fundamental premise of democratic government was jeopardized by the creeping control of corporate America, and when that control brought attendant decay in political standards and private ethics, then Montague turned to the primary mechanism as a countervailing popular force to restore equilibrium to the body politic.

Moreover, in his later life Montague remained fully aware that primary legislation was ineffectual in revitalizing government, unless it was accompanied by an intelligent suffrage. The failure of the parliamentary system, he once observed, "is due not so much to the nature of the system or its procedure as to the electorate. We must go deeper than parliamentary procedure and educate the people [to] higher ethical standards." [25] The good schools movement thus complemented the primary movement. Only with an educated citizenry could the primary mechanism serve its intended purpose.

---

25 *Compte Rendu de la XXVme Conference Tenue a Berlin du 23 au 28 Aout 1928* (Lausanne, 1928), Montague Papers.

XIII

———— ◆●◆ ————

A STATE AND NATIONAL
REPUTATION

THE conflict over the senatorial primary provided a central theme for Virginia politics from 1902 to 1904. By securing the primary the progressives hoped to bring about Martin's political downfall. To make certain that downfall, Montague had also endeavored, unsuccessfully, to mold his political following into a functioning alliance capable of effective opposition to the machine, both in the legislature and in the state Democratic convention of 1904. Most of all, however, he recognized the need for a concerted Independent opposition to Martin's reelection bid in 1905, and he sought to unify the various quarreling factions of the Independents behind one common candidacy—his own.

Montague's political interests during his first years as governor were not confined to state and local politics, however. On the national political scene Montague rose rapidly to a position of some prominence. In a strange alliance, he temporarily became the protégé of Thomas F. Ryan, a stalwart of Tammany and Wall Street who hoped to make Montague a leading spokesman for the Southern Democracy. Utilizing contacts afforded by Ryan and other Northern friends, Montague conducted several Northern forays from 1902 to 1904, speaking on behalf of state and national Democratic candidates. He also delivered addresses of a nonpolitical nature, on one such occasion receiving an honorary doctorate from Brown University. Within a few years he achieved a national recognition surpassed only by Senator Daniel among Virginians. The Virginia press praised his growing reputation with native pride. Many predicted for him a promising future career in the nation's political councils. Montague's national contacts were thus no handicap in his coming campaign against Martin.

For Montague and for Virginia politics the years from 1902 to 1904 were essentially a prelude to the senatorial contest of 1905. By the time of his 1901 victory, he had made a promising start in his fight to destroy the Martin machine. Even before that victory was won, he had turned his eyes to a more formidable challenge—Martin himself. Montague realized that he was the logical candidate to oppose Martin's reelection; Martin also realized it. Thus, battle lines were early drawn. Almost every political event of consequence from 1902 to 1904 had overtones of the impending conflict between the heads of the two dominant factions.

Factional rivalries were particularly aggravated in deliberations of the General Assembly, dominated as it was by the Martin organization. In matters pertaining to better schools, better roads, and election regulations, Montague felt himself continually hamstrung by a hostile legislature determined to discredit his administration. That Martin's control of the legislature was not absolute, however, was demonstrated by the bitter controversy which developed among several elements of his organization over a reapportionment measure enacted early in 1902. The measure, which was rumored to have received Martin's prior approval, made drastic alterations in the state's congressional districts, especially in the Sixth and the First. The First was Jones's district, and the Sixth, consisting of the Lynchburg-Roanoke areas, was represented by Peter J. Otey, a close friend of Daniel. Proponents of the bill argued that it aimed merely to render all Virginia districts safe from the Republicans.[1] Opponents charged that it also aimed at eliminating Jones and Otey from state politics by gerrymandering much of their political strength into other districts. The chief beneficiary of the bill, most people agreed, was Congressman Henry D. Flood, Martin's staunchest ally. When the bill was considered before a house committee, Otey, Glass, and Daniel all appeared to oppose the measure. In addition to testifying against the bill before

1 Republican counties of the Fifth and Tenth districts were given to Otey's "safer" Sixth District. Henry D. Flood to A. G. Preston, April 8, 1902, Flood Papers.

committee, Daniel also arranged a private conference with Governor Montague.[2]

Montague, befriending Jones and possibly sensing an opportunity to drive a wedge between the squabbling Martin factions, vetoed the bill four days after it passed the legislature in March, 1902. Observing that the Virginia constitution required that congressional districts be equal in population and geographically compact, Montague charged that the bill failed to meet either of the requirements. Rather, "the present system more nearly complies than the proposed changes." Wryly he observed that "unaccountable changes are to be wrought." Flood's Tenth District, then consisting of an ideal 185,000 population, would be reduced by 26,000, whereas the contiguous Ninth District, with a population of 227,000, would be left intact. Furthermore, the rearranged Tenth District resembled a tortuous worm, stretching from Highland County on the West Virginia border to within fifteen miles of North Carolina and touching seven of the other nine districts in its course. Montague termed these and other changes "a violation of State and Federal law and inimical to the best interests of the Commonwealth." [3]

Montague's veto was easily the most important political topic of the day. Though technically based on constitutional grounds, it was a very practical setback to Flood and Swanson. Congratulations poured into his office. A Newport News resident commented, "We wanted reapportionment here but glory in your nerve, you couldn't have done otherwise, and your friends are with you." Most important, Congressmen Jones, Otey, Lamb, and Rixey all defended Montague's move. From the other camp, veiled threats were heard that Montague's right to veto the measure would be contested in the courts on the ground that apportioning the districts was strictly a legislative matter. Although the threat persisted for some time, nothing concrete resulted. Rumors that the Virginia senate would reap vengeance by refusing to confirm Montague's appointments to the corporation commission were likewise discredited.[4] Montague's boldest use of the veto had

2   Richmond *Evening Leader,* March 25, April 5, 1902; Doss, "John Warwick Daniel," 294–96. It was a fear of provoking this sort of interorganization wrangle that had earlier convinced Martin not to press for reapportionment (James Hay to Flood, Jan. 21, 1901, Flood Papers).
3   Richmond *Evening Leader,* March 29, April 3, 1902.
4   W. P. Johnson to Montague, April 3, 1902; Montague to John Lamb, April 20, 1902; Lamb to Montague, April 25, 1902; all in Montague Papers. W. P. Barksdale to Flood, April 8, 1902, Flood Papers; Richmond *Evening Leader,* June 13, 1902.

resulted in a notable victory for the Independents. At the time, at least, he seemed to have weakened the solidarity of Martin's machine.[5]

Although, as Montague's veto demonstrated, Martin's organization occasionally lacked cohesion, the Independents, in their political pursuits, suffered from an almost complete absence of central direction or discipline. Montague's attempts to provide that direction attained only limited success. His eagerness to enter the fray against Martin was, ironically, frustrated and hampered by his friends, not his enemies. Three other Independents aspired to carrying the battle emblem, and not until late 1904 were all three eliminated, making the path clear.

Montague initially seemed to have clear sailing. Evidently, after the 1901 election, the Virginia public automatically expected him to lead the Independents against Martin four years later, particularly since the main theme of his addresses had been a criticism of Martin's domination in Virginia politics. As early as June, 1902, the Richmond *Evening Leader* observed, "Every well-posted politician looks upon Gov. Montague as a strong competitor for Sen. Martin's seat." Similar speculations continued into the fall: "Already the lines are beginning to settle for the great Senatorial battle of 1905, when Governor Montague and Senator Martin will oppose one another and hug on the political field in a death grapple. . . . It will be a final struggle for mastery and control of the Democratic party." Martin himself looked to Montague as his probable opponent as early as 1901.[6]

Montague's private correspondence helped circulate such rumors. To numerous acquaintances and inquirers he sent letters of which the following is typical: "As yet I have arrived at no fixed conclusion save that I deem it of essential importance that Sen. Martin be not

5 Factional rivalry was also evident in the Democratic State Central Committee, which had been restaffed in 1901 by the same convention that had nominated Montague. Montague's dominating influence on the committee appeared evident when that body in 1902 and 1903 arbitrated local factional disputes in the Norfolk area. In the city of Norfolk the pro-Montague clique, led by W. W. Dey, received recognition as the official Democratic organization, and in Norfolk County, George W. Jones, a Montague supporter who often communicated with the governor on political matters, obtained recognition for his "Straightout" faction against the "fusionists," a group of white Democrats and Negro Republicans. Montague lost control of the committee, however, after the state convention of 1904. Richmond *Evening Leader*, Jan. 28 and 29, March 3 and 4, 1902; Richmond *News Leader*, June 26, 1903.

6 Richmond *Evening Leader*, June 16, Nov. 27, 1902; Martin to Francis Rives Lassiter, Aug. 21, 1901, Lassiter Papers.

returned to the U.S. Senate. I think the interests of Virginia have been greatly corrupted and retarded by his political influence." To more intimate friends he confided, "While I do not formally announce my candidacy I will be pleased if you will further my name as you may see fit in a quiet way." By fall of 1902 he definitely had decided to make the race, barring unforeseen developments. Hesitating to announce his candidacy officially so soon after entering office, he nevertheless felt it necessary to indulge in fence-mending, since even at that early date he found Martin's friends active.[7]

In January, 1903, on his way to New York Montague stopped briefly in Washington, evidently attempting to arrange a conference of Virginia's congressional Independents, now including the freshman Congressman, Carter Glass. Glass, however, declined to participate "in any Congressional junta, interfering in state elections. . . . this was the very ground on which Montague had fought Swanson and was a thing he (Glass), himself had deprecated." Despite such rumblings of discontent among some of his 1901 followers, Montague, in sharp contrast to his usual pessimistic appraisal of Martin's hold on state politics, expressed confidence in eventual victory: "Martin's defeat," he predicted, "ought to be accomplished with less effort than was expended in the defeat of Mr. Swanson." [8]

This rosy optimism was to suffer severe setbacks from subsequent events. On Thanksgiving Day, 1902, it was reported from the Southwest that former Governor Tyler would probably enter the senatorial race. Tyler, who suffered ignominious defeat at the hands of Martin in 1899, had longed for an opportunity to take revenge. Rumors were circulated that he felt his previous fight against the machine had been largely responsible for Montague's 1901 victory and that Montague should now stand aside for him. In addition, he considered Montague incapable of defeating Martin.[9]

Pro-Martin newspapers hailed Tyler's rumored candidacy as rendering certain the Senator's reelection. Montague himself confessed that Tyler's threat was "a weight upon me." In March, 1903, he wrote to E. T. Brady of Abingdon, asking, "Do you know of any way

---

7   Montague to J. M. Barker, May 3, 1902; Montague to Camm Patteson, Sept. 3, 1902; Montague to J. W. Bowdoin, Sept. 13, 1902; Montague to S. H. Hansbrough, Sept. 22, 1902; all in Montague Papers.

8   A. C. Braxton to C. V. Meredith, Jan. 24, 1903, Braxton Papers; Montague to W. W. Pendleton, Nov. 8, 1902, Montague Papers.

9   Richmond *Evening Leader,* Nov. 27, 1902; John S. Draper, Jr. to Montague, Feb. 28, 1903, Montague Papers.

by which Gov. Tyler can be prevented from entering the Senatorial race?" He bitterly lamented that though Tyler did not have a "ghost of a show," his candidacy would mean Martin's election.[10] As late as September, 1903, Tyler was still rumored to be considering the race, but his good sense seems to have erased any delusions of his being elected. By 1904 he was definitely eliminated.

A more formidable rival for the honors appeared in the person of A. C. Braxton, the man to whom Montague had made several offers of a position on the corporation commission. Braxton's authorship of the article in the new constitution which established the commission had given him a statewide reputation which engendered speculation on his political future. He had been mentioned as a gubernatorial candidate in 1905, or as a candidate against Daniel's reelection in 1903. Both prospects Braxton declined to consider.[11] The prospect of a race against the controversial Martin, however, was more inviting.

Braxton vacillated in making his decision on the 1905 Senate race. At first, he declined to seriously consider becoming a candidate. As late as December of 1902 he agreed that a third candidate would be considered an intruder in the Martin-Montague feud. The same month, however, he began contacting important state figures concerning their attitudes toward his potential candidacy, and by February, 1903, he asserted privately, "If the sentiment in my favor continues to grow as it apparently has done in the last few months, I think it very probable that I will consent to enter the race." By June, however, he had again tentatively decided not to run, and in a letter to the *Times Dispatch* he explained that he was not "at this time" a candidate. Braxton hoped a move away from Montague would yet occur in appreciable force; thus he left the door ajar for a potential draft which never developed.[12]

Braxton derived support chiefly from a hard core of Independents, many of whom had served with him in the constitutional convention. Braxton himself argued for his candidacy on the grounds that he had

10 Rockbridge County *News,* undated clipping, scrapbook, Martin Papers; Danville *Bee,* March 11, 1903, in scrapbook, Moore Collection. Montague to John S. Draper, Jr., March 7, 1903; Montague to E. T. Brady, March 7, 1903; Montague to George F. Walker, Feb. 6, 1903; all in Montague Papers.
11 Braxton to J. C. Wysor, Dec. 27, 1902, Braxton Papers.
12 Braxton to R. D. Haislip, March 26, 1902, June 4, 1904; Braxton to J. C. Wysor, Dec. 9, 1902; Braxton to C. V. Meredith, Dec. 18, 1902, June 9, 1903; Braxton to Joseph L. Barham, Feb. 2, 1903; Braxton to Edmund Pendleton, Feb. 9, 1903; all in Braxton Papers.

fewer enemies than either the Senator or the governor. Moreover, he felt that Montague would be unequal to a match with Martin: "Martin has his forces better in hand than Montague, and Montague has lost many friends by his appointments on the Corporation Commission, and in other respects, my impression is that, he has decidedly lost popularity in the last few months." In February, 1903, writing to J. C. Wysor, his staunchest supporter, he asserted: "Montague is certainly losing strength rapidly, as far as I can learn. His friends charge him with ingratitude and selfishness, and it is believed by many that he is in fact as much dominated by railroad influences as Martin is. However this may be, I think the impression is gaining strength that, in a fight between him and Martin, the latter would be successful." [13]

This charge that Montague was dominated by railroad influence cannot be substantiated,[14] but the fact that Braxton felt such animosity toward the man who had offered him the choicest patronage at his command is somewhat baffling. Writing to Edmund Pendleton in February, 1903, he complained, "If I do not [run], it will be because of Montague's persistency in staying in, and should he then get beaten, as he probably will, I trust that it may prove his quietus, as I do not think that he is a healthy element in Virginia politics." [15] This hostility toward Montague would continue through the 1905 campaign, long after Braxton himself had withdrawn as a candidate. Braxton's candidacy is indicative of a major split in the Independent ranks, one which Montague was unable to heal completely.

Montague did not share Braxton's opinion that he would make the better race against Martin. "Braxton," he alleged, "would make no better run than did Echols or Dick Marshall, save that he will take

13 Braxton to Wysor, Dec. 27, 1902, Feb. 3, 1903, *ibid.*
14 There is no doubt that Montague had contacts among railroad personnel. On Oct. 3, 1903, he sent congratulations to L. E. Johnson, evidently a personal acquaintance, on his election as president of the Norfolk and Western Railway: "I am gratified to know that your Company has taken a gentleman for its head who is so accurately apprised of the needs and wants of the State." Johnson replied (Oct. 5, 1903): "In performing the duties of this office it will be my pleasure to . . . aid and abet the interests of . . . Virginia. . . . I wish for you all the success that it is possible for any man to have . . . should you in the future desire political advancement, it will be a great pleasure to me to aid you in such manner as I possibly can." Montague's acquaintance with Johnson evidently secured the neutrality of the N & W in the 1905 campaign, but he encountered difficulties in attempting to keep the C & O and Southern from supporting Martin. All the above references are in Montague Papers.
15 Braxton to Pendleton, Feb. 2, 1903, Braxton Papers.

the vote from me and not from Martin." Montague's opinion was confirmed by an early report from Nevins Fishburne of Waynesboro that the leading men of his area opposed Braxton's idea to enter the race, favoring Montague instead. Montague maintained that it was entirely due to his 1901 election that the "slightest show" against Martin had been made possible: "It looks rather inconsistent that he [Braxton] should endeavor to reap the fruits of my doing." Furthermore, Montague believed that Braxton was being encouraged to run by Martin elements, "though Braxton may not be conscious of it." [16]

This opinion receives credence from subsequent developments; after relinquishing his ambition for the Senate, Braxton fell heir to another candidacy. Prominent Virginians began booming him for the Democratic vice-presidential nomination in 1904, and the most notable individual behind the move was Flood, Congressman from Braxton's Tenth District. In April, 1904, Montague joined Braxton's boosters at the urging of Alfred B. Williams, editor of the *News Leader;* Braxton thanked Williams for "what you have done in this connection." Flood undoubtedly wished to pacify a man too prominent for his own political safety, and Martin's machine may have desired to deepen the rift among the Virginia Independents. For his part, Montague probably wished to relieve himself of a potential senatorial opponent and at the same time pacify Braxton's pique. The Braxton boom collapsed, however, before the state convention in June, due largely to Daniel's opposition and Braxton's lack of enthusiasm. Still, his popularity was sufficiently strong to obtain his election as one of the "Big Four" delegates-at-large to the St. Louis Democratic convention.[17]

Montague was also selected as one of the Big Four at St. Louis. Still uncertain whether Braxton intended to run for the Senate, Montague closely watched his actions, communicating to Jones his observation that Braxton "was coddled by the Martin people in every way, and seemed to be so impressed with his importance and the weight of the Republic that he was not observant of lesser things no matter how deplorable." He predicted, however, that Braxton would not make the race: "I am under the impression that he has promised Martin

16 Montague to Munsey Slack, June 4, 1903; Montague to W. N. Fishburne, Jan. 28, 1903; Montague to E. D. Newman, Jan. 22, 1903; Fishburne to Montague, Feb. 5, 1902; all in Montague Papers.
17 Braxton to D. Q. Eggleston, April 25 and 29, 1904; Braxton to Alfred B. Williams, April 23, 1904; Braxton Papers; Weathers, "Allen Caperton Braxton," 101–104.

not to run and am further of the opinion that he will support Martin." [18] Montague's predictions were correct. Braxton made no further move to enter the game of politics, and during the 1905 election
he remained publicly neutral, though privately expressing hopes for a
Martin victory.

Throughout this period of indefinite candidacies, Montague's campaign was slowly developing. His continual handicap seems to have
been an inability to establish strong local organizations. Efforts to
displace incumbent assemblymen of Martin's faction seemed at first
unavailing, and in May, 1903, he wrote to Jones despairingly, "The
Martin people are very active, and it is very important that an organization be at once effected if Mr. Martin is to be opposed." The legislative situation, coupled with the threatened candidacies of Tyler and
Braxton, temporarily discouraged him: "Anti-Martin people seem to
be doing nothing whatever. My own life has been most irksome and
laborious for the past year. The continuous sessions of the Legislature, together with the Constitutional Convention, have made my life
anything but an easy one . . . yet [I am] willing to make any possible sacrifice to overthrow the political incubus."

By fall of 1903, his spirits had revived. The threat of other candidacies had diminished, and conversations with friends at the Hot
Springs state bar convention portrayed his prospects as "very encouraging." He enthusiastically resumed writing to acquaintances throughout the state, soliciting their support and asking for names of voters
favorable to his candidacy, "so that I can write to them freely." [19]

There yet remained a storm cloud on the horizon, however, a
cloud which did not lift entirely until several months after the state
Democratic convention in 1904. Congressman Jones, previously the
leader of the Independents and still a potent factor in state politics,
hesitated to admit that he had been replaced by the youthful Montague as the preeminent leader of the reformers. [20] His hesitancy

18 Montague to Jones, June 11, July 16, 1904, Montague Papers. Though
    Braxton swung to Martin, several of his supporters, including Wysor, his
    most prominent backer, supported Montague in 1905. While supporting
    Braxton in 1903 Wysor described Montague as a "very good, deserving
    man. I also think he is very fond of office." Wysor to Braxton, Jan. 27,
    1903, Braxton Papers.
19 Montague to Jones, May 14 and 25, 1903; Montague to J. Ogden Murray,
    Sept. 1, 1903; Montague to George B. Jones, Sept. 17, 1903; all in Mon-
    tague Papers.
20 Or as one observer put it, "Jones resents Montague's assuming that he,
    Montague, is entitled to the support of the reformers in Virginia; and

caused the governor to delay his official announcement for the senatorial race, a delay he once termed "fatal."

By virtue of his long and prominent service in state and national politics Jones always figured as a possible candidate for statewide positions. In late 1902 and early 1903 he therefore received mention in the state's press as a potential opponent to Martin in 1905. Concerned, Montague wrote to Delegate R. Walton Moore in January, 1903, asking him to feel out Jones as to his position: "W. A. Jones (I've heard) thinks it strange that I've never mentioned to him I contemplate making the race for the Senate. . . . I didn't know but that Jones would run also, and I thought he could more delicately tell me. I hear that he favors me but feels a little sore for the reason stated. . . . Tell him, if you think it wise, what I've told you." Moore spoke with Jones, and reported to Montague that Jones had decided to stand aside and give the governor a clear field.[21]

In several newspaper interviews, however, Jones declined to explicitly disavow his candidacy. Moore expressed mystification as to Jones's motives for such coyness. Montague hopefully surmised, however, that Jones would ultimately abandon any hope of entering the race: "I think . . . he would like to run. I am afraid that he is not giving me any support now, and his attitude is such as to cooperate with those who are endeavoring to make friction for my campaign. Consciously or unconsciously he hopes the tide may turn toward him. Of course you know this will not be."[22]

During the first half of 1904 the question of the senatorial election was temporarily set aside for a more immediate problem, the preservation of the primary. Montague and Jones cooperated closely in efforts to assure that the state convention would make no alteration in their favorite reform project. After the convention, however, Montague tried to convince Jones that the Independents should combine immediately upon a single candidate: "So far as I am individually concerned I am unwilling to make a fight . . . unless the matter can be disposed of very speedily. . . . The announcement should have gone out contemporaneously with the promulgation of the primary

---

Montague does so assume." Alexander Hamilton to Henry St. George Tucker, March 24, 1903, Tucker Papers.
21 Montague to Moore, Jan. 6, 1903, and Moore to Montague, June 3, 1903, Montague Papers.
22 Richmond *News Leader,* May 7, 1903; Moore to Montague, Oct. 21, 1903, and Montague to Moore, Oct. 23, 1903, Montague Papers.

plan, and the longer we wait the greater the impression will be created by the Martin people that the reason of the delay is to let the influence of the Convention . . . die out." [23]

Jones agreed to a conference on the matter with Montague and other Independents, including Moore, Delegate Camm Patteson, Meredith, and Stuart, but early efforts to arrange an acceptable date were unsuccessful. By mid-July Montague, growing increasingly restless, warned Jones that

> the opportunity and advantages which we have had are slipping rapidly away from us and we will soon find ourselves in the same plight that we did in the Tyler campaign [1899]. . . . I have felt, as you are perhaps aware, ambitious to make the fight, only, however, upon the condition that the anti-Martin people would give me united support. This ambition has been greatly weakened by the long delay in our campaign and the long continued activity of Mr. Martin in his. . . . unless something is done very soon I shall lose all interest in the matter, either for myself or anybody else, for I cannot undertake to assist in a futility.[24]

Not until August 29 was a secret Washington conference finally arranged among the state's leading Independents. The outcome was evidently such as Montague expected, for on September 2 he informed Camm Patteson: "I expect to announce for the Senate in a few days." And writing to Jones on September 13, he revealed that after consulting "with our people" in Chesterfield County, he had decided to announce his candidacy immediately: "There were so many rumors to the effect that Mr. Martin would have no opposition. . . . I had hoped to confer with you further about this, but I trust that what I have done meets your approval." Two weeks later he reported to Jones that response to his public announcement had been gratifying: "The fight can be won if we are energetic." [25]

Virginia's Independents had selected a worthy candidate. Tyler and Braxton never seriously challenged Montague's role as leader of the Independents; they threatened only to break off fringes of anti-machine strength. Jones, once described by Montague as a "genuine patriot, a refined gentleman, a brave independent and able man," [26] more nearly approached Montague in capability and surpassed him in

23 Montague to Jones, June 11, 1904, Montague Papers.
24 Montague to Jones, July 1, 1904, *ibid.*
25 Montague to Camm Patteson, Sept. 2, 1904, and Montague to Jones, Sept. 13 and 27, 1904, *ibid.*
26 Montague to Tucker, April 27, 1918, Tucker Papers.

political experience, but even he lacked something of Montague's personal magnetism. Moreover, as representative of the First District, he could not match Montague's statewide reputation and proven popularity. Montague had risen quickly, perhaps too quickly, to be accorded accolades throughout the Commonwealth. His prominence in the crusades for good roads, good schools, and the popular primary, were acknowledged and praised. As a leading spokesman for the new Virginia, he had attracted a large popular following. His endorsement by leaders of the Independents naturally followed. The political lines had been drawn. Virginia expectantly awaited a battle royal.

If Montague's rise to power in Virginia had been rapid, his climb to national recognition was meteoric. In but a few years he went from relative obscurity as an attorney general to the position of an intimate in the Democratic party councils—a spokesman for Southern Democrats.

Several factors explain this rise to prominence. Montague's 1901 campaign had attracted nationwide attention. Shortly after his election, the distant Chicago *Chronicle* nominated him for the senatorial race in 1905. More significantly, only seven months after his inauguration, he was invited to a "harmony dinner" held in New York by the Samuel J. Tilden Club. Important Northern representatives of both the gold and silver factions of the Democratic party attended; former President Cleveland and David B. Hill served as two of the speakers for the evening. Montague was the only prominent Southern Democrat present and the only speaker from south of New York state. The Brooklyn *Eagle,* favorably impressed by his address, characterized him as "handsome, cultivated, eloquent, prudent, progressive and straightforward." [27]

Montague's favorable reception resulted in numerous appeals from Northern Democrats to speak in the fall election campaigns of 1902. Invitations came not only from the national Democratic committee, but from individual Democratic candidates in such widely separated areas as Indiana, Wisconsin, Iowa, and Massachusetts. William A. Gaston, candidate for governor of Massachusetts, urgently appealed to Montague to address a rally in Boston. Gaston had met Montague at the Tilden banquet, and was greatly impressed by his magnetic

27 Dan B. Jesse to Montague, Nov. 9, 1904, Montague Papers; Richmond *Evening Leader,* June 20, 1902; unidentified clipping, scrapbook, Moore Collection.

personality and marked power as a speaker: "You must send him to
the Senate," he advised a Virginia news correspondent, "it would be
a fatal mistake not to." Montague accepted several invitations, including Gaston's. Only a lack of time and funds frustrated his desire to
accept more of them.[28]

Montague's masterful oratory was to be further utilized by his national party during the 1904 presidential elections, when he spoke at
points in New York, Pennsylvania, and Maryland, declining more invitations than he accepted. Out-of-state appearances of a nonpolitical
nature included an address delivered to the 1903 Jefferson memorial
banquet in Washington, and a speech entitled "The Supremacy and
Opportunity of the American Republic," presented before a Kansas
City audience in November of the same year. In June, 1903, he traveled to Rhode Island to address the graduating class of Brown University; it was there that he and another young Democrat, Woodrow
Wilson, received honorary doctorates.[29] The many national appeals
for Montague to speak prompted the *News Leader* to comment, on
December 21, 1903, "No man in the country has grown faster than
Governor Montague. . . . He has given the State abundant reasons
to be proud of him."

Many scores of invitations Montague found necessary to decline,
including several to address the New York State Bar Association, and
one to speak before the Union League of New York on the subject of
Lincoln—high tribute, indeed, for a Southerner. Montague himself

28 Richmond *Evening Leader,* Sept. 29, Oct. 29, 1902; Montague to Wil-
    liam A. Gaston, Oct. 23, 1902, Montague to Glass, Oct. 1, 1902; all in
    Montague Papers.
29 Richmond *News Leader,* Nov. 20, 1903, Oct. 18 and 31, 1904. Montague
    to A. B. Montague, June 23, 1903; Montague to C. D. Parker, Nov. 2,
    1903; Montague to Daniel McConville, Aug. 24, 1904; all in Montague
    Papers.
        In 1903 Montague delivered a particularly moving address on a Civil
    War theme to the American Bar Association at Hot Springs, Virginia. The
    Alexandria *Gazette* declared that Montague had "eclipsed all the speakers
    of the season by one of the most brilliant efforts ever made by a son of
    this . . . commonwealth." This glowing description was confirmed by an
    impartial visitor at the meeting, Frederick Pollock, a British jurist: "One
    of the best speeches I have ever heard was made by the Governor of
    Virginia, Mr. Montague. . . . On this occasion Governor Montague spoke
    of the history of his own State, on his own soil and in frank vindication
    of Virginia's honourable sons who had felt bound to put loyalty to their
    own State first; he spoke with feeling and eloquence and yet with such
    tact and courtesy that none of the many Northerners present could take
    offence." Alexandria (Va.) *Gazette,* Aug. 31, 1903, in scrapbook, Monta-
    gue Papers; Pollock, *For My Grandson* (London, 1933), 197–98.

estimated that he had received more requests for public addresses, within and without the state, than any public man in Virginia during the previous half-century. His reputation grew to such an extent that dispatches from St. Louis during the 1904 Democratic convention referred to him as one of the most eloquent men in the ranks of the young Democrats.[30]

This rise to national prominence was based chiefly on the governor's facile tongue and intellectual persuasiveness. But to an undetermined extent, Montague also benefited from friends in high places. Some of his Northern co-workers in the educational crusade—Ogden, George Foster Peabody, Albert Shaw, Lyman Abbott—were influential in Northern politics. Another Northerner who developed an intriguing relationship with Montague was Thomas Fortune Ryan, Wall Street financier, public utilities executive, and member of the tobacco trust. A Virginia orphan who ultimately acquired a fortune of fifty million dollars, Ryan carried weight in New York politics and the Tammany organization. In Montague he saw the embodiment of his desire to reunite the Northeastern and Southern wings of the Democratic party and thus dominate the 1904 Democratic convention. For a brief period from early 1903 through 1904 the two men worked in close cooperation.

After 1900 the national Democratic party seemed moribund and leaderless. William Jennings Bryan, the revivalistic champion of silver in the 1896 campaign, had lost some of his fervor by 1900. Only four mountain states joined the South in supporting him in the fall presidential election. Disillusionment with the Nebraskan pervaded the entire Democratic party, but especially the Southern branch. A move arose among both Southerners and Northerners to break the eight-year Southern-Western alliance and realign the party on a North-South axis, an axis more conservatively oriented along hard-money lines. Several names were proposed to head this new alliance—some preferred a third term for Cleveland, others favored Arthur Pue Gorman of Maryland, George Gray of Delaware, or Richard Olney of Massachusetts. The one who proved most acceptable was Judge Alton B. Parker, an "old-fashioned American type," a silent, conservative New York banker.[31]

---

30 Montague to H. H. Baker, Jan. 13, 1905, Montague Papers; Richmond *News Leader*, July 22, 1904.
31 Woodward, *Origins of the New South*, 458–59; Richard B. Doss, "Democrats in the Doldrums: Virginia and the Democratic National Convention of 1904," *Journal of Southern History*, XX (Nov., 1954), 513.

Ryan was one of the leaders spearheading the Parker movement. In January, 1903, he contributed an article to the *North American Review* entitled, "The Political Opportunity of the South," proposing that at the 1904 Democratic convention the South act as a unit to bring about a conservative nominee and platform, repudiating Bryanism and returning the party to its traditional stands for sound currency, economy in government, and a tariff for revenue only.[32] He challenged his native South to reassert herself nationally, to regain a position of prominence in national government councils. To help achieve this goal, Ryan turned to Montague as a promising young politician, attractive to Northern audiences and endowed with innate ability. Moreover, in a state where machine forces were inclined to support Arthur Gorman, Ryan undoubtedly hoped to convert Virginia's governor to the cause of Parker. Possibly, he envisioned Montague as Parker's running mate.

Montague's attitudes toward Parker and the 1904 convention were typical of many of his fellow Southern progressives. He had completely abandoned his earlier stand on free silver and considered obsolete Bryan's retention of the issue. Rejecting Bryan on the left, he also opposed William Randolph Hearst and Gorman on the right, men he considered corruptible. He ultimately decided, as did Braxton, Jones, Glass and other Virginia progressives, to support Parker as the "best man . . . very friendly to me," though admitting that victory for the ticket against the popular and progressive Theodore Roosevelt, whom he also admired, was not likely. Writing to Ryan in March, 1904, Montague expressed the wish that the South would "unite behind Parker. . . . perhaps not to win, but a defeat with him would leave the party intact and strong for four years hence, when we ought to win." [33] Montague's alliance with the Parker movement was therefore an alliance not motivated by any enthusiasm for the New York gentleman, but rather by a desire to establish national contacts with Democratic leaders, to develop a reputation which would not only aid him in his campaign for the Senate in 1905, but which would prove invaluable in his senatorial career afterward. Unquestionably, he also sincerely endorsed Ryan's campaign to revive the South's political importance.

32 Thomas F. Ryan, "The Political Opportunity of the South," *North American Review*, CLXXVI (1903), 161–72.
33 Doss, "Democrats in the Doldrums . . . ," 515; Jones to Montague, Nov. 9, 1904; Montague to W. B. Richards, April 18, 1904; Montague to Ryan, March 9, 1904; all in Montague Papers.

Ryan evidently selected Montague as his protégé on the basis of the latter's reputation and without benefit of a prior acquaintance. As a tax-paying resident of Nelson County, Virginia, he had naturally learned of Montague's oratorical feats in the 1901 campaign; as a resident of New York he may have attended the Tilden banquet of 1902 which featured Cleveland, David B. Hill, and Montague as speakers. At any rate, in late December, 1902, or early January, 1903, probably at the same time Montague made a northern trip with Tucker on educational matters, Ryan had an audience with Montague. This was about the same time that Ryan's article on "The Political Opportunity of the South" appeared in print. On January 5, Ryan wrote Montague, advising him not to accept an invitation to speak at a New York dinner the following month. "Wait till Congress adjourns," he urged, "before making an address on political questions. . . . The next speech made by you in this section of the country should be most carefully prepared and one which will put you far in advance of any Southern Democrat on the public questions of the day, and if I mistake not there will be much material furnished you by the time the present session . . . adjourns."

A week later Montague effusively replied that Ryan's interest in him was "the most surprising and gratifying event" of his career:

I take some consolation that you see in me a medium (indifferent though it be) to accomplish something for Virginia,—the purpose to help her bear her full responsibility to the Union, and to contribute her full share to its growth and glory. This purpose I cherish profoundly, and I am not hopeless that with your wise aid my efforts may be entirely unavailing.[34]

Though Montague made numerous addresses outside Virginia throughout 1903, his next important New York speech (and his most important national address while governor) was delivered in January, 1904. The occasion was a Democratic banquet held in honor of Mayor George B. McClellan of New York City. Invited to the affair were all the prominent Democratic notables of the industrial Northeast. Ryan had evidently participated in arranging the dinner, but when Cleveland, Gorman, and Parker declined to attend at the last minute, Ryan wrote Montague suggesting that he also absent himself from the affair:

I am anxious about your own political fortune, and while I don't now see how your coming will hurt there may be some risk. . . . The

34 Ryan to Montague, Jan. 5, 1903, and Montague to Ryan, Jan. 12, 1903, Montague Papers.

papers will expect you to state your preference as to the candidates, and it is my judgment that it would be unwise for you to take any risks till we know how strong you will be with the delegates from Virginia to the National Convention.

At this time Ryan feared that Cleveland was a certain candidate and would endanger Parker's chances in the Northeast. Thus he hoped for a Solid South as the determining balance of power in the convention. And he continued to view Montague as a spokesman for Southern sentiment.[35]

Despite Ryan's advice, Montague attended the McClellan dinner. The most notable visitors included former Governor Robert E. Patteson of Pennsylvania; Richard Olney of Massachusetts, the only prominent Cleveland man present; and former Governor David B. Hill of New York, leader of the anti-Cleveland Tammany forces. The Providence *Journal* commented, "If the dinner was intended to be . . . a Democratic love feast of national proportions, it served its purpose. Harmony was so thick you couldn't cut it with a razor." Hill, Olney, and Montague were the main speakers of the evening; Hill and Olney devoted the major portion of their addresses to foreign policy. Montague, dwelling on the role of the South in the party, called for the South to reassert herself nationally, "to affirmatively stand forth in behalf of the established and conservative principles of democracy . . . to not only ask, but to demand that issues which are dead should not be stirred up for our undoing. . . . The South should be treated not as a section, but as an integral part of our union." The candidate the South should unite behind, according to Montague, would be "courageous but not venturesome; zealous, but not picturesque; sober in judgment, but not fanatical in faith." All of these references, of course, were veiled jibes against Bryan and the silver issue. Such phraseology also conformed closely to the language used by Ryan in his article a year earlier.[36]

Montague's speech struck a responsive chord. The Chattanooga *Times* and the Montgomery *Advertiser* agreed that it voiced "the sentiment of the South." The Norfolk *Virginian-Pilot* described it as "a notable speech [which] demonstrates quite clearly Hon. Andrew Jackson Montague's capacity to keep his head above water in what-

---

35   Ryan to Montague, Jan. 2, 1904, *ibid.*
36   Providence (R.I.) *Journal*, Jan. 5, 1904; Norfolk *Virginian-Pilot*, Jan. 8, 1904; Staunton *Spectator and Vindicator*, Jan. 15, 1904; Richmond *News Leader*, Jan. 5, 1904.

ever company of his fellow citizens he may chance to fall." And Montague privately bragged that "no speech of the evening met with quite so much demonstrative approval as mine." [37]

In early 1904 Montague continued to inform Ryan concerning the Virginia political situation. The machine headed by Martin, Hay, and Flood favored Gorman, a man Montague criticized as having a "long career in the Senate without a single achievement and low standard in politics everywhere." But most of the state's Independents pledged for Parker as early as November of 1903; so did some machine men, including Swanson. By April, 1904, Daniel also had joined the drift to Parker.[38] In May, a month before Virginia's convention, Montague conveyed to Ryan his suspicions that Martin too had swung to Parker for expedient reasons. A Parker Club in Richmond, "started under the auspices of a very corrupt ward man of this city [Clyde W. Saunders]," was getting money from some of Parker's friends, but was actually a front in the fight against the primary. Ryan replied: "I have no doubt that the money you refer to came from the source named. Sen. Martin, whom I had never met, called to see me . . . seemed very strong in his support of Judge Parker. I was at a loss to understand it at the time, but what you indicate in your letter and the fact that he had a meeting with Parker the night of the day he saw me account for his attitude."

By June Montague could report that "Martin, Flood and Hay have abandoned Gorman. . . . There has been a good deal of money spent in Virginia on the delegation [to the state convention] by Mr. Martin or somebody; but if we succeed in carrying the primary, which is my main fight and which seems now more than probable, I will whip him before the people." [39]

At the 1904 Richmond state convention, Ryan, possibly with Montague's assistance, was selected as a delegate from his home Tenth District. At Richmond, Montague himself ran for one of the four positions as delegate-at-large for the coming St. Louis conven-

37 Staunton *Spectator and Vindicator*, Jan. 15, 1904; Richmond *News Leader*, Jan. 12, 1904; Montague to Philip F. Brown, Jan. 8, 1904, Montague Papers.

38 Montague to T. B. Thames, Nov. 16, 1903, Montague Papers; Doss, "Democrats in the Doldrums . . . ," 515. Ironically, of the state's major political figures, Montague alone seems to have taken no public position regarding Parker, other than through private correspondence.

39 Montague to Ryan, May 30, June 4, 1904, and Ryan to Montague, May 31, 1904, Montague Papers.

tion. In the balloting, Daniel led the list of the "Big Four" with 1,414 votes; Martin following with 1,387; Montague with 1,057; and Braxton with 938. Two minor candidates were eliminated. The vote reflected the complexion of the convention. Martin controlled it, but not with an iron hand. He and Daniel fought to keep the convention uninstructed as to Parker, and though Braxton, Jones, Glass, and Montague all favored instruction, Martin won on a test vote, 818 to 728.[40]

As one of the delegates to the national convention, Montague desired "to get upon the Committee on Resolutions, but a majority of our delegation is perhaps for Martin and I think he will oppose me." At St. Louis he was shunted into the honorary position of vice-president of the delegation, whereas Daniel, Martin, and Braxton figured prominently in the convention's deliberations. Under the unit rule the delegation went solidly for Parker, and the New Yorker was nominated.[41]

With Parker's nomination realized, Montague devoted considerable time in the final campaign, both in Virginia and the North, speaking for the nominee. Still, as he had predicted long before, Parker suffered defeat by a mammoth margin; only Maryland outside of the South joined that region in voting Democratic. Montague wrote Jones: "Our defeat of course I expected. I expected snow, but not at such a depth . . . [perhaps it can be] accounted for by prosperity. Roosevelt is a vigorous and progressive man; he makes mistakes but stands in the open, and this appeals to the people." [42]

Montague's close political connections with Ryan evidently ceased shortly after the 1904 campaign. If Ryan had ever entertained notions of pushing Montague as Parker's running mate, the hostility of the Virginia delegation toward Montague, personally, probably defeated such a purpose. Possibly, Ryan analyzed the strength of Martin's faction at the Virginia convention and concluded that Martin would be unbeatable in 1905—that Montague would not become the prominent Southern spokesman he had envisioned. Perhaps he concluded that Montague's usefulness had terminated once Parker had

40 Richmond *News Leader,* June 10, 1904; Doss, "Democrats in the Doldrums . . . ," 517. Ryan did not attend the Richmond convention, explaining to Montague that it would "give people more to talk about money influence." Ryan to Montague, June 6, 1904, Montague Papers.

41 Montague to Ryan, June 13, 1904, and Montague to Charles R. Hughes, March 14, 1905, Montague Papers.

42 Montague to Jones, Nov. 11, 1904, *ibid.*

been nominated. Whatever his reasons, Ryan soon severed his relationship with the Independent wing of Virginia's Democracy. By 1908 he had aligned with Martin's organization, and by 1912 he placed himself forthrightly against the Wilsonian campaign then being championed by most Southern progressives, including Montague. Montague's former connections with the man must then have proved embarrassing.[43]

Montague's brief association with Ryan can be explained by no other motivation than political ambition and a desire to see a renewed Southern power in the national Democratic party. Ryan, a typical "robber baron," had indulged in all the financial manipulations characteristic of the breed. However, it is true that in Virginia Ryan did much for "religion, education and philanthropy," and such a progressive as Braxton rated him as "a high man of patriotic motives." [44] Montague himself may have entertained such an opinion. It is also true that aside from an offer to advise Montague on personal investments in the New York stock market, no evidence exists that Ryan's friendship with the governor entailed any promise of financial subsidy in the 1905 race.[45]

Still, the entire connection savors of expediency. Essentially, Ryan represented a reaction to the progressive movement as expressed on a national scale; in making this alliance, Montague was thus cutting against the grain of his record as a Virginia progressive. Evidently, he sincerely felt that Parker was the best possible condidate, but in joining Ryan and the Parker cause, he was not so much concerned with the 1904 election as with elections to come. Aiding Montague in his climb to a national reputation, Ryan provided extremely valuable contacts, giving him personal access to some of the nation's preeminent statesmen. Had Montague been victorious in his 1905 senatorial campaign these national connections, combined with his natural ability, would have made possible a successful and influential career as Senator. His star might have risen even higher in the political spectrum.

Even before the 1904 campaign Montague's ascending national

---

43 Ryan remained personally friendly, however, at least as late as 1906, when he applauded Montague's decision not to leave Virginia. Ryan to Montague, Jan. 8, 1906, Montague Papers.
44 *Dictionary of American Biography* (New York, 1928–37), XVI, 266; Brooklyn (N.Y.) *Daily Eagle*, Jan. 30, 1903; Braxton to Samuel W. Williams, April 23, 1904, Braxton Papers.
45 Montague to Ryan, Jan. 12, 1903, Montague Papers.

reputation had led to speculation in some quarters as to his candidacy for high national office. In January of 1903 the Brooklyn *Daily Eagle* had nominated Olney as a Democratic candidate for the presidency in 1904. Mentioned as vice-presidential possibilities were "Governor Montague, of Virginia, or Governor Aycock, of North Carolina, progressive statesmen, born since the war or children at the time of the war . . . at once conservative and progressive." After his 1904 address at the McClellan banquet a Boston paper declared that "Montague of Virginia, who has many friends in New York . . . is regarded in the East as likely to be named for second place on the Democratic national ticket." [46]

Montague was also suggested seriously by some as a future contender for the presidency. The Reverend T. B. Thames, pastor of the First Baptist Church in Elizabeth, New Jersey, even suggested that he enter the race in 1904. Later, in 1906 the Baltimore *Sun,* fearful of another Bryan nomination for the presidency in 1908, reminded the party that other able individuals were available. Foremost in their speculation was Montague, "recognized . . . in the North as a man of vigorous intellect, with high ideals—a clear-headed, practical statesman, who gave Virginia an admirable administration as governor." [47] Douglas Southall Freeman, writing after Montague's death, praised his "high capacity, restless energy and imagination. . . . There was a time, thirty years ago, when most observers would have said that if any Southern Democrat had a chance to become President of the United States, Jack Montague had." Certain it was that in 1905 he had a larger following for that office than "had rallied at that time to his fellow-Southerner, who would become president, Woodrow Wilson." [48] Had Montague been granted more years of seasoning, of experience, in the Senate, his future would have seemed limitless. Walter Hines Page, one of his admirers, described him in 1912 to President-elect Wilson as "the best Governor Virginia has had in our day, and too honest and clean to commend himself to the political machine. . . . I can think of no other man of public experience, who (though not of distinguished origin) so well represents the old (genuine) Southern gentleman and statesman class. . . . His mind

46   Richmond *News Leader,* Feb. 3, 1903; Brooklyn *Daily Eagle,* Jan. 29, 1903; Boston *Herald,* Jan. 5, 1904, in scrapbook, Montague Papers.
47   T. B. Thames to Montague, Nov. 13, 1903, Montague Papers; Baltimore *Sun,* clipping sent by R. L. Montague to Montague, Sept. 10, 1906, Montague Papers.
48   Richmond *News Leader,* Jan. 25, 1937.

is keen and clear. It is furnished, too. He has read and thought." [49]

On an April day in 1905, Montague spoke to a receptive audience in St. Louis; the occasion was "Virginia day" at the World's Fair. Two English visitors listened as the governor spoke, with his usual excellence, on Virginia's historical heritage. After the address, one of the visitors remarked upon the comparative youth of both Montague and President Roosevelt. "I venture the assertion," he announced, "that if Governor Montague lives and continues to grow in favor he may be your President." [50]

An article entitled "Montague's Endless Chain" made its way through Virginia's and the nation's newspapers early that year. The analogy referred to Montague's unbroken succession of public offices from district attorney, to attorney general, to governor. And now he was campaigning—some thought successfully—to take a seat in the United States Senate. "Who knows after?" was the inevitable question. [51]

Though Montague may have asked himself the question, he did not daydream. He first proposed to forge the Senate link in the chain. The stirring campaign of 1905, possibly Virginia's most dramatic political fight of the twentieth century, was about to begin.

49 Page to Wilson, Nov. 27, 1912, in Woodrow Wilson Papers, Manuscripts Division, Library of Congress.
50 Staunton *Spectator and Vindicator*, April 21. 1905.   51 *Ibid.*

XIV

CAMPAIGN FOR SENATOR,
1905

> I am a young man, born since the war, yielding to none in
> national patriotism and hope for national perpetuity; but I
> am like thousands of young men throughout the South who
> have never been permitted to share in the responsibilities
> of national government . . . a condition of intellectual and
> moral servitude. I love every spot of the American Union;
> it should be a Union of affection, genuine fellowship, broad,
> patient, catholic, and enduring.
> MONTAGUE to GEORGE T. LEMON, December, 1904

IN Virginia politics the year 1905 was a year of decision. The fomenting rivalry of a decade had reached its culmination. From 1897 to 1904 an indecisive struggle had been waged between the two hostile Democratic factions for political mastery of the state. Notable victories had come to each; yet neither had completely vanquished the other. But in 1905 the inconsistent Virginia electorate would be faced with a clear-cut decision. Martin and Montague, the respective generals of the contending armies, met in personal combat while their lieutenants watched with anticipation. The result of this personal battle would determine the course to be traveled by the Old Dominion for years to come.

Who would win? Supporters of both candidates exuded supreme optimism at various times, and though he was occasionally beset with doubts, Montague personally maintained a calm confidence in ultimate victory. Several factors seemed to confirm this assurance. First of all, Martin lacked familiarity with the public. His previous elections had come via the legislature, not the people, and only occasionally had he addressed Democratic party gatherings. While Martin's personal popularity was thus an unknown factor, Montague's was proven. Had Montague not achieved a resounding victory against the machine in 1901? Had he not since that time served as the oratorical missionary for various reforms throughout Virginia? His 1901 platform had advocated the party primary, an employer's liability law, good schools, and good roads. Had not these two former objectives been realized with no assistance from Martin, and had not Montague contributed greatly to the growing reform agitation for the latter? Was it not logical that the most prominent advocate of these reforms should ride the crest of victory? Such was the basis of Montague's optimism. Such were the incentives for his campaign.

There was also cause for encouragement in the genuine ardor and loyalty of many of Montague's followers. Though his campaign was more intensively organized in 1905 than in 1901, and though Montague had become a more seasoned politician in the interim, his campaign of 1905 lost none of its aura of fresh amateurism. The tenor of his vast correspondence conclusively demonstrates that—in the minds of most of his followers at least—this was a battle against the Goliath, against political corruption; this was a crusade. Crandall Mackey urged Montague to "fight, fight, fight." No real issue existed, he intoned, save the "destruction of the Martin-Swanson machine . . . supported by every gambler, Sunday saloon keeper and crook in the State." Among the individuals in the reform element who supported Montague were Moore and Hunton, his close confidants in 1901, and A. H. Clement and E. P. Buford, both victims at different times of machine manipulation in their fights for legislative positions. William E. Dodd, the liberal-minded historian then teaching at Randolph Macon in Ashland, backed Montague as the man best able to eradicate the blight of the Martin organization. To one enthusiastic supporter, Montague affirmed, "My coming into political life in Virginia was induced by my earnest hostility to the ideals and stands which Mr. Martin held up to the people of this State." This flavor of a moral crusade permeated his campaign.[1]

The governor also received endorsement from two prominent state

1 Crandall Mackey to Montague, Feb. 13, 1905, and William E. Dodd to Montague, Oct. 14, 1904, Montague Papers.

figures in the reform faction, Henry St. George Tucker and Congressman William A. Jones. Jones had accepted Montague's leadership of the Independents with good grace, and offered his advice during the early part of the campaign. Montague was deprived, however, of Jones's assistance during the heat of the campaign because of an arrangement between the Congressman and Senator Daniel by which both agreed not to speak in the campaign. The agreement, initiated by Daniel, was especially agreeable to Jones, who left during the campaign for a congressional committee's tour of the Philippines. Still, Montague regretted his friend's inability to participate actively in the campaign.[2]

Though Montague thus retained the allegiances of many of the same persons who supported him in 1901, there were evidences of alarming defections from the ranks. Congressman John Lamb complained soon after the 1901 election that his support for Montague had injured him politically, and he gave no assistance to the governor in the fight for the primary. Attorney General William A. Anderson evidently supported Montague, but refused to publicize the fact. Lieutenant Governor Joseph E. Willard, then running for governor, scarcely communicated with Montague or his advisors. Former Governor Tyler opposed him openly.[3]

A more important example of defection can be cited in the case of A. C. Braxton's disenchantment with the governor. In 1905 Braxton privately supported Martin against Montague, though he took no active part in the campaign. Carter Glass, the vitriolic opponent of machine corruption and domination in 1901 also assumed a position of public neutrality in 1905. Though Montague and Glass conferred until as late as November, 1903, concerning the legislative elections of that year, Glass thereafter withdrew from the Martin-Montague rivalry. In January of 1905 Montague urged Jones to enlist Glass's aid: "I believe he is for me but don't know that he is willing to do anything." As late as April Glass had taken no move to indicate his preference: "He is now simply keeping quiet." Actually, Glass had decided to vote for Martin, and toward the end of the campaign expressed his views in a written appraisal which was published against his wishes.[4]

2 Montague to Tucker, March 20 and April 3, 1905, and Jones to Montague, undated, *ibid.*
3 Montague to Jones, May 18, 1904; Montague to John W. Hilldrup, Jan. 24, 1905; Montague to H. O. Humphreys, Sept. 28 and 30, 1904; all *ibid.*
4 Montague to Glass, Jan. 24, Nov. 9, 1903, May 24, 1904; Montague to

Handicapped by his inability to achieve solid support for his candidacy from the Independents, Montague was also unable to match Martin's prowess in erecting a strong campaign organization. He was hindered especially by a lack of finances, and those limited funds at his command were chiefly utilized in a mammoth mailing campaign. Beginning in February, 1905, and extending through April and into June, letters were sent in increasing volume to a majority of the state's Democratic electorate. Even so, Montague could not equal Martin's pace: "Martin this morning purchased $2,000 worth of postage stamps," reported Montague in early May, gloomily noting that his own letter campaign had necessarily been "less extensive." His inferior financial position was rendered even more acute when the Martin forces in the state Democratic committee assessed the candidates the cost of the primary. Montague's share amounted to $1,500.[5]

Response to Montague's letters was alternately encouraging and discouraging. Optimism was the prevalent tone, but disturbing reports were also in evidence, especially concerning the lack of organized activity by the Independents. As late as mid-July, only one month before the election, Lynch Montague, the governor's brother and campaign manager, bemoaned the fact that in Wythe, Giles, and Scott counties "we have no organization and are absolutely at the mercy of the machine." In Roanoke County "only half the precincts were ever organized for you," according to one Montague worker. "I personally got 20 people to vote for you, but one man can't do it all." [6]

Martin encountered few such difficulties. Beginning with a solid core of city and county officeholders, most of whom owed their election or selection to machine favor, Martin invariably obtained valuable local cooperation in the promotion of his campaign. Evidently, he also obtained sufficient financial backing, whether from the railroads, as Montague suspected, or from some other source. Aside from superior organization and finances, Martin also enjoyed the important support of the vast majority of the state's electoral judges,

---

Jones, Jan. 6, 1905; R. L. Montague to William D. Hix, April 22, 1905; all *ibid.* Rixey Smith and Norman Beasley, *Carter Glass, a Biography* (New York, 1939), 81.

5   R. L. Montague to J. H. Capers, Jr., June 28, 1905; Montague to R. J. Camp, May 9, 1905; Montague to Tucker, April 3, 1905; all in Montague Papers.

6   R. L. Montague to Creed M. Fulton, July 18, 1905; R. L. Montague to John W. Hilldrup, Aug. 12, 1905; O. L. Stearnes to Montague, Sept. 8, 1905; all *ibid.*

and on election day he reportedly had representatives in all thirteen hundred precincts of the state.[7]

But Martin's advantages were based not solely on superior organization. He also commanded a statewide popularity vastly underestimated by Montague and the Independents. As Virginia's Senator he had been unusually effective in obtaining appropriations for improvement of her waterways and port facilities. His businesslike efficiency in responding to individual pleas of his constituents had become almost legendary. That Martin possessed attractive personal qualities, an ability to inspire loyalty, and a talent for administrative detail, cannot be denied. Although he had rarely appeared before the Virginia populace in a speaking capacity, he nevertheless possessed the advantages of ten years' seniority, a well-known name, and a record of achievement for the Commonwealth.[8]

Montague hoped to pierce Martin's armor where it was weakest: the Senator's lack of a positive record of sponsorship for important national legislation. Only rarely had Martin taken clear-cut positions on major issues of the day. Basically, his ideology was not abreast of the times. He was usually out of sympathy with the reforms which swept Virginia and the country at the turn of the century. He demonstrated a reluctance and a hesitance in trying to adjust to the new circumstances, yet the adjustment was gradually made.

An indication of Martin's shifting attitudes toward the functions of government developed early in the 1905 campaign. As with Swanson in 1901, the charge was made by labor organizations that Martin had opposed several attempts in the Virginia Assembly to enact an employer's liability bill. Like Swanson, Martin denied the assertion: "I at no time antagonized the passage of the bill. . . . On the contrary I on every fitting and proper occasion expressed the opinion that legislation should be enacted abolishing the common law doctrine of nonliability of the employer from injuries." As proof of his sincerity, Martin pointed to his support of a similar bill before the United States Congress.[9]

Indeed, Martin did sponsor, in March, 1905, a Senate committee resolution to "consider what legislation should be enacted in relation

---

7 Eckenrode, "Virginia Since 1865," 309.
8 Martin had obtained $1,200,000 for the construction of a dry dock at Norfolk, $360,000 for an extension of Norfolk's harbor, and $750,000 to improve the James River.
9 Richmond *News Leader*, Jan. 28, 1905.

to the liability of railroad companies engaged in interstate traffic for injuries received by their employees when in discharge of duty." [10] Martin's favorable position on national regulation of railroad rates and toward employer's liability legislation was very possibly genuine. As early as March, 1901, he had voted to require Interstate Commerce Commission reports on employee injuries. And in January of 1905 H. R. Fuller, a national legislative representative of railroad unions, asserted that "The Senator has been fair to our interests. . . . I think our members throughout the State of Virginia will make no mistake in giving him their support." [11] Martin and other organization leaders usually assumed friendlier attitudes toward national reform legislation than toward efforts to reform Virginia internally. Internally, their political dominance rested on the status quo. Nationally, they were freer to take independent action.

Nevertheless, in Virginia's fight for an employer's liability law, Martin had evidently been in opposition. In 1900, when such a bill was being considered by the Assembly, the Legislative Board of Railway Employees planned a meeting with Martin at Murphy's Hotel in Richmond. Members of the committee traveled from all points of the state to discuss Martin's position on the measure, but the Senator forgot the engagement. And in the subsequent defeat of the bill by the Assembly, all Martin's friends, "save one," voted against it.[12]

Montague personally considered Martin's congressional resolution for the Senate committee investigation merely a ruse to delay effective legislation. As for Martin's avowed concern for the regulation of railroad rates, Montague was equally dubious. His suspicions had been heightened by the knowledge that Martin was one of only two Democratic Senators who had voted with some Republicans to subsidize the Pennsylvania Railroad's terminal in Washington with $3,000,000 rather than the $1,500,000 actually adopted. Since the Chesapeake and Ohio—a railway which possibly gave Martin financial backing in the 1905 campaign—was a subsidiary of the Pennyslvania, Martin's vote may have been a means of retaining railroad support, even while giving lip service to more comprehensive regulatory legislation of popular appeal. As the senatorial contest developed, Montague was

10 Dale A. Thorn, "The Martin-Montague Campaign of 1905" (MS in Department of History, University of Virginia, Charlottesville), 6.
11 H. R. Fuller to H. S. Brown, Feb. 23, 1905; Montague Papers.
12 Montague to W. I. Steele, Jan. 31, 1905, and Montague to J. B. Drissel, May 19, 1905, *ibid.*

to charge publicly that Martin's sudden interest in rate regulation just before his first popular election was mere opportunism, especially since his previous ten years in the Senate had witnessed scarcely a word from him on the subject. "Promises made in contemplation of matrimony," Montague argued, "should be carefully scanned." [13]

This initial controversy of the senatorial campaign had actually been a sidelight of the parallel race for governor, which found two of the candidates, Swanson and Lieutenant Governor Willard, exchanging accusations on the employer's liability issue. A third candidate for governor was State Senator William H. Mann, author of the Mann liquor law. Although Willard was generally considered a Montague man and Swanson and Mann were recognized as friends of Martin, little surface correlation seemed to exist between the senatorial and gubernatorial fights. Montague had had differences with Willard during their terms in office, differences which were not resolved to the governor's satisfaction. In June, 1903, he derisively complained that Willard seemed inclined to "run with the hare and hunt with the hounds, so far as I can judge." As late as May of 1904 he predicted to Philip F. Brown that "Mr. Willard, I suppose, if he votes would vote for some anti-Martin man [for the Senate], though what he would do later on I do not know. His position has not been very fully disclosed or very satisfactory to me." [14] Because of this estrangement, Montague evidently encouraged Tucker, his colleague in the Ogden movement, to enter the gubernatorial race. But when Tucker ultimately declined to run, Montague endorsed Willard. And in September, 1905, one month after both Montague and Willard had suffered defeat, Montague appointed the latter to the position on the corporation commission vacated by Fairfax. [15]

Martin and Swanson had closer associations in the 1905 campaign. While many Montague supporters steered clear of Willard's candidacy, all the big names in Martin's organization supported Swanson. After 1901 Swanson had participated regularly in the deliberations of the "inner council" of the organization, sharing, for example, the "retainer" fees awarded for legislative favors by E. P. Meaney of Ameri-

13 Montague to J. B. Drissel, May 19, 1905; "Record of Thomas S. Martin," (typescript), both *ibid.*
14 Montague to Joseph E. Willard, Feb. 12, 1903; Montague to R. Walton Moore, June 5, 1903; Montague to Philip F. Brown, May 23, 1904; Moore to Montague, Feb. 8, 1905; all *ibid.*
15 Unidentified clipping, scrapbook, Moore Collection; George Bryan to Henry St. George Tucker, Jan. 16, 1905, Tucker Papers.

can Telephone and Telegraph. Still, the "game cock," as Swanson was sometimes known, maintained a certain sprightly independence of action which evidently disturbed Martin. Rumor had it, at least, that Martin attempted to dissuade Swanson from the gubernatorial race in 1903. By March, 1904, however, Flood had pledged Swanson his aid, and in the 1905 campaign the Martin and Swanson forces cooperated closely behind the scenes.[16] Swanson emerged victorious in the three-way contest.

Aside from the publicity on the employer's liability controversy, the Senate race was relatively quiet during the first three months of 1905. Behind the scenes, however, organizational activity of the past three years was building to a climax. "Conspicuous and luminous" Montague buttons, bearing a "splendid likeness of the governor," were distributed to Montague workers in early February. The same month found Martin conducting conferences with his supporters in Richmond and elsewhere. Late in March he opened his headquarters in the capital city; Montague soon followed suit. Montague's headquarters bubbled with enthusiasm and confidence, and Montague predicted that he would obtain an "immense majority" if the elections were free of fraud. Martin reticently observed that he was "not without friends in every section." [17]

Montague delivered the initial salvo of the campaign with a speech at Spotsylvania courthouse on April 3. If the Virginia populace had expected a campaign filled with mild generalities and polite dinner toasts, Montague quickly dispelled such delusions. In this first speech and throughout the campaign he maintained a strong offensive against Martin personally and against his machine in general. Speaking at gatherings from the isolated Eastern Shore to the plateau country of the southwest, the governor relentlessly placed Martin and his record before the public. Some of Montague's advisors cautioned him against overplaying his hand; others applauded his tack and urged him to plunge the knife deeper.

Martin at first reacted passively. From his first speech early in April

16 Marshall McCormick to Henry St. George Tucker, Nov. 14, 1903, and J. Ogden Murray to Tucker, Nov. 21, 1903, Tucker Papers; Henry D. Flood to S. L. Ferguson, March 23, 1904, Flood Papers; Jim D. Patton to John W. Daniel, June 28, 1905, Daniel Papers. Patton mentions "Martin's and Swanson's headquarters" in Richmond.
17 Richmond *News Leader*, Feb. 11 and 20, March 18, 1905; Montague to Wyndham Robertson, Feb. 18, 1905, Montague Papers.

until he and Montague met in joint debate three months later, Martin relied on his own latent popularity to counteract Montague's incisive thrusts. Portraying himself as a hard-working Senator wounded by the venomous maligning of the rash and libelous Montague, he rarely mentioned the governor by name and, except to refute two or three charges, only occasionally criticized directly the latter's stands on important issues. Instead, his speeches concentrated on the value of his own senatorial accomplishments. During the early period of the campaign Montague appeared to attract the larger and more enthusiastic audiences, whereas Martin's tame delivery and defensive approach seemed to justify his reputation as a working, not a speaking, Senator.[18]

When he accepted Montague's challenge to a joint debate at King George courthouse in early July, however, Martin was forced to alter his tack. The governor's pointed queries in the debate forced the Senator to reply directly, and in so doing, Martin also leveled several serious charges against Montague. For the remainder of the campaign (which lasted until the primary election on August 22) Martin continued this offensive, while Montague, if anything, became even more denunciatory. As a speaker, Martin showed up well at the King George debate, and his subsequent tours of the state evidenced a greater confidence, a greater familiarity with his audiences. Although he did not approach Montague in diction and eloquence, he proved himself capable of holding his own in a speaking campaign.

The main issues raised by the two candidates did not focus upon specific national policies. In his platform, Montague advocated modification of the tariff, adequate regulation of railroad rates, a crusade against political graft and corporation contributions to political parties, "equal rights to all, special privilege to none," the submission of all causes of war to arbitration and the direct election of Senators. But Martin did not respond to the governor's attempt to make these issues a major factor in the campaign, except to emphasize his approval of railroad regulation. Instead, Martin concentrated on his record as an efficient public servant and procurer of appropriations. If his record was satisfactory to Virginia, he argued, why displace the man who had achieved it? The question was astute. Claude Bennett, Montague's research assistant in the Congressional Information Bureau, admitted, "In its practical accomplishment, Sen. Martin's rec-

18   Copy of Martin's speech at Front Royal, Va., June 7, 1905; R. L. Montague to J. T. Thornton, May 10, 1905; R. L. Montague to J. J. Powell, May 31, 1905; John Hart to Montague, May 25, 1905; all in Montague Papers.

ord is unusually good. . . . With so many appropriations and references he will certainly appeal to the people." [19]

Concerning Martin's attitude on important issues, Montague privately charged that Martin was in essence a Republican Senator; yet he found difficulty in proving the point. He could demonstrate that Martin had supported a protective tariff for white pine, that he had voted for government aid to the Pennsylvania Railroad depot in Washington, and that he had voted to subsidize the shipping industry; yet these actions hardly formed a convincing case. Montague himself lamented that Martin's record "does not show where he stands on any question of importance." Martin was culpable, not for what he had done, but for what he had failed to do.[20]

Most notably, Martin had failed to support the crusade for a senatorial primary. Consequently, Montague attempted to make his own advocacy of the reform and the Senator's hostility to it the chief issue of the campaign. This was his trump card. It was inconceivable to him that the Virginia electorate, overwhelmingly favorable to the primary, could consistently support the man who had endorsed the primary belatedly and half-heartedly. The form letter which was circulated throughout the state from Montague's headquarters emphasized his role in pushing the reform, and in almost every speech he contrasted his active sponsorship to Martin's nebulous position. In this, the first senatorial primary in Virginia's history, he challenged the electorate to "reward the man who has tried to give it to you, and . . . rebuke the man who has tried to withhold it from you." The United States Senate Montague repeatedly described as the "decaying branch of the congress," and the most obvious way to purge it of its corrupting influences was to make its members responsible to the people—not to corporate lobbies in state legislative halls.[21]

Martin at first made no reply to Montague's charge that he had consistently opposed the primary principle. From early April when the charge was first made until the King George joint debate in July, no word of protest or refutation was heard. Montague claimed that Martin's silence was tantamount to substantiation of his charges, but still Martin made no reply. When the two finally met in joint debate, however, the Senator could no longer ignore the issue.

The joint debate came on July 6; the location was an old brick

19   Claude C. Bennett to Montague, March 14 and 23, 1905, *ibid.*
20   Montague to Robert N. Harper, March 9, 1905, *ibid.;* Richmond *Times Dispatch*, May 28, 1905.
21   Richmond *Times Dispatch*, April 4 and 5, July 16, 1905.

courthouse in King George, a rural county bordering the Potomac south of Washington. Montague had challenged Martin, and the latter accepted, naming the terms. The two candidates, "crossing the mud-puddle at the door," entered the courthouse at 1:30 P.M., and Martin, with "a pad of paper in one hand [and a] stern countenance" sat six feet from Montague as the latter opened the first hour's discussion. A crowd of four hundred listened attentively.[22]

Several issues entered the debate, but a highlight of the verbal wrestle was the repartee concerning the primary. Summarizing the history of the primary movement and his part in it, Montague, "clasping his hands together, asked his first question of 'the junior Senator.' 'I would not take any advantage of the junior Senator . . . for a thousand seats in the Senate. But I would like to have his reply before I leave here. I ask him to say when and where and why he had done anything in this State for a primary.' "

When the time came to reply, Martin, speaking with "volleys of vigorous sentences," first asserted: "I have not discussed the primary before in this campaign. I do not attach [to it] that momentous importance. . . . I do not believe the sun will cease to shine whether senators are elected by the people or by honorable legislators, as has been done for one hundred and sixteen years." He continued by declaring that he had always honored and respected the state convention and state committee as the governing bodies of the party, and when they had adopted a primary as the party's mode of election, he had been satisfied with their decision. Had not his motion for the adoption of the primary in the 1904 convention proved his sincerity? As for his part in the 1897 Roanoke convention Martin admitted he had opposed the primary at that time, but for good reasons. The scheme, he said, had been "to strike Tom Martin down. It would saddle on me $10,000." This was in reference to the provision of the 1897 plan which would have assessed each senatorial candidate that amount.

In rebuttal Montague termed Martin's explanations evasive. "The senator says he is in favor of a primary, and moved an amendment at the last State convention. Well, why not? The tail gate was down, and anybody could get in the cart." Martin, he charged, had favored the primary only after the people had demanded it, and he had yet to support actively the national movement for the direct election of Senators. The point remained that he had done nothing to aid the cause, while "every friend he has in the State Senate fought the legali-

22 The description of the debate is derived chiefly from two sources: Washington *Post*, July 7, 1905; Richmond *Times Dispatch*, July 7, 1905.

zation of the primary. Let him line up his friends for legalization."
Here Montague had reference to the defeated Machen bill.

In his rebuttal Martin claimed that in 1899 he had issued a statement supporting the reform. As one paper related: " 'I never saw it,' interposed the governor. 'I circulated it from one end of this State to the other,' declared the Senator in high voice, gesturing at the governor, who sat in proud composure, waving a pasteboard fan." Martin also charged that of the sixteen votes against the Machen primary bill in the state senate, nine were cast by supporters of himself and seven by friends of Montague. Furthermore, he argued, if the primary issue were of such vital importance in the campaign, why should not Jones, the original proponent of the innovation, be the candidate, and not Montague? With these sentiments, the debate terminated.

Following the King George debate, Montague continued emphasizing the primary issue, aided now by Martin's admission that he had opposed the 1897 plan for pecuniary reasons. He also refuted Martin's fallacious claim that he had publicly supported the primary as early as 1899. For his part, Martin temporarily resumed his silence on the issue. At length, however, Montague's relentless attacks had their effect. On August 7 the Senator launched an offensive of his own, attempting to minimize the governor's role in obtaining the primary. Noting that Montague had been nominated for attorney general by the same convention that defeated the primary in 1897, Martin deduced, "Thus he controlled the convention. I was for another man, but he got nominated. . . . What did he do for the primary then? Nothing . . . he said not a word . . . profound silence." The same silence, charged Martin, had characterized Montague in the succeeding Norfolk and Richmond Democratic conventions, while at the latter it had been himself, not Montague, who had moved to readopt the primary.[23]

Martin deliberately distorted the record, ignoring the May conference of 1899, in which Montague played an important part, and the gubernatorial campaign of 1901, in which Montague repeatedly advocated a primary. The charge that Montague had been silent during the various conventions was technically true, but only because he had been a delegate to none of them. When Martin charged that Montague had done nothing for the primary, the governor tersely replied, "The senator uttered what he knew wasn't true." [24]

23 Richmond *Times Dispatch*, July 22, Aug. 8, 1905.
24 Staunton *Spectator and Vindicator*, Aug. 18, 1905.

Martin probably deceived few persons in attempting to pose as an original friend of the primary, and Montague undoubtedly won converts through his persistent emphasis of the issue. Yet by this very emphasis Martin had been forced to assume a position which differed little from Montague's own. Regardless of his past attitude, Martin was now committed to the primary principle. This transformation can be termed a Montague victory, but by removing a chief cause for criticism of Martin, it hampered the governor's campaign.

Montague also experienced difficulty in attacking Martin's public positions on two other important issues. The contagious enthusiasm of the 1905 May education campaign infected even the lukewarm junior Senator. In several addresses at school rallies, Martin seconded educators' pleas for a longer school term. Though nine months was too long, he said, five months was too short: "Get a boy to the common schools, to church and to public speaking, and he will be an educated man at thirty-five years or a fool." [25]

Martin also tardily endorsed the growing demand for better roads. In his first address of the campaign, delivered in Lunenburg County, the Senator declared he was in favor of federal aid to roads, expressing the belief that too much money had been spent in the North for pensions, public buildings, and harbors. And on April 17 he spoke in Southampton to one of the several good roads conventions held throughout the state. Montague, with good reason, viewed this rapid conversion to the good roads cause skeptically.[26] Noting that several highway bills were then pending before the Senate, Montague charged that Martin had been "as silent as the graves at Arlington" while these bills remained bottled up in committee. He also criticized the machine-dominated Virginia legislature for failing to enact his proposal for a state highway commission.[27] Nevertheless, Martin had again stolen Montague's thunder. By acquiescing to the popular

25 Doss, "John Warwick Daniel," 359; Richmond *Times Dispatch,* May 10, 1905.
26 A "Memorandum" written by Montague (Dec. 14, 1904, Montague Papers) states: "On yesterday at Fairfax Courthouse Sen. Lattimer of South Carolina said to me that at the time he introduced his bill for national aid for public highways, Sen. Martin . . . opposed . . . the same. He said that after sending out a good deal of literature on the subject, Sen. Martin came to him one day and remarked, 'If you will stop those constituents of mine from sending me from ten to fifteen letters a day on this subject I will vote for your steal.' "
27 Richmond *Times Dispatch,* April 11, 16 and 22, 1905.

movements of the day, he proved an elusive target for campaign oratory.

Of all Montague's attacks on Martin, the one that resulted in the most controversy, and the one that most vitally influenced the campaign, was the charge that Martin lacked the statesmanlike qualities of a Senator. In his first address at Spotsylvania, Montague declared that "Martin's record is insufficient to justify 18 years in the Senate. . . . He does the work of an executive clerk rather than that of a senator." In Martin's ten years in the Senate, claimed Montague, he had not authored one important law, nor had he vocally supported any law of consequence. Instead, he had performed the duties of a "business Senator," faithfully answering letters and running from one department to another on minor errands for his constituents. Montague called for the election of a Senator who could represent Virginia "as she had been represented in the best days of the Commonwealth," not one who served merely as a business agent.[28]

Montague's concern for the decline of Southern statecraft lay at the base of his desire to oust Martin from the Senate. From his earliest days at Richmond College he had preached reconciliation of the North and South so that the South could once again assume a prominent role in American government. And his "first political ambition" had arisen when as a boy he listened to a political conversation between his father and Senator R. M. T. Hunter at Inglewood.[29] His idealistic conception of statesmanship, derived from his environment, was not synthetically acquired in the flush of campaign. This conception, his grandest legacy from the Old South, was the catalytic agent in his rebellion against the Martin machine and in his subsequent role as a Southern progressive. Possessing an intense pride in his state, her people, and her history, he had viewed with revulsion the postwar deterioration of Virginia's politics, and the rise of men of narrow partisanship and mediocre intellect as her political leaders.

Born during the Civil War, Montague did not look upon that conflict as the irrevocable finale to the Southern statesmanship known to his father's generation. True to his youthful feeling that "no man is any account without conceit," Montague sincerely believed, despite a modest exterior in personal relationships, that he was qualified to help lead a resurgence of Southern statecraft. Not inconceivably, he

---

28 *Ibid.*, April 4, 1905; Montague to John M. Garnett, March 16, 1905, Montague Papers.
29 Montague to Stephen Hunter, Jan. 17, 1905, Montague Papers.

hoped someday to win the Presidency, to serve as a living symbol of sectional reconciliation, of the reentry of the South as an integral part of the American Union. In the 1905 campaign, however, his criticism of Martin's lack of statesmanship proved politically unwise. By calling for a return to Virginia's former senatorial greatness he indirectly advertised himself as capable of that greatness. Martin was to effectively satirize the egotistical implications of this self-glorification.

At first, most of Montague's advisors applauded his aggressive technique in condemning Martin's prosaic record. Others cautioned, however, that the gentlemanly Virginia Democracy, unaccustomed to public spats between candidates, would not tolerate bitter criticism of one Democrat by another.[30] Capitalizing on this prevailing sentiment, Martin complained in his first campaign address that he "did not initiate this method of campaign," he did not desire to engage in personal references to himself and his senatorial record, and he would not decry his adversary. But he had striven to merit the senatorial honor conferred upon him by Virginia, and he hoped his stewardship would be found acceptable. For Montague's platonic and unrealistic idea of statesmanship, Martin had only contempt:

> I do not recline in my toga . . . if you want that sort of statesman, vote for my opponent. . . . A statesman must do more than speechify. If any can say I have not done what they asked, I have failed as a Senator. The South is too sentimental. This is a practical age; we have been talking constitutions while they [the North] have been getting appropriations.[31]

Montague heatedly denied that he had unjustly maligned and abused Martin and his record: "If a respectful discussion of the record of a public servant is treason," he declared, "then I am guilty of that crime." The governor also disparaged Martin's utilitarian and materialistic philosophy of a Senator's duties: "It's time to make a change [in the Senate], and I tell you that the passage of an appro-

30 Henry St. George Tucker, while fully agreeing that Martin had debauched state politics, felt that Montague had shown poor taste in publicly terming Martin a "department-runner." Tucker to S. S. P. Patteson, April 13, 1905, Tucker Papers. In the Martin camp, at least one observer felt that Montague's "weak and childish" course would "boomerang," and that Martin should treat the charges with "silent contempt." William E. Allen to Henry D. Flood, April 7, 1905, Flood Papers. For his part, Congressman Jones approved of Montague's "line of attack," though cautioning him to "use as much tact as possible." Jones to Montague, April 4, 1905, Montague Papers.

31 Richmond *Times Dispatch*, April 8, 11, and 23, 1905.

priation bill will not solve the difficulty." If the procurement of appropriations were the sole function of a representative, he argued, Virginia would do better to send Republicans to Washington, since the members of that party controlled the Congress.[32]

Martin's attempt to ridicule Montague's lofty idealization of a Senator's duties was not favorably received by the state's press; neither, however, was Montague's attempt to label Martin a "department-runner." True, Martin did not have the makings of a great leader or statesman; his mind was too prosaic and unimaginative. But although most Virginians readily agreed that Martin was not an orator of Daniel's or Montague's stature and not a man of broad philosophic vision, they admired him for his efficiency and dispatch.[33] Montague deprecated the importance of Martin's perfunctory office work, yet the *News Leader* probably expressed the view of a majority when it asserted that both Martin and Montague had been "exceptionally efficient, energetic, and valuable in their respective and important places." [34] Perhaps, indeed, Montague's concept of the Senate and of statesmanship was overly romanticized, somewhat grandiose. Perhaps, as Martin claimed, he was naive in calling for a return to the "grand old days" of Senators William C. Rives and Hunter. Perhaps his nineteenth-century mugwump idealism was passé in the face of twentieth-century reality. Perhaps, in this sense, Martin was actually more representative of the "new South" and the "new Virginia" than was Montague. In any event, by attacking Martin's department-running, Montague had made the tactical mistake of attacking the Senator's forte. Martin made the most of that mistake.

Robert Beverley, a Montague supporter, advised the governor shortly after both candidates had begun their campaigns that his speeches would be more effective if he stopped attacking Martin's department-running, and concentrated instead on exposing Martin's connection with the railroads. "Only the large amounts of money spent by the railroads have kept them [the machine] with the whip handle." In reply Montague lamented:

> The trouble is in securing proof. We all know it, but the question is to prove it. . . . He [Martin] is denying now in his speech that he is

32 *Ibid.,* April 25, May 23 and 28, 1905, and campaign editorial, May 16, 1905.
33 Richmond *Times Dispatch,* June 23, 1905; Staunton *Spectator and Vindicator,* Aug. 11, 1905; Bear, "Life of Martin," 180.
34 Richmond *News Leader*, July 19, 1904.

a railroad man, although I have made no criticism upon this point so far. He states that all the railroad presidents of the state are against him. I know nothing of this, except I have heard that perhaps one railroad president will support me. Of course you understand it makes no difference who the president is, if the political department of the railroad is turned against the candidates, and I know the political departments of the railroads of Virginia are against me.[35]

Montague had earlier contracted a friendship with L. E. Johnson upon the latter's election as president of the Norfolk & Western late in 1903 (see Chapter XIII, n. 14), and this friendship was evidently instrumental in obtaining the neutrality of that road in 1905. Montague's contacts with certain officials of the Southern Railway, however, was to prove of no avail: "The Southern Railway and C & O seem to be active against me through their chief attorneys, but I do not know whether they will put any money in the campaign. I am inclined to think that the Norfolk and Western will remain neutral." By May of 1905, as the campaign progressed, Montague was not so doubtful: "There is a great deal of money against me. The railroads are putting it up. The talk of railroad presidents being for me is all stuff, and if they are, it is a blind in order to deceive the people while the railroads put up the money against me."[36] Though Montague regularly castigated Martin's initial 1893 election as being accomplished by devious methods, he never directly charged that Martin had continued to represent the railroads since that time. As he told his inquirer, proof was lacking.[37]

If Montague hesitated to attack Martin's uncertain alliance with railroads, he had no such qualms in denouncing Martin's machine. Corrupt tactics of petty politicians in both factions had continued (though in diminished intensity) to plague the Commonwealth's political scene throughout Montague's term in office. In the 1903 legislative elections, for example, Montague described the "most stupendous fraud . . . recently perpetrated in the Patrick County primary.

---

35 Robert Beverley to Montague, April 12, 1905, and Montague to Beverley, April 15, 1905, Montague Papers.
36 Montague to Wyndham B. Robertson, Feb. 18, 1905; Montague to W. K. Pace, May 22, 1905, Montague to Albert Shaw, Jan. 2, 1905; Montague to J. Henry Cochran, Jan. 6, 1905, all *ibid.*
37 Indicative of Martin's continuing contacts with railroad personnel is this appeal from W. T. Tinsley, Treasurer of Alleghany County: "We are bound to do something here to stop Montague. He [Martin] must send some good railroad man here to do the work and that quick." Tinsley to Henry D. Flood, March 3, 1905, Flood Papers.

Not more than three hundred votes were polled, yet the returns showed nine hundred for Judge Moore, Martin's candidate." Since the Machen bill to legalize the primary had failed to pass the legislature, Montague feared a repetition of such chicanery in the senatorial election. Thus, although criticism of the machine and machine tactics was not the paramount issue in Montague's 1905 campaign as it had been in 1901, it still found ample reference in his speeches, particularly as the final stages of the campaign neared.[38]

Montague especially excoriated Martin's domination of the legislature and the obstructive action of his friends in defeating good roads legislation and the Machen primary bill. At their King George debate he charged the machine with selfish partisanship, terming it a government "of friends, by friends, and for friends." In reply, Martin denied knowing anything whatever concerning the vast majority of legislative actions, stating further that if he possessed all the friends attributed to him, Montague was pursuing a vain hope in seeking his defeat.

Shortly after the joint debate, Montague spoke in Manchester, one of his strongholds. Here he reiterated his opposition to machine methods and domination. Speaking from the same platform he had used four years earlier, he declared that Martin's organization of 1901 had since grown even stronger and more dangerous: "A gentleman told me the other day, 'I am with you, but don't say anything about it; I am afraid.' " This the governor lambasted as a sordid example of the degrading influence of pressure politics. And he counseled, "You cannot break up the county rings unless you break up the state rings first." [39]

As he had with the primary issue, Martin, following the King George debate, attempted to meet Montague's charges with a counteroffensive. In a Pittsylvania County address, the Senator labeled Montague's criticisms as "cry-baby talk of a machine to hide the only real machine that exists." Montague, he charged, had built up an organization by virtue of his large appointive powers, and the two "cogs" of that machine in Pittsylvania were James L. Tredway and J. Hunt Hargrave. The next day Montague replied that he had appointed Hargrave to the Farmville Normal School board specifically because he was not a politician and would give the board nonpartisan service:

38 Montague to Jones, Sept. 17, 1903, Montague Papers.
39 Richmond *Times Dispatch,* July 16, 19, 22, and 25, 1905.

They say you can't prove there is any machine. This may be true for it lives of, by and for politics and usually in dark places, where the privileged few are set against the whole people. It does not desire to benefit the State so much as to down the Governor. . . . The secret of the machine in Virginia is, if you want anything from the Legislature, stand by Martin.

In his anger, Montague bitterly asserted that if the king of England manipulated elections as regularly as did the machine in Virginia, he would lose his crown within six months.[40]

Vitriol flowed as the campaign neared its climax. Although Montague had definitely been the more aggressive of the two candidates in the first half of the contest, the months of July and August found both equally caustic. As the weather became warmer, so did the campaign, so did the tempers.

Martin's temper had been especially on edge during the King George debate. On that July afternoon he made several serious charges which he later regretted. In his opening speech Montague had made his customary accusation that the Senate was a decaying institution, that many of its members were admittedly corrupt. The *Times Dispatch* recorded Martin's heated reply:

Why should my competitor be elected because Quay, Dietrich and Burton are corrupt? . . . Graft has come nearer my distinguished competitor than Washington. Under his very eyes it has occurred in the education bureau in Richmond. You have seen a book costing eighteen cents sold to the schools at seventy-five cents, and the profits go into the pockets of the clerk of the board. . . . Even the great Corporation Commission has been discredited in a way that must bring the blush to every thoughtful cheek. . . . My competitor might do well to keep his eyes on the graft nearer home and give himself less concern about the sins of senators in Washington. The sins are being taken care of in Washington.

Martin referred to two incidents which considerably embarrassed Montague. The first concerned the state board of education, of which Montague was a member. J. D. Eggleston, a candidate to replace Joseph W. Southall as the state superintendent of public instruction, charged early in his campaign that the price of school registers, which each of the state's nine thousand teachers were required to buy, was ridiculously exorbitant. The state board met on June 22, 1905, to consider the charges, Montague presiding. It developed that J. A. Mc-

40 *Ibid.*, July 18, 1905.

Gilvray, the second clerk in the department of public instruction, had collaborated with J. P. Thomas, principal of Richmond High School and the author of the register, in distributing the registers at a price of seventy-five cents each, while the cost of production was actually only eighteen to twenty cents; the two divided the resultant profit. When the board discovered the facts of the case, they immediately dismissed McGilvray, and Thomas resigned.[41]

Martin's criticism of Montague's role in the scandal was hardly justified, since McGilvray, the guilty party, was actually under the supervision of superintendent Southall, a Martin man. The eight-member board of education merely served in an advisory not an administrative capacity over the state department of public instruction. Even Eggleston, in making his charge, specifically exempted Montague and the state board from all blame for the incident.[42] At the King George debate Montague replied to Martin's criticisms by observing that he had continued the investigation "when other members of the board thought it should be discontinued and as a result the scandal has been unearthed. . . . I defy any one to say that I have not met corruption with a fearless front."

The other circumstance mentioned by Martin was more embarrassing. Beverley Crump, Montague's lawyer appointee on the corporation commission, had purchased a $100 share of stock in the Virginia Corporation Company; in addition, a clerk of the commission had purchased three shares. The purpose of the company was to draw up charters for those corporations applying to the corporation commission, and to present the same before the commission for approval. Crump argued that he had done a public service in buying the stock, since the technical draft work of the commission was facilitated. Critics, however, charged that Crump's stock in the company prejudiced his official actions when charters were presented for approval. Montague privately expressed "intense anxiety" concerning the controversy, terming Crump's action the "greatest indiscretion." [43]

This scandal had been uncovered in early June. By July, when Martin made his accusation against Montague, public opinion had largely rallied behind Crump. Thus, when Martin described not only

41 Overton, "Life of Eggleston," 216–21; Magruder, *Recent Administration in Virginia*, 27.
42 Prepared campaign editorial, July 1, 1905, Montague Papers.
43 Magruder, *Recent Administration in Virginia*, 158; McDanel, *The Virginia Constitutional Convention*, 85; Montague to W. G. Loving, June 2, 1905, Montague Papers

Crump, but the entire commission, in terms of disrespect, he did not voice popular opinion. Henry C. Stuart, one of the three commissioners, urged Montague not to shrink from defending Crump's honorable motives, emphasizing the fact that Crump had never profited "to the extent of a penny" from his investment. Stuart also suggested that Montague capitalize on Martin's critical references to the commission as a whole. The commission, "the guardian of the people's rights . . . against corporate influences," had provided for an increase in state revenues of one-half million dollars, and was currently in the process of formulating a system of freight rate regulations. Now Martin, in his first public reference to that body, had assailed its integrity.[44]

Accepting this advice, Montague publicly criticized Martin's indictment of the commission and defended Crump as a man of honor. The *Times Dispatch* joined in protest: "Sen. Martin cannot afford to let the matter rest where it is. Crump is a good citizen, and he has the interests of the State at heart. . . . Does he impugn the honor of Crump?" After much delay, Martin finally apologized for his remarks with the curt admission, "I shot off my tongue when I ought not to have done so." [45]

Such were the issues of the 1905 campaign.[46] As they developed, they alternately gave hope and discouragement to each candidate. Yet Montague generally maintained a rosy optimism that erased all personal doubt as to the eventual outcome. Encouraging reports from all sections of the state early in the campaign seemed to confirm this optimism. In late April, however, his canvass received a possibly fatal setback when he underwent an ear operation which left him seriously ill and incapacitated for a month. By May 22, however, he had fully recovered, and on that day he addressed a rally in the city of Bedford, where his reception was most encouraging. A week later he spoke to a tremendous gathering at the Academy of Music in Richmond, so

44 R. L. Montague to Montague, July 10, 1905, Montague Papers.
45 Richmond *Times Dispatch*, July 18, Aug. 19, 1905.
46 Another issue, inflated out of proportion, arose when Montague, hoping to drive a wedge between Martin and Senator Daniel, charged that the former had claimed credit for Congressional work actually performed by the latter. Montague was referring particularly to an act which had settled Virginia's long-standing claims against the federal government. The charge backfired when Daniel refuted it, praising Martin as "active, alert, and efficient." William A. Jones to Montague, March 20, 1905, Montague Papers; Richmond *Times Dispatch*, April 6, 1905.

large that a full five hundred voters were turned away. In pointed reference to Martin, Montague began his remarks with the comment, "I have not the distinction of having represented you in the Senate for ten years and never faced an audience in your beautiful city." After he had spoken for two hours, Montague looked at his watch as if to close his remarks when a voice from the crowd cried, "Go on; tomorrow is Sunday." Montague's headquarters claimed that the enthusiasm evidenced by the crowd "badly frightened the opposition. . . . It was the turning point of the campaign." [47]

Reports from Martin's camp told a different story. Although early in the canvass Martin's confidence was dampened by poor audiences, by June, even before the debate with Montague, reports emanating from his Richmond headquarters exuded confidence. "Jim" Patton reported to Daniel on June 12 that Martin had just returned from a tour of the Valley, where he found "everything satisfactory." On June 16 the same individual related that after conferring with "several members of the State Committee," he found all of them "to be very certain that Martin will carry the State by a very decided majority." Patton thought that "Martin ought to make a little better canvass than he is making," but that in general "he is organizing his forces very well." [48]

Meanwhile, in the Montague quarters a similar confidence prevailed throughout the month of June and into July. On July 1 Montague's brother cheerfully noted that the Martin forces had reduced their former predictions of a victory margin from 25,000 to only 10,000 or 15,000: "They say they'll take Richmond by 500 votes. We expect to carry the city by 1,500 to 2,000." [49]

Spurred by the dramatic King George debate, the campaign shifted to high gear in July. The impact of that debate is difficult to determine. Several of Martin's statements worked to his disadvantage, but in general the Senator held his own against the eloquent Montague. Martin sympathizers, evidently surprised and pleased when their man emerged relatively unscathed, broadcast news of his "victory" throughout the state. One firsthand observer of the debate, however, assured Montague that the debate "has gained you strong ground.

---

47 R. L. Montague to Henry O. Humphreys, May 26, 1905, and R. L. Montague to John M. Tabb, May 31, 1905, Montague Papers; Richmond *Times Dispatch,* May 28, 1905.
48 Patton to John W. Daniel, June 12, 16, and 28, 1905, Daniel Papers.
49 R. L. Montague to Benjamin T. Gunter, July 1, 1905, Montague Papers.

. . . The doubtful ones since yesterday are out and out Montague men." And C. V. Meredith felt that Montague had "smoked Martin out of many positions, which he has heretofore occupied by silence. . . . He lied when he said he favored the primary 6 years ago." The fact that Montague carried that county in the August primary gives some credence to these evaluations.[50]

Nevertheless, others viewing the spectacle felt that Martin had by no means come off second best. The correspondent for the Washington *Post* asserted that when Montague made his half-hour rebuttal, "They [the crowd] made more noise than it seemed possible for his supporters to make, and for a while the meeting seemed going the governor's way." But when Martin spoke, the crowd slowly "came around," and in a "short while he had captured the crowd as much as his predecessor had done." Perhaps most conclusively, Montague himself, in a letter to his wife shortly after the debate, admitted, "I was quite below par when time came to speak, which I had to do under terms dishonorable to my competitor." Montague felt the terms were "dishonorable" since, in effect, Martin had one and one-half hours for rebuttal to his half-hour. (Montague spoke first for an hour, Martin followed for an hour, Montague and Martin concluded with a half-hour each.) For once, Montague's eloquence had failed him. That failure came at a critical moment in his campaign.[51]

Even though the King George debate thus somewhat deflated Montague's reputation for oratorical prowess, his headquarters seemed to become even more optimistic as the fateful day of August 22 arrived. On July 31, Lynch Montague claimed, "We are unwilling to concede to Martin but one of the ten congressional districts. . . . Gov. Montague confidently expects from ten to twenty thousand majority. . . . Bragging is a Martin game." On August 3 Lynch jubilantly proclaimed, "We have them on the run." And on the same day Montague asserted, "Nothing but fraud can defeat me." [52]

The threat of fraud had worried Montague for some time. As early as March 24 he had expressed the fear that Martin would pay the poll

---

50   Staunton *Spectator and Vindicator,* July 14, 1905; T. W. Boggs to Montague, July 6, 1905; Meredith to Montague, July 8, 1905; R. L. Montague to Frank Buford, July 10, 1905; all in Montague Papers.

51   Washington *Post,* July 7, 1905; Montague to his wife, July 8, 1905, in possession of Mrs. Janet M. Nunnally.

52   R. L. Montague to C. L. Scott, July 31, 1905; R. L. Montague to J. S. Phillips, Aug. 3, 1905; A. J. Montague to J. W. Shepard, Aug. 3, 1905; all in Montague Papers.

taxes of his supporters. These fears were confirmed when M. S. Whitlock wrote from Wise County reporting that the "Martinites" were getting a list of all Democratic voters who were unregistered and whose poll taxes were unpaid. He suggested that Montague send him $100 so that he could devote his entire "time and talent" to the interest of the campaign: "It shall be an everlasting secret with me." When Montague replied that the Barksdale Pure Elections Law prohibited such expenditures, Whitlock replied knowingly that he was "aware of the fact . . . but the like is being done as you know." [53]

Particularly dangerous was Martin's organizational control of most of the electoral machinery in the various counties. At a Montague rally in Petersburg, Lynch Montague overheard two gentlemen claim it was "all fixed" how Dinwiddie County would go. He subsequently wrote to Rennie Butterworth, a Dinwiddie resident, asking him to watch for infractions: "we have no judges in the county friendly to us." To avert possible corruption, Montague's headquarters attempted to designate one person in each county who would name Montague watchers for each precinct. By August 14, Lynch reiterated the belief that fraud was the only thing to be feared, "and we think we have that scotched." [54]

For all their optimism and self-assurance, Montague and his supporters proved to be poor prophets. Senator Martin was much more astute when he wrote to his wife near the end of July: "I never missed you more than since we parted at the Depot here yesterday morning. It seems a week. . . . I had a very successful trip to Mecklenburg—found good audiences and strong support. I got back here to breakfast and find a heavy mail with encouraging reports . . . We will win a great victory and it is yours." [55]

On the morning following the election, Thomas Staples Martin issued the statement: "When this campaign commenced the cry of my competitor was back to the people. We have been back to the people and I am satisfied with the verdict of the people." Martin had achieved a victory, the scope of which was surprising even to his ardent supporters. He carried every district in the state, sixty-six of the one hundred counties, and thirteen of the eighteen cities. Such sup-

53 Montague to R. C. Blackford, March 24, 1905; and M. S. Whitlock to Montague, April 6, 10, and 13, 1905; *ibid.*
54 R. L. Montague to Rennie Butterworth, Aug. 4, 1905; R. L. Montague to John W. Hilldrup, Aug. 12, 1905; R. L. Montague to C. T. Baskerville, Aug. 14, 1905; all *ibid.*
55 Martin to his wife, July 30, 1905, Martin Papers.

posed Montague strongholds as Danville and Richmond fell before the Martin onslaught. Martin's total vote reached nearly 47,000, whereas Montague amassed approximately 36,000, a percentage of fifty-six to forty-four. Montague commented, "I have kept the faith, though my fight has been in vain." [56]

Why had Montague lost? Why had the Virginia populace rebuffed the man described as "one of the best known Governors in the U.S.?" [57] Why had this "man of the people" been rejected by the people?

One possible explanation lies in the fact that the voters' verdict was not entirely unclouded. To some extent, at least, the fraud Montague feared was real. "Men were allowed to vote who had no particle of right to vote, and others deprived from voting who had a perfect right to vote," declared the Staunton *Spectator and Vindicator.* One disconsolate Montague supporter wrote from Danville: "Nearly all the whiskey people here were for you, but the Martin people went to them and told them that if they did not vote for Martin they would carry the town dry. . . . The people they could not change and buy they got to leave town . . . one fourth that voted for you are afraid to tell it. . . . If this kind of stuff these leaders here call Democracy I am no Democrat." From Patrick County Montague received a detailed list of complaints encompassing a wide gamut of irregularities, including ballot box stuffing.[58]

So numerous were the complaints that Montague seriously considered demanding a recount: "The conditions in your county are the same throughout the state . . . otherwise I could have been easily nominated. . . . The Barksdale Law did not stand in the way of the extravagent [*sic*] use of money to overthrow the wishes of the people. . . . Collect your facts . . . perhaps I'll use them after the November elections." But later, when H. H. Baker wrote from Frederick County that the Montague majorities in certain precincts had been mysteriously converted to Martin majorities, Montague replied,

---

56   Richmond *Times Dispatch,* Aug. 23, 1905; New Market *Shenandoah Valley,* Aug. 24, 1905; Montague to John W. Jenkins, Aug. 23, 1905, Montague Papers. Martin's margins were largest in the Fourth, Fifth, and Ninth districts; smallest in the First, Third, and Sixth.

57   Richmond *Times Dispatch,* April 14, 1905.

58   Staunton *Spectator and Vindicator,* Aug. 25, 1905. E. A. Croston to Montague, Aug. 30, 1905; R. A. Finnell to Montague, Aug. 23, 1905; W. B. Farmer to Montague, Aug. 24, 1905; all in Montague Papers.

"I do not know that you need bother about the re-count. . . . It would be well enough if re-counts could be secured elsewhere. I neither complain nor explain. Time will do both." [59]

Stung by his defeat, Montague probably exaggerated the importance of fraud in causing it, but he did not exaggerate the importance of Martin's machine organization. In the short space of four years he had been unable to equal Martin's organizational mastery. Less than half the precincts of the state had any semblance of a Montague organization, whereas Martin's many workers were "never . . . more earnest or more thorough. . . . To the political workers who got out his vote . . . must be ascribed largely the majorities he received." Montague's oratory may have captivated thousands, but it did not conquer the courthouse rings.[60]

Other factors than superior organization and possible fraud, however, must help to explain Martin's decisive triumph. One of these, certainly, was the Senator's seniority and experience. In the opinion of the *Times Dispatch* the typical voter had asked this question: "Was there sufficient reason for turning one prominent man out in order that another might be put in? Possession proved nine tenths of the law." To followers of Martin, moreover, Montague's bitter accusations provoked equally bitter resentment. William Henry Mann, chafing under Montague's denunciation of the machine, exploded, "Montague is the greatest demagogue of the generation—He comes nearer to fulfilling Machiavelli's conception of a leader than any other man within my view, and from the ready and skilful manner in which he assumes all the political virtues without really possessing any of them, leads me to think that he must have knelt at the shrine of the crafty Florentine." Others felt that Montague, although a good man, was "overdoing the part of a reformer and idealist. . . . He simply wants a job that is held by another man." [61] Montague, of course, would have challenged this latter analysis, but to deny that his ambition was a paramount factor in creating his bitter antipathy to Martin would be to deny an elementary characteristic of human nature.

59 Montague to W. L. Duval, Aug. 26, 1905; Montague to J. B. Burwell, Aug. 26, 1905; H. H. Baker to Montague, Aug. 28, 1905; Montague to Baker, Sept. 4, 1905; all in Montague Papers.
60 Montague to A. H. McCue, Aug. 25, 1905, and O. L. Stearnes to Montague, Sept. 8, 1905, *ibid.*
61 Richmond *Times Dispatch*, Aug. 24, 1905; W. H. Mann to Francis Rives Lassiter, May 24, 1905, Lassiter Papers; Bland (Va.) *Messenger,* Aug. 3, 1905, in scrapbook, Montague Papers.

Other explanations for Montague's defeat can be enumerated briefly. The temperance crusade was beginning to make itself felt in state elections, and James Cannon of the temperance forces had allowed the Martin organization to circulate a letter criticizing the governor for pardoning several men convicted under the Sunday closing law.[62] Montague's action in calling out 80 per cent of the state militia to protect a Negro rapist was censured by one voter who claimed to speak for numerous others in his neighborhood.[63] His action in calling the militia to suppress violence in the Richmond transit strike was similarly unpopular among labor forces, and Martin, by moving in his direction, robbed him of effective campaign issues such as schools, roads, and the primary.

Another factor, not to be overlooked, is the probability that Montague's supporters in 1905 did not vote in as large a proportion as the better-organized Martin men. From two areas of the state, at least, this was apparently the case; according to one correspondent, one-third of the state's Democrats failed to vote.[64] The decline in the total state electorate, both white and Negro, may also help explain Montague's defeat. In the 1901 November election Montague alone had received a total of 117,000 Democratic votes—this in a campaign the final result of which was never seriously in doubt. In the 1905 primary, when the battle raged furiously until the very day of decision, the total Democratic primary vote reached only 83,000. Martin's hard core of party workers and officeholders thus naturally carried more weight.

In the final analysis, the ultimate cause of Montague's defeat must be traced to developments preceding the 1905 campaign. Since 1901, the governor had evidently suffered from a steady decline in popularity. Although he attracted a loyal band of followers, he failed to win the confidence of a considerable number of Independent leaders, Glass and Braxton being the most notable. O. L. Stearnes attributed Montague's defeat partially to the fact that "In so far as your personal popularity is concerned, you entered this contest at the worst possible time—at the lowest ebb of the tide." Montague later complained that he had fought his 1905 campaign almost singlehandedly, with little organized assistance from his friends. A. F. Thomas of

62 James Cannon to E. F. Sheffey, May 26, 1905, quoted in Lucius Gregory to Montague, Aug. 1, 1905, Montague Papers.
63 J. R. Bondurant to Montague, Jan. 6, 1905, *ibid.*
64 South Boston *News,* Aug. 31, 1905, in scrapbook, Moore Collection; O. L. Stearnes to Montague, Sept. 8, 1905, Montague Papers.

Lynchburg corroborated his diagnosis in a letter five years later: "Several years ago your friends deserted you, I among the number. This, in my judgment, was a deplorable mistake. For a long time I have realized it, and I am glad to say that others are coming to see that they, too, erred." [65]

Why this desertion? Did Montague's efforts to create an organization to combat Martin smack too much of a personal machine? Did the modest façade of his personality appear hypocritical when contrasted with the somewhat pompous tone of his call for a revival of senatorial greatness? Did his earlier flirtation with Thomas F. Ryan convince some of the reformers that he too was merely an ambitious opportunist, ready to sell his political principles to the highest bidder? Or was the defection simply a case of envy? With Braxton and Tyler, jealousy and resentment were probably determining factors. Others, including Carter Glass, may have deduced that a victory for the youthful Montague would forever close the avenue to their own political advancement.

Had Montague failed as governor? No, that would be too severe an indictment. His seeming disinclination to push strongly for his program in the General Assembly can be most legitimately criticized as evidence of weakness, yet the circumstances involved—an Assembly dominated by a faction bent on destroying the governor—made effective leadership of that body well-nigh impossible. Moreover, the Virginia governmental structure reflected the lingering colonial resentment of executive power by relegating the governor to a position relatively less powerful than that of the legislature. In the context of his times, then, Montague had perhaps exerted more energy and influence than the average Virginia governor. In the 1905 campaign critics rarely charged him with weakness, inability, or misconduct in office; rather, he was denounced for his partisanship and his overweening ambition. His supporters, on the other hand, praised him for his vigorous espousal of major reforms, for his clean and efficient conduct of office. Many journals seemed to take special pride in the nationwide attention he had brought to himself and to his state.

The reason for Independent disaffection toward Montague's cause remains elusive. Few people positively disliked the governor. Friend and foe alike testified to the magnetism of his personality, the charm of his manner, the extent of his knowledge and ability. And it must

65   O. L. Stearnes to Montague, Sept. 8, 1905; Montague to Machen, Feb. 6, 1911; A. F. Thomas to Montague, March 8, 1910, all in Montague Papers.

again be emphasized that many did accept his leadership without question. Yet there existed a self-effacing, unassertive side to his nature that seemed to weaken his role as superior. The political "outs" nearly always find difficulty in combining against the "ins," yet strong leaders occasionally do produce such unity by the sheer force of their own wills. Perhaps Montague was too rhetorical, too sophisticated, too eloquent, too idealistic—insufficiently hard, resolute, commandeering, callous. Often typed by his friends and colleagues as a "gentleman" of the old school, he had risen to political power at a time when gentlemanly traits were no longer an asset. Whatever the reasons, Montague's campaign was lost, not only because Martin managed a superbly organized canvass but also because the governor was unable to effect a similar solidarity among the ranks of the Independents. Unable to successfully associate his own personality and ambition with the general hostility felt by most progressives toward Martin, he had, in this respect at least, failed as a leader. In his inability to coalesce Martin's opposition, his higher political ambitions were forever blocked. The dreams dreamed at Inglewood would remain unfulfilled. And personal scars of the defeat would never completely heal.

Following the climax of Montague's defeat, the remainder of his term as governor witnessed little of consequence. In October and November, he actively participated in the campaign which preceded the general elections, proclaiming that he was a Democrat "in defeat and victory." In December he accepted the position of dean of the University of Richmond law school, and as he prepared to leave office a month later, he felt that his public career had ended.[66] On January 10, 1906, he delivered his last message to the legislature, and on inauguration day, January 31, in fine irony he escorted Governor-elect Claude A. Swanson down the aisle of the chamber of the House of Delegates. On February 1 he and his family left the governor's mansion and moved to a Grove Avenue residence in Richmond. Like a nova, Montague's star had burned brilliantly for a time, and then quickly faded.

During the course of the 1905 campaign Montague once proclaimed to a Hampton audience: "I have done one good thing. I have enabled you to hear the voice of your junior senator, which has never

66 Richmond *Times Dispatch,* Sept. 29, Oct. 19, 1905; Montague to Lyman Abbott, Jan. 22, 1906, Montague Papers.

been heard before." [67] Therein lies the true significance of Montague's 1905 campaign, and, indeed, of his term as governor. For though defeated and bereft of political power, Montague's administration left a Virginia considerably different from the one he had found when first elected. The years of his term in office were essentially years of transition. The reforms he sought, the goals he set, were not all obtained, even during his lifetime. Yet the brief interim from 1902 to 1906 witnessed a promising beginning.

Montague had helped shock Virginia out of her post-Civil War inertia. By performing the role of the critic, by publicizing from the rostrum the faults and weaknesses of the Old Virginia, he had materially assisted the various reform movements that gradually transformed the Commonwealth into a New Dominion. By helping to convert the public to the causes of good schools, good roads, and the preferential primary, he had helped force the political hierarchy to abandon its aloofness, to take cognizance of changing public opinion. As a result, though Montague failed in his efforts to displace that hierarchy, he had made it more democratic, more amenable, more responsive to the people and their needs. This was his victory.

His last address to the legislature was an auspicious occasion. From 1904 to 1906 the governor had supervised the addition of two new wings to Virginia's ancient capitol building. The task had been completed just before the legislature convened. The modern surroundings seemed symbolic of a new Virginia. Montague added yet another innovation to the proceedings by personally delivering his message; no Virginia governor since the Revolution had done so.[68]

The content of Montague's message, his valedictory to the Commonwealth, was bold, daring, and progressive. He called upon the state to adopt a wide variety of reforms and improvements: a better system of prison parole, increased appropriations for mental institutions, a new hospital for epileptics, a general board of charities and corrections, a school for the colored deaf and blind, and a reformatory for youthful delinquents. He advocated a comprehensive civil service system for all state employees so that "efficiency and character can be removed . . . from political considerations." He recommended that the state bear the expense of primary elections, that the judges of elections be selected impartially, and that campaign contributions by corporations be prohibited. He renewed his suggestions for

67 Richmond *Times Dispatch*, July 2, 1905.
68 Richmond *News Leader,* Jan. 10, 1906.

a highway commission, and for increased state aid to the development of public schools; he gave strong and urgent reasons for compulsory education. Near the close of his address, he urged the state to establish an immigration commission to help Virginia compete with Northern states in attracting the stream of European immigrants. "The State needs immigration, for she can easily support a population of 10,000,000." Such was the optimism, and the vision, of Andrew Jackson Montague.

The last paragraph of Montague's message is a fitting conclusion to his career as governor. His words best reveal the role he played—as spokesman for the new Virginia:

> Great opportunities are fast coming to Virginia and we must grasp them with the spirit of enterprise and progress. The demands of the hour cannot be met by past traditions or excused by past misfortunes; but we should rather count these things as the energizing call for the renewal of our most patriotic efforts to place our beloved Commonwealth in the forefront of the extraordinary, economic, intellectual and moral forces now at play in the world.
>
> A. J. MONTAGUE

XV

THE NATIONAL PROGRESSIVE

THE thirty years which elapsed between Montague's departure from the governor's mansion in 1906 and his death in 1937 were in a sense anticlimactic. True, they were for him years of intense activity, public service, and real contribution—as educator, foreign diplomat, Congressman, and constitutional lawyer. Still, Montague's closing career presents a picture of talent unused, ambition unrealized and eventually extinguished. The vigorous drive which had fired the campaigns of 1901 and 1905 continued for a time to motivate the redheaded former governor, however. He maintained his position as an active Independent in Virginia politics; he continued his role as spokesman of the South before Northern audiences, for a time serving as an adviser to President Theodore Roosevelt on issues affecting the South; he later helped promote the prenomination fight for Wilson in Virginia, and entertained futile hopes of either a Cabinet appointment or a Supreme Court position. Finally, as a Wilsonian Congressman elected in 1912, he contributed his share toward the enactment of the New Freedom, the legislative climax to the progressive movement both on a state and a national level. By the end of the Wilson era, his desire for reform had been satisfied and his yearning for political advancement stilled. After 1921 he no longer played an important role in Virginia or national politics.[1]

1 Considerably more detail pertaining to the material in Chapters XV and XVI can be found in William Larsen, "Andrew Jackson Montague, the

Following his term as governor, Montague had accepted a position as dean of the law school at the University of Richmond. After three years of lecturing on constitutional law and bankruptcy, he resigned to turn to a more lucrative private law practice, establishing a partnership with his brother in Richmond. Their legal business consisted mainly of large corporate suits, frequently involving pleas before the Virginia Supreme Court.[2]

While dean at Richmond, Montague had retained his contacts with a coterie of Northern educational leaders and philanthropists, including Albert Shaw, Lyman Abbott, Robert Ogden, George Foster Peabody, and W. A. Putnam. Other academic friends of national prominence included the historians William Dodd, James Ford Rhodes, William A. Dunning, William MacDonald, A. B. Hart, and S. C. Mitchell. (Mitchell was a leader of Virginia's educational crusade and later became president of the University of South Carolina.) Several of these men had an exceptional admiration for Montague's character and ability and encouraged him to continue his role as spokesman for the South, a role he had successfully assumed while he was governor.[3] That Montague himself desired to continue in this role is indicated by his acceptance of numerous speaking invitations, including appearances at Harvard University in 1907 (where he spoke on "The South of Today") and before the Pennsylvania Bar Association in 1911. Montague's speech at Harvard made a favorable impression on President Charles W. Eliot, who had only recently returned from a visit to Tuskegee Institute in Alabama and was "really gloomy" over the prospects for race relations in the South. In the opinion of one observer, at least, Montague had "once and for all changed Pres. Eliot's hopelessness about the South: he spoke of you [Montague] as the one Southern statesman he knew and he builds high hopes on your power for good." [4]

The historian Dodd took a special interest in Montague. From his University of Chicago location he wrote numerous epistles of weari-

---

Making of a Southern Progressive" (Ph.D. dissertation, University of Virginia, 1961), 589 ff.

2   In 1910, for example, Montague's firm represented the Carnegie Trust Company in its suit against the Security Life Insurance Company of America, a suit involving voting trusts. Montague to Alfred Thom, Oct. 10, 1910, Montague Papers.

3   S. C. Mitchell to Montague, Dec. 8, 1908, July 26, 1910, *ibid.*

4   The *Harvard Crimson,* March 8, 1907; Nancy Joy to Montague, Feb. 17, March 28, 1907, Montague Papers.

some length, analyzing Southern politics and Montague's progressive position therein. At Dodd's recommendation, the University of Chicago in 1909 invited Montague to deliver an address to its faculty and student body; Montague responded with a scholarly analysis of "The South and the Nation." In a remarkably candid display of introspection for a Southern politician, he traced briefly the South's history from its early nationalism, through its "intensely conservative," proslavery sectionalism, and through the war and painful adjustments which followed. In postwar developments he described significant indications of a renewed Southern nationalistic feeling. "Slow tides of immigration," a growing industrialism, the establishment of improved transportation and communications, the formation of communal life and the development of a belief in popular education—all these factors had gradually created a new South, a South ready to resume her rightful place in the American union. What direction the South's new political evolution would take—whether "toward conservatism or liberalism . . . reactionary or progressive"—Montague declined to predict. But he did assert that differences among Southern politicians toward national issues, "the growth of flexibility in [Southern] public sentiment," demonstrated that the South was prepared once again to contribute to the nation's councils. The nation, he concluded, "does need the South's larger service; and the South has need to do that service." [5]

In a small way Montague himself had given his services to the national government. In May, 1906, only four months after his term as governor ended, Secretary of State Elihu Root advised him of his appointment as an American delegate to a Pan-American conference in Rio de Janeiro. Montague quickly accepted, and traveled with five other delegates to the ninety-day meeting in Brazil. At the conference a wide variety of subjects—banking, customs, trade, communications, quarantine, international law, naturalization—were discussed. Montague's particular assignment concerned copyrights, trademarks and patents, and the need for uniform law and mutual guarantees among the American nations.[6]

Later, in 1909, Montague received an appointment by President William Howard Taft to the Third International Conference in Maritime Law, meeting at Brussels. This conference was "empowered to

5 A. J. Montague, "The South and the Nation," 93–101, Montague Papers.
6 Root to Montague, May 10, 1906; Robert Bacon to Montague, May 18, 1906; Charles R. Dean to Montague, May 19, 1906; all *ibid*.

assist in making and adopting treaties on collisions and salvage, ship-owners' liabilities, liens and mortgages and other kindred subjects." The United States group especially endeavored to have adopted a collision treaty, whereby liability damages for maritime collisions would be awarded "proportionate to fault." Concrete accomplishments of the conference were not impressive, but the experience proved a valuable one for Montague.[7]

Montague's reputation as an expert on international law had been partly responsible for these appointments. But more important, both Presidents Roosevelt and Taft had approved the selections personally. Exactly when Montague and Roosevelt first met cannot be determined, but in early 1905 the two corresponded as friends; in the fall of 1905 Montague served as official host to the President on the initiation of the latter's Southern tour. Montague admired Roosevelt for his progressive stands on public issues, and Roosevelt on several occasions expressed a highly favorable opinion of the governor.[8] For a time, Montague became an adviser to Roosevelt on Southern political topics. For example, late in 1906, when the President was preparing his annual message to Congress, he turned to Montague for advice in the phrasing of that portion of his speech dealing with the race problem in the South, particularly in reference to lynching. Montague returned the draft of the message with his approval and some minor suggestions which Roosevelt adopted. Though the message strongly condemned lynching, the President had hesitated to suggest the establishment of a federal lynching commission until he consulted "with the Southern members whom you [Clark Howell] and I and men like ex-Governor Montague and Judge Jones feel to be really disinterested and patriotic, with the necessary courage to make their virtue count for something." [9]

By taking Montague into his confidence, Roosevelt hoped to enlist his support in attempting to develop a two-party system in the South,

7   William H. Taft to Lyman Abbott, May 22, 1909, and Alvey A. Adee to Montague, Sept. 11, 1909, *ibid.;* Richmond *Evening Journal,* Sept. 16, 1909.
8   In 1909, when Montague congratulated Roosevelt on a successful administration, Roosevelt replied, "Yours is one of the letters that I most prize, for I believe in you, honor you and I am fond of you, and I value greatly your good opinion." Roosevelt to Montague, March 10, 1909, Montague Papers.
9   Roosevelt to Montague, April 1, 1905, quoted in Elting E. Morison (ed.), *The Letters of Theodore Roosevelt* (6 vols.; Cambridge, 1951), IV, 1155; Roosevelt to Clark Howell, Oct. 26, Nov. 5, 1906, quoted *ibid.,* V, 472, 487; Roosevelt to Montague, March 10, 1909, Montague Papers.

an aim shared by Taft, his heir to the presidency. In the 1908 presidential campaign Roosevelt made a special effort to woo Montague from the Democratic camp to the support of Taft. As recalled by Montague and verified by Roosevelt three years later, these were the circumstances:

> I [Montague] did take luncheon with President Roosevelt in May or thereabouts, 1908. The President did then substantially say that he believed that a large element of the Democratic party in the South, including myself, approved some of his progressive policies; that he desired above everything to see a division among the Southern people upon national questions, and he then expressed a desire to have me act in sympathy with his view, provided the Republican party took a progressive stand and nominated a progressive candidate. My prompt reply was that however high my personal regard may have been for Mr. Roosevelt, and it is very high, I could not accept or entertain his suggestion.[10]

If Montague had been prompt in his reply to Roosevelt, he had demonstrated much indecision earlier. The perennial loser, Bryan, was likely to become the 1908 Democratic nominee, and his proposal for government ownership of railroads, among other things, had not endeared him as a candidate to the more conservative Montague. Moreover, Montague despaired of the future of the Democratic party in the South:

> It has ceased to be a party in any great sense, having no distinctive policies to maintain or principles to inspire. . . . The negro and consequent ballotbox corruption have destroyed the vigor and vision of the South. We have become so narrow that we recognize neither duty nor opportunity, and we fear, or feign to fear, the negro without ballot as much as the negro with ballot. . . . The issues between the parties are now so obscure, or so vaguely defined . . . that the country awaits . . . the platforms of the next national conventions.[11]

Montague's continuing disenchantment with the Virginia party of Martin, Swanson, Flood, et al., the fact that the Martin organization had climbed on the Bryan bandwagon, and the seeming attractiveness of Taft as a progressive presidential candidate had led to his serious consideration of a break with the party of his heritage. In April, 1908, he conveyed his feelings to Walter Hines Page, who strongly encouraged the disassociation. Wrote Montague:

10 Roosevelt to Montague, Aug. 31, 1911, Montague Papers. Roosevelt quoted a newspaper clipping of Montague's account in verifying the incident.
11 Montague to F. E. Montague, Dec. 12, 1907, ibid.

I have been searching and struggling for some weeks for a light of duty which has thus far shone only dimly upon my path. . . . The political conditions in the South, as you well know, are wretched . . . . The Southern Democracy seems a dead sea and is moved by no currents. Our ship has no guiding hand; her crew is squandering the larder, knowing no charts and on the outlook for no luminary. . . . into this South great political parties must come, and come they will, the interesting question being who will first cry the way and take the lead. . . . The South now seems wholly given over to the detail of politics, the genius of which is office-getting, not office-serving . . . . our one party . . . has driven a great people from the orbit of national responsibility and national opportunity until we in the South are outside of the great currents of the republic and of the world as well.[12]

In this same letter, however, Montague confessed that in the South, "respectability and Democracy are synonymous, and our party affiliations inexorable." Would he not "utterly fail," he asked, if he engaged in an abortive and solitary effort to alter the pattern? This practical consideration proved decisive, for one month later, as indicated, he declined the President's personal invitation to change his affiliation. Later, he campaigned for Bryan in the final election.[13]

Although Montague thus adhered to his Democratic heritage, he continued to maintain friendly relations with both Roosevelt and Taft. When Montague congratulated Taft on his election in November, 1908, Taft replied by asserting, "Nothing in the campaign has been of more interest to me than the stirring up of public opinion and public discussion in the South. I sincerely hope that four years may make some progress in a movement in which I hope for your sympathy." Montague's 1909 diplomatic appointment by the new President indicates further their amicability. In August, 1910, after returning from the Brussels conference, Montague wrote Taft, briefly reviewing the work of the first session, then adding, "Perhaps an impartial opinion upon some Southern questions may at some time be of interest and service to you, and if so, I beg that you will command me." To this entreaty, Taft replied, "I shall be glad to see you in Washington when I come back and talk over the Southern questions with you." [14]

Montague's desire to confer personally with Taft was probably motivated partially by his candidacy for appointment to the newly

12   Montague to Page, April 30, 1908, *ibid.*
13   Unidentified clipping, Oct. 31, 1908, *ibid.*
14   Taft to Montague, Nov. 30, 1908, Aug. 25, 1910, and Montague to Taft, Aug. 22, 1910, *ibid.*

created Commerce Court established by the Mann-Elkins Act of 1910. Early in 1910, in an attempt to obtain Roosevelt's influence, he reaffirmed his friendship with the former President through an exchange of congenial letters. At Roosevelt's invitation, Montague later visited him in New York. Roosevelt declined to ask favors of Taft, however, and despite powerful recommendations from such Northern friends as Ogden, Abbott, Dodd, and MacDonald, Taft did not place Montague on the bench.[15]

Montague's failure to win this appointment evidently ended his relationship with Taft, who was coming under increasing attack from progressives of his own Republican party. Indeed, even while seeking judicial appointment, Montague privately expressed disillusionment with the man he had almost supported in 1908, and sympathy for the Republican insurgents.[16] Roosevelt shared this disillusionment, and shortly after his return from Europe in June of 1910 he assumed tacit leadership of Taft's opposition. Thus, letters written between Montague and Roosevelt from December, 1910, to September, 1911, assume possible significance. In December Roosevelt urged Montague to visit him in New York, and in January he again invited Montague to lunch with him and the other staff members of *Outlook* (a weekly news journal edited by Lyman Abbott, for which Roosevelt was a contributing editor) whenever he came to that city. Later, in September, Montague thanked Roosevelt for "your kind letter which increases my appreciation of your delicacy of feeling and generosity of conduct as well as your sense of fair play." He also promised to see Roosevelt when next he was in New York.[17] Whether these visits were made cannot be definitely determined, but the mutual respect between the two men, and their close relationship as late as 1911, lend credence to the oral testimony of Montague's three children (based upon a lost handwritten letter) that Roosevelt asked Montague to run as his vice-presidential candidate in 1912. Roosevelt's papers do reveal that as late as July of 1912, with preparations then under way for a Progressive third-party convention, the

15 Roosevelt to Montague, April 2, July 13, 1910; Lyman Abbott to Montague, June 22, 1910; William MacDonald to Montague, July 2, 1910; Robert C. Ogden to Montague, Nov. 22, 1910; all *ibid*.

16 Montague to W. H. Page, April 12, 1910, and Montague to William Dodd, Oct. 17, 1910, *ibid*.

17 Roosevelt to Montague, Dec. 13, 1910; Frank Harper (Roosevelt's Secretary) to Montague, Jan. 4, 1911; Montague to Roosevelt, Sept. 8, 1911; all *ibid*.

former President expressed a preference for a Southern nominee, "if we can get the right type of man." [18]

Although Montague had thus established a close rapport with the more progressive elements of the Republican party, a complete alliance was never consummated. Taft continued his swing to the right, and Roosevelt's efforts to free his party from Taft's domination were doomed to failure. More important, Montague's own Democratic party seemed at last to be freeing itself from the domination of the unpalatable Bryan. As early as January, 1910, Montague relayed to Dodd his hope that "there may be a breaking of the timber, and some chance for a revivified democratic party upon a sound issue of tariff reform, economy in government expenses, fidelity in official life and the exercise of governmental powers in the interest of the people." Finally, with the rise of Woodrow Wilson as a potential Democratic nominee for the presidency, Montague could return to his party's ranks with enthusiasm.[19]

Montague had known Wilson for several years. They had met at least as early as 1904, when both men received honorary doctorates from Brown University. Wilson, a Southerner, a man of integrity and of idealism—urbane in manner, polished in speech, progressive yet moderate in political temperament—easily appealed to Montague's ideals of statesmanship. Consequently, Montague became one of the earliest sponsors of Wilson's candidacy in Virginia. As early as April, 1910, he wrote Wilson, asking for a copy of one of his speeches. Throughout 1911 he corresponded fairly frequently with the New Jersey governor, encouraging him in his campaign for the nomination, describing in detail the nature and extent of Wilson's strength in Virginia, and giving advice on how best to handle the Virginia phase of his preconvention canvass. Evidently, he served as one of Wilson's major confidants in the Old Dominion, as well as a prominent orator at Wilson rallies.[20]

The Wilson movement in Virginia, endorsed by the state's progressives, coincided with yet another struggle of that faction with the Vir-

18 Nunnally and Moore interviews, and a brief conversation with R. Latané Montague, Montague's son, Dec., 1959, Urbanna, Va.; Roosevelt to John C. Schaffer, July 20, 1912, in Theodore Roosevelt Papers, Manuscripts Division, Library of Congress.
19 Montague to Dodd, Jan. 13, 1910, Montague Papers.
20 Montague to Wilson, April 21, 1910, Nov. 9, 1910, June 5, 1911, Sept. 14, 1911, Sept. 25, 1911, Oct. 4, 1911; and Wilson to Montague, Nov. 10, 1910, June 6, 1911, Sept. 27, 1911; all ibid.

ginia Democratic machine. In 1911 Martin, again up for reelection, faced opposition in the person of Congressman Jones, Montague's old ally. A second senatorial contest developed between the newly installed Senator Swanson (appointed to succeed Daniel in 1910) and the vitriolic Congressman, Carter Glass. The resulting primary fight exceeded even that of 1905 in personal bitterness and acrimony.[21]

Montague, Tucker, John Garland Pollard and others joined in the formation of a Virginia Democratic League which helped direct the campaign against the machine and which organized a speaking canvass by leading Independents, Montague among them. In the final campaign month of August, Montague stumped the state, echoing Jones's line of attack against Martin's organization. In a speech at Staunton he charged that the machine had maintained power by a systematic confederation of all the officeholders and employees of state, city, and county governments into a compact union which arbitrarily excluded from political advancement "all who inquire into or oppose the action of any official" of the organization. Montague also charged that the machine callously continued to tolerate corrupt elections throughout the Commonwealth. Jones's and Glass's fight against ring rule, he declared, was the same fight he had waged six years previously.[22]

Results of the September primary indicated that neither Jones nor Glass could match Montague as an opponent of the organization. Martin and Swanson sailed to an easy victory, defeating their opponents by two-to-one margins. Montague wrote to Dodd, "I am very disconsolate and distressed. I have done the best I could . . . but it all seems to count for nothing." [23]

Montague had attempted to correlate his fight for Jones and Glass with his concurrent support for Wilson. Indeed, he once urged Wilson

21 Montague had given some consideration to making the race, but found public support lacking. He later gave enthusiastic support to Jones, but supported Glass simply "because he would not vote for Swanson 'under any circumstances.'" Montague to John B. Robertson, Nov. 1, 1910, and Robertson to Montague, Nov. 14, 1910, *ibid.;* Harold E. Cox, "The Jones-Martin Senatorial Campaign of 1911," *Essays in History,* I (University of Virginia, 1954), 40.

22 Cox, "The Jones-Martin Senatorial Campaign of 1911," 42–44; typed copy of Montague's speech, delivered Aug. 11, 1911, Montague papers. The most sensational incident of the campaign occurred when Jones produced letters which strongly indicated that Martin had distributed railroad monies to legislators in 1893, thus facilitating his election to the Senate.

23 Quoted in Woodward, *Origins of the New South,* 480.

to enter the primary embroilment on the side of the Independents, and on every possible occasion in his 1911 speaking tour, he highly praised the New Jersey governor. Most Virginia Independents ultimately joined Montague in supporting Wilson, whereas Martin and most machine leaders made determined efforts to dampen Wilson sentiment. Although the vast majority of Virginians (judged by journalistic opinion) favored Wilson, at the Norfolk Democratic convention held in May, 1912, Martin was able to keep the Virginia delegation uninstructed. And at the national Baltimore convention, for forty-two tedious ballots Martin and a majority of the Virginia delegation divided their votes between Oscar W. Underwood of Alabama and Champ Clark of Missouri. A small minority favored Wilson. After the forty-second ballot, however, though Wilson's nomination was still not assured, Martin sensed the ultimate outcome, called a caucus, and announced his support of the governor. On the forty-sixth ballot Wilson was nominated.[24]

Montague expressed delight with Wilson's selection, though he regretted that Virginia had not been united behind the winner. "Had a good fight been made," he commented in a letter to George Foster Peabody, "he would easily have commanded the entire delegation in this state." Montague had not attended the national convention which nominated his favorite, as he was occupied at the time with his own fight for nomination to a lesser office—that of Virginia's Third District Congressman. His decision to reenter competitive politics had been made with difficulty. Montague had reason to believe that a Cabinet position would be forthcoming in the event of a Democratic presidential victory, and a possible defeat in a congressional primary endangered his chance for appointment. Nevertheless, confident that his future political promotion would best be obtained from the vantage point of a public office, he determined to make the race.[25]

Apprehension of possible defeat naturally existed, since the Third District incumbent, John Lamb, was a strongly entrenched veteran of political wars. As chairman of the House Agricultural Committee, he

24   Martin to Hay, May 8 and 14, 1912, and Byrd to Hay, March 24, 1911, James Hay Papers, Alderman Library, University of Virginia, Charlottesville; Norfolk *Ledger Dispatch,* May 24, 1912, Richmond *Times Dispatch,* June 28, July 5, 1912, and New York *Times,* July 2, 1912, all in scrapbook, Martin Papers.

25   Montague to Peabody, Jan. 20, 1913, Montague Papers. An unidentified Washington correspondent, "Jim," reported that "Wilson thinks most kindly of you . . . in the event of his election you are likely to be Secy of State." "Jim" to Montague, Jan. 12, 1912, *ibid.*

also possessed all the advantages of seniority. Moreover, though not firmly wedded to Martin, Lamb evidently received unobtrusive machine support in his fight for renomination. Montague on the other hand possessed the advantages of a superior intellect, persuasive oratory, and a favorable reputation as governor. He capitalized on the prevailing Wilsonian sentiment in the state by making his advocacy of the New Jersey governor a main feature of his speaking canvass. He also sounded a progressive tone by calling for public congressional committee meetings, for Philippine independence, for a more flexible system of national finance, and for ratification of the constitutional amendment then pending which provided for the direct election of Senators. In a brief summer campaign, spirited but not acrimonious, Montague emerged triumphant by a safe margin of 1,500 votes in a total of 9,500.[26] He would remain the Richmond area Congressman for the next quarter-century.

In the national presidential campaign of 1912 which followed, Montague conducted a speaking tour of the North, concentrating most heavily on the states of Pennsylvania and New York. Though he thus contributed his small part in Virginia and the nation toward a Wilson victory, the prospects of a Cabinet post did not materialize. Montague had been suggested to Wilson for appointment either as Secretary of State or as Attorney General. In November, 1912, evidently upon Wilson's request, Walter Hines Page compiled a descriptive list of potential appointees, including Montague:

> His professional qualifications lie outside my range of judgment, but I know that he is regarded by good lawyers as a good lawyer. . . . I am sure of his ethical soundness—he's an honest, high-minded, right-minded gentleman, and a precise and cultivated man. He was the best Governor Virginia has had in our day, and too honest and clean to commend himself to the political machine. . . . I can think of no other man of public experience, who (though not of distinguished origin) so well represents the old (genuine) Southern gentleman and statesman class.[27]

Messages from Montague's Northern friends voiced their confidence in his appointment, but the call did not come. Nevertheless, as a victorious freshman Congressman riding the Wilsonian tide, Mon-

26 R. L. Montague, III, "The Red Fox Runs Straight," 45–62; Richmond *Times Dispatch,* July 13, 17, 23, and 31, Aug. 16, 1912.
27 Page to Wilson, Nov. 27, 1912, Woodrow Wilson Papers. Edward M. House's list of Cabinet possibilities, however, did not include Montague. Whether he was ever seriously considered by Wilson cannot be determined. House to Wilson, Jan. 9, 1913, Wilson Papers.

tague expressed himself as anxious to promote the success of the new administration. And Peabody proclaimed the expectation that he would take a place in Congress "as the voice of Virginia, a voice for which many have longed during these years of machine representation." [28] Though the transfer had been made to the lower, not the upper, branch of the Congress, the son of Middlesex had at last arrived in Washington.

From 1913 to 1920 Montague continued his role as Southern and national progressive, enthusiastically supporting Wilson's foreign and domestic program almost in its entirety. Joseph P. Tumulty, Wilson's private secretary, reminisced two decades after the Wilson era, "I recall with pleasure our association during my days at the White House. Surely, Woodrow Wilson had no more loyal or devoted friend than you." [29]

Wilson and Montague had many similarities of background and ideology. Both were Southerners and native Virginians; both had established records as reform governors of their respective states; both had maintained close academic affinities. In their political ideologies, both had reacted against the decay in American statesmanship which followed the Civil War, and both resented the alarming mastery acquired by moneyed interests over the nation's economy and the organs of government. Acting from a similar motivation, both aspired to lift government from its miasma of self-seeking special-interest groups, and to restore the ideal of public service to public servants.

The two were similar in yet another respect: a basic strain of conservatism which tempered their progressivism. Indeed, the conservative strain of their thinking had antedated their progressivism; Wilson did not "change colors" until 1910 or after. Neither Wilson nor Montague can be termed radicals; neither desired to abandon past tradition for the mere sake of change. To the contrary, Montague's chief desire was to restore the virtues of nineteenth-century antebellum America, not to initiate a new social or economic order. He, like Wilson, retained traditional attitudes toward several of the more ambitious reforms of the period; thus we have the apparent paradox of two progressive reformers opposing woman suffrage. Wilson's philosophy, in both its conservative and liberal aspects, finds an amazing

28 Peabody to Montague, Jan. 1 and 24, 1913, and Mitchell to Montague, Jan. 7, 1913, Montague Papers.
29 Tumulty to Montague, March 24, 1933, *ibid.*

correlation in Montague's legislative record from 1913 to 1920.[30]

The substance of that record, in both its progressive and conservative aspects, can be briefly recounted. In the new Congress which met in special session shortly after Wilson's inauguration, Montague, at his own request, was awarded a seat on the Committee on Interstate and Foreign Commerce, one of the most important committees in the House. This was the committee originally responsible for the bill creating the Federal Trade Commission, which bill, together with its complement, the Clayton Antitrust Act, constituted one of the three most important domestic enactments during Wilson's first term. Assigned to the subcommittee which framed the bill, Montague faithfully attended preliminary hearings, "gave thorough study of the bills presented," consulted Wilson himself at one point, and drafted portions of the measure as finally reported to the House floor. In the ensuing debate he spoke at length defending the bill's merits.[31]

The basic provisions of the bill reported were these: a Federal Trade Commission consisting of three members was established to investigate violations of antitrust laws, to require systematic annual reports by all corporations having greater capital than five million dollars, to assist the courts in supervising the enforcement of decisions in trust cases, and to make recommendations to the Attorney General for antitrust prosecutions. No independent remedial power was granted the commission itself.[32]

In House debate, Montague argued that the bill would effectively aid in the restoration of competition in American business; that the unfair means of competition practiced by large corporations against smaller ones, especially the cutthroat manipulation of prices, would be effectively exposed by the trade commission; and that with subsequent corrective action taken either by the courts, the Executive, or the Congress, the tendency toward monopoly would be arrested and reversed. In answer to those who desired to give the commission independent power to coerce recalcitrant corporations, Montague argued that this entailed an improper delegation of legislative and judicial authority. In conclusion, he advised the House to test the com-

---

30 Arthur S. Link, *Wilson, the New Freedom* (Princeton, 1956), 241–43, and *passim.*
31 Clipping, July 22, 1936, in scrapbook, Moore Collection; Montague to R. L. Montague, March 4, 1914, and R. L. Montague to T. C. Commins, May 25, 1914, Montague Papers.
32 *House Report No. 533,* 63rd Cong., 2nd Sess., II, *passim.*

mission "by actual experience . . . before enacting more comprehensive and radical legislation." [33]

Montague's stand on this phase of antitrust legislation was thus definitely a moderate one, reflecting both his desire for reform and his constitutional caution. He wanted regulation, not regimentation. He completely opposed, for example, proposals that the commission fix prices of big business products. President Wilson also feared that a commission authorized to issue "cease and desist" orders would possess dangerous powers. But both Wilson's and Montague's original wishes were overruled when the Senate considerably enlarged the powers of the commission. The House, including Montague, accepted the alterations.[34]

Montague's support of Wilson on the question of trust regulation was but one example of his comprehensive endorsement of all facets of the New Freedom. On several occasions he delivered polished speeches on the floor of the House in defense of major items in that program, speeches notable for their scholarly depth of research in constitutional and international law. In September, 1913, for example, he lectured the House at length, defending the constitutional power of the government to establish the Federal Reserve System of regional banks, which Wilson desired. In the same month, in a more partisan address, he applauded the tariff reductions contained in the Underwood bill as a "redemption of Democratic promises . . . plainly heeding the call of the greatest good to the greatest number." In other endeavors, he worked for Wilson's compromise amendment to the Clayton Act, which declared that labor unions were not to be construed as illegal combinations in restraint of trade under the antitrust laws. He supported pension measures for families of Spanish-American War veterans. He favored prohibition of interstate trade in goods manufactured by child labor. Finally, he sanctioned and helped formulate in committee the Adamson Railroad Act, which established an eight-hour day and provided other compensations to railroad employees.[35]

33 *Congressional Record*, 63rd Cong., 2nd Sess., LI, 8984 ff.
34 Link, *Wilson, The New Freedom*, 436–38; Richmond *Times Dispatch*, Oct. 19, 1914.
35 *Congressional Record*, 63rd Cong., 1st Sess., L, 5625 ff., 5090 ff.; 63rd Cong., 2nd Sess., LI, 3646, 6909, 12771 ff.; 63rd Cong., 3rd Sess., LII, 248; 64th Cong., 1st Sess., LIII, 2035. See also Dewey W. Grantham, Jr., "Virginia Congressional Leaders and the New Freedom, 1913–1917," *Virginia Magazine of History and Biography*, LVI (July, 1948), 306–309; Richmond

On matters of foreign policy, Montague also supported Wilson when he advocated repeal of the tolls exemption granted American vessels trading through the Panama Canal. This exemption constituted a direct violation of the 1901 Hay-Pauncefote Treaty between Britain and the United States, and Montague, in a scholarly dissertation on international law, argued for repeal on the basis of the sanctity of treaties as solemn agreements between nations. In a day's debate characterized by "verbal artillery," his address received a favorable review by the press, the New York *World* evaluating it as "perhaps the best that was made." Shortly afterward, the Richmond *Times Dispatch* asserted that the speech had achieved for Montague a "prominent place seldom accomplished by men serving their first terms in the House." [36]

In another important address on foreign policy Montague supported a bill offered in 1914 by his friend and ally, Congressman Jones, which declared the intention of the United States to grant the Philippines eventual independence. The Filipino people, he warned would have their independence, "whether by voluntary action on our part or by the exercise of force on their part." Dismissing Republican arguments that representatives of the United States must remain indefinitely in the islands to educate and protect the residents, Montague solemnly averred that "every time a book is put into one hand of a Filipino boy, sooner or later, if you withhold his independence, there will be a sword in the other hand." [37]

Such sentiments reflected Montague's basic progressive outlook. This was the spirit which pervaded his attitude toward Wilson's New Freedom; this was the spirit which had pervaded his administration as Virginia's governor. But another facet existed in Montague's political thinking, one equally high-minded but more conservative, more legalistic. On some occasions, this conservative bent was to run directly counter to his own liberal inclinations and to the national reforms of the day.

This conservatism was evidenced in matters involving conflict between federal and state jurisdictions. "The hope and the genius of our system," Montague once declared, "consist in the better balancing

---

Times Dispatch, June 12, 1914; Richmond *Evening Journal,* April 17, 1913.

36 Richmond *Times Dispatch,* March 7 and 30, April 14, 1914; R. L. Montague to Joseph Willard, April 3, 1914, Montague Papers.

37 *Congressional Record,* 63rd Cong., 2nd Sess., LI, 16623 ff.

and adjustment of these two powers and jurisdictions than ever before accomplished by man." Acting on this belief, he opposed an amendment to a general dams bill before Congress in 1914 which allowed the government to levy a tax on the sale of electricity produced from dams on interstate waterways. This he labeled an improper extension of the federal power to regulate interstate commerce, since the states were the actual owners of the country's rivers, and the federal government possessed only the right to intervene in matters of navigation.[38]

Montague's belief in decentralized government also influenced his thinking on several reforms of the day. During his eight years under Wilson he consistently opposed all efforts to pass a constitutional amendment for woman suffrage, on the premise that matters of suffrage should be left to the individual states. He also opposed efforts in 1914 to enact national prohibition, even though Virginia had gone "dry" that same year.[39] In these stands Montague ran diametrically against prevailing national trends, but he also closely approximated Wilson's positions on the same issues. Like Montague, Wilson initially opposed both prohibition and woman suffrage. And in his composite record we have, in the words of Arthur S. Link,

> the anomaly of a progressive in conflict with reformers and radicals. . . . To the extent that they [Wilsonian-Democrats] championed popular democracy and rebelled against a status quo that favored the wealthy, they were progressives . . . They wanted impartial government with a modicum of federal regulation, rather than dynamic, positive federal intervention and participation in economic and social affairs. With their state-rights view of the Constitution, these liberal Democrats tended to suspect any attempts to commit the federal government to projects of social amelioration, because such intervention implied an invasion of the police power heretofore exercised almost exclusively by the states.[40]

Such an evaluation aptly describes Montague, the minor Congressional lieutenant, as well as Wilson, the leader and President.

In the four years of Wilson's second term, Montague continued to support the President's legislative program. The American entry into the World War almost coincided with Wilson's second inauguration; subsequently, the original tenets of the New Freedom were forgotten

38 Richmond *Times Dispatch,* June 14, 1914; *Congressional Record,* 63rd Cong., 2nd Sess., LI, 12771 ff.
39 Richmond *Times Dispatch,* Sept. 13 and 23, 1914, June 24, 1915; *Congressional Record,* 63rd Cong., 3rd Sess., LII, 1482.
40 Link, *Wilson, the New Freedom,* 241, 256–59.

as the nation concentrated its entire energy toward the war effort. Montague endorsed every important measure designed to strengthen military effectiveness (before the outbreak of war he had favored Wilson's preparedness program as well), and as a member of the Committee on Foreign Commerce, he was personally entrusted with the drafting and supervision of the important Trading with the Enemy Act which passed Congress in 1917. The catalytic impetus of the wartime emergency produced far-reaching extensions of government power, including government administration of railroads. Montague accepted this extension from the standpoint of military exigency, but he expressed increasing concern that wartime emergency measures would become permanently embedded in Congressional statutes. Specifically, he feared that once control of the country's railroads had been assumed by the government, permanent nationalization would result. Consequently, in hearings on the railroad bill before his House committee, he urged his colleagues to limit government control to one year following the war. The committee instead fixed a duration of two years.[41]

Montague continued to believe that public transportation facilities should be regulated in the public interest, however, and early in 1920 he sponsored a bill to prohibit the abandonment of coastwise and inland waterborne commerce routes without the consent of the Interstate Commerce Commission. His decision to introduce the bill was motivated by the Old Dominion Steamship Company's discontinuing certain of its less profitable routes in eastern Virginia. Montague, "persuaded that the railroads are back of this abandonment," privately termed it a "clumsy affront to public sentiment," and a "rather ruthless disregard of public interest by this corporation and perhaps others so soon after being turned over to private control. . . . [There must be] a scrupulous regard given to the protection and development of the commerce of the people." In his opinion, "Private ownership is now undergoing its final trial and test, and unless public sentiment can be satisfied, government ownership will ensue within the next few years," a development he labeled a potential castastrophe.[42] Montague's attitude toward regulation of transportation facilities thus revealed not only his continuing insistence that the pub-

---

41 New York *Times*, Jan. 10, Feb. 2, July 3, 1918; *Congressional Record,* 65th Cong., 2nd Sess., LVI, 2635 ff.
42 *Congressional Record,* 66th Cong., 2nd Sess., LIX, 3992; Montague to J. Scott Parrish, March 6, 1920, and Montague to George Bryan, March 5, 1920, Montague Papers.

lic's rights be safeguarded, but also his firm belief in the efficacy of private enterprise as a dynamic force in the American economy. In general, he felt that federal regulation had achieved a satisfactory degree of protection for the public; further inroads of socialism he would oppose vigorously. His career as a full-fledged progressive had ended.

By 1920 Montague had also reached the end of his active career as a Virginia Independent. As a freshman Congressman, he was one of three Virginia Independents in the House, and as such he figured in the battle for Wilson's patronage which ensued between the organization and antiorganization wings of the party. But as his statewide popularity declined, and as the cleavages between the organization and antiorganization wings of the Virginia Democracy became less sharply delineated, his influence in Virginia's political picture slowly contracted to the confines of his own district. His personal popularity had reached its apex in 1901, and the years following his 1905 defeat by Martin would see no revival of that former eminence.

Senator Martin, one of Wilson's most persistent early antagonists, had shifted to Wilson at a critical moment in the 1912 convention, but too late, some feared, to benefit politically. Leaders of the organization looked with trepidation upon the spectre of a vengeful President parceling out all patronage, the lifeblood of any machine, into the receptive hands of Glass, Jones, and Montague, the triumvirate of Independent leaders in the House. And the "antis," seeking to break the machine's stranglehold on state politics and government, anxiously awaited such an overt demonstration of partiality from a grateful candidate. A protracted fight for recognition developed.[43]

Wilson attempted to conciliate both factions in their quest for patronage, though he naturally inclined to favor his Virginia supporters. As party leader, however, the President had to deal with Martin and Swanson in the Senate (Martin was sufficiently respected there to become Senate Democratic leader later in Wilson's administration), where the Democratic majority was perilously thin. Montague recognized Wilson's dilemma when he wrote to Peabody in April, 1913:

> The Virginia situation may not be properly understood or disposed of by the President. I fear he will have to so accommodate himself with the senators that the progressives . . . in Virginia will be discouraged and disheartened . . . whereas a proper recognition would easily turn the scales in this State. Indeed the ranking file [sic] of the machine will

43 Richmond *Times Dispatch*, July 3, 1912.

be only too eager to leave the machine if they saw it no longer effective in securing patronage.[44]

At first, Wilson managed to appease both factions. When Jones, Glass, and Montague endorsed former Lieutenant Governor Willard for an ambassadorial post, the machine forces countered by supporting Thomas Nelson Page for a similar post. Wilson, perplexed and undecided, at length delivered an ultimatum to both parties to adjust their differences and come up with a mutual candidate. "When the ultimatum came the Virginians got together . . . decided that it would be foolish to take two bites at one apple and came to a quick conclusion to ask for two apples." Wilson condescendingly submitted, awarded Page an ambassadorship to Italy, and gave Willard the minister's post in Spain. Both factions were content.[45]

The appointments of Page and Willard, however, were but the initial foray. Much more important to both factions was a package of seven appointments to the offices of district attorney, U.S. marshal, and collectors of revenue and customs. Montague, Glass, and Jones each sponsored their favorites for particular positions, and the machine forces did likewise. For many months Wilson remained discreetly silent as to his preferences, while Glass, Montague, Martin, and Swanson all made personal visits on behalf of their respective candidates. Each faction found the other's nominees anathema, and Wilson was described as at "his wit's end to find a way to deliver." [46]

The delivery came on March 21, 1914. The upshot was an almost complete victory for the machine; six of its seven candidates received the presidential nod. The only exception was the nominee for revenue collector of the west; this went to John M. Hart as an indication of Wilson's esteem for Glass. Montague had particularly campaigned for T. P. Davie for collector of customs, to no avail. As Montague's brother informed Willard, Wilson's appointments did not represent the President's personal preferences in the matter; they represented a pragmatic acceptance of political realities. The Martin organization was Virginia's political reality.[47]

44 Montague to Peabody, April 3, 1913, Montague Papers.
45 Richmond *Evening Journal*, March 13 and 19, 1913; Montague to Glass, Feb. 20, 1913, Montague Papers.
46 R. L. Montague to Willard, Nov. 15, 1913, Montague Papers; Richmond *Evening Journal*, May 9, 1913; Richmond *News Leader*, Dec. 6, 1913; Richmond *Times Dispatch*, March 3, 8, 14, and 15, 1914.
47 Montague to Woodrow Wilson, Aug. 4, 1913, and R. L. Montague to Willard, April 3, 1914, Montague Papers; Roanoke *World News*, March 21, 1914, in scrapbook, Martin Papers.

A potent argument always used by the machine in the intraparty wrangle for patronage was that the cries of Glass, Montague, and Jones merely represented the protests of the "outs" against the "ins" —that Martin and Swanson more truly represented the sentiment of the Virginia electorate, and should be so recognized. The antimachine forces realized the strength of this argument and in 1913 made successful efforts to achieve a few victories of their own.

Henry C. Stuart, Montague's appointee to the corporation commission in 1903, had canvassed for the 1913 gubernatorial nomination as early as 1911. By corralling pledges far in advance of other potential candidates, he brought effective pressure on local politicos, who in turn conveyed reports to machine leaders. As a result, the machine wisely decided to field no candidate in opposition. As an Independent, Montague gave Stuart his warm endorsement ("I have confidence in his judgment and patriotism"), and in private correspondence urged his nomination.[48]

Glass, Jones, and Montague also scored a victory in 1913 by convincing John Garland Pollard, a young Richmond lawyer, to run against the incumbent attorney general, Samuel W. Williams, a machine man. In a dynamic speaking tour of the state, Pollard presented a platform dedicated to curbing electoral malpractices, to providing for the impartial selection of election judges, to instituting a presidential primary in Virginia, and to ending the fee system of paying local officials. In response, the Virginia electorate rewarded him with a narrow margin of 32,261 votes to Williams' 31,187. Against direct machine opposition, the Independents had won their first statewide victory since Montague's nomination in 1901.[49]

The following year the machine received another possible setback when Montague easily won his campaign for reelection. Montague had given unwavering support to Wilson during his first term in office, and his general performance seemed so satisfactory that opposition to his reelection at first appeared unlikely. However, on April 14, 1914, Louis O. Wendenburg, a state senator from Henrico County, filed for the district primary to be held on June 16. As state senator, Wendenburg was known primarily for his prolabor leanings, but, paradoxi-

48 J. N. Bauserman to Hay, Jan. 17, 1911, Hay Papers; Baltimore *Evening News*, June 13, 1913, in scrapbook, Martin Papers; Montague to Walter Ryland, April 3, 1913, Montague Papers.

49 John Stewart Bryan to Montague, May 30, 1913, Moore Collection; Richmond *Evening Journal*, June 5, 1913; Richmond *News Leader*, July 11, 14, 18, and 21, Aug. 6, 7, and 8, 1913.

cally, his hesitant entrance into the race had evidently been encouraged by organization men. Once Montague's reelection became assured, however, the machine abandoned Wendenburg, and the latter's chief support came from certain labor elements and disgruntled former supporters of Lamb, Montague's vanquished opponent of 1912. The outcome was never in doubt. Several spirited Richmond speeches in the week prior to the election featured charges by Wendenburg that Montague had antilabor sympathies, charges which Montague refuted with little difficulty. On election day Wendenburg went down to defeat by a plurality of four to one.[50]

So emphatic was Montague's triumph that for fourteen years he faced no further opposition to his renomination in a Democratic primary, and only slight opposition from Republican and minor-party candidates in general elections. But of more immediate importance, his victory strengthened his hand among the Virginia progressives who were shortly to advocate his nomination to the United States Supreme Court.

Montague had never relinquished his ambitions for high federal office. Though honored to represent his district in the House of Representatives, he always felt himself limited in that body. Since a seat in the Senate now seemed unlikely, his aspirations turned more and more to the judiciary where his incisive legal mind, his term as Virginia's attorney general, his position as dean of Richmond College's law school, and his experience in the Rio de Janeiro and Brussels conferences gave him ample qualifications. Accordingly, early in January, 1916, upon the death of Associate Justice Joseph R. Lamar of the Supreme Court, Montague's candidacy for the vacancy was laid before President Wilson. Presenting the application were Governor Stuart and a delegation of prominent Virginians, including Pollard, Glass, and Meredith. The move was applauded by the Richmond bar and press, and by such legal dignitaries as Judge William L. Marbury of Maryland, who was also mentioned for the post.[51]

Hope for a united endorsement from Virginia's two factions did not materialize, however. Since the call for Montague's nomination had been sounded by individuals none too friendly to Martin, the Senator could not afford to let Montague's candidacy go unopposed.

---

50 R. L. Montague to Willard, April 15, June 18, 1914, Montague Papers; Richmond *Times Dispatch,* June 7, 13, and 14, 1914.
51 Richmond *Times Dispatch,* Jan. 8 and 9, 1914; J. J. Darlington to William L. Marbury, Jan. 7, 1916, Montague Papers.

Within a few days after Stuart announced Montague's availability, Martin countered by launching a similar campaign for Joseph L. Kelly, a judge of the state supreme court. Senator Swanson, six Virginia representatives in the House, and four justices of the state supreme court all endorsed Kelly. Petitioned by both Virginia factions, Wilson refused to commit himself, though he professed "highest and sincerest esteem" for Montague's qualifications. But the consequences of Martin's move were obvious. As the Norfolk *Virginian-Pilot* dispassionately observed, "If we can not agree among ourselves to present at Washington the name of one candidate . . . we can scarcely expect the President to heed the voice of divided council." In opposing Montague, Martin had effectively killed his chances of nomination, while his support for Kelly, causing as it did a "divided council," could never have succeeded. On January 28, Wilson confounded all political factions everywhere by appointing Louis Brandeis.[52]

Circumstances and the Virginia machine had combined once again to thwart Montague's hope for federal appointment. His unsuccessful candidacy for the Supreme Court proved to be the last event in which he figured prominently as a Virginia Independent. In 1916 he was occasionally mentioned as an opponent to Swanson's reelection to the Senate, but he did not consider the prospect seriously. The personable Swanson had proven his popularity in the 1911 campaign, while his later support of Wilson's legislative program removed legitimate grounds for criticism. These factors also discouraged other Virginia Independents, including Stuart, Tucker and Glass, from making the race. Swanson's subsequent renomination was the first unopposed machine victory since Daniel's last election in 1904.[53]

The machine suffered a significant setback in 1917, however, when J. Taylor Ellyson, a candidate backed by important figures in the organization, lost to Westmoreland Davis, a representative of agricultural interests who was an Independent in politics, although not closely associated with the Independent faction in Congress. Finishing third in the race was Pollard, the man sponsored by that faction.

52 Richmond *Virginian,* Jan. 11 and 13, 1916; Bristol *Herald,* Jan. 8, 1916; Danville *Register,* Jan. 15, 1916; all in scrapbook, Martin Papers. Richmond *Times Dispatch,* Jan. 12 and 18, 1916. As late as the 1930's Montague received mention as a Supreme Court appointee.
53 Richmond *Virginian,* Dec. 14, 1915; Alexandria *Gazette,* Dec. 18, 1915; Roanoke *Times,* Dec. 16, 1915; all in scrapbook, Martin Papers. Richmond *Times Dispatch,* June 2, 1916.

Ellyson's defeat can be credited to the increasing importance played by the issue of prohibition in Virginia politics. Both Pollard and Ellyson were "dry's," whereas Davis was a moderate on the question; the prohibition vote was divided, and Davis benefited accordingly.[54]

Davis faced one of his most important decisions as governor when the longtime head of the Virginia machine, Thomas Staples Martin, died in 1919 after a lengthy illness. Speculation immediately arose as to whom Governor Davis would appoint to fill the vacancy. Among possible appointees mentioned by a *Times Dispatch* editorial were Tucker, the Independent candidate for governor in 1909, Glass, now Secretary of the Treasury under Wilson, and Montague, "one of the strongest men of the State." Davis surprised some prognosticators by selecting Glass, who many suspected would prefer to remain in the Cabinet. The appointment, however, was a natural one: "Mr. Glass always has been an avowed enemy of the . . . machine. The attitude of the Governor is no less hostile to the old leaders of the party." In choosing a man of his own political allegiances, therefore, Davis had turned to the most prominent Independent available. Glass, not Montague, fit that description.[55]

Davis' hope that Glass, as Senator, would strengthen the antiorganization elements of the Virginia Democracy proved illusory. Glass enjoyed such formidable popularity that Flood, the organization's heir apparent, decided not to oppose his election in 1920. Unable to dislodge Glass, the machine endeavored to convert him. By October of 1922 Glass could declare to Swanson, his bitter opponent in 1911, that the outstanding circumstance of his brief service in the Senate had been "the restoration of our former intimate friendship." And in the gubernatorial election of 1925 Glass gave unstinting support to the organization's candidate, the young reformer, Harry Flood Byrd.[56] The disgruntled Davis, himself an unsuccessful opponent to Swanson in 1922, was later to wish remorsefully that he had appointed Montague rather than Glass.[57]

54 Eckenrode, "Virginia Since 1865," 364–65; Roanoke *Times,* July 22, 1917, scrapbook, in John R. Saunders Papers, Alderman Library, University of Virginia, Charlottesville.
55 Richmond *Times Dispatch,* Nov. 14 and 16, 1919.
56 Richmond *News Leader,* Jan. 1, 1920; Glass to Swanson, Oct. 26, 1922; Glass to Byrd, Aug. 6, 1925; Byrd to Glass, Aug. 9, 1925; all in Carter Glass Papers, Alderman Library, University of Virginia, Charlottesville.
57 Moore interview. Davis made this admission to Mrs. John R. Saunders, who was Mrs. Montague's sister.

For Montague the appointment of Glass ended all serious political ambition.[58] The zeal that had characterized his 1901 and 1905 campaigns had diminished year by year, as hoped-for appointments failed to materialize, and as the Virginia organization became increasingly invulnerable. As a Wilsonian Congressman he had performed creditably, had won the respect of his colleagues, and had been entrusted with the formulation of significant legislation. But the magic oratory and magnetism of the youth, which had promised such a meteoric future, had somehow failed to bring the expected dividends. In the House of Representatives Jack Montague was not in his element. There his powers as an oratorical spokesman became enervated in the routine of committee government. Once, when a movement developed to increase the House membership to five hundred representatives, Montague proposed instead that the number be reduced. A legislative body composed of so many individuals, he lamented, became "necessarily extravagant, clumsy, and unwieldy in operation." [59] In such a forum, Montague felt inhibited and restricted. In such a body his political ambitions remained unfulfilled.

If Glass's appointment marked the final disappointment of Montague's ambitions, it also marked a period of transition for Independent leadership generally. Glass had made his peace with the machine. Jones, the veteran Independent, had died in 1918. Pollard, the most liberal of the Virginia progressives in 1914, eventually ran successfully for governor in 1929 with machine backing. Montague never overtly joined with the organization, but he no longer actively opposed it. As they grew older, leaders of the progressives became more conservative, lost influence, or were absorbed by the organization. The machine, on the other hand, by virtue of its strength, attracted the most capable of Virginia's aspiring politicians. Martin, the most astute of them all in his day, was shortly succeeded as head of the organization by his peer, Harry Flood Byrd. By a sagacious policy of compromise and by a gradual purging of its corrupting features, the Virginia Democratic organization developed an aura of permanent invincibility.

---

58 In 1920 Montague considered running for the Senate in 1922, but only if, as rumored, Swanson retired. Swanson did not retire, however. *Richmond News Leader*, Dec. 4, 1920.
59 *Congressional Record*, 66th Cong., 3rd Sess., LX, 1632.

XVI

CONSTITUTIONAL LAWYER
AND
INTERNATIONAL SPOKESMAN

THE closing phase of Montague's life is in some respects tinged with melancholy. With Glass's appointment to the Senate in 1919, he had been deprived of his last serious opportunity for political advancement in Virginia. Likewise, the Republican domination of the national government in the 1920's made impossible any creative contribution in high administrative office. Consequently, the former progressive governor, the Wilsonian reformer, became in his last years conservative, philosophical, somewhat detached. Time had its effect. Age thinned his hair and expanded his waistline. In the last five years of his life his general health broke down, and this provoked one last political challenge in the congressional election of 1936—a challenge the veteran of so many political wars managed to weather, but by a pathetically small margin. Death came in 1937 to a man weary in mind and body, disillusioned with his dream of a revived standard of American citizenship and with his hopes for a harmonious international community of nations.

In another sense, though, the closing chapter of Montague's career presents a pleasing panorama of unobtrusive service as Congressman and spokesman for international understanding. Purged of ambition but not of idealism, Montague, in his last years, attained honors unsought but not undeserved. As a frequent representative to international conferences and as a leading official in several world peace organizations, he raised a sometimes lonely voice for international goodwill and cooperation in solving the problems attendant to the postwar era. And as an increasingly conservative representative in Congress, he won the esteem and respect of his colleagues for his legal acumen and unbiased statesmanship. An industrious, congenial, but unassuming Congressman, he never became a figure of national prominence. Although in the early Wilson years he had assumed a role as oratorical spokesman for much of the New Freedom legislation, in his last sixteen years in Congress he made few major addresses to the House—and those made were chiefly upon technical points of law and constitutional interpretation. Nevertheless, as a diligent committee member, he participated in formulating much constructive legislation.

A member of the important House Commerce committee in the Wilson era, Montague had helped draft the Trading with the Enemy Act, the Adamson Act providing an eight-hour work day for trainmen, and various compensation measures for veterans, longshoremen, and government employees. Later, in 1921, he was transferred at his own request to the House Judiciary Committee, a committee which better enabled him to utilize his vast store of legal knowledge and experience, but which largely removed him from public notice. His concrete accomplishments while on this committee were many. In 1922 he piloted through the House a crime bill to simplify the procedure of prosecution for interstate freight thefts. In 1926, when serious charges were brought against George W. English, a district judge for eastern Illinois, Montague and other members of the committee convinced the House to indict English, thus bringing him before the Senate for impeachment proceedings. Montague was later appointed one of the managers for the Senate trial; so well did the prosecution prepare its case that English voluntarily retired rather than face almost certain conviction. In 1932 Montague contributed to the drafting of the La Guardia Bill restricting the frequent use made by the courts of the injunction technique in curbing labor strikes. He voted for its passage, and was appointed one of three conferees to compromise differences with the Senate's version. In 1932 he also assisted in the drafting of the federal antikidnaping bill which passed Congress in reaction to the famous Lindbergh incident, and during the 1930's he was personally credited with adding a total of fifteen "anti-crime" bills to the federal code.[1]

1 *Congressional Record,* 67th Cong., 2nd Sess., LXII, 7980; 69th Cong., 1st Sess., LXVII, 6714–16, 6977, 7679–80; 71st Cong., 2nd Sess., LXXII,

Montague's tireless and painstaking work on the judiciary committee won the admiration of his colleagues, several of whom lavishly praised him as a man of "erudition and keenness," and "a scholar in every sense of the word." Outside of the committee Montague also earned the respect of the general House membership. In retrospect, Congressmen Sam Rayburn, Joseph W. Martin, Jr., Carl Vinson, John W. McCormack, Emmanuel Celler, Colgate Darden, and others all remembered him as a man of polished manners, ability, industry and absolute integrity.[2] On more than one occasion, effusive personal tributes were expressed from the House floor itself. Indeed, after the death of Speaker Henry T. Rainey of Illinois in 1934, Montague received some mention for the Speakership, but his declining health precluded his filling such a position of responsibility, even if he could have obtained it.

Outside of his committee activity, Montague took no important part in the formulation of legislation. Nevertheless, to trace the continuing evolution of his political attitudes, a brief review of his voting record during these final years is valuable.

Toward the end of the Wilson era Montague had displayed a growing conservative bent—especially a fear that socialistic expedients rendered necessary in wartime would become permanently embedded in statute law. After the war the United States returned to "normalcy" under Harding, Coolidge, and Hoover, and Montague's apprehensions partially subsided. He still raised occasional warnings against the dangers of the erosion of state sovereignty and of government interference in private enterprise. But he also supported measures to protect the public interest in various phases of the economy and to preserve a balance of power between management and labor in industry. Toward the end of the Republican era, he shifted somewhat to the left in approving several strong steps taken to counteract the effects of the Depression. During the 1920's, then, Montague generally adhered to a middle-of-the-road policy.

Specific instances of Montague's more progressive attitudes include his support of two key bills enacted by the "Farm Bloc": the Grain

---

10052; 72nd Cong., 1st Sess., LXXV, 5511, 5720, 13290–300; 73rd Cong., 2nd Sess., LXXVIII, 8224, 8774–77; 74th Cong., 1st Sess., LXXIX, 11355; Richmond *Times Dispatch,* Aug. 5, 1928.

2   Letters from these men and others to the author (February and March, 1960), all describe Montague in this light. See also *Congressional Record,* 68th Cong., 1st Sess., LXV, 7685–86; 74th Cong., 1st Sess., LXXIX, 8199, 11351; 75th Cong., 1st Sess., LXXXI, Appendix, 1262, 1279, 1322, 2495.

Futures Act, which gave the Secretary of Agriculture sweeping powers of regulation over the grain stock exchanges; and the Packers and Stockyards Act, which was designed to "preserve competition among packers and to compel commission merchants and the stockyards to charge only reasonable rates." He also approved of measures establishing arbitration machinery for settlement of labor-management disputes in railroads, and providing flood control on the Mississippi River. He took an active part in obtaining anti-injunction legislation for labor unions; in 1932 he voted for Philippine independence, and in 1933, for repeal of prohibition.[3]

On the conservative side of the ledger, Montague in 1922 opposed a bill making lynching a federal crime. He consistently resisted all efforts in the 1920's to involve the United States in water-power projects, specifically the Muscle Shoals and Boulder Dam programs. Finally, in 1924, 1927, and 1928, he voted against the McNary-Haugen Bill, which provided government price supports for various agricultural products.[4]

Montague criticized all these bills on constitutional grounds. Every Congressman, he maintained, was "duty-bound" to vote against any item of legislation contravening the Constitution. Thus he opposed the antilynching legislation solely on the grounds that it constituted an invasion of the fundamental police powers reserved to the states. And he cogently argued that the Constitution authorized only the improvement of navigation on interstate waterways, not the harnessing of water power and the production of electricity. The latter was particularly objectionable, he felt, since it brought the federal government into competition with private industry. When Montague took the House floor to oppose the lynching bill, he admitted his criticisms were "largely of a constitutional character. Oh, I know it is said that this is the old cry. But I would to God it were oftener heard in this House."

3 *Congressional Record*, 67th Cong., 1st Sess., LXI, 1429, 2035, 5448; 67th Cong., 4th Sess., LXIV, 1861 ff., 4112, 5013, 8156; 68th Cong., 1st Sess., LXV, 5918, 8952; 69th Cong., 1st Sess., LXVII, 5646–47; 70th Cong., 1st Sess., LXIX, 7123; 71st Cong., 2nd Sess., LXXII, 341; 72nd Cong., 2nd Sess., LXXVI, 1768, 4516; Richmond *Times Dispatch*, Nov. 3, 1922.

4 *Congressional Record*, 67th Cong., 2nd Sess., LXII, 1303–1306, 9861; 68th Cong., 1st Sess., LXV, 3776, 3925; 69th Cong., 2nd Sess., LXVIII, 4098; 70th Cong., 1st Sess., LXIX, 8233–34, 9647, 9957; Richmond *Times Dispatch*, July 24, 1928; New York *Times*, Jan. 18, 1922.

As Montague claimed, he was not a strict constructionist of the Constitution. From the standpoint of his nineteenth-century background, he was distinctly a nationalist, a disciple not of Calhoun and John Taylor, but of John Marshall. As late as 1909 he had urged an emphasis on state duties, not states rights. But in the twentieth-century age of industry, when the federal government began assuming powers not strictly derived from the Constitution, either explicit or implied, Montague's conservative pleas for self-restraint became the dominant strain of his constitutional thinking. And his call for moderation in defining constitutional authority became more and more a lonely cry in the Congress. He was now a representative of the "old school." The evolution from conservative, to progressive, to conservative, had come full circle.

With the advent of the Depression, Montague's drift toward conservatism was partially reversed. As the impact of the Depression grew increasingly serious during Hoover's administration, he supported bills granting additional capital to the Federal Land Banks, making emergency appropriations for highway construction, distributing surplus wheat and cotton for relief of the unemployed, providing federal aid directly to impoverished individuals, and promoting a vast expansion of public works. And in his 1930 campaign for reelection, he criticized the Republican attitude toward the Depression as myopic: "Our Republican friends had eyes that did not see, and ears that did not hear." [5]

Montague's later reaction to Roosevelt's "New Deal" was in keeping with the flexible, moderate conservatism which characterized his twelve years under Harding, Coolidge, and Hoover. An admirer of Roosevelt personally, he never became a vocal exponent of the New Deal, but he did give his personal support to several of the more important legislative objectives of the Roosevelt administration. Specifically, he voted for the establishment of the Home Owners Loan Corporation in 1933, the Securities Exchange Act of 1934, and the Public Utility Holding Company Act of 1935; he welcomed the reciprocal trade program enacted in 1934, and he opposed balancing the budget "at the expense of suffering or starvation." Most significantly, he supported the Social Security Act of 1935. In his 1936 campaign for reelection, Montague praised the general accomplishments of

5 *Congressional Record,* 72nd Cong., 1st Sess., LXXV, 966, 4892, 12243, 13210; unidentified clipping, 1930, scrapbook, Moore Collection.

Roosevelt and his administration: "His head is all right and his heart is all right. I think those two attributes show what kind of a man he is." [6]

But Montague's support of specific items in Roosevelt's program does not label him a thoroughgoing New Dealer. On the contrary, his opposition to other phases of that program, though muted, indicates his disenchantment with the radical inclinations of the aristocrat from New York. In April, 1935, for example, he opposed the act establishing the Works Progress Administration, a cornerstone in the "second New Deal," designed to combat the still pressing problem of unemployment. He continued his resistance to a Tennessee Valley Authority, and he voted against the Guffey-Vinson Bituminous Coal Act which established for the mining industry a code of regulations pertaining to safety standards and hours of labor. Repeated absences caused by poor health enabled him to avoid public commitment on such important New Deal agencies as the National Recovery Administration and the Agricultural Adjustment Act, and he took no position on the Wagner Labor Act of 1935. Even though Richmond newspapers criticized his poor voting record on major issues, Montague declined to reveal his attitudes. Thomas Walsh, his secretary, probably best reflected Montague's own state of indecision in a letter he wrote the "Governor" near the end of 1933. Reviewing the political scene, Walsh observed: "I still doubt the success of the NRA, the AAA, the PWA, etc. . . . Our whole form of Government has been turned upside down . . . the sanctity of contracts means nothing. . . . The old system did not work—I hope the new one will." [7]

As a Congressman in the New Deal era Montague had lost his youthful faith in absolutes and tangibles. One of his colleagues later recalled that he recognized "that a new day had come for industry, labor and agriculture." [8] He realized vaguely that his own intellectual heritage, a conservative-progressive legacy of the nineteenth century, did not neatly fit the new conditions. And although he showed an in-

6 *Congressional Record,* 73rd Cong., 2nd Sess., LXXVIII, 8115, 10547, and index, HR6975; 74th Cong., 1st Sess., LXXIX, 3479, 3981, 6068–69, 10637–39; Richmond *Times Dispatch,* Nov. 7, 1932, July 5, 1936; Richmond *News Leader,* Jan. 7, 1935; Montague to D. B. Morrissett, Feb. 22, 1935, Montague Papers.
7 *Congressional Record,* 74th Cong., 1st Sess., LXXIX, 5150, 11039; Thomas Walsh to Montague, Oct. 25, 1933, Aug. 31, 1935, Montague Papers.
8 *Congressional Record,* 75th Cong., 1st Sess., LXXXI, Appendix, 1520.

clination to change his mode of thinking, he never made the complete evolution from a Wilsonian progressive to a Roosevelt liberal.

Concerning domestic affairs, Montague's career as Congressman thus ended in a haze of mental indecision and evasion. In the arena of international relations, however, his star had a brighter setting. As a leader promoting the development of international law, the establishment of international mediation machinery, and the resolution of international differences, Montague displayed his innate idealism at its mellow maturity. Motivated by the very simple desire to improve the world for posterity, in his last years he diverted his creative energies from domestic to international problems. Aside from his reputation as a constitutional lawyer, no feature of his later years in Congress was more prominent than his role as spokesman for worldwide understanding.

Montague's interest and concern for international relations had early origins. He had studied international law at the University of Virginia, and in 1891 he contributed to the Richmond *Times* an article discussing at length the Bering Sea controversy involving international rights over the sealing waters in the Alaskan area. He had displayed an active interest in the Hague peace conference which met in 1899, and in the American Conference on International Arbitration which met in 1904. His participation in the Rio de Janeiro and Brussels conferences on international law helped establish his reputation as a thinker on international problems, which in 1910 resulted in his appointment as trustee of the Carnegie Endowment for International Peace, a position he held until 1935. From 1917 through 1923 he served as assistant treasurer for the organization and from 1923 to 1929 as its full treasurer.[9]

While he was in Congress, Montague filled several significant positions in organizations promoting international understanding. In 1914 he became one of thirteen men appointed by the Congress to represent the American Group of the Interparliamentary Union at its annual meeting held at The Hague. In 1917 he became President of the American Society for the Judicial Settlement of International Dis-

---

9 Danville *Register*, April 15, 1891, in scrapbook, Moore Collection; *The Second American Conference on International Arbitration* (Washington, 1904), 118, Montague Papers; *Biographical Directory of the American Congress, 1774–1949* (Washington, 1950), 1577.

putes, a sadly incongruous position in view of the world conflict then raging. On the floor of Congress itself, Montague had given unstinting support to Wilson's prewar defense of international law, as well as to his postwar goal of a League of Nations. And from 1920 to 1924 he served as President of the American Peace Society, a venerable organization founded in 1828, which aimed at educating public opinion "in opposition to war as a means of settling international differences." Toward this end, the society called occasional peace congresses, published a monthly periodical (the *Advocate of Peace*), and subsidized permanent commissions to study methods of facilitating amicable international relations.[10]

At the same time that Montague officiated as president of the peace society, he also served as vice-president of the American Group of the Interparliamentary Union. The Union was an association composed of parliamentary bodies throughout the world, representatives of which met annually to discuss mutual problems of parliamentary government, security and disarmament, codification of international law, colonial problems, and tariff policies. In view of the American refusal to join the League of Nations, Montague felt that the role of the Union was particularly important. "This is about the leading instrumentality," he commented at one of the conferences, "by which the American nation can touch elbows with its friends of all other nations." Consequently, in the decade of the twenties he attended the annual conventions regularly—at Stockholm in 1921, Vienna in 1922, London in 1924, Paris in 1927, and Geneva in 1929. At all of these conferences he participated in debates. At some he made formal addresses. According to several reports, his address at the 1929 Geneva meeting, in which he discussed the implications of the Kellogg-Briand Peace Pact, was the highlight of that conference.[11]

Shortly after the Geneva conference, Senator Theodore E. Burton,

10 *Biographical Directory of Congress,* 1577; *Annual Report of the Directors of the American Peace Society* (Washington, 1921), *passim,* Moore Collection; Edson L. Whitney, *The American Peace Society, a Centennial History* (Washington, 1929), 260, 310.

11 "The Interparliamentary Union" (handbook of the American Group, 1914), *passim,* Montague Papers; New York *Times,* Oct. 1, 1922, Sept. 10, 1924, Sept. 27, 1927, Aug. 30, 1929; Manley O. Hudson to Montague, Sept. 6, 1929, Montague Papers. As might be expected, Montague took a dim view of those aspects of foreign policy in the 20's that, as he saw it, jeopardized international accord—especially the American high tariff policy, and the American attitude toward the European debt-reparations situation.

long the president of the American Group, died. In 1930 Montague was formally elected his successor. Later, he received an additional honor by being selected one of only four members serving with Secretary General Christian L. Lang on the executive committee which was responsible for the Union's worldwide direction. Since Montague was isolated fom the European continent and unable to attend committee meetings regularly, the post was primarily an honorary one, indicative of the esteem in which he was held by the Union's leadership.[12]

Montague inherited the presidency at an inopportune time. The optimism which pervaded the world with the signing of the Kellogg Pact in 1928 quickly disappeared when Japan invaded and occupied Manchuria in 1931–32. The worldwide Depression aggravated the tense European reparations situation, and the League of Nations proved ineffectual as a force for preserving peace. Though Montague and others hoped that the Interparliamentary Union might help, in a small way, to stem the apparent collapse of international diplomatic machinery, their hopes proved futile. At home the Congress, spurred by an economy drive, in 1933 cut its small annual contribution to the Union, and for the first time the American Group was unable to send a delegation to the annual conference in Madrid. A serious illness prevented Montague's personal attendance as well.[13]

Efforts by Montague in 1934 to convince Roosevelt and Secretary of State Cordell Hull to encourage Congress to subsidize American participation were similarly unavailing. Only by obtaining a grant of $5,000 from the Carnegie Endowment was he able to defray expenses for a small American delegation to the Istanbul conference of that year.[14] Plagued by poor health, Montague finally resigned his position as president in 1935. Various circumstances—the Depression, a Congress preoccupied with domestic problems, his own health —had combined to handicap his brief administration. Still, prior to his prolonged illnesses he had pursued a vigorous role as unofficial American ambassador of goodwill, a role lauded by many of his foreign colleagues in the Union. Though composed of many internationally prominent figures, the Interparliamentary Union acted in an advisory capacity only. Still, it served as a forum for the meeting of

12 Clipping, March, 1930, scrapbook, Moore Collection; Montague to Arthur D. Call, July 14, 1933, Montague Papers.
13 Arthur D. Call to Montague, July 14 and 29, Nov. 1, 1933, and Leopold Boissier to Montague, Aug. 31, 1933, Montague Papers.
14 Hull to Montague, May 12 and 21, 1934; Montague to Hull, May 14, 1934; Tom Walsh to Montague, Aug. 14, 1934, all *ibid.*

minds and for the formulation of world opinion. It reflected the genuine efforts of a band of men dedicated to the search for a better world through international cooperation. The course of history would prove their labors to be futile, perhaps naive. But their failure does not tarnish the essential nobility of their endeavor.

Montague's earlier record as a Wilsonian Congressman, his prominent activity on the House Commerce and Judiciary committees, his reputation as a constitutional lawyer par excellence, and his impressive role as an international spokesman—all these factors brought to him a personal popularity in the Third District which almost automatically insured his reelections through the years. From 1914 to 1928 he faced no rivals within his own party, and in the latter year D. C. O'Flaherty, a Democratic challenger, went down to defeat by a five-to-one majority. For its part, the Republican party never provided serious opposition in final elections.[15]

In 1936, however, the story was different. Spirited opposition to Montague's renomination developed in the person of David E. Satterfield—a young Richmond lawyer who was for twelve years Richmond's commonwealth's attorney, and campaign manager in 1933 for the successful candidate for governor, George C. Peery. Satterfield had considered running against Montague as early as 1930, but had wisely deferred to the Congressman's formidable reputation and experience. By 1936, however, Montague's continued absences from Congress had raised the legitimate question of his physical ability to serve, and Satterfield, after personally informing the "Governor" of his decision, announced his candidacy. Montague, somewhat reluctantly, accepted the challenge.[16]

The political lines drawn by the campaign had no overt correlation to the statewide cleavage between machine and antimachine forces. Montague appears to have taken little part in factional fights after the Wilson era. His brother-in-law, John R. Saunders, an organization man, served as Virginia's attorney general throughout the twenties, and his lifelong friend, Pollard, was elected governor in 1929 with machine backing. But Satterfield, his 1936 opponent, had been the successful manager in 1933 for George C. Peery, the organi-

15   Richmond *Times Dispatch,* Nov. 5, 1918; Oct. 29, Nov. 3, 1920; Nov. 5 and 8, 1922; Nov. 4 and 5, 1924; Nov. 3, 1926; Aug. 5, 6, 7, and 8, 1928, Nov. 5, 1930; Nov. 5, 7, and 10, 1932; Nov. 5, 6, and 7, 1934.
16   *Ibid.,* June 28, July 11, 1936.

zation candidate whom Montague criticized during the campaign for opposing old-age pensions. More important, Montague was friendly with Lieutenant Governor James H. Price, who was hostile to the Byrd organization. Thus, Montague's action in announcing his support of Price's candidacy for governor in 1935 could not have been well received by the organization.[17]

The Montague-Satterfield campaign proved unexpectedly heated. Satterfield's platform was concisely drawn: he supported old-age pensions; he attacked deficit spending and much of the New Deal program; he advocated federal development of the James River; he favored an extension of federal aid to farmers. The major issue, however, was simple: Montague was old and feeble; Satterfield was young and able.[18]

Montague replied to Satterfield's thrusts by reviewing in detail his many accomplishments in Congress; by arguing that his seniority had proven valuable to the Third District and Virginia; by defending his physical vigor as the best he had enjoyed in five years; and by questioning Satterfield's qualifications for the position. He pointed with justifiable pride to a long list of appropriations which he had obtained for the Third District, a list sufficiently impressive to have evoked envious comment from Senator Martin himself. "I am seeking reelection for no selfish interest," Montague declared, "but because I am deeply interested in the promotion of some public matters which I should like to see completed before I am removed from the picture."[19]

The challenger nearly ousted the incumbent. In the primary held on August 4, Montague defeated Satterfield by a margin of only about 500 votes in a total of 24,000. Though his edge was perilously thin, it was nevertheless evenly distributed. He carried all the nine po-

---

17 Richmond *Times Dispatch,* Sept. 14, 1932, July 8, 1936; Montague to Pollard, May 2, 1930, April 1, May 14, 1935; Price to Montague, April 17, 1935, all in Montague Papers.

18 Richmond *Times Dispatch,* June 23 and 28, July 19, 23, and 26, Aug. 2, 1936.

19 *Ibid.,* July 19, 23, and 31, 1936. Montague had done extremely well in garnering appropriations for his district. From 1913 to 1936 he had obtained $4,400,000 for improvements in the James River, $150,000 for the Mattaponi, York, and Pamunkey rivers, $2,500,000 for Richmond post-office buildings, and smaller amounts for a post office at West Point. He had also been instrumental in bringing the Reserve Bank to Richmond in 1914 and in creating two federal parks, the Colonial National Monument, and the Seven Days Battlefield Park. Richmond *News Leader,* July 4, 1936; list of "Appropriations secured for the Third District," Montague Papers.

litical subdivisions of the district save one, Chesterfield County.[20]

Montague had won his last Democratic fight, but the satisfaction of victory provided only a brief interlude of good health. By December the veteran had once again suffered a lapse of energy: "Governor Montague remains about the same as when you saw him. . . . It is a pity he is unable to regain his strength," wrote his secretary to a friend.[21] Montague had never enjoyed robust health. A wide variety of brief minor illnesses had attended him throughout his life. As he approached old age, his physical constitution had simply deteriorated. Although a serious operation in 1933 had corrected a bladder ailment, he continued to suffer from a weak heart and poor circulation. Just prior to his 1936 campaign he had recovered from pneumonia.

During these declining years Montague spent most of his time with his wife in Urbanna, a small village on the Rappahannock River in Middlesex County. In 1934 he had purchased and remodeled an eighteenth-century home there, christened "Sandwich." And there, in his native Middlesex, he spent many hours fishing and relaxing in a vain attempt at recuperation. To the end, he retained his courteous charm, his modest, cheerful deportment, his impeccable manners. Though old and infirm, he still rose from his chair whenever his wife or daughters entered his room or study. A spokesman for the "New Virginia," Montague retained always the gentility of the Old South, a past era of sentiment and honor. The heritage of Inglewood would never die.

When the Seventy-fifth Congress convened on January 6, 1937, Montague was not present to take his oath of office. Congressman Otis Bland, his friend and Virginia colleague, was appointed to administer the oath at Montague's Urbanna home. Bland subsequently journeyed to Middlesex and performed the assignment. Two weeks later Montague's daughters were summoned to Urbanna; his son, a Marine Corps officer, was away at sea. Death came quickly, but not unexpectedly, from a heart attack on the morning of the twenty-fourth.

Public and private expressions of condolence were numerous and evidently heartfelt. Speaker of the House William B. Bankhead praised Montague as "a man of culture. . . . He belonged to the old school of statesmen which is rapidly passing." *World Affairs,* a

20   Richmond *Times Dispatch,* Aug. 5 and 6, 1936, Jan. 29, 1937. Contradictory accounts place the margin between 250 and 700 votes.
21   Call to unknown, Dec. 4, 1936, Montague Papers. Nunnally interview.

publication of the American Peace Society, recalled that he had labored "with marked ability, judicial sincerity and a quiet persuasiveness that led all privileged to associate with him to admire and respect not only his views but his rich and fructifying personality." Secretary of State Cordell Hull wrote Montague's widow: "Governor Montague was one of the ablest men with whom it has been my good fortune to come in contact at the national capital. I never knew a person who possessed more fine qualities than he, nor a more intense patriot." The *Times Dispatch* described the "Red Fox of Middlesex" as a fox "of a brilliant color, sharply differentiated from the common run of foxes all his long life, even in the congressional years." [22]

The funeral was held on January 26. Though Montague had requested that no special House committee be appointed, there were in attendance Congressmen from Florida, Ohio, Arkansas, and Texas. Also present were the governor of Virginia and his staff. Tribute to his legal reputation was shown by the attendance of Justices McReynolds and Van Devanter of the Supreme Court. After a brief sermon by Reverend Dr. Beverly D. Tucker, rector of St. Paul's Church in Richmond, Montague was buried in Christ Church cemetery in Middlesex, near a knoll overlooking the Rappahannock. Three words engraved on his tombstone serve as his epitaph: JURIST STATESMAN PATRIOT.

22 Richmond *Times Dispatch* and Richmond *News Leader,* Jan. 25, 1937; *World Affairs,* C (March, 1937), Moore Collection; Cordell Hull to Mrs. Montague, Jan. 27, 1937, Moore Collection.

XVII

EPILOGUE

ANDREW JACKSON MONTAGUE left no monuments behind him. Despite his significant contributions to his state, twenty-five years after his death his name and accomplishments have passed almost into oblivion. A portrait in the State Capitol, a Montague Avenue in Danville, a favorable reputation among a few political veterans, an occasional reference in history books—little remains to save his life and name from complete obscurity. His statewide prominence endured too brief a period to create for him a lasting reputation. As governor, his most notable accomplishments resulted from his active efforts on behalf of the Virginia campaigns for better schools, for better roads, and for the direct senatorial primary. As the foremost advocate of all three crusades he contributed a valuable impetus which probably hastened the day when these reforms reached fruition.

Still, though Montague's role as a spokesman cannot lightly be dismissed, in all three crusades he only slightly anticipated the current trends of the day. He added his endorsement to the crescendo of voices speaking for education in the South, but even without his aid the Ogden campaign would probably have attained ultimate success in Virginia. With a gradual return of prosperity, the Southern states would also have inevitably looked to the improvement of their public roads. And, in helping to institute the direct primary in Virginia, Montague reflected the nationwide move toward a more popular democracy, a move which culminated with the Seventeenth Amendment's adoption in 1913. In a larger perspective, then, Montague was merely one of a phalanx of similarly minded individuals fighting for reform and for their conception of progress.

If Montague did not make Southern history, he mirrored it. It is as a representative of his time that he becomes significant and illustrative; it is as a prototype of his age and his generation that a study of his life becomes meaningful. Fighting machine government, calling for clean elections, striving to revive Virginia statecraft and to instill in Virginians an elevated standard of citizenship through public education, Montague helped crystallize the thinking, the reactions, and the psychology of the many individuals who comprised the Southern progressive movement. And though the leaders of that movement rarely succeeded in winning permanent political power, they did succeed in their primary aim to spur their Southland toward political and economic progress. In an industrial age of rapid change, they articulated and guided the popular demand for restraint of big business, for improvement of state services, and for purification of electoral processes. As critics of the established order, they forced complacent political leaders to acknowledge the need for change and reform—a service which was vital to the function of a healthy democracy.

These Southern progressives had paradoxical motivations. They believed in human progress, in individual worth, in the utilization of government not only to protect the people's rights and liberties, but to provide for their welfare. Yet these men were no levelers, no socialists. In true Jeffersonian tradition, they would provide equality of opportunity to all; they would strive to alleviate human suffering and depravity. But, also following the Jeffersonian dream, they would cherish intellect and superior attainment. They would not ennoble the common, the vulgar, the average. In providing equal opportunity to every individual, they would insist that actual equality be earned. Thus, in the South, denial of suffrage to the illiterate served to maintain the standards of democracy at a high level and to obviate the temptation for demagoguery among officeholders. Yet, while restricting the electorate, Southern progressives simultaneously strengthened Southern education, providing the opportunity for every individual to grow to his utmost capacity, to "burgeon out all that there is within him." Through education, the individual would thus be afforded the means to earn his suffrage and to enjoy the full status of citizenship in a mature democracy.

Montague's background and political development exemplified that of his progressive contemporaries. The son of the secessionist Civil War lieutenant governor of Virginia, he inherited an idealistic tradition of public service and political conservatism. A devout Baptist, he also developed a serious, moralistic, humanitarian nature. A Victorian in thought and action, he idealized the home, the family, the emotions, and the intellect. Taking his cue from Scott and Dickens he cherished manners, sentiment, and the delightful surroundings of a cultured and intelligent society. "A warm home with books, bright firesides and sanctified by the care of wife and children"—this to Montague was the most a man could desire. All these attributes he found epitomized in the surroundings of his heritage, the Old South.

But Montague was not only a product of the Old South. His birth occurred even as the old order was facing its crucial challenge in the War Between the States. His boyhood and young manhood were comparatively free from the intense bitterness found among many veterans of that conflict. He early nurtured a genuine desire for sectional reconciliation. In the context of his age, he was distinctly a nationalist. If he idealized the character and deportment of Southern statesmen, he did not idealize the forces and developments which had brought on the war. The entrenched institution of slavery he regarded as having had a perverse and pernicious influence on Southern thinking. And he once privately confided his conviction that the South's defeat in the war had been providential.

Montague's heritage from the Old South, then, was not so much a legacy of ideology as of a way of life—belief in dignity in human relationships, love of classical learning, idealization of government and public service, advocacy of individual freedom under law. These influences served to mold the young Montague, to shape his basic personality and character.

Montague's Old South background also led him to reject the cruder phases of the New South which he encountered as student, lawyer, and young politician. While yet a student, his chief fear had been that constitutional government would be subjected to the whimsical wishes of the ignorant Negro electorate newly enfranchised following the war, an electorate which constituted a majority of the voting population in many Virginia counties. Montague always retained his disdain for an uninformed electorate, but as Virginia's political morality slowly degenerated, he came to detest even more the type of petty politician which an electoral system characterized by bribery, dishonesty, and corruption inevitably produced. Most of all, he regretted the appearance on the Virginia scene of a tightly knit group of machine politicians who condoned and exploited election malpractices as a means of maintaining white supremacy and who enjoyed the financial support of railroads and corporations, a support rewarded by legislative favors and immunity from harsh restrictive legislation. Montague sympathized with the Democratic desire to maintain white government throughout the Commonwealth, but he could not look with equanimity upon the methods used to insure that supremacy. And he lamented as well the emergence of a cohesive factional machine which eventually controlled the Virginia legislature and which played a vital role in shaping the political destiny of any aspirant for public office. Montague had long opposed the principle of monopoly in business as potentially dangerous, not only to the public but ultimately to the monopoly itself, in discouraging initiative and retarding invention and improvement. He opposed political monopoly for the same reasons—only healthy and untrammeled competition could keep a democracy alive and vibrant. He furnished the Virginia Democratic machine the most vigorous direct competition it ever encountered.

In his reaction to these phases of the New South, Montague demonstrated all the traits of the typical Southern progressive. Resenting the incubus of machine domination and desiring to restore integrity to Virginia's politics, he first joined those who proposed that the power to select United States Senators be taken from the General Assembly (where that power had been so abused in 1893) and be given to the people at large. In an open election, he felt confident that entrenched politicians such as Martin would be rejected by the people and that the machine itself would disintegrate. A freer political atmosphere in which men rose by virtue of their own merit would be restored.

As a second solution to the problems of the new Virginia, Montague also joined in attacking the canker of electoral corruption. Illiterates of both races had helped debauch democratic processes, stimulating widespread practices of vote buying and ballot box stuffing. Corrective legislation proved meaningless, since those responsible for enforcement were themselves culpable. The only effective solution to the impasse seemed to rest with suffrage reform. By establishing literacy as a qualification for voting, Montague and some Southern progressives hoped to remove the shibboleth of white supremacy from elections, to make elections cleaner, and to eliminate the need for machine solidarity. Combined with suffrage reform was the complementary campaign to curb all monetary contributions by corporations and railroads, which furnished the backbone of the Virginia machine. By disfranchising the illiterate and minimizing the importance of corporations and political machines in elections, Montague hoped to remove the price tag, with all its connotations, from Virginia politics and to establish talent as the sole criterion in the building of a new Southern statesmanship.

As a third curative for the South's ills, Montague and the Southern progressives advocated a strong system of public education. In a sense, this too was a corollary of disfranchisement, for only with the race issue subdued could greater attention be given to the solutions of other problems, including the woeful deficiencies in Southern public education. An adequate education, on the other hand, would instill good citizenship and ultimately bring universal suffrage. More than once Montague asserted the necessity for universal education if universal suffrage were to be made feasible. He recognized the need for improved educational facilities if Virginians were to compete in the new age of commerce and industry. And he argued that the state was responsible for giving every individual, Negro and white, equal opportunity to realize his potential. By urging universal education, he advocated an education suited to the individual, one that would aid him both practically and intellectually—one that would, most of all, instill within him industry, character, ideals, and citizenship. The end result would be a better individual and a better Virginia.

Possessing such motives, Montague joined in the mainstream of the Southern progressive movement. The men who sponsored this movement were basically idealistic and altruistic. They were also politically ambitious, and this served to make their zeal for reform all the more intense. So it was with Montague. In his youth he had harbored an ambition almost intoxicating in its potency. Cherishing as he did a desire to contribute toward a national renaissance of Southern leadership, he chafed at the political conditions which barred the candidacies of those individuals not willing to speak "the language of the tribe," or to accept passively machine domination of state affairs. In fighting such domination, he was not averse to formulating expedient alliances of his own. A practical politician as well as an idealist and statesman, he fought fire with fire. If by rationalization he equated his personal ambitions with the Independents' crusade to dismember

Martin's organization, and if he consequently overplayed the part of
the reformer, still his motives were basically genuine and his egotism
was fully justified. During his four years as governor he led the Independents at a time when their fortunes seemed brightest.

Partly because of jealousy among other aspiring Independents,
partly because of his cautious role as an administrator, partly because
of his overweening ambition, Montague was unable to win united
Independent support for his leadership. Even so, no other figure of
that faction could seriously challenge his statewide popularity. In his
1905 fight against Martin, therefore, he personally carried the cause
of the Independents in the most crucial test of strength ever faced by
the Virginia organization. In the long history of that organization,
now extending over seventy years, Montague came as close as any
contestant to displacing a major leader of the machine in a direct contest. If his 1905 campaign had been successful, not only would his
personal career have attained its full flower, but the head of Virginia's
political hierarchy would have been deposed and the course of Virginia's political development significantly altered. His defeat, however, signaled a gradual decline in Independent fortunes and leadership, which, with some exceptions, has continued to the present day.

Speculation is at best risky, but if testimony of his House colleagues can be accepted, Montague would have made valuable contributions as Senator. Even without a seat in the Senate he was prominently mentioned as a possible appointee to Wilson's Cabinet and to
the Supreme Court. Few Virginia governors since the Civil War have
had the breadth of cultivated learning, the largeness of vision, or the
power of eloquence that Montague had. He may not have possessed
an unusual intellect, but he developed that which he had to an unusual extent. Throughout his long life and career he retained a love of
books and a love of learning. Though he was fond of sports, especially fishing and hunting, his most natural occupation was the seden-
tary one of reader and scholar. His intellectual interests encompassed
a wide diversity of subjects and earned for him two honorary doctorates from prominent American universities. An English acquaintance
once commented to Montague's wife, "Your husband's mind is like a
well-ordered desk; he can reach up to any pigeon-hole, and take
down any subject he wants." This mind and these interests, combined
with Montague's personal charm and magnetism, gave promise to

some of his early associates of a brilliant and productive future. Had the results of the senatorial election been reversed, Montague might indeed have realized these expectations.

Thwarted in his higher ambitions, Montague played a prominent role only during his term as Virginia's governor, performing creditably in promoting the crusades for schools, roads, and the senatorial primary. As a vigorous Independent, challenging the right of the dominant organization to govern the Commonwealth, he also rendered service vital to any democracy—that of creating or promoting political dissent. By carrying his forceful arguments and his personal cause to the people, he forced Martin to abandon his aloof senatorial perch. By subjecting Martin to his first popular election, he forced him to take cognizance of the various reforms championed by the progressives and, consequently, to endorse most of them. Though the Virginia public rejected Montague's ambition for personal advancement, that public and the Democratic machine eventually accepted his reforms. Montague served as a catalytic agent, causing the machine to shift its ideological base—making it more compromising, more representative, more effective, more responsive to Virginia's needs. Ironically, in the process, he rendered the organization even more impregnable.

Following his term as governor, Montague remained ambitious, but he never again played a truly important role in state or national politics. His flirtation with the Republicans Roosevelt and Taft paid no substantial dividends, and the prospects of a Cabinet appointment in reward for his Virginia campaign for Wilson never materialized. In the House of Representatives he functioned capably as an active, industrious, but unpublicized Congressman. As a freshman representative he gave absolute support to Wilson's New Freedom, and showed promise of development as a committee leader. But his years of productive seniority came in the ebb tide of Democratic favor during the 1920's. His attention was naturally diverted, therefore, from the congressional to the international scene, where he served admirably as an unofficial ambassador of goodwill to various conferences in European capitals. With the renewed advent of Democratic power in 1933 he was no longer physically able to give effective service. Moreover, he found the New Deal, at least in some respects, incompatible with his increasingly conservative political complexion.

To the end Montague retained his idealism, his sentiment, his scholarly bent. But he lost his enthusiasm, his optimism, and his ambition. In the words of Colgate Darden, a congressional colleague, "Some of the fire and daring which according to all accounts so marked him in the early days had given way to a philosophical detachment and serenity which made him most attractive." The serenity, however, did not signify complacency, for in a sense Montague felt that he and his generation had failed. His previous faith in the efficacy of education, for example, turned to disillusionment; in his opinion, education had not served to improve the morals and character of the populace, nor had it promoted a revived standard of political citizenship. Near the end of his life, the deteriorating international situation seemed to indicate failure for his and others' aim to create a new world of international accord under law. And the devastating effects of the Depression unsettled his confident faith in the American dream. Some of his last words to his daughter were both regretful and despairing, "I had hoped to leave my children in a better world. God only knows what awaits you."

Montague, the "elder statesman," never found complete satisfaction with his service in the House, and the wound of his 1905 senatorial defeat never completely healed. When assured by friends that he had done his state honor through his performance as Congressman, he would "shake his fine head and say, 'No, the House is too large for a man to do anything. In the Senate it is different.' In his own heart," as Douglas Southall Freeman has said, "he felt that circumstance, a subtle conspirator against man's wisest planning, had thwarted him. Perhaps it had . . . but it never could sour the sweetness of his spirit."

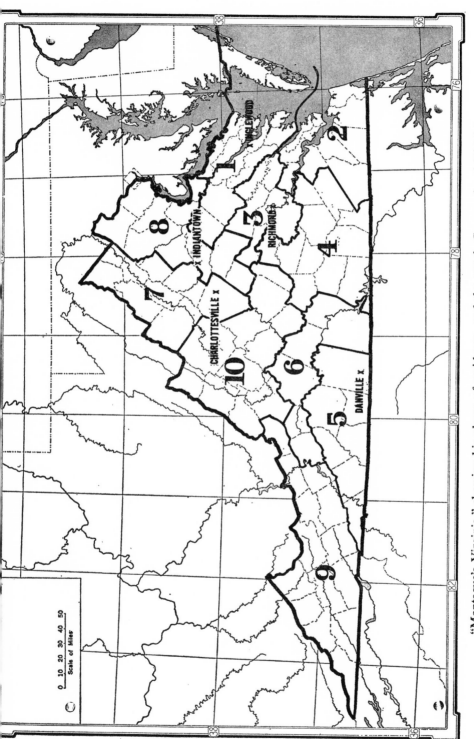

"Montague's Virginia," showing his places of residence, and the state's Congressional Districts during his tenure as attorney general and governor.

CRITICAL ESSAY ON AUTHORITIES

MANUSCRIPTS

This biography has been derived largely from primary sources, especially manuscript collections. The Andrew Jackson Montague Papers in the Virginia State Library at Richmond have provided the most valuable single contribution. This is a vast collection of letters, scrapbooks, and miscellaneous documents and pamphlets, some conveniently arranged chronologically and alphabetically, some unsorted and unarranged. The collection is most complete and conveniently arranged for the period from 1897 through 1914. Letters before 1900 are chiefly of an impersonal nature, and a considerable portion of Montague's congressional papers (after 1914) have been destroyed.

The second most valuable manuscript collection for this study has been a collection of Montague papers in the possession of his daughter, Mrs. Gay Montague Moore, who resides in Gloucester County, Virginia. Consisting of numerous letters, scrapbooks, and miscellaneous documents, it contains papers pertinent to all phases of Montague's life, but is especially valuable for his family background and early life. Particularly helpful was a large assortment of letters written by Montague to his fiancée from 1884 to 1889.

Several manuscript collections of Montague's Virginia contemporaries are essential for a political history of the period. The most voluminous is that of Henry Delaware Flood, located in the Library of Congress. Flood was Senator Thomas S. Martin's trusted confidant, and his excellently indexed papers, which extend from the 1890's into the Wilson era, provide the best insight into the workings of the Virginia organization. Also helpful for an analysis of the organization in the 1890's and early 1900's are various manuscript collections of Martin's political friends: the Francis Rives Lassiter Papers, located at Duke University (Lassiter was Montague's opponent for the attorney general nomination in 1897); the William Bibb Papers, located in Alderman Library at the University of Virginia, Charlottesville (Bibb was a minor figure in Virginia politics but a longtime member of the state Democratic central committee, and a loyal follower of Martin); the John Warwick Daniel Papers, also in Alderman Library (Daniel, U.S. Senator from Virginia, preceded Martin to power but later cooperated with him, at the same time preserving a certain independence; his papers are of uneven value but touch fairly comprehensively on most topics of interest during Montague's prominence in Virginia politics); the James Hay Papers, Alderman Library (this is a small collection of a Congressman from Virginia who was one of the inner coterie of machine leaders in the early 1900's); and the J. Taylor Ellyson Papers, Alderman Library (Ellyson was state chairman of the party for several decades, and unsuccessful candidate for the gubernatorial nomination in 1897 and 1917).

Manuscript collections of representatives of the Independent faction of Virginia's Democratic party include the William A. Anderson Papers, the Allen Caperton Braxton Papers, the Carter Glass Papers, all in Alderman Library; and the Henry St. George Tucker Papers, University of North Carolina library. Although Glass was a prominent Virginia politician in the early 1900's, his papers are valuable only for the years after Montague's governorship. Tucker's papers are rich in material relating to the Ogden educational movement but are disappointingly lacking in material directly relating to Montague's role in Virginia politics, although the two were cordial political friends throughout their lives (Tucker was the Independents' choice for governor in 1909). Anderson was elected attorney general in 1901, the year of Montague's gubernatorial election, but the majority of his papers pertains to legal and business matters. They are most helpful in describing in detail the movement for a senatorial primary in 1899. Braxton was a prominent figure in the Virginia constitutional convention in 1901, and thereafter a leader of that Independent faction dissatisfied with Montague's domination. His collection is extensive, well-indexed, and very helpful.

Other manuscript collections of less value include the E. P. Buford

Papers, the John L. Hurt Papers, the John R. Saunders Papers, and the Micajah Woods Papers, all located at the Alderman Library; and the Charles T. Lassiter Papers, located in Duke University library. All of the above individuals were minor figures in Virginia politics in the 1890's and early 1900's.

Unfortunately, collections for three of the most important Virginia politicians of the era are either extremely inadequate or nonexistent —William A. Jones, Montague's close ally in the Independent faction; Claude A. Swanson, unsuccessful opponent of Montague in the 1901 election, later a Virginia governor and U.S. Senator; and Senator Thomas S. Martin himself. A small collection of Martin's papers in Alderman Library at the University of Virginia is valuable chiefly for its scrapbook material.

For references to Montague's role in national politics, the large collections of the Theodore Roosevelt and Woodrow Wilson papers in the Manuscripts Division of the Library of Congress were utilized.

NEWSPAPERS

Newspapers afforded the second most important source for this biography, especially for the election of 1897, for the May conference of 1899, for the years of Montague's governorship, 1902–1906, and for the factional rivalry in Virginia politics from 1913 to 1916. Virginia journals of the day were predominantly Democratic in affiliation, reflecting this bias in reporting as well as in editorials. The best were those of the state's political and cultural capital, Richmond. Reference has been made to all of the following: Richmond *Dispatch,* Richmond *Evening Journal,* Richmond *Evening Leader,* Richmond *News Leader,* Richmond *State,* Richmond *Times,* Richmond *Times Dispatch.* For Montague's four years as governor the *Evening Leader,* the *Dispatch,* the *News Leader,* and the *Times Dispatch* were especially helpful.

Research in smaller newspapers published throughout the Commonwealth provided a contrasting, and usually more partisan, point of view: Berryville *Clarke Courier,* Harrisonburg *Rockingham Register,* Lynchburg *Daily Advance,* Lynchburg *News,* New Market *Shenandoah Valley,* Staunton *Daily News,* Staunton *Spectator and Vindicator.*

In addition, mention should be made of the wealth of scrapbook material available and utilized—in the two Montague collections, the Martin Papers, and the Anderson Papers. These scrapbooks made possible a wide and convenient sampling of newspaper material from many minor Virginia organs, whose files are presently incomplete or nonexistent, as well as more important Danville, Roanoke, and Norfolk dailies, among others. The scrapbooks in Montague's collections also include numerous clippings from important out-of-state journals.

THESES AND DISSERTATIONS

Of secondary source works, the most extensively utilized have been unpublished theses and dissertations, most of them produced at the University of Virginia. Biographical studies of Montague's Virginia contemporaries include: James Adam Bear, "Thomas S. Martin, a Study in the Virginia Democracy" (M.A. thesis, University of Virginia, 1955); Bear's thesis, a realistic appraisal of Montague's arch political enemy, covers only the first portion of Martin's political career. Richard B. Doss, "John Warwick Daniel, a Study in the Virginia Democracy" (Ph.D. dissertation, University of Virginia, 1955), is an elaboration of his thesis, a mammoth work, covering in considerable detail Daniel's role in state and national politics from the 1870's to 1911. This was a very helpful reference. John H. Moore, "The Life of James Gaven Field, Virginia Populist (1826–1902)" (M.A. thesis, University of Virginia, 1953), though technically a biography of Field, is also a history of Virginia Populism and a digest of Virginia politics in the 1880's and 1890's—useful as a reference to general political developments. Victor D. Weathers, "The Political Career of Allen Caperton Braxton" (M.A. thesis, University of Virginia, 1956), and Harold G. Wheatley, "The Political Career of William Atkinson Jones" (M.A. thesis, University of Virginia, 1953) briefly describe the careers of two other Independents, aligned with Montague. Weathers' study goes into exhaustive detail on Braxton's work in the Virginia constitutional convention, but is also helpful in portraying Braxton's role in Virginia politics thereafter. Wheatley's work is especially helpful in describing Jones's important role in the senatorial primary reform movement. Lois G. Moore's study of "William Alexander Anderson, Attorney General of Virginia, 1902–1910" (M.A. thesis, University of Virginia, 1959), is concerned chiefly with legal matters and the routine of the office of Virginia's attorney general.

Mention might be made of the author's two earlier studies of Montague (William Edward Larsen, "Governor Andrew Jackson Montague, Spokesman for the New Virginia," M.A. thesis, University of

Virginia, 1958; and "Governor Andrew Jackson Montague of Virginia, the Making of a Southern Progressive, 1862–1937," Ph.D. dissertation, University of Virginia, 1961). The former work concentrates entirely on Montague's four years as governor, the latter is an expanded biography. Both contain considerably more narrative detail than does this present abridged version, especially for the first six and last two chapters of this volume.

A nearly completed dissertation by Henry C. Ferrell on Claude A. Swanson was unfortunately unavailable at this writing, although the author has read portions of it. Mr. Ferrell takes a much more charitable view of Swanson, and a much dimmer view of Montague, than does the author.

Two unpublished studies of a general nature have been useful in providing background material: H. J. Eckenrode, "Virginia Since 1865, a Political History" (manuscript in Alderman Library, University of Virginia), and Herman L. Horn, "The Growth and Development of the Democratic Party in Virginia Since 1890" (Ph.D. dissertation, Duke University, 1949).

Unpublished theses and dissertations upon various phases of Virginia's good roads and good schools movements include the following: Byron M. Flory, "The Development of Secondary Education in Virginia" (M.A. thesis, University of Virginia, 1925); Elizabeth H. Kepner, "Education in Virginia under Dr. Joseph W. Southall, 1898–1906" (M.A. thesis, University of Virginia, 1939); Richard A. Meade, "A History of the Constitutional Provisions for Education in Virginia" (Ph.D. dissertation, University of Virginia, 1941); Edward F. Overton, "A Study of the Life and Work of Joseph Dupuy Eggleston, Junior" (Ph.D. dissertation, University of Virginia, 1943); Marjorie F. Underhill, "The Virginia Phase of the Ogden Movement" (M.A. thesis, University of Virginia, 1952); Rudyard B. Goode, "The Distribution and Disposition of Highway Funds in Virginia" (Ph.D. dissertation, University of Virginia, 1953); Susie C. Palmer, "The Development of Virginia Highways" (M.A. thesis, University of Virginia, 1930).

BOOKS AND ARTICLES

For purposes of convenience, published books and articles used in this study can be roughly divided into five categories: (1) general works on Virginia history; (2) works on Virginia history before 1900; (3) works on Virginia history after 1900; (4) general and specific works on the Southern scene, especially pertaining to the Southern phase of the progressive movement; (5) works useful for specific information on Montague's life. Unpublished works already cited are listed here in the categories where they were most helpful.

General reference works on Virginia history include: Richard L. Morton, *History of Virginia,* 6 vols. (Chicago, 1924); Robert C. Glass and Carter Glass, Jr., *Virginia Democracy, a History of the Achievements of the Party and Its Leaders in the Mother of Commonwealths, the Old Dominion,* 3 vols. (Springfield, 1937). Also of value are two works edited by Lyon G. Tyler: *Men of Mark in Virginia,* 5 vols. (Washington, 1906–1909), and *Encyclopedia of Virginia Biography,* 5 vols. (New York, 1915). The Eckenrode manuscript cited above was also valuable in this area.

General and specialized studies of Virginia history before 1900 include: Allen W. Moger, *The Rebuilding of the Old Dominion* (New York, 1940)—Moger's work is an overview of Virginia's political history from Reconstruction to the turn of the century; Robert E. Martin, *Disfranchisement of the Negro in Virginia* (Washington, 1938); Richard L. Morton, *The Negro in Virginia Politics, 1865– 1902* (Charlottesville, 1919); Charles C. Pearson, *The Readjuster Movement in Virginia* (Yale University, 1917); William C. Pendleton, *Political History of Appalachian Virginia, 1776–1927* (Dayton, Virginia, 1927)—Pendleton's work is almost unique among published studies of recent Virginia history in the sense that he writes from a Republican viewpoint; William L. Royall, *History of the Virginia Debt Controversy* (Richmond, 1897); William DuBois Sheldon, *Populism in the Old Dominion, 1885–1900* (Princeton, N.J., 1935); Charles E. Wynes, *Race Relations in Virginia 1870–1902* (Charlottesville, 1961); Richard McIlwaine, *Memories of Three Score Years and Ten* (New York, 1908); Allen W. Moger, "The Rift in the Virginia Democracy in 1896," *Journal of Southern History,* IV (August, 1938), 295–317; and Harry E. Poindexter, "The Virginia Democracy in 1897, Silver-Plated Conservatism," *Essays in History,* II (Charlottesville, 1955), 5–27. Mr. Poindexter's article was especially pertinent for an analysis of Montague's 1897 campaign. For pre-1900 Virginia history, see also the theses and dissertations by Moore, Bear, Doss, and Wheatley mentioned above.

Two published works on Virginia history and government after 1900 were especially useful for this study: Ralph C. McDanel, *The Virginia Constitutional Convention of 1901–1902* (Baltimore, 1928), and F. A. Magruder, *Recent Administration in Virginia* (Baltimore, 1912). Helpful published articles on specific phases of Virginia political history after 1900 include: John Ritchie, "The Gubernatorial Campaign in Virginia in 1901," *Essays in History*, II (Charlottesville, 1955), 53–70; Richard B. Doss, "Democrats in the Doldrums: Virginia and the Democratic National Convention of 1904," *Journal of Southern History*, XX (1954), 511–29; Harold E. Cox, "The Jones-Martin Senatorial Campaign of 1911," *Essays in History*, I (Charlottesville, 1954), 38–56; Robert L. Montague, III, "The Red Fox Runs Straight," *Essays in History*, III (Charlottesville, 1956), 45–62; and Dewey W. Grantham, Jr., "Virginia Congressional Leaders and the New Freedom, 1913–1917," *Virginia Magazine of History and Biography*, LVI (July, 1948), 304–13. For post-1900 political history, see also the unpublished manuscripts by Doss, Wheatley, Weathers, Eckenrode, and Horn cited above.

Published biographies and memoirs of important Virginia contemporaries of Montague are few; among them are two works pertaining to Bishop James Cannon, the man most ardently involved in Virginia's temperance crusade: James Cannon, Jr., *Bishop Cannon's Own Story—Life as I Have Seen It* (Durham, N.C., 1955); and Virginius Dabney, *Dry Messiah, the Life of Bishop Cannon* (New York, 1949). There are also two pertinent biographies of Carter Glass: James E. Palmer, *Carter Glass, Unreconstructed Rebel* (Roanoke, 1938), and Rixey Smith and Norman Beasley, *Carter Glass, a Biography* (New York, 1939).

Several published works touch upon phases of Virginia's educational development after 1900: Walter R. Bowie, *Sunrise in the South, the Life of Mary-Cooke Branch Munford* (Richmond, 1912); J. L. Blair Buck, *The Development of Public Schools in Virginia, 1607–1942* (Richmond, 1952); Cornelius J. Heatwole, *A History of Education in Virginia* (New York, 1916); Richard McIlwaine, *Addresses and Papers Bearing Chiefly on Education* (Richmond, 1908); Dumas Malone, *Edwin A. Alderman, a Biography* (New York, 1940). The theses and dissertations by Underhill and others mentioned above also provide information on this subject.

Several excellent survey works recreate the general scene of recent Southern history; some of them offer objective, factual history, others interpretative analyses: Philip A. Bruce, *The Rise of the New South* (Philadelphia, 1905); Virginius Dabney, *Liberalism in the South* (Chapel Hill, 1932); Benjamin B. Kendrick and Alexander M.

Arnett, *The South Looks at Its Past* (Chapel Hill, 1935); V. O. Key, Jr., *Southern Politics in State and Nation* (New York, 1950); Francis Butler Simkins, *The South Old and New* (New York, 1947); and C. Vann Woodward, *Origins of the New South, 1877–1913* (Baton Rouge, 1951).

Specialized studies of phases of the Southern progressive movement include several works relating to developments in Southern education: Charles W. Dabney, *Universal Education in the South*, 2 vols. (Chapel Hill, 1936); Louis R. Harlan, *Separate and Unequal, Public School Campaigns and Racism in the Southern Seaboard States, 1901–1915* (Chapel Hill, 1958); and Philip W. Wilson, *An Unofficial Statesman, Robert C. Ogden* (Garden City, 1924). Dabney and Wilson (as well as Bowie, Underhill, and most historians of Virginia educational developments) take the traditionally charitable view of the general Ogden movement, whereas Harlan, rewriting history from a modern egalitarian premise, emphasizes that it benefited chiefly the white population.

Other phases of the Southern progressive movement have received specialized study: Elizabeth H. Davidson, *Child Labor Legislation in the Southern Textile States* (Chapel Hill, 1939); Maxwell Ferguson, *State Regulation of Railroads in the South* (New York, 1916); C. Vann Woodward, *The Strange Career of Jim Crow* (2nd ed., New York, 1962); Arthur S. Link, "The Progressive Movement in the South, 1870–1914," *North Carolina Historical Review,* XXIII (1946), 172–95; Jane Zimmerman, "The Penal Reform Movement in the South During the Progressive Era, 1890–1917," *Journal of Southern History,* XVII (1951), 462-92.

Biographies of Southern progressive leaders, contemporaries of Montague, include an old work, R. D. W. Connor and Clarence Poe, *The Life and Speeches of Charles Brantley Aycock* (Garden City, 1912), and three recent scholarly productions: Dewey W. Grantham, Jr., *Hoke Smith and the Politics of the New South* (Baton Rouge, 1958); Robert C. Cotner, *James Stephen Hogg, a Biography* (Austin, Texas, 1959); and Oliver H. Orr, Jr., *Charles Brantley Aycock* (Chapel Hill, 1961).

Other works utilized contain specific information on phases of Montague's life: L. Beatrice W. Hairston, *A Brief History of Danville, Virginia, 1728–1954* (Richmond, 1955); Benjamin Simpson, *Men, Places, and Things* (Dance Brothers, 1891); George W. Montague, *History and Genealogy of Peter Montague of Nansemond and*

Lancaster Counties, Virginia, and His Descendants, 1621–1894 (Amherst, Massachusetts, 1894); Frederick Pollock, For My Grandson (London, 1933); Thomas F. Ryan, "The Political Opportunity of the South," North American Review, CLXXVI (1903), 161–72; Edson L. Whitney, The American Peace Society, a Centennial History (Washington, 1929); Annual Reports of the Directors of the American Peace Society (Washington, 1921–1923); Catalogue of Students of the University of Virginia Summer Law Class for 1884 (Charlottesville, 1884).

INTERVIEWS AND LETTERS

Several interviews with Montague's children gave insight into the personality of their father, as well as contributing factual information about his early life and career. Interviews with Gay Montague Moore at Toddsbury, Gloucester County, Virginia, December, 1959, and June, 1960; with Janet Montague Nunnally at Deltaville, Middlesex County, Virginia, June, 1960; and a brief conversation with R. Latané Montague at Urbanna, Virginia, December, 1959, were invaluable.

Letters from several individuals made possible a reconstruction of Montague's early years at Indiantown: from Mrs. Catesby Willis Stewart, Fredericksburg (March 11 and March 28, 1960); from Miss Nellie Norman, Culpeper (March 6 and April 3, 1960); and from Mrs. Edgar O. Willis, Jr., Culpeper (March 23, 1960).

DOCUMENTS

With two exceptions, public documents have not provided important source material. The exceptions: Annual Report of the Attorney-General to the Governor of Virginia, 1898, 1899, 1900, 1901 (Richmond, 1898–1901); and the always valuable Congressional Record, L–LXXXI, 63rd through the 75th Congresses (Washington, 1913–37).

INDEX